Keep this book. You will need it and use it throughout your career.

About the American Hotel & Lodging Association (AH&LA)

Founded in 1910, AH&LA is the trade association representing the lodging industry in the United States. AH&LA is a federation of state lodging associations throughout the United States with 11,000 lodging properties worldwide as members. The association offers its members assistance with governmental affairs representation, communications, marketing, hospitality operations, training and education, technology issues, and more. For information, call 202-289-3100.

LODGING, the management magazine of AH&LA, is a "living textbook" for hospitality students that provides timely features, industry news, and vital lodging information.

About the Educational Institute of AH&LA (EI)

An affiliate of AH&LA, the Educational Institute is the world's largest source of quality training and educational materials for the lodging industry. EI develops textbooks and courses that are used in more than 1,200 colleges and un'   ldwide, and also offers courses to individuals through its Distance Learnin
rely on EI for training resources that focus on every aspe
try-tested videos, CD-ROMs, seminars, and skills guid
skill level. EI also offers professional certification for the
information about EI's products and services, call 800-

D1534615

About the American Hotel & Lodging Educational Foundation (AH&LEF)

An affiliate of AH&LA, the American Hotel & Lodging Educational Foundation provides financial support that enhances the stability, prosperity, and growth of the lodging industry through educational and research programs. AH&LEF has awarded millions of dollars in scholarship funds for students pursuing higher education in hospitality management. AH&LEF has also funded research projects on topics important to the industry, including occupational safety and health, turnover and diversity, and best practices in the U.S. lodging industry. For information, go to www.ahlef.org.

SPA:
A COMPREHENSIVE
INTRODUCTION

Educational Institute Books

SPA:
A COMPREHENSIVE
INTRODUCTION

Elizabeth M. Johnson
Bridgette M. Redman

International SPA Association Foundation
Lexington, Kentucky

American
Hotel & Lodging
Educational Institute

The International SPA Association Foundation is the 501(c)3 foundation of the International SPA Association and was created in 1999 to serve the educational and research needs of the spa industry. The ISPA Foundation's mission is to improve and enhance the value of the spa experience; its vision is to advance spa culture to sustain health and well-being. The ISPA Foundation's objectives include being the educational source for the spa industry, establishing definitive research that validates spa industry related topics, and creating an endowment that sustains the ISPA Foundation in perpetuity.

Disclaimer

This publication is designed to provide accurate and authoritative information in regard to the subject matter covered. It is sold with the understanding that the publisher is not engaged in rendering legal, accounting, or other professional service. If legal advice or other expert assistance is required, the services of a competent professional person should be sought.
— *From the Declaration of Principles jointly adopted by the American Bar Association and a Committee of Publishers and Associations*

The authors are solely responsible for the contents of this publication. All views expressed herein are solely those of the authors and do not necessarily reflect the views of the Internatioanl SPA Association Foundation (ISPA), American Hotel & Lodging Educational Institute (the Institute), or the American Hotel & Lodging Association (AH&LA).

Nothing contained in this publication shall constitute a standard, an endorsement, or a recommendation of ISPA, the Institute, or AH&LA. ISPA, the Institute, and AH&LA disclaim any liability with respect to the use of any information, procedure, or product, or reliance thereon by any member of the hospitality industry.

©2008
By the INTERNATIONAL SPA ASSOCIATION
FOUNDATION
2365 Harrodsburg Road, Suite A325
Lexington, KY 40504 USA

Published by
The AMERICAN HOTEL & LODGING
EDUCATIONAL INSTITUTE
2113 N. High Street
Lansing, Michigan 48906-4221

The American Hotel & Lodging
Educational Institute is a nonprofit
educational foundation.

Printed in the United States of America
    3 4 5 6 7 8 9 11

ISBN 978-0-86612-323-5

Contents

DEDICATION

This text is dedicated to the pioneers of the spa industry who have contributed so much to the explosive growth of spa. It is in honor of those who have dedicated their passion and creativity to heal the spirit of people in the past, today, and in the future.

Preface

The International SPA Association and the ISPA Foundation recognize that with the rapid growth in the spa industry around the world, education is extremely important in order for the industry to continue to thrive and serve humanity. To provide for the successful future of the industry, ISPA and the ISPA Foundation have created *Spa: A Comprehensive Introduction*, which provides a strong foundation of knowledge for anyone interested in learning about the spa community.

Spa: A Comprehensive Introduction represents an important step in the sustainability of the spa industry. The global spa industry has experienced a great deal of change. Some countries have seen phenomenal growth in the industry; in other areas, this growth is just beginning. As the industry continues to evolve and as more consumers learn of the benefits of spas and healthy lifestyles, the industry needs to be ready for them. To sustain the spa industry, it is imperative that new spa professionals enter the industry with an informed vision and understanding of the business and philosophy of spas.

This book combines the wisdom and experience of a diverse group of seasoned industry professionals to provide a cross-cultural view of the world of spa. It takes a comprehensive look at subjects ranging from the history and cultural development of spa to spa terminology and financial considerations. The text examines today's spa industry and introduces students to spa careers. In addition, it takes readers through a typical day from a spa director's perspective, examines the qualities of an outstanding spa experience, and discusses industry trends and future directions.

The dichotomy of the "business" of spa and the "higher purpose" of the spa experience can be challenging. Balance—a word that is often used in the spa industry—is essential. With the right balance, one can manage a profitable business and serve the higher purpose of wellness through the spa experience.

Acknowledgements

Spa: A Comprehensive Introduction provides extensive and unbiased education on the global spa industry. Many spa industry professionals were involved in this monumental effort and their passion and enthusiasm is remarkable. They have devoted their valuable time and knowledge for the greater good of this project and their efforts are clearly visible in the quality of this text.

Spa: A Comprehensive Introduction Task Force

The ISPA Foundation is grateful to John Korpi for his vision for this project and for the critical role he played in its development. The ISPA Foundation thanks and commends him and the committee for sharing their knowledge and expertise and for their untiring devotion to the completion of this task. The committee responsible for this inaugural edition is:

Sharilyn Abbajay
Founder/General Manager
Abbajay & Associates, LLC

Ann Moloney Brown
Spa Director
Spa Shiki

Jane Crebbin-Bailey
Partner
HCB Associates

Jonathan Paul DeVierville, PhD, MSW
Owner/Director
Alamo Plaza Spa at the historic Menger Hotel

Greg Hagin
Partner
LH Connects

Jaime A. Huffman, MPH, LMBT
Executive Spa Director
The Grove Park Inn Resort & Spa

John Korpi
Principal
SpaQuest International

Jeremy McCarthy
Director, Spa Operations and Development
Starwood Hotels & Resorts Worldwide Inc.

Edwin Neill III
President
Neill Corporation

Jim Root
President
Glen Ivy Hot Springs, Inc.

The ISPA Foundation is honored and grateful to have worked with Elizabeth Johnson and Bridgette Redman as the co-authors of this book. Their experience and knowledge in writing, editing, storytelling, and developing industry-specific textbooks have helped shape this publication into the valuable resource it is today.

Contributors

This project would not have been accomplished without the assistance of several other contributors who provided content, shared stories, answered questions, and provided quotes. Their valuable advice, thoughts, and wisdom were instrumental to the development of this project and their service is gratefully acknowledged.

Dr. Brent Bauer, Mayo Clinic

Mary Bemis, *Organic Spa*

Steven Bernstein, Enchantment Resort

Jennifer Bondurant, CatchPhrase Communications

Anne Bramham, ASTECC

Wendy Clark, I-Bella

Cathy Cluff, The Oaks at Ojai

Sheila Cluff, The Oaks at Ojai

Angela Cortright, Spa Gregorie's

Misty Crawford, Paris Parker Salon and Spa Group

Bill Chrismer, Gentleman's Quarters

Sara Cruncleton, Ihloff Salon & Spa

Jason de Caprio, Noelle Spa for Beauty and Wellness

Peter de Caprio, Noelle Spa for Beauty and Wellness

Chris Fields, Red Door Spas

Darlene Fiske, The Fiske Group: Public Relations & Marketing Strategies

Tara Grodjesk, TARA Spa Therapy

Sean Handler, Solace Spa/Boyne USA

Cheryl Hartsough, Gurney's Inn Resort & Spa

Celeste Hilling, Skin Authority

Laurie Hostetler, The Kerr House

Tinka Hrounpas, MD

Thad Hyland, Harbor View Hotel & Resort

Annika Jackson, Enchantment Resort

Michelle Kinney, Alvadora Spa

Debra Koerner, imassage, Inc.

Karen Korpi, The Ritz-Carlton Hotel Company, LLC

Hannelore Leavy, Day Spa Association

Ginny Michel Lopis, The Lodge at Woodloch

John E. Lopis, The Lodge at Woodloch

Wanda Love, Santé Spa

Pam McNair, Gadabout SalonSpas

Dawn Panepinto, Retail Lifestyle Division, Neill Corporation

Frank Pitsikalis, Enablez/ResortSuite

Larry Prochazka, Robbins Research Institute

Paula Provenzano, Essentially Spa Consulting

Bonnie Prudden, Bonnie Prudden Myotherapy

Patricia Ruble, Pilates Lifestyle.biz

Sylvia Sepielli, Sylvia Planning and Design

Sharon Shugart, Hot Springs National Park

Loren Stone, Sovereign Hospitality

Ruth Stricker, The Marsh: A Center for Balance and Fitness

Michael Tompkins, Miraval Resort

Elaine Trahan, Paris Parker Salons and Spas

Henk Verschuur, Thermae Bath Spa

Jana Westerbeke, Gadabout SalonSpas

Enid Whittaker, Bonnie Prudden Myotherapy

Peer Review

Professional authors were engaged to write this text, and the task force of experienced and dedicated industry professionals supplied their time and expertise to guide the development of the content. Once compiled, the chapters were sent through a peer review process. A variety of professionals from around the world were asked to participate in this process and provide feedback on the content and relevance of the text. Each of our peer reviewers has unique industry experience and insights that significantly strengthened this course. Many are educators at colleges or within the industry and all are dedicated professionals who selflessly gave of their time. We thank them for their commitment to higher education and for helping to create such a strong foundation for our future.

Dr. Brent Bauer, Mayo Clinic

Mary Bemis, *Organic Spa*

Cathy Cluff, The Oaks at Ojai

Angela Cortright, Spa Gregorie's

Simone P. Doudna, Hilton Americas Houston Skyline Spa and Healthclub

Thor Holm, Ginn Hammock Beach Resort

Jesper Houggard, Serena Spa Pvt. Ltd.

Lori Hutchinson, Hutchinson Consulting

Victoria Liu, Sparks Academy, Taiwan

Calvin Martin, Calvin Martin & Company, PLLC

Jack Morrison, Elmcrest College

Craig A. Schmantowsky, Lynn University

Sylvia Sepielli, Sylvia Planning And Design (SPAD)

Deborah Smith, Smith Club & Spa Specialists

Ruth Stricker, The Marsh, A Center for Balance and Fitness

Mary Tabacchi Ph.D., Cornell University

Mindy Terry, Creative Spa Concepts

Diane Trieste, Strategic Spa Solutions, LLC

LaRae Verros, The Ambage

Deborah Waldvogel, The Ambage

Shenyn Wang, Orient Retreat Spa

Jennifer Wayland-Smith, Golden Door Spa at the Boulders

Mary Wisnom, Florida Gulf Coast University

Partners

This book would not have been possible without the support, vision, and wisdom of other important partners and resources.

The International SPA Association was a vital partner and proponent of the development of *Spa: A Comprehensive Introduction*. ISPA is recognized worldwide as the leading professional organization and voice of the spa industry and their sponsorship, support, and involvement of this book reinforces that position. The authors are grateful for the assistance of many members of ISPA's staff, including Becky Brooks, Debra Locker, Shelby Jones, and especially Stefanie Ashley, former director of research and development for ISPA.

The ISPA Foundation would also like to thank the American Hotel & Lodging Educational Institute for editing and publishing this textbook. We are grateful for their continued support of ISPA Foundation initiatives and the spa industry.

2008 ISPA Foundation Board of Directors

Edwin Neill III, President

Ruth Stricker, Vice President

Cathy Cluff, Secretary

Calvin Martin, Treasurer

Brent A. Bauer, MD

Jean Kolb, ISPA Vice Chairman

John Korpi

Thad Hyland

Howard Murad, MD

Jim Root, ISPA Chairman

Sylvia Sepielli

Deborah Szekely, Honorary Member

Jennifer Wayland-Smith

Shenyn Wang

International SPA Association Foundation
2365 Harrodsburg Road, Ste. A325
Lexington, KY 40504 USA
1.888.651.4772 or 1.859.226.4326
ispafoundation@ispastaff.com
www.experienceispa.com

Chapter 1 Outline

Philosophy
    Evolution and Culture of Spa
    Today's Philosophy of Spa
    Defining Mind, Body, and Spirit
Defining Spa
    Global Definitions
    ISPA Definition
Variations of Spa
    Types of Spa
    Typical Spa Services
Spa-Goers
    Spa-Goers' Philosophies
    Spa Drivers
Interpretation of Spa
    The Four Rs of Spa
    Domains of Spa
Business and Philosophy of Spa Working in
    Harmony
    Wisdom for Spa Professionals
    Drawing on a Legacy
    Vision First
Expression and Emotional Responses
    Day Makers
    Community
Value of Spa

Competencies

1. Describe how the philosophy of spa and the integration of mind, body, and spirit have evolved from the beginning of time. (pp. 4–9)

2. Define spa and list the variations of spa types and services. (pp. 9–17)

3. Describe spa-goers and what drives them to use a spa. (pp. 17–22)

4. Explain why spas are important to people and what the domains of spa are. (pp. 22–25)

5. Describe how the business and philosophy of spa can work in harmony. (pp. 26–30)

6. Identify the emotional responses that spa professionals and guests have to spas. (pp. 30–32)

1

Philosophy of Spa

She watched as the guest slowly opened her eyes and the corners of her lips rose into an easy grin. As Elena, the spa manager, quietly placed a glass of cucumber water on the table next to where the guest was resting in one of the Winter Garden's chaise lounges, the guest reached her hand out and touched Elena's arm. "Have I been lying here long?" she asked softly. "I feel so sublime, like time has stopped."

Elena smiled at Mrs. Markovitch, who earlier that day had complained about how hectic her life was and how she felt enslaved by her cell phone and e-mail. She wished her calls and e-mails would stop for a few days so that she could get more work done. She regretted signing her children up for so many extra-curricular activities. She was not able to get more housework done because when she wasn't at work, she was constantly running from one place to another.

"The last time I was sick," Mrs. Markovitch had told Elena upon arriving at the spa for a three-day visit, "I was lying in bed, miserable, and wishing the world would stop while I was sick. There was so much to do and it was piling up while I lay in bed doing nothing. It was then that I realized I was wishing for time to stand still for the wrong reasons. I wanted it to stand still so that I could do more, not less."

Elena was pleased that Mrs. Markovitch seemed to have escaped that guilt, at least for the moment. "You're welcome to lie here as long as you wish. Everyone needs to stop and take time not just to get things done on your to-do list but to truly take care of yourself. To breathe."

"It feels so indulgent to just take care of myself," Mrs. Markovitch said.

"Yet, if you don't take care of yourself, how will you be able to help others? It's like in an airplane. The flight attendants tell you that in case of a loss of cabin pressure to put your oxygen mask on first and then help your children. You won't be there to take care of your children unless you take care of yourself. And taking care of yourself is just what you're doing now."

Mrs. Markovitch nodded and took a sip of the cold, refreshing water. "How can I hold onto this—this feeling of deep contentment and peace as well as this philosophy of taking care of myself? How can I take this home with me?"

With that she motioned to her surroundings in the lush winter garden of the spa. Her husband was taking a fitness walk along the sea and she had the winter garden to herself. She'd been lying in a white robe on the softly cushioned reclining chair. With her hair still oily from her last treatment, she breathed in the exotic aromas used on her skin.

Before Elena could answer, Mrs. Markovitch continued. "Look at this," she said, stretching down over her knees and rubbing her feet. "Normally, my feet are aching all the time. Now they're relaxed. No aches. No pains. They're like velvet to the touch. I'm actually thinking about myself physically in a positive way rather than thinking about how much I hurt or how ugly I feel. This morning in yoga, I was so self-conscious about my body. By the end, the consciousness had turned to its power, its grace, its possibilities. My tension melted away into a new flexibility. The movements were so graceful and powerful. I can't remember the last time I thought of myself so positively. It feels so much better than being obsessed with my aching body or the extra ten pounds I've gained. Instead, while I'm here, I can focus on how soft my skin is, my inner strength, balance, and grace. It opens up new possibilities to what I can achieve."

Elena nodded, *"It's powerful, isn't it?"*

They both looked at the horizon as the sun began to set. Together, they took a deep breath, taking in the oxygen from the green, luscious plants around them.

"I'm almost nervous to leave the sanctuary of this winter garden. If I leave, will I lose this newfound wisdom and peace? How can I take it with me? Or can I stay here in this magical place forever?"

Elena nodded wisely. *"Spa is a place to meet yourself. The meaning of spa is within you and it will always be with you, to seek out and find anywhere. But if you do find yourself back in a place where you don't want to be, you can always take time and pause at any spa—to reconnect. We are here to help you in your journey. We are your sanctuary to meet yourself."*

Philosophy

Philosophy is often considered a foundation upon which people build their knowledge and belief structures. The Greek word for **philosophy** translates to "love of wisdom." It is appropriate then, that this text begins its exploration of spa by delving beyond the business models and types of treatments to take a close look at the wisdom and "why" of spa. Spa philosophy encompasses the deeper meaning and sacred significance of spa.

Spa is ancient in its origin; the ideas behind spa reach back through the ages. This historic tradition, based on the health and wellness of the total person, has stimulated and catalyzed the modern spa world. Spa has experienced rapid growth over the past three decades as spa philosophy has permeated modern culture.

Devoted spa professionals have embraced the wisdom at the very core of spa. It is a wisdom that is committed to the wellness of all humanity. Spa wisdom believes that spas can create places in which people can renew their heart and spirit, rejuvenate their minds, refresh their bodies, and regenerate their souls. Spa is a place where people find physical, emotional, mental, and spiritual healing.

Spa creates a safe time and place to observe and listen to the creative spirit. It is a place where ideas can be inspired and revealed.

Evolution and Culture of Spa

Spa existed in all cultures of the world long before the word "spa" was applied to its current day uses. Today's spas encompass many types of healing and philosophies that can be traced back through time. These include:

- Wellness focused on the total person—physical, mental, social, and spiritual
- Bathing and water rituals
- Herbal remedies
- Massage therapy
- Thalassotherapy
- Hydrotherapy
- Exercise
- Diet

Spa began with the search for healthy living using water and herbal remedies. Then came the development of bathing rituals and the use of mud and other natural substances from the earth and sea. From there, various spa treatments were developed including massage, fitness movements, and skin treatments. The history and evolution are key in understanding today's philosophies of spa.

A quick look at the evolution of spa culture includes these highlights:

- Around 3100 B.C.E., two rituals and therapies began to be practiced that have survived to the modern era: the Egyptian civilization began to practice water therapies and herbal remedies. The nearby civilization of Babylonians also established bathing in rivers and applying hot and cold compresses.

- Water rituals played a role in many cultures from the Greek practice of cold water bathing to Persian steam and mud baths to the Hebrew ritual purification and bathing in the Dead Sea.

- Ayurvedic medicine began thousands of years ago, though the exact dates are disputed. It is a philosophy that provides the foundation for many therapies in spas today. The word Ayurveda is a combination of two words meaning "long life" and "knowledge," together translating as "knowledge of a long life" or "knowledge of life." One of the ancient Indian Ayurvedic texts, the *Charaka Samhita*, defines life as the "combination of the body, sense organs, mind, and soul, the factor responsible for preventing decay and death, which sustains the body over time, and guides the process of rebirth." It is a system of medicine that is designed to promote healthy living and offer therapies related to physical, mental, social, and spiritual harmony.

- When the Greeks introduced water treatments to the Romans in 300 B.C.E., this concept led to the building of spas throughout Roman territory.

- Thailand's (then Siam) massage therapy tradition began around 100 B.C.E., when Buddhism first arrived there.

- Modern thalassotherapy is traced to Dr. Richard Russell of Brighton who, in 1750 C.E., published "De Tabe Glanduri" in which he wrote, "The sea washes away all the evils of mankind."

- Swedish physiologist Per Henrick Ling developed modern massage techniques known as Swedish massage in 1806.

- The first modern hydrotherapy spa was founded in 1829 in Grafenberg, Germany.

- In 1934, Elizabeth Arden, born Florence Nightingale Graham, founded the first day spa in Maine, United States. She brought in high quality skin care and esthetics.

- Six years later, Rancho La Puerta, the first of the American destination spas in the modern era, was established.

- Dr. Kenneth Cooper coined the word "aerobics" in 1968 and published a book about the system of exercise that helps prevent coronary heart disease.

- A year later, Judi Sheppard Missett developed Jazzercise, a series of dance routines to improve cardiovascular health.

- In the years that followed, several diets were introduced, including the low-carbohydrate Atkins diet; the Pritikin program, which advocated whole grains, fruits, vegetables, and low fats; and the Scarsdale diet, a high-protein, low-carb diet.

- More recently, the importance of proper nutrition and regular exercise has entered the mainstream as an important life consideration.[1]

All of these historical events contribute to the spa philosophy, a philosophy that draws upon many great traditions to nurture and rejuvenate people's bodies, souls, and minds today.

Today's Philosophy of Spa

A spa is the epitome of the old adage "an ounce of prevention is worth a pound of cure." In a world where many people spend more time and money on preventive maintenance for their cars than on themselves, spas offer a balance and the chance to recalculate the equation to focus on personal well-being.

People go to spas to rest, relax, and become spiritually or physically replenished. It's a chance to get away from work, obligations, telephones, e-mails, doorbells, and everyday stress, giving guests time for themselves. Spas provide stress-free, noncompetitive experiences in settings that promote rest and relaxation.

Spa is the love or deeper appreciation of one's self through education, knowledge, and/or wisdom about oneself and one's potential. It is about beauty, health, wellness, fitness, mental health, and spiritual journeys—a time and space for guests to be the best they can be. It's a time to heal—and learn how to continue to heal.

Spa is everywhere now. It is in the grocery aisle with spa cuisine offerings that are healthy, wholesome, and free of additives and chemicals. It is in the medical community where massage therapies are now being offered at hospitals to reduce the effects of chemotherapy, improve cardiovascular health, and help injured muscles heal. It is in people's homes as they begin to bring elements of the spa into their interior design for a more peaceful escape from the stresses of daily life. It has even expanded to residential communities built around spas where people can experience the benefits of the spa lifestyle daily.

Spa Snapshot: Why are spas important to the world and to the individual?

Spas are one of the few places to escape the daily demands of life. With technology advances and the iphone/BlackBerry craze just getting more and more robust, it will become harder and harder to "turn off." Spas give people the permission to do just that.

—*Darlene Fiske, Owner, The Fiske Group: Public Relations & Marketing Strategies*

Spas are the great equalizer and balancer, offering a secret path to enlightenment. Our world is full of stress, war, and negativity. However, everyone's actions are their own choice. Spas provide a space to renew and re-energize; spas provide a platform for education including answers to better health, nutrition, self-esteem, relationships; spas provide an environment where creativity and new ideas can flourish.

—*Sean Handler, Director of Sales, Solace Spa/Boyne USA*

People are seeking a return to the more simple things in life, including a holistic approach to health and wellness, which a spa lifestyle can help provide. This is more of a New World phenomenon, as the Europeans and other cultures have long embraced 'spa' as a lifestyle, while North Americans viewed it as an indulgence for many years. There is a change afoot now to overcome that indulgence/pampering image and focus on the wellness component.

—*Wanda Love, Director of Sales & Marketing, Santé Spa*

Spas reinforce the direction society is heading. As we become more conscientious about self-care and preventive medicine, people will look for sources to achieve their new enlightened goals, such as spas.

—*Debra Koerner, Chief Operating Officer, imassage, Inc.*

Spas are a place to relax and receive the positive power of touch. Stress is a proven killer, and spa is a power dose of healing.

—*Angela Cortright, Owner, Spa Gregorie's*

Studies have shown that over 90 percent of disease and illness is stress related and high stress has also been unequivocally linked to aging. Although we cannot eliminate anxiety and pressure altogether from our busy lifestyles, regular spa services can help to manage our stress levels and therefore can decrease our anxiety, provide us with more energy, improve our circulation, decrease the aging process, and create a sense of overall well-being and peace.

—*Sara Cruncleton, Spa Director, Ihloff Salon & Spa*

What is the spa lifestyle? It is a way of living that is focused on the whole person and on balance. What spas have to offer to everyone goes deeper than a simple massage or a pedicure. It goes beyond any given treatment. Rather, the spa lifestyle springs from the reasons these treatments are offered. The spa lifestyle is about living fully, with harmony of the body, mind, heart, and spirit.

Top athletes understand the positive effects of spa treatments on exerted muscles. Cancer patients are finding a much-needed place for reprieve at spas. Families are enjoying spas together as quality time to bond and relax. Teens are going in groups and learning lifestyle lessons on skin care and proper nutrition. Man's best friends have even clawed their way into spas with the creation of pet spas focused on grooming and pampering dogs and cats.

"Spas are absolutely mainstream. Everyone is busier than ever before and they're realizing they must take time out to recharge their batteries and de-stress," said International Spa Association (ISPA) President Lynne Walker McNees. "People no longer see spas as pampering, but instead as a requisite to stay healthy. The two main reasons that people go to spas are to relieve stress and feel relaxed."

Spas have become places of learning. They offer services and programs to align the body and mind, so that the guest can leave with a new commitment to healthy living. The spa philosophy is about teaching life lessons. Guests can enrich their lives with each visit. They can learn how to live healthier lives, experience encouragement about their minds and bodies, and have their spirit lifted.

Defining Mind, Body, and Spirit

The spa world often talks about attending to the needs of **mind, body, and spirit.** What do these key words mean in the spa world?

Mind. Intellectual growth and an understanding of the world about oneself are key components of healthy living. The brain has powers far beyond what people are able to understand and it directs the health and well-being of the body. Spas often offer education and awareness training that can lead people toward healthier lives.

Body. The body refers to the physical vessel that each person is granted during this lifetime. Spas have long worked at helping people develop healthy habits that nurture and strengthen the body, along with enhancing physical appearance.

Spirit. Spirit can be defined in many ways, though at its essence, it is about integration and connection. Dr. Andrew Weil, a pioneer of integrative medicine, defines spirit by writing, "The essence of spirituality is connectedness, an inner sense that we are not random, isolated creatures, but part of something sacred and infinitely larger than ourselves." He also writes, "As humans, we are not intended to achieve full health as isolated, separate beings. Health is wholeness, and wholeness implies connectedness—to family, friends, tribe, nation, humanity, the Earth, and whatever higher power you conceive of as the creator of the universe." Spas help people to make those connections—whether to other people, to nature, to waters, to the community, or to themselves. They provide a place for reflection and for inspiration.

While spa looks at the whole person and serves the needs of the whole person, individual spas are not designed to be all things to all people. Not all spas cater to

Spas exist to nurture the mind, body, and spirit. Such things as meditation help to focus the spirit while other treatments are geared toward feeding and healing the body and mind.

mind, body, and spirit. Some spas specialize in a particular area, focusing on fitness or in spiritual reflection. Others might have an educational focus.

At their core, though, spas and the professionals who work in them look at a person as a whole—mind, body, and spirit—even if their direct treatments may appear to cater to only one component. Many in the spa industry believe the three are uniquely tied together as a unified tri-force, with one affecting the other.

Defining Spa

Most of the world begins its definition of spa with water. Without water, most say, there is no spa. The original spas—mineral springs and hot springs—have been a part of relaxation and healing in many cultures for millennia. Towns with hot springs grew into popular destinations for holiday retreats.

Today the original concept of a spa as a place with healing waters has widened and moved beyond just the waters. Spas have expanded from places dedicated to just the taking of waters into modern day spas, club spas, cruise spas, hotel and health resort spas offering just about everything for what relaxes, energizes, or ails a person. Contemporary spas cater to people who want to lose weight, get in shape, relax, or luxuriate with pampering treatments. They offer all, or the key elements, of a healthy lifestyle, including nutritious food, fitness activities, face

Ruth Stricker: Treating the Spirit, Mind, and Body

While working as a family physician in a Native American hospital in the Southwest, Carl Hammerschlag was introduced to a patient named Santiago, a Pueblo priest and clan chief, who asked him where he had learned how to heal. Hammerschlag responded almost by rote, rattling off his medical education, internship, and certification.

The old man replied, "Do you know how to dance?"

To humor Santiago, Hammerschlag shuffled his feet at the priest's bedside. Despite his condition, Santiago got up and demonstrated the proper steps. "You must be able to dance if you are to heal people," he admonished the young doctor. "I can teach you my steps, but you will have to hear your own music."

—Carl A. Hammerschlag, M.D.,
The Dancing Healer: A Doctor's Journey of Healing with Native Americans, 1989

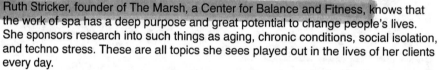

Ruth Stricker, founder of The Marsh, a Center for Balance and Fitness, knows that the work of spa has a deep purpose and great potential to change people's lives. She sponsors research into such things as aging, chronic conditions, social isolation, and techno stress. These are all topics she sees played out in the lives of her clients every day.

For her, the Carl Hammerschlag story of Native American dance is emblematic of the spa industry.

"I think we try to provide the music instead of listening to where people are and reading the front page of the newspaper," said Stricker, "but I think we're getting more serious. I think we're in an ideal position for people who need encouragement and the element of hope. People are socially isolated, so the socialization part of spa is important. I see a great future for us."

At 73, Stricker is just as passionate about wellness as she was 52 years ago when she first started in the fitness world, working with such fitness leaders as Bonnie Prudden and Dr. Kenneth Cooper. She described how she eventually encountered an entire generation of people who felt ripped-off by the fitness movement because it didn't change their lives and simply fed into narcissism.

It was then that she realized that it wasn't enough to have just a fit body; you needed a well mind and spirit. She has centered her life's work on that idea. She says she has watched as people's lives have evolved and how their wellness is closely knit to the things that are going on in their lives.

Stricker calls The Marsh a medical spa because of the way her staff works together to treat not just ailments, but the entire person. The staff includes five holistic physical therapists, a myotherapist, a cardiologist, personal trainers, acupuncturists, and massage therapists.

"Our massage therapists work very hard with a personal trainer," she explained. "For instance, if someone is having treatments of some kind in the spa for a bad back or a bad knee and then they go downstairs and get on a treadmill with their body out

Profile (continued)

of alignment, there is going to be an issue. We need to talk about that together. Massage therapists are in tune with patients and have knowledge of the body."

Her staff attempts to blend different treatments, recognizing that a treatment for one health challenge or person won't necessarily work for another.

"We don't compete. Acupuncture might be right for one and physical therapy for another. We're just laying out the big cafeteria plan for the clients. But the staff does all meet and talk with each other about these things," she said. "My fear is that integrated medicine will move to where allopathic was—that it will be a 'fix me' situation. We have to be more empowered ourselves as personal advocates to take charge of our lives and our health."

She has also seen body work such as craniosacral therapy, Trager, and healing touch change people's lives. She described how a man came into her spa who had run the gamut of weight loss treatments, diets, and surgeries. He wasn't able to walk the length of the hall and she didn't have a chair that could fit him comfortably. When he started with body work, all sorts of things came out about his past and how he was abused.

"It's amazing what comes out, but you have to be almost a pro at psychology to work with these people. You have to know what you're doing when you open someone up that way. We have mental health workers on our staff now and it's really important," she said. "It's a sense of community, a sense of being heard. Where can you be heard? We react rather than internalize things because we have to get back to an e-mail, a fax machine, or a cell phone. It's all good, but we pay a price."

and body treatments, medical evaluations, behavioral management counseling, nutrition education, stress management, holistic health, spiritual growth, movement therapy, exercise physiology, and more. Spa treatments promote physical appearance—helping people to look good and feel better about themselves. For many people, there is a connection between their self-esteem, sense of self-value, and looking good. Positive mental effects contribute to physical health.

Spas exist in all shapes and sizes: at a mountaintop retreat, in the heart of the city, on a tropical island, in a desert oasis, or in the countryside. Their nurturing services are found from Iceland to Australia and all points in between. What they have in common is that they all specialize in wellness. To one degree or another, each addresses physical, emotional, and spiritual needs. Some have distinct specialties while others can tailor an experience to individual guest preferences.

The term "spa" is used in many different ways. It can refer to an individual spa—the physical building and location in which people go to receive a variety of services related to health, well-being, relaxation, and beauty. ("Maria went to visit the Seasons Spa.") It can refer to the philosophy of spa which encompasses all that spa stands for throughout time and the world. ("Spa has made the world a better place by nurturing people's souls.") It can also refer to the world of spa, a shorthand way of referring to all the individuals and businesses that use, maintain, manage, support, or otherwise deal with spas. ("The spa convention offered educational seminars along with a vendor showcase.")

Water is the heart and soul of spa. In ways both symbolic and practical, water defines the renewal and rejuvenation that takes place throughout the spa world.

Global Definitions

For many throughout the world, spa has become synonymous with wellness. The English word for spa is becoming more and more common around the world. Exhibit 1 shows the many words used for spa in languages from around the world.

ISPA Definition

The International SPA Association (ISPA) has published the following definition of spa: "Spas are places devoted to enhancing overall well-being through a variety of professional services that encourage the renewal of mind, body, and spirit."

Ultimately, ISPA points out, the spa experience is unique for each person, which is why each spa offers different services and treatments. Despite their variety of offerings, spas all have one thing in common—they specialize in renewal and rejuvenation.

ISPA further defines the spa experience as "your time to relax, reflect, revitalize, and rejoice." More people are experiencing spas because of the lasting benefits of learning to live a healthier lifestyle—and because of the sheer enjoyment of going to a spa and receiving services.

Exhibit 1   Spa in Many Languages

Dansk (Danish)
n. - spa, kursted, kurbad, mineralholdig kilde

Nederlands (Dutch)
n. - kuuroord

Français (French)
n. - station thermale, thermes (d'une station thermale), hôtel ou ville touristique
très en vogue, (US) buffet (de restauration)

Deutsch (German)
n. - Bad, Badeort, Mineralquelle

Ελληνική (Greek)
n. - ιαματική πηγή, λουτρόπολη, λουτρά

Italiano (Italian)
n. - stazione termale

Português (Portuguese)
n. - balneário (m), estação de águas (f)

Русский (Russian)
n. - минеральный источник, курорт с минеральными водами, лечиться на
водах, ездить на воды

Español (Spanish)
n. - balneario, estación termal

Svenska (Swedish)
n. - hälsobrunn

中文（简体）(Chinese (Simplified))
n. - 矿泉, 矿泉治疗地, 温泉水疗

中文（繁體）(Chinese (Traditional))
n. - 礦泉, 礦泉治療地, 溫泉水療

한국어 (Korean)
n. - 광천, (온천지의) 호텔, 약방 겸 음료 및 경식사 판매점

日本語 (Japanese)
n. - 鉱泉, 温泉, 温泉地

العربية (Arabic)
n. - (المسا) أجتمع الأعداد نبيين, مياه معدنية

There are many places today that add the word "spa" to their name that would not fit under ISPA's definition of a spa. A hair salon would not become a spa simply by adding a manicure table. A doctor's office that performs microdermabrasion is not automatically a spa. Rather those are places that are offering a spa service. It takes more than one or two services to make an authentic spa.

Variations of Spa

There are many approaches to spa throughout the world and each spa provides services according to its own unique vision and mission. As the number of spa locations increased dramatically during the 1990s and into this century, classifications became necessary to categorize the array of spa experiences being offered in the market.

Types of Spa

ISPA defines the following as the main classifications of spas:

Destination Spa: A destination spa is a facility with the primary purpose of guiding individual spa-goers to develop healthy habits. Historically a seven-day stay, this lifestyle transformation can be accomplished by providing a comprehensive program that includes spa services, physical fitness activities, wellness education, healthful cuisine, and special interest programming.

Resort/Hotel Spa: A spa within a resort or hotel providing professionally administered spa services, fitness and wellness components, and spa cuisine choices.

Day Spa: A spa offering a variety of professionally administered spa services to clients on a day use basis.

Medical Spa: A facility that operates under the full-time, on-site supervision of a licensed health care professional whose primary purpose is to provide comprehensive medical and wellness care in an environment that integrates spa services with complementary and/or alternative therapies and treatments. The facility operates within the scope of practice of its staff, which can include both esthetic/cosmetic and prevention/wellness procedures and services.

Mineral Springs Spa: A facility that operates a spa offering an on-site source of natural mineral, thermal, or sea water used in professionally administered hydrotherapy treatments.

Club/Fitness Spa: A facility with the primary purpose of fitness and which offers a variety of professionally administered spa services on a day use basis.

Cruise Ship Spa: A spa aboard a cruise ship providing professionally administered spa services, fitness and wellness components, and spa cuisine choices.

In Europe, Visit Britain created its own classifications of spas as part of a standards-setting initiative. These categories include:

- **Day Spa:** A stand-alone spa, offering individual treatments in day and half-day packages.

- **Hotel Spa:** A spa within the boundaries of a property where the primary business is a hotel.

- **Salon Spa:** A facility that offers individual pampering and beauty treatments. They are usually found in cities.

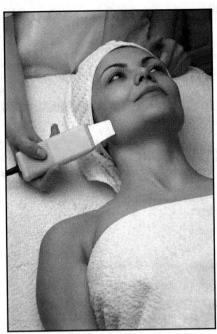

A medical spa guest receives an ultra-sound skin cleaning. Medical spas offer integrative care along with complementary treatments.

- **Sport and Fitness Spa:** A spa within a facility with the primary purpose of fitness.
- **Natural Spa:** A spa offering a naturally occurring on-site source of mineral, thermal, or sea water, or peat, mud, and other natural elements that are used in treatments.
- **Destination Spa:** A spa with the sole purpose of providing guests with lifestyle improvements and health enhancement through professionally administered spa services, physical fitness, education, and nutritional advice on a residential basis.
- **Resort Spa:** A spa within a defined and branded resort where the primary business is to create an environment dedicated to leisure and relaxation. The spa offers health, well-being, and pampering services administered by professionally qualified personnel on a residential or day visit basis.
- **Medi-Spa:** A spa where qualified medical staff administer medically prescribed treatments.

As spas continue to grow to meet new needs and try new business models, other forms will emerge. Various organizations and spas will use different labels to define themselves. A few other spa types include:

- *Residential spas*: Residential communities built around a spa that provides access exclusively to residents. Some have arrangements similar to golf-development communities.

- *Dental spas*: Some dentists have transformed their offices into spa-like environments to pamper their patients with spa services.

- *Mobile spas*: Spa professionals bring spa services to the guest, rather than the guest coming to the spa.

- *Eco-spas*: Those developing eco-spas believe that the health of the planet is tied up with personal health. Eco-spas offer organic treatments and try to ensure that their practices are in harmony with the environment. They keep nature in balance as a way of helping to keep their guests in balance.

People turn to spas with a variety of needs. Different spas allow guests to concentrate on an area of emphasis such as:

- *Fitness*—Guests can work out in fitness classes, enjoy invigorating body treatments, participate in outdoor sports activities, or sign up for programs to lose weight, get fit, or adopt healthier lifestyles.

- *Stress management*—Guests can learn relaxation techniques, how to manage stress, and other strategies for feeling more in balance and in control.

- *Peace of mind*—Guests can pursue a spiritual journey of introspection and reflection through meditation, yoga, tai chi, qigong, and other practices or activities that lead to serenity, understanding, and self-acceptance.

- *Pampering and pleasure*—Guests indulge their senses with massages, facials, mud or aromatherapy baths, and other delightful treatments as they enjoy a completely relaxing vacation or time out.

- *Health and wellness*—Guests can explore their health, learn to deal with issues such as smoking or medical concerns, and discover how lifestyle choices can lead to optimal wellness.

Typical Spa Services

Spas often strive to offer their own signature treatments with protocols varying from spa to spa. Spa guests will often choose spas based on the services that they offer as well as the philosophies that they practice.

Common treatments offered by spas include (some treatments appear in multiple categories):

- **Massage:** Swedish, deep tissue, sports, acupressure, reflexology, shiatsu, Thai, hot stone

- **Asian bodywork therapy:** acupressure, shiatsu, ashiatsu, reflexology, Tuina, Jin Shin Do, Thai, Reiki, polarity

- **Hydrotherapy:** balneotherapy, thalassotherapy, watsu, Scotch hose, Vichy shower, Swiss shower, sauna, steam room, hydrotherapy bath

- **Body treatments:** mud wrap, herbal wrap, salt glow, seaweed wrap, loofah scrub, fango wrap, Javanese lulur, aromatherapy wrap
- **Facials:** deep cleansing, anti-aging, vitamin, oxygen, microdermabrasion
- **Fitness:** yoga, personal training, tai chi, aerobics, hiking, meditation, fitness evaluation or analysis, Pilates
- **Salon treatments:** manicures, pedicures, paraffin dips, hair cutting and styling, hair removal
- **Lifestyle classes:** a wide range of subjects including fitness, wellness, nutrition, stress relief, better sleep, spirituality, etc.
- **Medical treatments:** surgical procedures, myotherapy, laser treatment, Botox, microdermabrasion, acupuncture
- **Energy work:** craniosacral massage, Reiki, polarity, chakra balancing, crystal therapy, healing touch

Spa-Goers

When spa-goers talk about spa, the language they use includes such words as:

- Stress-free
- Get-away
- Fun
- Pampering
- Serene
- Calming
- Tranquility
- Peaceful
- Nurturing
- Holistic

These images and associations create exceedingly high expectations among guests for their visits to spas. They expect from spas deep gratification, or something close to it. Their high expectations derive, in part, from the way the word "spa" stands in their minds as a symbolic promise of unusually meaningful and pleasurable life experiences.

Though any given spa experience may be evaluated differently, the term "spa" itself conjures shared meanings and images in the minds of most. The term inspires images of conscientious and professional staff, technicians, and therapists. It also conjures up images of sensually pleasing, relaxing environments, and ambience.

More than anything, however, spa-goers asked to reflect on the term "spa" describe occasions when they were transported out of the realm of ordinary human experience and temporarily transformed into worthy recipients of care and considerate attention. These idealized associations are held in common by spa-goers

Exhibit 2   Average North American Spa-Goer

The typical spa-goer is:

- Female (69 percent U.S., 71 percent Canada).
- Non-minority (85 percent U.S., 70 percent Canada).
- In her early to mid-40s (average age of spa-goers in both countries is approximately 44).
- Someone who has been going to spas for more than a year, but less than nine years (60 percent U.S., 55 percent Canada).
- Someone whose first visit was to a day spa (49 percent U.S., 60 percent Canada).
- Someone who on her first visit, had a body massage (68 percent U.S., 45 percent Canada) or facial (13 percent U.S., 20 percent Canada).
- Someone who over time has added other services, especially manicure in the past year (57 percent U.S., 54 percent Canada), pedicure (56 percent U.S., 52 percent Canada), and deep tissue massage (48 percent U.S., 33 percent Canada).

Source: 2006 ISPA Spa-Goer Survey

who routinely cultivate their souls at spas, by those who intermittently retreat to spas from the grind of modern life, and those who seek rare experiences of being pampered at spas.

In the United States and Canada, about one in every four adults has visited a spa. Although women are much more likely than men to go to spas, the number of men has been growing as spa services have expanded to cater to men with more male-oriented services.[2]

Spa-goers typically enter the world of spa through day spas, which remain the most frequently visited type of spa. However, resort and hotel spas also enjoy considerable use, and are benefiting from trends that have guests incorporating spas and spa cuisine into their vacation plans.

Exhibit 2 shows a profile of an average spa-goer based on statistically most common characteristics.

Spa-Goers' Philosophies

Not all who go to spas participate in the spa world to the same degree. Spa-goers appear to fall into three distinct segments, depending on how involved they are in the world of spas. The Hartman Group, a market research firm specializing in consumer lifestyle trends, has made these delineations over the past several years as they have researched the spa industry and profiled spa users on behalf of ISPA. See Exhibit 3.

Core spa-goers. At the heart of the spa world is a relatively small segment of **core spa-goers** who believe that learning about and going to spas is important to their lifestyle. They view cosmetic services as superficial and approach spas with more therapeutic ends in mind.

Exhibit 3 Spa Participants

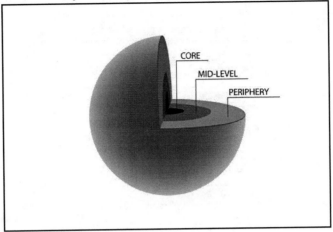

Source: ISPA 2006 Spa-Goer Study

Participation at the core of the spa world generally means incorporating spa visits into a more comprehensive or holistic wellness regimen. Although not above indulgences, these spa-goers participate in the spa experience primarily to "get work done," to transcend the physical, and address the mind and spirit as well. Their agenda is such that price takes a back seat to qualities of the spa setting, training of the staff, and overall ambience. Core spa-goers are not seeking luxury. Rather, they want every experience from arrival to departure orchestrated to carry them seamlessly through a process of rejuvenation or self-improvement.

Periphery spa-goers. At the other extreme is a **periphery** segment of **spa-goers** who enjoy going to spas but otherwise show little interest in them. They typically seek indulgent and cosmetic services to make them feel special and look beautiful. These spa-goers typically have little serious attachment to the world of spas and are generally very price sensitive, which may prevent them from trying services not aimed at improving appearance.

The experience of spas is rather limited for periphery spa-goers, and they tend not to associate their visits to spas with a health or wellness agenda. Their level of participation in the spa world is essentially peripheral to the core philosophy, values, attitudes, sensibilities, and behaviors that define the spa world.

Mid-level spa-goers. Between these two segments is the largest group: **mid-level spa-goers** who are interested in learning more about spas but lack the commitment and passion of the core spa-goers. They strive to strike a balance between pure pampering and transformative mind, body, and spirit experiences.

The mid-level is characterized by spa-goers looking to blend their wellness and spa-going behaviors. There are limits to what they will spend on untried services because their larger objective is to escape rather than work on themselves. From a marketing perspective, this segment holds the greatest potential for growth in the industry.

Exhibit 4   Average Number of Spa Visits in the Past 12 Months (By Spa Type)

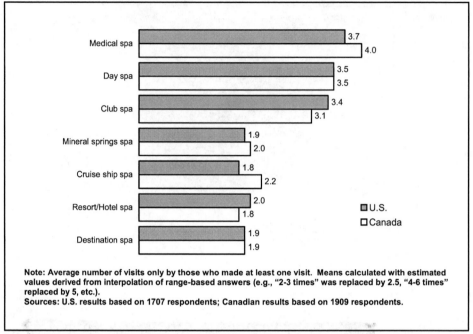

Note: Average number of visits only by those who made at least one visit. Means calculated with estimated values derived from interpolation of range-based answers (e.g., "2-3 times" was replaced by 2.5, "4-6 times" replaced by 5, etc.).
Sources: U.S. results based on 1707 respondents; Canadian results based on 1909 respondents.

Source: ISPA 2006 Spa-Goer Study

Exhibit 4 shows how frequently all groups attend specific types of spas.

Spa Drivers

Three primary drivers have emerged as reasons that people use spas:

- Indulgence
- Escape
- Work

Indulgence. Indulgence is the driver most commonly found among those who use spas intermittently. It is also what brings the largest number of people to spas. Typical indulgence services include non-clinical massage, hot stone massage, hydrotherapy, body polish, body scrubs, body wraps, complex facial treatments, thermal baths, steam rooms, aromatherapy, hydrotherapy, and Reiki. Exhibit 5 lists some of the terms typically used by people who go to spas for personal indulgence.

Escape. Escape is a key element for guests who are not using spa services for physically therapeutic purposes. Spas provide one of the few service venues where a sense of escape from the demands of everyday life becomes possible. While "going out on the town" may help people escape some mental stress, it is still a highly social occasion. Spas, on the other hand, offer a place of intense escape where

Exhibit 5   Themes of Indulgence

The ISPA Consumer Trends Report found the common vocabulary often used by people who go to spas to indulge themselves:

- Fun
- Indulgence
- Playfulness
- Decadent
- Pampering
- Letting go
- Joy
- Heavenly
- Treat
- Enjoyment
- Time for me
- Being good to myself

Source: 2004 ISPA Consumer Trends Report

no socializing is required. Regular spa-goers may demand an experience with no interruptions, no cell phone rings, no conversation from the therapist, no external noises, and quiet, relaxing waiting and treatment rooms.

Common escape-oriented services include facials, massages, hot stone massages, hydrotherapy, body polish, body scrubs, body wraps, mud wraps, week-long destination visits, and extensive, multiservice treatment packages. Exhibit 6 lists some of the language used by people seeking an escape through a spa experience.

Work. Work is the opposite of indulgence, though the line between the two has blurred for many. Seeking out work that is fun is increasingly legitimate. Hard work is often valued, and sacrificing fun for the sake of achieving more or earning more is deeply rooted in the American way of life. The concept of work extends metaphorically to individual conditions, a deep cultural driver in American middle class life characterized by the desire to constantly improve oneself and one's domestic surroundings through sustained effort. Along with the gym and places of worship, those attracted to the spa world have added spas to the list of places where the critical work of self-betterment gets done.

Work can relate to the improvement and maintenance of one's physical or cosmetic self. Such things as facials or pedicures address highly visible parts of the body, as do anti-aging skin treatments. However, work goes beyond the cosmetic appearance to the restoration of a lost emotional state and to increased fitness. Spa users may be looking to reduce stress or recover from a trauma.

Work ranges from maintenance to self-improvement and transformation. At the most intense level, some spa users and many spa therapists view spa as a spiritual experience that is important to their emotional and spiritual well-being. Spas are

Exhibit 6   Themes of Escape

Words commonly used by people for whom spas represent an escape:

- Calm
- Escape
- Peacefulness
- Release
- Time-out
- Enveloping
- Relief
- Rest
- Quiet
- Seclusion
- Cocooning
- Tranquility

Source: 2004 ISPA Consumer Trends Report

Exhibit 7   Themes of Work

Language associated with the "work" driver includes:

- Confident
- Relaxed
- Upkeep/maintenance
- Young
- Physical therapy
- Invigorated
- Refreshed
- Energized
- Prevention
- Rejuvenated
- Renewed
- Replenished
- Duty
- Cleansed
- Detoxed
- Holistic
- Rebirth
- Journey
- Healing

Source: 2004 ISPA Consumer Trends Report

not only about treatment for these people, but about re-creating themselves, being reborn, or finding regeneration.

Typical services associated with work include facials, pedicures, manicures, massage, body scrubs, thermal baths, Thai massage, nutrition seminars, special mud wraps, ritual bathing, floating services, and four-hand massages. People who go to spas for the purpose of work often use the vocabulary found in Exhibit 7.

Interpretation of Spa

While spa professionals can research those using spas, people will continue to approach the spa world with their own interpretations. Individuals will come to spas with different needs and receive different benefits. Spas will offer a variety of services and build their mission around those needs they can best meet.

Exhibit 8   Benefits You Personally Seek or Highly Value on Most Spa Visits

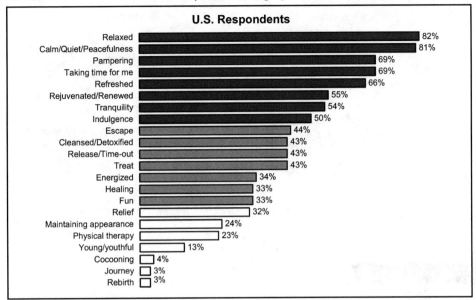

U.S. Respondents

Benefit	%
Relaxed	82%
Calm/Quiet/Peacefulness	81%
Pampering	69%
Taking time for me	69%
Refreshed	66%
Rejuvenated/Renewed	55%
Tranquility	54%
Indulgence	50%
Escape	44%
Cleansed/Detoxified	43%
Release/Time-out	43%
Treat	43%
Energized	34%
Healing	33%
Fun	33%
Relief	32%
Maintaining appearance	24%
Physical therapy	23%
Young/youthful	13%
Cocooning	4%
Journey	3%
Rebirth	3%

Source: ISPA 2006 Spa-Goer Study

The Four Rs of Spa

The benefits guests receive from spas may be summarized in the four Rs:

- Relax
- Reflect
- Revitalize
- Rejoice

Each person has different ways to achieve these results, and spas provide many of the means along with a nurturing, supportive environment.

Spa guests seek out these benefits whether they are visiting a day spa or taking a spa vacation. When on a spa vacation, the three most important benefits cited are relaxing and relieving stress, getting a break from the day-to-day environment, and being pampered. See Exhibit 8.

Body massage is the most common spa treatment initially experienced by spa-goers in the United States. Manicures and pedicures are about twice as likely to be gateway experiences for Canadians. Women are much more likely than men to have started out with spa services that enhance their appearance, focusing on those elements that are most often on display. Exhibit 9 shows the most common spa treatments initially experienced by spa-goers.

Gender accounts for many differences in the reasons given by spa-goers for going to spas and choosing their treatments. See Exhibit 10 for more details.

There are also differences in the use of spa treatments according to age. See Exhibit 11.

Exhibit 9   What Was the First Spa Treatment You Ever Received?

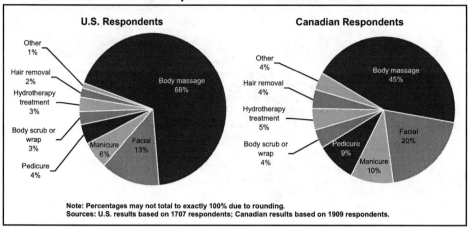

Note: Percentages may not total to exactly 100% due to rounding.
Sources: U.S. results based on 1707 respondents; Canadian results based on 1909 respondents.

Source: ISPA 2006 Spa-Goer Study

Domains of Spa

In 2001, ISPA introduced the domains of spa as expressed in Exhibit 12. The circle concept was developed for ISPA by Robin Zill, founder of TouchAmerica, and illustrates how the elements found in spa work together for total wellness. It's a concept that continues to resonate and describe the role that spas play. These elements include:

- Waters: The internal and external use of water in its many forms.
- Nourishment: What people feed themselves including food, herbals, supplements, and medicine.
- Movement: Vitality and energy through movement, exercise, stretching, and fitness.
- Touch: Connectivity and communication embraced through touch, massage, and bodywork.
- Integration: The personal and social relationship between mind, body, spirit, and environment.
- Aesthetics: Our concept of beauty and how botanical agents relate to the biochemical components of the body.
- Environment: Location, placement, weather patterns, water constitution, natural agents, and social responsibility.
- Cultural expression: The spiritual belief systems, the value of art, and the scientific and political views of the time.
- Social contribution: Commerce, volunteer efforts, and intention as they relate to well-being.
- Time, space, rhythms: The perception of space and time and its relationship to natural cycles and rhythms.

Exhibit 10   Gender Differences Among American and Canadian Spa-goers

- In both the United States and Canada, women are much more likely than men to receive manicures, pedicures, and facials.
- These results are consistent with the traditional cultural emphases placed on women's appearance and men's performance. Because women typically devote more time and effort than men to managing their outward appearance, it is not surprising to find them more often taking advantage of spa services oriented to those parts of the body that are typically "on stage." Conversely, male spa-goers in Canada are more likely to explore various forms of healing massage and the martial art of tai chi.
- Society in both countries is giving greater recognition to men's appearance, which may lead to great growth potential for spa treatments designed to enhance men's appearance, as long as marketing these treatments to men does not suggest an overtly feminine experience.
- Men are much more likely than women (especially in Canada) to mention physical ailments as a reason for going to spas. Women, on the other hand, are more likely to give entirely different reasons, including working on their appearance or self-confidence, or having an opportunity to get away with friends.
- Men are more likely to respond favorably to messages directed at their physical well-being than those touting other spa benefits (at least initially). Although women are also interested in soothing sore joints and muscles, they are open to appeals to improve their appearance.

Source: ISPA 2006 Spa-Goer Study

Exhibit 11   Age Differences in Spa Services Experienced

- In the U.S., those 35 and older are significantly more likely than younger users to attend lifestyle classes.
- In Canada, those 35 to 54 are significantly more likely than other age groups to choose deep tissue massage, while those 35 and older are more likely than younger users to engage in energy work.
- Not all of these differences may be attributed to the aging process since some are apparent in only one country. If aging truly influenced participation, similar patterns would be expected in both countries. Instead, it seems more likely that cultural, or possibly marketing, differences between the two countries may explain the differences. Reasons for going to spas do not vary much by age. In fact, the only motivation consistently related to age is to soothe sore joints and muscles. Understandably, this reason is given by a much larger percentage of older guests. One key practical consideration—lack of time—prevents some younger spa-goers from going to spas more often. Older spa-goers may not find the lack of time to be a significant barrier to visiting spas, and may be more likely than younger spa-goers to feel they already go to spas as often as they want.

Source: ISPA 2006 Spa-Goer Study

Exhibit 12   The 10 Elements of the Spa Experience

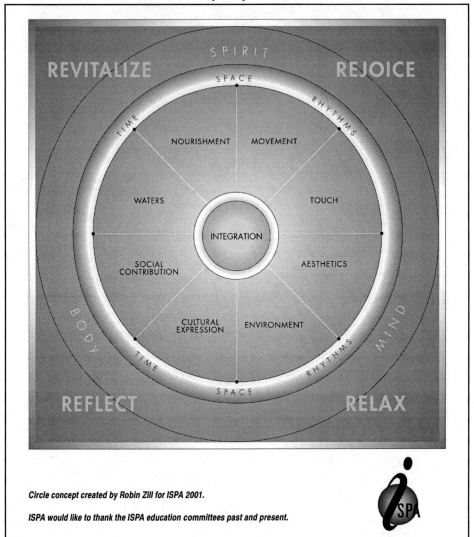

Circle concept created by Robin Zill for ISPA 2001.

ISPA would like to thank the ISPA education committees past and present.

Business and Philosophy of Spa Working in Harmony

While spas are about healing people, they are also businesses that can survive to do good work only if financially stable and operating on a sound business model. Spa professionals have the challenge of ensuring that they operate as a business while staying true to the mission of spa.

Just as spas teach balance to their guests, they themselves must practice balance by keeping the business and philosophy working in harmony. Spas exist to put other people first and care for them. It is a service to humanity that goes beyond profit and spa professionals must enjoy doing it to be successful.

How does a spa go about keeping its "spa-ness" without becoming simply a retail provider of services? It begins with spa professionals. Spa professionals have to believe in and be connected to the spa concept and the spa experience. Business development begins with personal development. They also have to have sincere conversations with their guests and find out what their guests need and desire.

In the 1950s and 1960s, people involved in the spa industry were purposeful. The people founding and running spas were doing so from the heart to serve a perceived human need. Their intention was improving the health and wellness of the guests they served. Then, when large hotel and resort brands became involved with including spa facilities in their new resort developments in the 1980s, the purpose suddenly changed. The priority of serving guest needs fell below such concerns as increasing the percentage of double occupancy, increasing revenue per available room, and generating significant additional revenue. Departmental profit took over in these venues and to many people the spa industry was simply a commercial business.

Certainly, there were a handful of top hospitality executives who understood how the health and wellness focus of a spa could positively influence the culture of the company, such as Mandarin Oriental Hotels. More often than not, however, it was a case of attracting the female business traveler, or being selected as the site of those national and regional meetings that had made the conscious decision to use only properties that had a spa, that drove the development decision process.

With the dramatic growth in the spa industry from 1999 to 2004, there was a growth in the number of spas that were financially driven and lacked a true believer who embodied the spa vision. To some, the soul of the spa became commercialized. However, as the new century dawned, spas in all segments began re-evaluating their missions and reaffirming the need for purposeful work.

Wisdom for Spa Professionals

I slept and dreamed that life was joy
I awoke and saw that life was service
I acted and behold, service was joy
—*Rabindranath Tagore*

Stephen R. Covey, a renowned author of inspirational leadership books, explains that there are Five Ages of Civilization: hunters/gatherers, agrarian society, industrial age, information/knowledge, and wisdom. Society is currently in the information age, which is rapidly transforming into the knowledge worker age. It is transforming so quickly that it requires continual reinvestment in education and training for any spa professional to stay current. Much of this will be gained through experience and purposeful education aimed at acquiring the new mind-set and skill-set required to anticipate and accommodate the realities of the new age. This will aid in a gradual morph into an age of wisdom, when information and knowledge are principled and driven by purpose.

Information is not wisdom. Nor is knowledge wisdom. The more a person knows, the more they learn that they don't know. As American philosopher and

Financial stability and good business sense are two key factors that help a spa carry out its mission.

historian Will Durant says, "Education is a progressive discovery of our own ignorance."

As Covey says, "Wisdom is the beneficial use of knowledge; wisdom is information and knowledge impregnated with higher purpose and principles. Wisdom teaches us to respect all people, to celebrate their differences, to be guided by a single ethic—service above self."

Spas that are financially successful have discovered that their success lies in doing good. They serve human needs and do well by doing good.

Drawing on a Legacy

Although it would be difficult to create a course in wisdom and experience, it is possible to learn from those who have come before. Spa professionals who learn to respect tradition and the pioneers in the industry will come away with a deeper wisdom and understanding of the spa world in which they work. There is a rich legacy for those entering the industry.

It is that person-to-person inspiration that has helped the spa world to grow. One often-told story is that of Mel Zuckerman, founder of Canyon Ranch, and the inspiration he received from Sheila Cluff, the owner of The Oaks at Ojai. In 1977, Mel was an overweight homebuilder who visited the The Oaks at Ojai for a week. He said that on the first day it took him just under a half hour to walk a mile. The fitness director there kept working with him until, by the tenth day, he could jog a mile and a half in 11 minutes and 38 seconds. He called his wife and said he was going to stay a few more weeks. After those few weeks, he called his wife and asked her to join him, saying, "I've found what I want to do for the rest of my life."

It was a life-changing experience for not only Mel Zuckerman, but for the spa world. He left the Oaks and founded a destination spa called Canyon Ranch, which has grown into a spa empire that now includes two resort spas and three club spas.

Vision First

A spa's philosophy is the North Star that guides the spa, while trends and guests are the winds and currents that may redirect its path. It is important that spa professionals synchronize their business components with their spa philosophy, as that philosophy is the reference point for all they do. Meanwhile, they monitor trends and listen to their guests to help keep them from wandering unknowingly off course.

There are so many choices in today's world of spas. With so many options for consumers, spas can stand out by creating a unique philosophy and a culture within the spa that embodies its mission. This provides the road map for the decisions spa professionals make every day—from the environment they choose, to the people they hire, to the retail products they sell, to the treatments offered, to the education they provide their staff and clients.

When a spa builds its philosophy, it is creating an extension of its brand through the spa environment. A theme for an environment further strengthens the clarity of the spa's philosophy to both its guests and staff. There are many ways to develop or further define a theme. For example:

- Geographic influences: high desert, northern lake, ocean, Asian, elevated mountains, etc.

- Treatment theme: Asian, modern, Ayurvedic, Native American, sports-focused, medical, holistic, Eastern, ancient rituals, etc.

- Focus on core business component: a synergistic tie-in with the ocean, golf, natural springs, mineral springs, retirement communities, country club communities, alternative or holistic medical practice, adventure, hiking, mountains, etc.

Ensuring that the spa's treatment menu, retail offerings, décor, and theme are in synch with its philosophy creates points of difference between the spa and its competition. The more complete an approach, the more likely there are to be points of difference. These make it easier for guests to express their delight in the spa to others and to describe the nature of the spa when referring to it. As for staff, the clearer the points of difference, the simpler it is to hire individuals aligned with the spa philosophy.

Finding and defining this philosophy begins with the definition of the spa's mission and core values.

The Spa's Vision. Having a **vision** for a spa is particularly significant because of the dramatic evolution the spa world has experienced. When modern spas first began, the primary discussion was always the vision of the spa: What would the spa do? What needs would it serve? How would it meet those needs? When spa growth began to accelerate, some spas ignored the cornerstone of establishing the vision and mission. Instead, the spa was established simply to provide guests with massage and skin care services or a place to work out. Other establishments added spa services in an attempt to take advantage of the spa caché. However, a spa's vision is essential to its success. While a mission describes how the business acts in the present, vision is the conviction about how the spa will look in the future. Spa professionals need to know what the spa's vision is and how it will continue to fulfill its mission into the future.

The Spa's Mission. The following questions are those that guide spa professionals to an explicit statement about their **mission** and culture:

- What is the purpose of the spa?

- Who are the target clients and what are their profiles?

- What are the target clients looking for in choosing a spa?

- What does their spa represent to them?

- How does the spa want to be perceived?

- What are the spa's core values?

The spa's purpose is synonymous with its mission. It represents what the spa wants to be known for and its philosophy.

The mission of the spa provides the foundation for the choices made throughout the spa: its décor, the types of treatments offered, who it hires, its retail selection, its marketing, and more.

The Spa's Core Values. The spa's mission is linked to its **core values**—the guiding principles for all decisions made by the staff.

Core values underlie the behaviors the spa encourages in its staff to support the mission and bring it to life. Core values give spas the boundaries in which to operate.

Expression and Emotional Responses

One spa professional described the spa experience as a chance to "go in good and come out better." Guests who go to spas want to do work and accomplish something, but someone else has to do it for them. They go to a spa and connect with the therapist or the technician to receive the service.

Receiving a spa service is the act of being nurtured by someone. The spa guest comes in with some sort of need—whether it is beauty, escape, respite from pain, or a need for quiet time. Their need makes each spa service an individual experience.

The spa professional has the challenge of meeting the guest wherever he or she may be. It is a challenge that most spa professionals relish. There are many points of entry to the spa. Some people decide early in their careers that they want to work in spas, offering healing and rejuvenation to others. Other spa professionals enter the industry from the corporate world, with the thought that there has to be something better.

A career in spas is not for everyone. It is a calling, not just a business. It is soulful, purposeful work.

Day Makers

David Wagner, a world-renowned hair stylist, artist, entrepreneur, and author, coined a phrase that has become popular across the world. He insists that his profession is not about quality service and styling hair. Rather, it is his personal mission to make someone's day while performing those services. He published a book, *Life as a Daymaker: How to Change the World by Simply Making Someone's Day.*

Wagner told a story about how he did a woman's hair who couldn't afford his service. Through talking to her, he discovered that she was about to kill herself and was getting a hairstyle so that she'd look great in the casket. He ended up saving her life.

Daymaker is a perfect descriptor for the spa industry: it is a soulful industry of "day makers." Every day, around the world, spas are in the business of making someone's day. The purposeful work of spas is to lift people's spirit. Spas do not exist to sell massage and nail appointments, but to make sure that when guests leave, they are uplifted. Hair styling, massages, and manicures are about a physical and emotional uplifting. Facials can make guests want to take better care of themselves. These services "make the day" for guests.

Community

In many cultures, early spas centered around communal bathing, a tradition that has continued to this day in many places. For example, residents of Iceland engage in communal bathing in the country's many hot mineral springs every day. It is as much a part of the Icelandic culture as going to the pub in England, drinking wine in cafés in France, or having coffee in a coffee shop in America.

While the modern spa industry often focuses on the private elements of escape for spa-goers, the idea of communal "spa-ing" has returned and is catching on. Spas have created group experiences where people can come and connect with their partners, their families, their friends, and even with people they have yet to meet.

Many spas have installed large bathing areas where people can take the waters together. Other spas have built communal areas where guests can visit steam rooms, relax, or even watch television.

Guests are turning to spas for such social gatherings as bridal showers, birthday and anniversary parties, team building, and couples treatments. In some places, spas are becoming the new bars and offering singles' nights. Families are coming to the spa together to engage in services, spend quality time together, and take classes.

Value of Spa

Spas have survived and thrived throughout history because of the value they offer to individuals and society. They have blazed the trail of whole body wellness by

This luxury spa creates a sense of community by offering wet lounges in a serene environment.

caring for the body, mind, and spirit. They have explored methods of healing and relaxation that appeal to the whole person.

They have also added value to the world economy, with spas growing exponentially and having a profound financial impact. Spas have proven to be profitable, viable businesses by engaging in meaningful, purposeful work.

This book will not impart everything one needs to know to become a successful spa professional, but readers can develop a heightened awareness of their worthy purposes and principles that can, over time, bring them to wisdom.

Endnotes

1. Jane Crebbin-Bailey, John Harcup, and John Harrington, *The Spa Book: The Official Guide to Spa Therapy* (London, UK: Thompson Learning, 2005), p. 4.

2 ISPA 2006 Spa-Goer Study, International SPA Association, 2006, p. 7.

 ## Key Terms

club spa—A facility with the primary purpose of fitness that offers spa services on a day use basis.

core spa-goer—Guests who believe that learning about and going to spas is important to their lifestyle.

core values—The guiding principles and behaviors that guide decision-making.

day spa—A spa offering professionally administered spa services on a day use basis.

daymaker—A profession that is about making someone's day while performing services or providing an experience.

destination spa—A facility with the primary purpose of guiding individual spa-goers to develop healthy habits.

escape—The desire to go to spas to get away from the everyday stresses and demands of life.

fitness spa—A facility with the primary purpose of fitness that offers spa services on a day use basis.

indulgence—The desire to go to spas to be pampered and to treat oneself.

medical spa—A spa offering comprehensive medical and wellness care under the on-site supervision of a licensed health care professional.

mid-level spa-goers—Guests who are interested in learning more about spas, but lack the commitment and passion of the core spa-goers.

mind-body-spirit—A connection between the mental, physical, and spiritual.

mineral springs spa—A spa with an on-site source of natural mineral, thermal, or sea water used in hydrotherapy treatments.

mission—An explicit statement that sets forth the purpose of the spa.

periphery spa-goers—Guests who enjoy going to spas but otherwise show little interest in them.

philosophy—Love of wisdom, a foundation upon which people build their knowledge and belief structures.

resort/hotel spa—A spa within a resort or hotel.

vision—Having a dream for where the spa is going to go in the future.

work—The desire to go to spas to heal or somehow improve oneself, whether that be physically, spiritually, or mentally.

 Review Questions

1. What is philosophy?
2. How could the philosophy of spa be described today?
3. How do spas nurture the mind, body, and spirit?
4. What are the different ways that the term "spa" can be used?
5. What is the ISPA definition of spa?

6. What are the main classifications of spa?

7. What are the differences between core spa-goers, periphery spa-goers, and mid-level spa-goers?

8. What are the three primary drivers for people who use spas?

9. What are the four R's of spa?

10. What are the domains of spa?

11. What is the difference between vision and mission?

12. How does the term "daymaker" apply to spas?

Internet Sites

For more information, visit the following Internet sites. Remember that Internet addresses can change without notice. If the site is no longer there, you can use a search engine to look for additional sites.

American Holistic Medical Association
www.holisticmedicine.org

American Massage Therapy
  Association
www.amtamassage.org

Asia Pacific Spa and Wellness Council
www.spawellnesscouncil.com

Associated Bodywork and Massage
  Professionals
www.abmp.com/home/index.html

The Ayurvedic Institute
www.ayurveda.com

British International Spa Association
www.spaassociation.org.uk/2.html

CIDESCO
www.cidesco.com

The Day Spa Association
www.dayspaassociation.com

Destination Spa Group
www.destinationspagroup.com/index.html

International SPA Association
www.experienceispa.com/ISPA

Medical Spa Association
www.medicalspaassociation.org

Medical Spa Society
www.medicalspasociety.com

National Coalition of Estheticians,
  Manufacturers/Distributors, and
  Associations
www.ncea.tv

Spa Management Journal
www.spamanagement.com

The Spa Association
www.thespaassociation.com

Chapter 2 Outline

The Origin of Spa: Water
The First Civilizations
    Early Civilizations of the Fertile
        Crescent
    Ancient Egyptian Civilization
    Hebrew Civilization
    Early Greek and Minoan Civilizations
    Ancient Indian Civilization
    Ancient Chinese and Japanese
        Civilizations
Western Civilizations and Spa Cultures
    Classical Greek Civilization
    Roman Spa Culture
    Spa Cultures of Europe
New World Spa Cultures
    American Spas in the Twentieth
        Century
    New Spa Design and Research during
        the 1930s
    The Second World War, Physical
        Medicine, and Spa Rehabilitation
The Beginnings of the Contemporary Spa
    Era

Competencies

1. Describe the importance of water and water rituals to the following ancient cultures: Egyptian, Hebrew, Minoan, Indian, Chinese, and Japanese. (pp. 37–43)

2. Describe the similarities and differences between the ancient Greek and Roman styles of bathing and spa culture. (pp. 43–47)

3. Discuss how religious and political issues affected the development and popularity of spas in Europe. (pp. 47–51)

4. Identify the people involved in the development of American spas in the eighteenth, nineteenth, and early twentieth centuries. (pp. 51–58))

2

A History of Spa and Spa Cultures

Much of the content of this chapter was provided by spa historian Jonathan Paul de Vierville, Ph.D., LCSW-ACP, LPC, TRMT, professor of history and humanities, St. Philips College, San Antonio, Texas; director of the Alamo Plaza Spa at the Menger Hotel; and founder of the Hot Wells Institute. The authors gratefully acknowledge his expertise and insight.

WHILE MANY PEOPLE may think of spas as a modern development of the Western world, the essentials of spa have their roots in human history as far back as the beginning of time. People have always sought out the places where water springs from the earth in order to experience water's healing properties and restorative qualities. Other aspects of spa, in particular the human touch of massage and the use of natural ingredients like mud, seaweed, herbs, and plant oils, have also been used in many civilizations over the centuries. By studying the roots of spa cultures and traditions throughout history, spa professionals can better understand and appreciate the richness of the modern spa environment in which they live and work.

This chapter explores the origins of spa and spa practices from antiquity through the middle of the twentieth century, which many spa historians identify as the beginning of the modern, or contemporary, spa era.

The Origin of Spa: Water

Water is the core foundation of spa, both in the places where water is found: a spring, well, pool, pond, lake, river, or the sea, and in the forms it takes: snow and ice; cold, cool, tepid, warm and hot liquid; gaseous fog; steam; and hot vapors. Numerous cultures in numerous eras have discovered and rediscovered that the "taking of the waters" enhances life in many facets: physically, mentally, medically, aesthetically, socially, therapeutically, and spiritually.

There is much evidence for spas and spa culture well before written history. All civilizations appear to have incorporated "taking of the waters" as a common healing practice. Throughout history, cultures around the world have found that "the waters" are a primary source for healthy living. The waters are also useful and valuable for the sick and diseased. Historically, "taking of the waters" in the form of bathing in hot, warm, tepid, cool, and cold waters, along with mineral, gaseous, saline, sea, and fresh waters have served to preserve health, prevent illness, and treat disease. Balneology, the study of baths and bathing, and balneotherapy, the use of baths and bathing for healing and wellness, bring into play

37

The Meaning of "Spa"

There is no certain or single origin for the word "spa." One possible derivation is from the three letters 'S' 'P' 'A' allegedly scrawled as graffiti on the walls of ancient Roman public baths. The coded message can be deciphered as the Latin *Salude Per Aqua*, which translates freely as "health or healing through water." Like most graffiti, however, the meaning of 'S' 'P' 'A' can be further interpreted in multiple ways, such as:

- *Sanus Per Aquam*

- *Salus Per Aquam*

- *Sanare Per Aquam*

- *Senare Per Aqua*

- *Sulsu Par Aqua*

The original Latin rendition is historically untraceable. What is unmistakable, however, is that contained within all renditions of 'S' 'P' 'A' not only are health, hygiene, and healing involved, but most importantly these are accomplished with, by, for, and through *aqua*—water and "taking the waters."

Other possible etymological origins for the *Spa* word can be traced from the diminutive form of the Latin verb: *spargere*, to pour forth. Roman legions made a practice of building their military camps and colonies at hot springs like Baden-Baden, Bath, Budapest, and other places where natural thermal springs and mineral water fountains poured forth.

Spa found its way into the English language through the old Walloon (old Belgian) word *espa*, meaning fountain. From *espa*, the English derived *spaw*. In 1326, a little village located in the Ardennes Mountains in eastern Belgium attained the name *Spa* when hot mineral waters were rediscovered and therapeutic baths developed for their medicinal treatments. When William Slingsby discovered the sulphur springs of Tewhit at Harrogate in England in 1551, he compared these natural sulphur mineral waters to the *Spa* waters of Belgium and the word stuck.

---

some of the oldest therapeutic methods and health care practices that make use of the preventative, therapeutic, and restorative powers of water.[1]

The First Civilizations

Along with nomadic Stone Age and Bronze Age societies, the earliest civilizations in Mesopotamia, Egypt, India, Crete, and China all used water for religious rituals as well as individual and social healing rites. The earliest written sources of history include accounts of the sick using purification baths in healing waters along with drinking from medicinal fountains. Within ancient springs, wells, and stone bath works, archeologists have found votive tablets and sculptures along with an abundance of artifacts that evidence wide use of the waters for health, regenerative, curative, and therapeutic practices. With all this evidence, scholars have gained an impression of ancient spa cultures and their different types, forms, and methods of purification baths and ritual bathing.

Early Civilizations of the Fertile Crescent

Around 4000 B.C.E. (c. 6,000 years ago) the Sumerians migrated south from Eurasia onto the arable plain of the Tigris and Euphrates river valley, known as the Fertile Crescent. Here they mixed with the local races and ethnic tribes and began to form the first organized cities of civilization. The urban life and social organization of these cities needed agricultural irrigation canals, city water supplies, and sewage discharge systems—all vital to survival in these arid river cities. Water supplies and irrigation were essential because for eight months of each year there was no rain. The ingenuity that led to the creation of sophisticated water delivery systems also paved the way for the culture to integrate water rituals and **purification rites** into its societal practices.

As empires were won and lost in early Mesopotamia, ritual bathing and seasonal purification rites developed religious and political importance. This civilization also used massage rituals; a Sumerian clay tablet dating from 2100 B.C.E. describes a massage technique that used herbal mixtures, rubbing, and friction.[2] During this time, people developed important centers for religious pilgrimage and worship, with social institutions using temple waters and social bathing rituals for cleansing and purification.

Ancient Egyptian Civilization

Around the same time that Mesopotamian cities were growing, a narrow strip of land on either side of the long Nile River running through what is modern day Egypt was being slowly united into a kingdom. More than 5,200 years ago the unification of Upper and Lower Egypt (c. 3200 B.C.E.) began; later this was followed by the Old Kingdom (c. 2770 to c. 2200 B.C.E), Middle Kingdom (c. 2050 to 1789 B.C.E.), and New Kingdom (c. 1560 to 1087 B.C.E.). Along with all their temples, tombs, and pyramids, the pharaohs of these kingdoms desired elaborate washings and royal bathing in this life, as well as final washes, baths, wraps, and burials for the next.

Egyptians worshipped the water of the Nile as a deity. Bathing was practiced as a sacred and symbolic rite of fertilization, since this is what the river waters did naturally every year by fertilizing the fields. The earliest Biblical account of bathing refers to the daughter of the Pharaoh and her attendants going down into the Nile where they found the baby Moses. In their sophisticated temple complexes, Egyptian priests ritually washed themselves in cool clean water several times a day before their services and prayers. This practice was later adopted by visiting Greeks. Along with the lengthy Egyptian bathing tradition, early Egyptian estheticians developed special bath cosmetics and additives including herbs, potions, and milk.

Hebrew Civilization

Sometime around 1250 B.C.E., Moses led the Hebrew tribes out of Egypt and began his journey through the wilderness. Alone and high in the mountains, it is said Moses heard the voice and words of God in an announcement that provided the Ten Commandments. Later these commandments, with the help of priests and scribes, became the basis for the Torah. The Torah, which forms the first five books of the

The sacred lake at the temple of Karnak in Egypt was used by the temple's priests for ritual ablutions and purification rites.

Christian Bible's Old Testament, frequently cites the religious need, use, and rite of bathing for both sanitary and healing processes. The Hebrews believed that **ablution** rituals and baths of immersions constituted an essential component for attaining a state of moral purity. The patriarchs, including Moses, Jacob, Aaron, and many others regularly practiced bathing for bodily cleansing and spiritual purification.

One example of healing baths was the prophet Elisha's treatment prescription for Namaan the leper to bathe seven times in the Jordan River. Among the Hebrews, Moses established the practice of bathing as a religious duty. It was the custom among the Israelites to "dip in the Jordan" to prevent the scourge of leprosy and other diseases. Herod resorted to the thermal baths of Calirrohoe near the Dead Sea for his disease.[3] In the Christian New Testament, references are made to the Jordan, the pool at Siloam, and the pool at Bethesda (also called Bethsaida), as sources of healing and purification.

Early Greek and Minoan Civilizations

Near the end of the third millennium B.C.E and a thousand years before Moses left Egypt, early Minoan rulers from Crete sailed widely about the Mediterranean and maintained contact and trade with the ancient Egyptians. A translated hieroglyphics mural in an ancient Egyptian tomb gives the original name of the Bronze Age people of Crete: Keftiu.

Not only were the Minoans (or Keftiuan) great sailors, they were also mighty builders of large palaces like those at Knossos and several other well-watered

The palace of Knossos on Crete featured indoor plumbing, fountains, and baths.

locations on the island of Crete. These multi-story, 1,300-room complexes were decorated with colorfully-painted frescos and featured broad stone-covered plazas surrounded by large shaded landscaped gardens. Inside these royal houses, builders installed the first indoor plumbing systems with terra cotta pipes and gravity-fed running water for spigots, fountains used for the Queen's baths, and an adjoining room with a flush toilet.

These ancient Minoan baths in the palace at Knossos might be considered the first truly European spa, since according to myth, Princess Europa, the Cretan queen and daughter of Agenor and Telephassa of Phoenicia, named the continent of Europe after herself.

Throughout the cities, states, and nations of the ancient world, social bathing provided a ritual act of civil hospitality for warriors and travelers. In the *Iliad* and *Odyssey*, Homer speaks of the bathing habits of his many heroes. Hercules was indebted to Minerva and Vulcan for the refreshing influence of warm baths. Althenaeus writes of the custom of antiquity for women and virgins to assist strangers in their ablutions.

Ancient Indian Civilization

During the same time that the ancient Minoan (or Keftiuan) island culture was flourishing, another ancient civilization emerged within the Indus River valley (c. 3200 to c. 1600 B.C.E.). Here the first great pre-classical Indian civilization built huge complex cities at Mohenjo-Daro (Pakistan) and Harappa. These ancient

Indian urban centers covered areas four times the size of those in either Meso-potamia or the Old Kingdom Egypt. Mohenjo-Daro and Harappa each counted populations estimated at more than 30,000 people. Within a two-mile circumfer-ence wall, each city included a citadel, market, and residential areas laid out on a rectangular grid plan. Both cities were constructed with elaborate and effective drainage systems. The internal plan of many houses included areas for bathing and cleaning. There was also a specially designed central public area for a Great Bath. The Great Bath was the most impressive feature of the Mohenjo-Daro's cita-del and included a large pool structure surrounded by smaller module rooms that served as part of a ritual complex.

Around 1200 B.C.E. and lasting until about 800 B.C.E., spiritual men of India wrote what today are known as the sacred *Vedas*. These Vedic texts reflected a reac-tion against excessive emphasis on sacrifice, accumulation of wealth and power, and offered hope for an afterlife in a garden of paradise. The *Vedas* attached great importance to purification baths and showed the minuteness of detail for bathing. In the *Vedas of Susrotas*, water is often spoken of as an article of treatment and as an antidote for illness, and the number and timing of the baths are exactly regulated.[4]

The Vedas also described other practices familiar to spa practitioners today, including massage, meditation, breathing exercises, and healthy eating. During the second century B.C.E., the Indian teacher Patanjali created what is considered the first yoga manual, which described the steps for bringing one's mind and thoughts under control through the practices of meditation, breathing, and asanas—yoga positions.[5]

Ancient Chinese and Japanese Civilizations

Similar to early civilizations in Mesopotamia, Egypt, and India, ancient China emerged, developed, and evolved over three and a half millennia (2100 B.C.E. to 1644 C.E.) along major Asian river valleys and trade routes. The ancient Chinese shared common and enduring religious philosophies based upon a view that humankind stands between Heaven and Earth. Humanity is continually working to harmonize its place within the cosmos through a complementary balancing of the active Yang and passive Yin forces of nature. Confucius (551 to 479 B.C.E.) in his *Analects* taught the virtue and conservation of traditions. Other classical works during these early times, such as the *Book of Changes* or *Book of Divination* (today known as the *I-Ching*), *Book of Poetry*, *Spring and Autumn Annals*, and especially the *Book of Rite*, taught the benefit of rites, rituals, and rules of etiquette, purifica-tion and contemplation, especially for the emperors, ruling class, and those need-ing to honor the spirits of their ancestors. During this time there was a turning to nature for wisdom. Temples and sanctuaries with bathing pools and meditation gazeboes were built at mountain springs and along lake and river shores.

An example of this early spa culture of China is found at the Imperial Baths of the T'ang Dynasty (619 to 901 C.E.). Built on the site of a thermal spring source, the Imperial Baths consisted of a complex of wood and stone bathhouses with con-stantly flowing warm water pools named the Crown Prince Pool (for the Emperor), Lotus (also Crabapple) Pool, and Constellation (also Star) Pool where T'ang emper-ors and their court officials came for leisure, bathing, and regeneration.

The yumomi ceremony at Kusatsu onsen in Japan cools the hot springs water to a suitable bathing temperature without diluting the water.

The book known as *The Yellow Emperor's Classic of Internal Medicine* (Huang Di Nei Jing), written around 500 B.C.E., describes other facets of Chinese health practices that formed the basis for Traditional Chinese Medicine (TCM). Acupuncture, the use of herbs, working with the body's meridians, and massage are all described as part of a holistic view of health and well-being.[6] Mind-body exercises, including tai chi and qigong, have also been part of Chinese wellness for many centuries. Many of these practices migrated from China to Japan by way of Korea in the sixth century of the Common Era. In Japan, they were known by the term "kampo," meaning "the Chinese way," indicating their country of origin.

Ritual bathing has always been a tradition in Japan, which has more than 3,000 hot springs. Around these springs, called *onsen*, the Japanese built places for public bathing in the mineral-enriched heated springs. *Ryokan*, or inns, were built around *onsen* beginning in the twelfth century, providing those who came to experience the *onsen* with lodging, food, and a variety of public and private bathing opportunities. Many of these *onsen*, still active today, trace their origins back to the early years of the Common Era. Records indicate that Prince Shotoku visited Dogo Spa in 596 C.E. Kusatsu Onsen in Gunma prefecture, was discovered by Minamoto no Yoritomo, a shogun of the Kamakura period. Just as Roman baths were used to soothe the weary muscles of Roman soldiers, so *onsen* were used by the Japanese samurai.

Western Civilizations and Spa Cultures

The spa cultures of Greece and Rome during classical antiquity and the development of hot and cold bathing and water-based therapies throughout Europe during the Middle Ages and Renaissance form the foundation of many spa practices of today.

Classical Greek Civilization

The spa culture of classical Greece in many ways resembles some of the **destination spas** of the modern age. Spa culture as a means for individual health and social regeneration was an important community process practiced thoroughly by the ancient Greeks. Freeborn Greeks practiced spa culture by regular exercising in gymnastic activities, while also exercising their minds with repeated mental, educational, and academic recitations. Massage was also part of this culture and was considered part of an athlete's regimen for good health. Alexander the Great (356 to 323 B.C.E.) was served by a personal massage specialist, and the physicians Hippocrates and Galen wrote about the use of massage before and after physical exercise.[7]

One of the earliest classical Greek spa culture facilities is found in the complex of buildings at the pilgrimage site of The Oracle of Delphi. Here near the Castillian Springs, the Greeks built a *gymnasium, xystos* (track), and *palestra* (column and partially covered court yard) with an adjoining *loutron* (cold water washroom), and *ephebeum* (a large area with seating for educational and social functions).

Although the ancient origins of spa culture can be traced from much earlier Neolithic, Bronze, and Iron Age societies, the classical foundations, basic development, and greatest expression of the classical healing arts and sciences are found among the stories and sanctuaries inscribed and dedicated to Asklepios (also Asclepios or Aesculapius), the ancient pan-Hellenic god-savior-hero-man of healing and medicine. For nearly a millennium (between the sixth century B.C.E. until the fifth century C.E.), numerous temples for places of pilgrimage were built and dedicated to Asklepios.

The Greeks built these spa facilities across the land and on the islands at natural spring sources and rural forest resort areas, as well as at the edge of cities, such as Athens. These healing temple complexes normally included an amphitheater for dramatic theater and facilities for bathing, cleansing, and purification, with lodging dormitories (clinics) for sleeping and dreaming. Known as Asclepieia or Asclepieion, these special sleep and healing dream temples served as sanctuaries for personal health, social health, and spiritual education.

As a cultural organization and civil institution, the network of Asclepieia served the Greek (and later Roman) world for nearly a millennium as public health care institutions dedicated to high spirituality and artistic beauty. The general therapeutic assumption made in the art and science of healing in the Asclepieia was that active contemplation and reflection on the beauty and harmony found in masterpieces of architecture, sculpture, and painting brought harmony and health to the individual. Enjoyment of the true, the good, the beautiful, and the divine are all important factors for elevating and enhancing human consciousness.

The best-known and archeologically-preserved Asclepieion is the Sanctuary and Hieron (Temple) at Epidauros in Argolid. The Hieron of Epidauros, like the Oracle at Delphi, became one of the most important and famous ancient sanctuaries for the adherents and practitioners of Asklepios. Many notable persons from the classical world visited Epidauros, including Plato, who wrote about the early healing practices and ideas in the *Symposium, Ion, Phaedros, The Republic,* and *The Laws.*

In 86 B.C.E., the Roman General Sulla sacked the Hieron of Epidauros during his war against King Mithridates. Later in the second century C.E., the Roman

The academy of Askliepion on the island of Kos served as a healing temple for the ancient Greeks.

senator Antonious, at his own expense, repaired the old and constructed several new buildings. At this time (150 C.E.), the Roman travel writer Pausanias visited Epidauros and observed the prosperous sanctuary that later hosted Emperor Marcus Aurelius (161 to 180 C.E.). During classical times, the Hieron of Epidauros included more than 30 structures, including the Great Spring and Fountain, a gymnasium, library, sacred housing for priests, nearly a dozen temples to various deities, a sacred plaza, and a theater that seated 14,000 spectators.

Later, Hippocrates on the Island of Kos, Galen at Pergamum, and many other communities built similar sacred sleep and dreaming complexes all around the Mediterranean, including one on the island in the middle of the Tiber River running through the center of Rome. Classical civilizations established the basic bath forms and bathing processes for individual and social renewal—that is, for total regeneration and mind-body therapeutics.

Roman Spa Culture

While the Greeks considered bathing, sleeping, and dreaming essential to health and healing, the Romans considered bathing more as an open social process and central civil function with activities that included leisure, conversation, and exercise. Roman culture moved the bathing practices of the Greeks toward a more social, collective, and publicly refined level and placed it in a complex of buildings called a *thermae*. The Roman *thermae* consisted of a series of specifically-arranged dry and moist rooms with different temperature airs and waters including tepid, warm, and hot-air pools followed with a frigid bath followed by an after-bath

This ancient seaside resort and thermal spa complex near the Bay of Naples, Italy, was visited by numerous Romans prior to the eruption of Mt. Vesuvius. (Courtesy of Jonathan Paul de Vierville (www.spacultures.com))

resting area. Roman baths could be found wherever the Roman armies traveled to conquer other peoples, such as in Bath, England, where Romans built *thermae* at a site sacred to the Celtic goddess, Sul.

Among the larger Roman *thermae*, walking areas were built with space for libraries, lecture rooms, art and sculpture galleries, multipurpose meeting and ceremonial halls, shaded parks and promenades, small theaters, indoor athletic halls, and, occasionally, sports stadiums. Massages and rubdowns were offered in the Roman baths, and Aulus Cornelius Celsus (25 B.C.E. to 50 C.E.) described common massage techniques including friction, rubbing, brushing, and cupping as ways to prevent and treat disease in his medical encyclopedia, *De Medicina*.

Following the wane of the western Roman Empire, the eastern Empire centered in Constantinople (modern day Istanbul) continued building on the tradition of the Roman baths. Here in the sixth century C.E. and with the birth and spread of Islamic culture, the Roman bath took on modifications. Islamic culture replaced the active games and athletics of the Romans with scrubs and massages, which became a central part to the traditional "Turkish bath" or *hammam*. *Hammam* were often elaborate and beautiful, with domes, octagonal pools, and ornate mosaics. The *hammam* was often an annex to a mosque and bathing was done in compliance with Islamic rules for purification and hygiene. They were also a place to socialize, with separate *hammam* for women and men.

Spa Cultures of Europe

During the European Middle Ages, Charlemagne's Aachen and Bonaventura's Poretta developed grand healing pools around thermal springs, along with Baden-Baden, Germany; Bath, England; and Spa, Belgium. As early as 740 C.E., the Benedictine Abbey of Pfäfers in Switzerland served as a spiritual and cultural center. Here the mountain monks operated the Baths of Pfäfers, where during the Renaissance the new Humanists came to meet and talk. In 1535, Theophrastus of Hohenheim, better known as Paracelsus, lived at Bad Pfäfers, where he practiced his healing arts. In 1630, the gorge was drained and at the beginning of the eighteenth century (1704 to 1716) new baroque bath buildings were built to serve the increasing number of patients. By the nineteenth century, the thermal waters were piped down to the more accessible town of Bad Ragaz, four kilometers away from the monastery. Bad Ragaz developed into a major health resort spa. Similar aquatic histories and traditions are found at other European spas including Aix-les-Bains, Evian-les-Bains, Vichy, Baden-Baden, Montecatini Terme, Albano, San Pellegrino, Karlsbad, Marienbad, Franzbad, and many more.

European spa towns experienced peaks and valleys of popularity in response to the religious and political climate of the time. In England, many natural springs were regarded as "holy wells" and were overseen by priests, nuns, and monks. In 1449, the bishop of Bath and Wells ordered those who used the hot springs to wear smocks or shifts, rather than bathing in the nude. Nude bathing was not only considered immoral, but was believed to spread diseases like syphilis, leprosy, and plague, making the springs places of illness rather than healing.[8]

In the sixteenth century, England's King Henry VIII ordered the closing of dozens of springs and holy wells, because of their Roman Catholic heritage. In response, Spa in Belgium became a meeting place for English Catholic dissidents, which in turn led to a 1571 law requiring English citizens to apply for a license in order to visit Spa.[9] Then, in a reversal of Henry VIII's closing of English baths, places like Bath, Buxton, and Harrogate were opened once again to keep English subjects at home rather than going abroad to experience the baths. A century later, Charles II, who had frequented French spas during his nine-year exile, revived the popularity of the spas at Bath, Epsom, and Tunbridge Wells when he returned to England in 1660.[10] During England's Regency period (1790 to 1820), visiting places like Bath and Buxton to "take the waters" was as much a social pastime for wealthy Britons as it was a medical therapy, as illustrated in the novels of Jane Austen.

Other places in Europe also built communities for health and relaxation around the flowing waters of mineral and thermal springs. An Italian spa directory, *De Balneis*, was compiled in 1553 and listed more than 200 springs throughout Europe, including Germany, Italy, and Switzerland.[11] French spa towns came into prominence in the seventeenth century, including those at Forges-Normandy, Vichy, and Plombieres. By the eighteenth century, Aix-la-Chappelle was renowned for its hot sulfur springs and in the 1890s, the hot springs of Aix-les-Bains, where

Profile

The natural spring fountain in front of the Cross Bath at the Thermae Bath Spa, Bath, England, sits on the spot where the ancient Celts worshipped the goddess Sul, and where the Romans built Aquae Sulis, a Roman bath. (Photo by Matt Cardy. Courtesy of Thermae Bath Spa.)

Thermae Bath Spa, England

The hot springs of Bath, England, have been a place of worship, a place of healing, and a place for socializing for centuries. The ancient Celts worshipped the goddess Sul at the place where the hot mineral waters bubbled up from the earth. When the Romans conquered Britain in the first century of the Common Era, they built thermae at the site. In the twelfth century, the bishop of Wells, England, built a bath in Bath. And in the eighteenth century, additional buildings were built, both for bathing and for drinking the mineral waters. By 1978, though, the spas in Bath closed, ending more than 2,000 years of spa culture in Bath.

In 2001, Henk Verschuur, managing director of Thermae Development Company, proposed a project to revitalize Bath with a new spa built on the historic sites of Bath. When the Thermae Bath Spa opened in 2006, it was a historic moment.

"I am a passionate believer in the special nature and benefits of the naturally warm, mineral-rich waters," said Verschuur, who also developed Thermae 2000 in Valkenburg, Holland. "My vision was to make the Bath spa a success based on my philosophy and concepts, thus providing real impetus to the revival of spa culture in the U.K. On a personal level, I wanted to give people, residents of Bath and visitors alike, the opportunity again to bathe in the thermal waters."

Verschuur's project combined old and new into a unique vision of spa.

Profile *(continued)*

"It was important to respect Bath's rich spa history, yet provide facilities that today's spa-goers would enjoy. By restoring five historic buildings and constructing one new building of modern design, we achieved a balance between respecting history and developing a twenty-first century spa experience," said Verschuur. "We still retain the names of the historic buildings, such as the Cross Bath, the Hot Bath, and the Hetling Pump Room, but have given them a new lease on life with a contemporary feel."

Verschuur has an interest in spa history and the role that thermal waters have played in the development of destinations like Baden Baden, Karlstadt, and of course, Bath.

"I am particularly interested in the Roman period and their ambition to bring their bathing culture to Celtic Britain," he said. "It is amazing to see the sophistication of the bathing complexes that they built in order to make use of natural thermal waters. The fact that the original Roman plumbing still functions in the Roman baths museum in Bath and at other European sites is testament to their engineering skills.

"I am happy that Thermae Bath Spa is playing an important role in advancing Bath's rich spa history and making a positive contribution to the future of this World Heritage city," he said.

ruins of medieval baths bore witness to the site's long history, once again became a popular location with spa-goers.

The Czech Republic and Slovakia, with more than 2,000 mineral and thermal springs, have a long history of spa culture. Hot springs and therapeutic muds at Piestany, Slovakia, were used by Germanic and Old Slavic civilizations, and a spa was established for medical use as early as 1546. Karlovy Vary, also known as Karlsbad, in what is now the Czech Republic, is built around thermal springs that have been used for healing since the sixteenth century. By the eighteenth and nineteenth centuries, that city, like Bath in England, had become a social and cultural hub as well as a center for medical treatment.

Hungary, too, has a long-lived spa culture built around its thermal mineral springs. In Budapest, the Kiraly Medicinal Bath dates from 1565. Built by the Pasha of Buda Arslan, the spa—an Ottoman bathing palace—reflects the influence of the Turks, as does the Ruda Medicinal Bath and Pool, built in 1550. Other spas in Budapest, such as the Szechenyi Spa, emerged during the surge in spa popularity in the nineteenth century.

Thalassotherapy, referring to the therapeutic use of seawater, was reintroduced in Europe in the eighteenth and nineteenth centuries, although for centuries, many cultures had found healing and wellness through the practice of bathing in the ocean or salt water, such as the Dead Sea. Englishman Richard Russell of Brighton advocated sea bathing in his book *De Tabe Gladulari*, and Dr. John Latham founded a marine hospital in Margate on England's east coast in 1791. In 1899, Dr. Louis Bagot, a French doctor, discovered that when people with arthritis bathed in heated seawater, they regained much of their mobility. Bagot worked with French biologist Rene Quinton, whose research found that blood plasma and seawater had extremely close chemical compositions.[12]

Karlovy Vary (Karlsbad) in the Czech Republic, was built around thermal springs used for healing since the sixteenth century.

In Silesia, in what is now the Czech Republic, an uneducated farmer named Vincent Priessnitz developed what is now recognized as **hydrotherapy**—the internal and external use of water for healing. As a means of recovering from a farm accident, Priessnitz created a regimen called "the cold water cure" or "the Priessnitz cure," which consisted of wrapping the body in wet sheets, taking cold baths, and practicing a regimen of fresh air, healthy diet, and exercise. He set up a **sanatorium** in Graefenberg in the Jesenik Mountains in 1829, where he treated several patients. By 1842, there were nearly 50 such hydropathic centers in Germany, Hungary, Russia, and Poland. Some of those who received the water cure took the knowledge and practice to England, throughout Europe, and to the United States.[13]

These practitioners included Father Sebastian Kneipp, a Bavarian priest whose book, "My Water Cure," published in 1886, described his system of hydrotherapy, lifestyle changes, and healthy diet. Dr. William Winternitz, the "father of scientific hydropathy," taught at a clinic in Vienna, Austria, in the 1860s, where American John Harvey Keith Kellogg learned the techniques that he later introduced at his sanatorium in Battle Creek, Michigan.[14]

Water therapies were not the only spa practices developing in Europe in the eighteenth and nineteenth centuries. Massage techniques were developed by Swedish physiologist Per Henrik Ling in the 1800s, and Dutch doctor Johan Mezgner also developed a system of massage therapy for injury rehabilitation.[15] Also in the 1800s, Eastern practices like yoga came to Europe and Great Britain by way of soldiers, educators, and government officials returning from living in

Vincent Priessnitz observed the way animals bathed their injuries in springs and adapted their methods to heal his own injuries. He then established the first hydrotherapy sanatorium where patients were treated with fresh air, healthy diet, exercise, and cold water treatments. (Courtesy of Jonathan Paul de Vierville (www.spacultures.com))

Father Sebastian Kneipp wrote "My Water Cure," which described a hydrotherapy system that also included healthy diet and lifestyle changes. The Kneipp Kur is still practiced today. (Courtesy of Jonathan Paul de Vierville (www.spacultures.com))

India. Western scholars also began translating ancient Indian texts, and Indian *swamis*, or holy men, visited Europe and the United States to demonstrate yoga and other practices used for health and wellness.[16]

In 1876, Dr. Erwin Baelz, a German doctor, was invited by the Japanese government to teach at Tokyo Medical School. During the 27 years he spent in Japan, Baelz studied the therapeutic waters of Kusatsu *onsen* and reported on them to the German Medical Society. He recommended Kusatsu as a "world class spa resort," comparable to the spa at Karlsbad (Karlovy Vary), leading to the *onsen's* popularity among Western European travelers.

New World Spa Cultures

The tradition of European spa cultures is lengthy; so is America's. Mayan and Aztec archeological sites in Central America and Mexico have unearthed ruins of sweat bath houses called *temazcalli*, the oldest of which date from 1350 B.C.E. They were used as medical facilities, treating a variety of medical conditions under the guidance of a trained healer called a *temazcalera,* who selected herbs and determined the levels of heat and humidity needed to treat her patients. When Friar Diego Duran wrote a history of Mexico in 1567, he included a description of the temazcalli, which bear many similarities to Finnish saunas, Turkish *hammam,* and American Indian sweat lodges.

In the 1600s, in what became the United States, English, Dutch, and French colonists built their stone huts and wooden tubs near wilderness healing springs frequented by Native Americans. During the 1700s, natural philosophers like Drs. John De Normandie (1721 to 1805) and Benjamin Rush (1746 to 1813) traveled to various colonial mineral springs and thermal sources and pools to analyze the waters for their chemical and medicinal virtues. In Virginia, Thomas Jefferson rode his horse to the distant Warm Springs Valley, the farthest West he ever traveled, and wrote descriptions and details on the healing mineral springs and pools in his *Notes on the State of Virginia.* Jefferson also studied Palladio's ancient Roman drawings and used them to design the historic Sweet Springs Spa in West Virginia.

In the decades between the War of 1812 and the Civil War, major health reforms swept the nation and numerous hydropathic (cold water) establishments, institutes, and medical colleges were built for the practice of cold water bathing. Some spa doctors like John Bell (1796 to 1872) and Daniel Drake (1785 to 1852) traveled to distant frontier springs the Native Americans were still using. Others like Drs. Thomas Goode at The Homestead and John Jennings Moorman (1802 to 1883) at The Greenbrier, in the Virginias, developed notable medical reputations for their mineral water and spa treatments.

Following the Civil War and during the Era of Reconstruction, spa doctors like Dr. George G. Walton (1839 to 1889) analyzed many newly-discovered frontier springs and constructed elaborate scientific and comprehensive classification systems based upon the current knowledge of geography, climatology, mineralogy, chemistry, and geology. At the same time, the American Medical Association Committee on Sanitaria and Springs published its first national report on sanitaria in 1880, classifying the nation's 646 known springs and mineral water pools.

American Spas in the Twentieth Century

At the beginning of the twentieth century, medical men like Simon Baruch (1840 to 1921), John Harvey Kellogg (1852 to 1943), and Guy Hinsdale (1858 to 1948) regularly conducted clinical hydrotherapeutic experiments and prescribed balneotherapy for their patients. These spa doctors also recommended **climatotherapeutics** and sent their patients to mountain springs where clean air and sunshine provided healthy environments. Kellogg, (of breakfast cereal fame) who directed the Battle Creek Sanatorium in Michigan, published an enormous methodical work on *Rational Hydrotherapy.* This 1,217-page tome included the technical theory and practice of hydrotherapy based on a systematic physiological system for every possible type of internal and external spa water treatment. He also authored a major text on *The Art of Massage* in 1895.

While most spa doctors wrote about and prescribed the internal and external curative benefits of the spa water(s), baths, and pools, they usually placed limited

When Uncle Sam Bathed the World

Hot Springs National Park in Arkansas has been part of the United States since the time of the Louisiana Purchase. In 1832, Congress set aside land around the hot springs for future government use, but didn't develop it. Private developers built hotels and bathhouses to take advantage of the springs, which also attracted people from all walks of life seeking medical relief from the healing waters.

Sharon Shugart, Hot Springs National Park's historian, is fascinated by events that shaped the park's destiny after the Civil War. During that time, people who couldn't afford to stay in the hotels and use the bathhouses in the town of Hot Springs pitched tents on the western slope of Hot Springs Mountain and congregated around areas where the springs bubbled up from the earth. Places like Mud Hole, Corn Hole, and Ral Hole became known as "Ral City."

"Ral was short for neuralgia, a nerve complaint that described many diseases, including syphilis," Shugart explained. "The hotel and bathhouse owners claimed the land, even though it technically belonged to the U.S. government."

In 1875, the U.S. Court of Claims ruled against all claimants seeking possession of the hot springs, and the government took control, making Hot Springs the first and only federal government spa. At first, government officials tried to oust the people of Ral City from the park's land, but they raised a protest that went all the way to Congress. In 1877, Congress passed an act requiring the government to "provide and maintain a

People who couldn't afford to pay to visit the bathhouses of Hot Springs, Arkansas, set up camp at Corn Hole. Although many people tried to run them off the land, a Congressional act declared in 1877 that the government had to provide and maintain a number of free baths for the use of the indigent. (Courtesy of the National Park Service, Hot Springs National Park collections.)

(continued)

When Uncle Sam Bathed the World *(continued)*

number of free baths for the use of the indigent," leading to the creation of a series of free government bathhouses that continued to operate into the twentieth century.

"It was very democratic. It proved that even people who didn't have money had a right to bathe at the springs," said Shugart. "Everybody had access, whether they could afford it or not."

Once the government stepped in to develop Hot Springs, building new piping and channeling the spring water more effectively to town, it became a popular destination. Opera singers, soldiers, politicians, baseball players—everyone came to Hot Springs.

"Posters declared 'Uncle Sam Bathes the World' at Hot Springs," said Shugart. "The government aspect was really played up. It was inspected, clean, regulated. People had a lot of confidence because of that."

Throughout the 1880s, elaborate bathhouses were built along Bathhouse Row in the town of Hot Springs National Park, and from 1892 through 1923, these structures were renovated to the heights of elegance—with marble floors, stained glass windows, billiards rooms, bowling alleys, beauty shops, and exercise rooms.

By the 1960s, though, hot springs bathing was no longer a popular activity, and between 1962 and 1985, most of the bathhouses closed, with the exception of the Buckstaff Bathhouse, which remains in continuous operation since 1912.

The twenty-first century has seen a revival of Hot Springs National Park. Many of the structures are on the National Historic Register and are in the process of renovation. The Fordyce Bathhouse, built in 1915, is now the park's visitor center and museum. The Quapaw Bathhouse, completed in 1922 and closed in 1984, reopened in 2008 as the Quapaw Baths and Spa, combining many of the original bathhouse's historic elements with modern features and accommodations.

emphasis on water exercise. As early as 1911, however, Charles LeRoy Lowman (1879 to 1977) began using therapeutic tubs to treat cerebral palsied patients and patients with involuntary spasms. Lowman, who in 1913 founded the Orthopaedic Hospital in Los Angeles, visited the Spaulding School for Crippled Children in Chicago, where he observed paralyzed patients exercising in a wooden tank. When he returned to California, he transformed the hospital's lily pond into two therapeutic pools. One fresh-water pool was used for therapy with paralyzed and poliomyelitis patients; the other pool was filled with saline water and used to treat patients with infectious diseases.[17] At Warm Springs, Georgia, LeRoy Hubbard developed his famous tank and in 1924 received his most famous aquatic patient, Franklin D. Roosevelt. Still a private citizen, Roosevelt traveled to Georgia where he exercised his legs, which had been withered by polio. A decade later as president of a nation deep in Depression, film newsreels showed Roosevelt performing therapeutic water exercises as he worked not only to heal himself but to lift public morale.

New Spa Design and Research during the 1930s

Before the Great Depression of the 1930s, America's spas, like the national economy, experienced rapid expansion. When the stock market crashed in 1929, little immediate impact was felt by many resort spas. In fact, the psychological effects of the Depression benefited the publicly-owned spas at Saratoga Springs, New York, and

John Harvey Kellogg of breakfast cereal fame, established a sanitarium in Battle Creek, Michigan, in the late 1800s. He wrote books on hydrotherapy and massage. (Courtesy of Jonathan Paul de Vierville (www.spacultures.com))

Hot Springs, Arkansas. More people visited spas to relieve their anxieties and the wealthy, who could no longer afford travel to Europe, chose American resort spas.[19]

During the Depression years, investigators researched the physical, psychiatric, thermal, mechanical, chemical, mineral, electrical, and radioactive qualities of nature's spa waters. Local and national medical organizations held special meetings and conducted special spa tours. A wealth of information, research, and articles on health resort medicine, spa therapies, and treatments appeared in professional journals.

In 1933, America's healing spa waters were officially recognized with the establishment of Simon Baruch Research Institute of Balneology at Saratoga Springs Spa. One of the first activities of the Baruch Research Institute was to issue a series of scientific spa and balneological bulletins: *The Publications of Saratoga Spa*. At Hot Springs National Park in Arkansas another group of spa doctors, including Louis G. Martin, Euclid Smith, George B. Fletcher, and Nelda King, a physical therapist at the Maurice Baths, spoke and published on the benefits of *Pool Therapy* and *UnderWater Physiotherapy*.

Everything Old is New Again

According to an August 2007 Associated Press article[18], several "new" spas have opened or will open on the sites of former historic spas. They include:

- The West Baden Springs Hotel and Spa in southern Indiana, a National Historic Landmark that had been closed for 75 years.

- The Bedford Springs Resort in Bedford, Pennsylvania, situated next to mineral springs that have drawn visitors since the 1790s.

- Quapaw Bathhouse in Hot Springs, Arkansas, where the National Park Service approved a private developer to create at new spa on the site of an 85-year-old bathhouse where people came to take the waters.

American spas are not the only new-old spas. In England, the historic Bath spa has reopened as the Thermae Bath Spa, and in Buxton, the University of Derby, Buxton Campus, uses the historic spa to train professionals studying spa management.

In 1936, President Franklin D. Roosevelt traveled by special presidential train to Hot Springs, where he visited the Army and Navy Hospital and Bath House Row. The same year, Dr. Albert W. Wallace described in the *Journal of the American Medical Association (JAMA)* America's health resort spas and their full medical potential. Wallace listed ten universal and necessary spa features:

1. Proper use of mineral springs and climates

2. Competent medical supervision

3. Proper dietary regimen

4. Systematic rest

5. Regulated exercise

6. Proper knowledge of the patient's reserve and limits

7. Spa therapies including physical-, electro-, helio-, and hydro-procedures administered by competent attendants

8. Planning and regulation of the patient's day

9. Psychic elevation of the morale

10. Development of a proper philosophy toward the disease from which the patient suffered[20]

In the basement pool of the Maurice Bath House at Hot Springs, Arkansas, a warm swimming pool was installed in the 1930s for special underwater physical therapy exercises and pool therapy treatments with chronic arthritic patients. At the 16th Congress of Physical Therapy in 1937, a three-page editorial titled "American Health Resorts" appeared in the *Archives* and a "Committee on Spas and Health Resorts in the United States" was established. The committee's first action established a formal outline for a national survey. Physicians toured spas at French Lick; Battle Creek and Mount Clemens, Michigan; and Glens Springs,

Richfield Springs, Sharon Springs, and Saratoga Springs, New York. The group drafted a resolution calling for the American Medical Association to establish a "Council on Spas and Health Resorts."

The AMA understood the therapeutic significance and growing interest in spas and appointed its own committee, but the trustees did not like the historical reputation of America's spas and insisted that the only suitable term was "health resort," not "spa." The *JAMA* published numerous articles affirming "health resort" therapy for "chronic disabling conditions including those affecting the heart and circulation, rheumatic disorders, ailments of the stomach, intestinal tract, gallbladder and liver, nervous conditions, certain disorders of the skin, and some metabolic diseases."[21]

The Second World War, Physical Medicine, and Spa Rehabilitation

Similar to the Depression, World War II resulted in benefits for American spas, but dramatically changed their course of both public and private development. Although there were hundreds of health resort and spa facilities located at thousands of hot and mineral springs throughout the country, there was no national organization or health resort bureau. What made matters worse was the increased internal politics among medical specializations and their territorialism.

American medicine was unable to develop comprehensive areas of responsibility that included the multidisciplinary and interdisciplinary practice of health resort medicine, spa services, programs, activities, treatments, and therapies. The AMA did define certain minimum health resort standards based upon established scientific procedures, but any medical references, especially to spa therapy and natural therapeutic agents and thermal resources, were generally forgotten as American medicine rushed to meet the immediate needs of the war.

The war forced major changes on America's spas and their treatment methods. The Army, Navy, and Veterans' Administration commandeered some of the best spas and resorts and turned them into military hospitals for physical therapy and rehabilitation programs.[22] Several American spas offered medically supervised regimens; a few orthopedic and mental hospitals practiced hydrotherapy. The military hospitals at Hot Springs, Arkansas; Glenwood Springs, Colorado; and Saratoga Springs operated institutional spa rehabilitation centers. A report from the Commission on Physical Medicine's subcommittee for Medical Hydrology and Health Resorts recommended the establishment of spa rehabilitation centers throughout the country at health resorts. Along with war veterans, spa rehabilitation centers could treat patients injured in industrial jobs, patients suffering from chronic degenerative diseases, and patients in post-hospital convalescence.

Unfortunately, the Committee on Physical Medicine did not include any of these recommendations in its final report. The interest and organizational support for health resort medicine and spa therapy diminished significantly at the war's end.

The Beginnings of the Contemporary Spa Era ——————

While the medical view of spa therapy and health resort medicine was on the decline, a new era in the world of spa began to develop in the 1940s, with an

The Army Navy Hospital at Hot Springs National Park, Arkansas. The man in the foreground is getting a jug full of natural thermal mineral waters to take with him to his hotel and home. (Courtesy of Jonathan Paul de Vierville.)

emphasis on physical fitness, personal development, self improvement, and wellness—not focused on the eradication of disease, but on the optimization of good health. The contemporary spa began to take shape, but still retained ties to its ancient and global heritage. Modern spas in many forms began to develop into what people today recognize as spa, incorporating and expanding on the practices and traditions of the rich history of the world's spa cultures.

In many ways, spa has come full circle, renewing and revitalizing thousands of years of spa culture to share with new generations of spa-goers. The mission of spa today remains as it has been throughout time—promoting health, healing, and physical, mental, and spiritual restoration to enhance people's lives.

A Timeline of Spa History

3100–300 BCE	Egyptian civilization practices water therapy and herbal remedies, similar to those used in spas today
1800–1500 BCE	Babylonian culture establishes bathing in rivers and the application of hot and cold 'compresses'
1000 BCE	Earliest known writings on Chinese medicine, much of which is still practiced
700–200 BCE	Greeks practice cold water bathing
600–300 BCE	Persians introduce steam and mud baths
300 BCE	Greeks introduce water treatments to the Roman Empire
200 BCE	Hebrews practice purification ritual by water through immersion in the Dead Sea
100 BCE	Thailand's (then Siam) tradition of massage and healing dates from the time Buddhism first arrived in Thailand from India
76 CE	Romans build a principal spa in Bath (Aquae Sulis) in Britain
211 CE	Romans discover the thermal springs in Baden-Baden (Aqua Aureliae) in Germany, which are still in commercial operation today
800 CE	Ottoman Empire builds Turkish baths
1326 CE	A curative, iron-bearing spring is discovered at Spa in Belgium that proves to be a spring used by the Romans before 100 AD named Sulsu Par Aqua
1336 CE	First "shower" developed in the baths of Bormio in Italy
1449 CE	Bishop of Bath proclaims that nude, mixed bathing profanes God's "holy gift of water." Bathers made to wear smocks while taking the waters in Bath
1536–1540 CE	Henry VIII of England closes hot baths and holy wells due to their implication in the "superstition and religion of Rome" (i.e., Catholicism)
1669 CE	*Natural Bathes,* by Thomas Guiddott, lists the minerals contained in water for the first time
1750 CE	Dr. Richard Russell of Brighton publishes *De Tabe Glanduri* in which he claims "The sea washes away all the evils of mankind," the first modern recognition of thalassotherapy
1806 CE	Modern massage techniques known as Swedish massage are developed by Swedish physiologist Per Henrick Ling
1826 CE	John Arnold of Rhode Island opens the first U.S. "pleasure resort" in Saratoga, New York. Saratoga is a Mohawk Indian word for "the place of the medicine waters of the great spirit"

(continued)

	A Timeline of Spa History *(continued)*
1829 CE	Vincent Priessnitz establishes the first modern hydrotherapy spa, with a health package of treatments involving fresh air, cold water, diet, and exercise, in Graefenberg, Germany (now the Czech Republic)
1861 CE	Dr. William Winternitz, known as the father of scientific hydrotherapy, opens a clinic and Institute of Hydrotherapy in Vienna, Austria
1870 CE	A Dutch doctor, Johann Mezgner, uses massage in rehabilitation, which becomes accepted in many countries, especially Germany and the United States
1880 CE	Father Sebastian Kneipp starts practicing hydrotherapy for the benefit of the poor in Bad Worishofen, Germany. His treatment center still operates today
1924 CE	The first facility for remedial exercise in water, the Hubbard Tank, developed by American orthopedic surgeon L. W. Hubbard, famous for treating Franklin D. Roosevelt, who suffered from polio

Source: Jane Crebbin-Bailey, John Harcup, and John Harrington, *The Spa Book: The Official Guide to Spa Therapy* (London, UK: Thompson Learning, 2005) p. xv–xvii.

Endnotes

1. Vladimir Krizek, "History of Balneotherapy" in Sidney Licht, M.D., ed. *Medical Hydrology*, 7th Volume of Physical Medicine Library (New Haven, Conn., 1963).

2. Patricia J. Benjamin, and Frances M. Tappan, *Tappan's Handbook of Healing Massage Techniques*, 4th ed. (Upper Saddle River, N.J.: Pearson Education, 2005), p. 21.

3. James K. Crook, *The Mineral Waters of the United States and Their Therapeutic Uses* (New York: Lea Brothers & Company, 1899).

4. Curran Pope, *Practical Hydrotherapy: A Manual for Students and Practitioners* (Cincinnati: Cincinnati Medical Book Company, 1909), p. 1.

5. Howard Kent, *The Complete Illustrated Guide to Yoga* (Lanham, Md.: Element Books, 1999), p. 13.

6. Benjamin and Tappan, p. 22.

7. Benjamin and Tappan, 23.

8. Jane Crebbin-Bailey, John Harcup, and John Harrington, *The Spa Book: The Official Guide to Spa Therapy* (London, UK: Thompson Learning, 2005) p. 4.

9. Crebbin-Bailey et al., p. 5.

10. Crebbin-Bailey et al., pp. 8–9.

11. Crebbin-Bailey et al., p. 5.

12. Crebbin-Bailey et al., pp. 11–12.

13. Crebbin-Bailey et al., pp. 14–15.

14. Crebbin-Bailey et al., pp. 24–25.

15. Benjamin and Tappan, pp. 25–26.

16. Kent, p. 14.

17. Charles L. Lowman, *Technique of Underwater Gymnastics: A Study in Practical Application* (Los Angeles: American Publications, Inc., 1937), p. 4.

18. Beth J. Harpaz, "New Spas Look to History for Inspiration," AP Travel Editor, August 14, 2007.

19. Robert S. Conte, *The History of the Greenbrier, America's Resort* (Charleston, W.Va.: Pictorial Histories Publishing Co., 1989), pp. 121–126.

20. Albert W. Wallace, "The Modern Health Resort, An Appraisal of Its Possibilities," *Journal of the American Medical Association*, vol. 107, no. 6 (August 8, 1936), p. 419.

21. Bernard Fantus, "Our Insufficiently Appreciated American Spas and Health Resorts," *JAMA*, vol. 110, no. 1 (1938), pp. 40–42.

22. "The Utilization of Health Resorts for Military Reconstruction," *JAMA*, vol. 123, no. 9 (October 30, 1943), p. 564.

 **Key Terms**

ablution—Washing the body or body parts, often as part of a religious rite.

climatotherapeutics—Treatment of illness through the use of air and climate, temperature, atmospheric pressure, humidity, air purity, light, and sun.

destination spa—A spa offering a multi-day, inclusive program of body treatments, mind enrichments, stress reduction, and spa cuisine for the purpose of health and wellness.

hydrotherapy—The internal and external use of water for healing.

purification rites—Religious rituals that use the physical act of washing or bathing to signify a cleansing of a person's spiritual state of being.

sanatorium—Also spelled sanitarium, a health resort or medical facility designed for long-term treatment of disease (such as tuberculosis) or to promote wellness and healing.

thalassotherapy—The therapeutic use of seawater.

 Review Questions

1. What are balneology and balneotherapy?

2. How did the spa culture manifest itself in the ancient Egyptian civilization?

3. What type of therapies could be found in the Hebrew, Greek, Minoan, and Indian civilizations?

4. How did the Chinese and Japanese incorporate water and bathing into their culture?

5. What did the Greeks contribute to spa history?

6. What did the Romans contribute to spa history?

7. How did spa cultures develop in Europe?

8. What were some of the early American spas in the twentieth century?

9. How did the Depression and World War II affect the success of spas?

10. What were spa rehabilitation centers?

 Internet Sites

For more information, visit the following Internet sites. Remember that Internet addresses can change without notice. If the site is no longer there, you can use a search engine to look for additional sites.

Father Sebastian Kneipp
www.kneipp.de/en/
kneipp_philosophy.html

The Greenbrier, White Sulphur
  Springs, West Virginia
www.greenbrier.com/site

The Homestead, Hot Springs, Virginia
http://thehomestead.com

Hot Springs National Park, Arkansas
www.nps.gov/hosp

Kusatsu Onsen, Japan
www.kusatsu-onsen.org

Quapaw Baths and Spa, Hot Springs,
  Arkansas
www.quapawbaths.com

Saratoga Springs, New York
www.saratoga.com/aboutsaratoga/
history/

Thermae Bath Spa, England
www.thermabathspa.com

Warm Springs, Georgia
www.warmspringsga.com/
warmsprings.htm#springs

West Baden Springs Resort, French
  Lick, Indiana
www.frenchlick.com/west_baden/
west_baden.asp

Chapter 3 Outline

Competencies

1. Trace the early development of contemporary spa. (pp. 65–67)

2. Describe the transitions that spas made during the early years of the contemporary period. (pp. 67–85)

3. Explain how spas today have proliferated and the organizations that have sprung up to support them. (pp. 85–94)

4. Describe how spas have developed brands and new concepts in the past several years. (pp. 94–100)

5. Identify how spa culture has influenced the rest of society, particularly service, cuisine, medicine, fitness, and hospitality. (pp. 100–109)

3

Contemporary Spa

The MODERN SPA ERA saw spas shift from their ancient medical and spiritual emphasis to today's corporate model that primarily focuses on beauty, fitness, and wellness. While wellness and relaxation have always been the cornerstones of a spa's holistic experience, the historical **European model** had come to emphasize taking the waters and retreating to pastoral and natural setting for weeks and even months at a time. Food was luxurious and abundant, and doctors routinely recommended spas as a way to cleanse and heal the body away from the rigors of everyday urban life.

In the early part of the twentieth century, medical discoveries started to replace clinical interest in spas and their powers of natural healing. Public hospitals started replacing spas and the medical establishment became guarded about spa treatments as a health response for many years. It wasn't until the last decade of the twentieth century that the public once again began to recognize the medical, health, and healing values of spas.

The contemporary spa period began during and shortly after World War II and continues to the present. This period in the spa industry began with a very regimented and rigid schedule-oriented spa program and gradually progressed to include a wide variety of applications, alterations, and modifications of the traditional spa culture and spa ethic. The most notable feature of this period was an explosive growth in spa usage with more people than ever using spas as part of an overall focus on wellness. On the commercial side, spas have flourished as the number of people using them has grown. Hotels that once saw swimming pools and fitness centers as a must-have amenity now look at spas in the same manner. In fact, many of today's consumers value the inclusion of a spa more than a golf course when selecting a vacation hotel or property to host a conference. The fitness and salon industries have incorporated various components of spa into their business models to enhance profitability and address consumer demand for these services.

Today, spas are combinations of ancient traditions and modern technologies. The modern spa is a place where people can go to practice preventive medicine, discover healthy lifestyles, and to relax. As they've grown in popularity, they've become accessible to a broader spectrum of the population who celebrate themselves, their inner and outer beauty, and their own dedication to a lifestyle that includes proactive wellness practices.

This chapter will explore the journey that spas have made from the mid-1940s to the present while also exploring the contemporary elements of spa, their types, and modern trends.

reflections

John and Ginny Lopis: Why Go to a Spa?

John and Ginny Lopis are founders of JGL, a spa design, development, and management team in the United States. They have both held top management positions at several of

the finest resorts in the country. They launched the Doral Saturnia International Spa Resort in Miami and were directors at Canyon Ranch Health Resort in Arizona. They were two of the founders of International SPA Association (ISPA). They are also the founders and owners of The Lodge at Woodloch.

Twenty-five years ago, losing weight was a major motivating factor for visiting spas. Guests were weighed and measured on check-in so that there could be a comparison made at the end of the visit to demonstrate success. The guest experience was characterized by small portions of food to meet a calorie count that was considered a "weight loss diet." Most guests met with a staff person to help plan their program, i.e., who helped them to determine their daily calorie count and to plan classes and activities that would help to burn calories in order to lose weight.

It was because of this focus that spas carried the label of "fat farm" for many years. At a popular destination spa in the Southwest, we designed a lifestyle program targeting executives, where they could experience the immediate benefits of the lifestyle changes we were teaching. We began with a full medical work-up, from weighing and measuring to blood work and stress test. We welcomed groups of 12 highly successful executives and professionals from business and industry, plus celebrities in entertainment. Our program repeated the full medical exam at the end of the week to demonstrate how dramatically the body could respond to diet, exercise, and relaxation sessions.

Despite the intense exercise and focus on weight loss in programs like this, occasionally a guest would lose inches, but not pounds. Because of the extensive pre- and post-testing on this special program, our guests were able to see results beyond the usual weight loss comparison typically available. In our first program, we all learned more about our guests' considerable obsession with weight loss and what it meant to them as a measure of personal success or failure. At the end of the lifestyle program, one of the young female executives who had worked so hard during the week received her very favorable test results including lowered blood pressure, improved levels of triglycerides and cholesterol, and even favorable changes in body measurements. This young powerhouse of a person who had impressed us all with her presence and strength all week long stepped onto the scale and when the balance bar didn't confirm the expected weight loss, she burst into tears. We had just demonstrated that she was measurably healthier and looked better than when she arrived, but without the confirming weight loss; the stigma of failure was overwhelming.

Today, we no longer weigh and measure guests on the way in and out. With the current shift from weight loss to the battle with stress, we now hear self-proclaimed success with the simple assertion of our guests when they say, "I feel great."

Entering the Contemporary Period

It was at a place called Muscle Beach in Santa Monica, California, where the first stirrings of the modern fitness movement began. Each weekend, thousands of spectators would line up to watch stunts and gymnastic events performed by the sea in the late 1930s. Many people recognize this as the birthplace of the contemporary fitness movement, which included such pioneers as Vic Tanney, founder of Vic Tanney Health Spas; Jack LaLanne, founder of clubs which were eventually sold to Bally; Joe Gold, founder of Gold's Gym and World Gym; and Harold Zinkin, inventor of the Universal Gym. Here they first gathered to put on muscle shows of physical feats in what was a boost to the morale of many people during the war years. The popularity of the beach grew and people became increasingly interested in various fitness activities such as weightlifting and gymnastics.

With the country moving on after the war, and the baby boom beginning in the late 1940s, modern medicine turned its focus to new and more scientific developments. With the war machine mostly dismantled, science went to battle with disease, developing a very effective, albeit reactive approach to fighting disease through targeted allopathic medicine. The general public very gradually began to take its own interest in fitness and wellness, and their associated benefits, and a new concept of spa began its life along with the rest of the baby boomers.

There were many pioneers in the contemporary spa movement. In their respective arenas, these people had a profound impact on their passion of helping people and on their industry. Mostly these people were creating as they went, following their passion and finding ways to share it with others. Their businesses were the outgrowth of their powerful personal visions, which became embodied in their businesses and available to others. These contemporary spa pioneers have literally touched millions of lives, and helped many thousands change for the better. These pioneers include people like Deborah and Alex Szekely, Mel Zuckerman, Jeffrey Joseph, Noel de Caprio, John Grey, Sheila Cluff, John and Ginny Lopis, and Ruth Stricker.

Transitions

In the United States, many spas followed the classical European tradition of taking the waters. Such historic spas as the Greenbrier, Saratoga Springs, The Homestead, Glenwood Hot Springs, and French Lick and West Baden Springs were all centered around mineral springs. As traditional medicine developed more treatments, drugs began to replace traditional water cures, leading to the waning of spas in America.

The renaissance and renewal of wider public interest in spas, especially in the United States and Canada, can be directly linked to the emergence and development of the health movement and fitness boom of the 1960s and 1970s. As the fitness fascination took hold, some spa professionals began to notice that there were "fit" people who were not "well." This shifted the paradigm from merely being physical toward a focus on wellness and emotional well-being, which in turn, opened and broadened the way from fitness clubs to the contemporary spa.

Spa Snapshot: What spa pioneer has been an inspiration to you and why?

In the destination spa category, Canyon Ranch Spa stands out as a great example of consistency in delivering an excellent customer experience. Their programs are flexible and allow the spa customer to customize their experience easily.

—*Wendy Clark, President, I-Bella*

Deborah Evans. I always look back at moments in my life that have helped me get to where I am today, and although I did not work with Deborah Evans directly, she helped shape the first spa that I worked at from a "fat farm" mentality to the beginnings of an award-winning destination spa. Without her vision, Lake Austin Spa Resort would not be what it is today and I would not have had the experiences I did without the seeds that she planted in Austin so long ago. As the general manager of the spa, she also encouraged her staff to participate in ISPA and it was under her leadership that I attended my first conference in Dallas. After she left the spa, I watched her take on project after project with a fearless vigor and she has always been an inspiration to me for those reasons.

—*Darlene Fiske, Owner, The Fiske Group: Public Relations & Marketing Strategies*

Hands down, the great pioneer of spas has to be Deborah Szekely for her incredible vision. Without brown-nosing as my boss will never read this, I'm inspired by the owner of the spas I work with in Canada, Dr. Wendy Smeltzer. She opened the first medical spa in Canada in 1998, leaving a busy medical practice to follow her heart. She has been relentless in her pursuit to improve the safety and hygiene standards of the Canadian spa industry.

—*Wanda Love, Director of Sales & Marketing, Santé Spa*

Deborah Szekely—she is a visionary and is so in touch with what is fundamentally important. I also admire Jim Root—he is a great blend of leadership and compassion.

—*Angela Cortright, Owner, Spa Gregorie's*

One of the central figures in this shift from fitness to spa was Sheila Cluff, a professional figure skater and high school physical education teacher. Cluff introduced "cardiovascular dance" to the world in the 1950s. Later her methods were refined by fitness practitioners, including Dr. Kenneth Cooper and Jacki Sorensen, and would come to be called aerobics. Cluff went on to found The Oaks at Ojai in 1977. This American fitness movement would lead many people to see and think

Fitness grew in popularity in the United States in the 1960s and 1970s. Much of the early spa movement came out of a desire to augment fitness with wellness.

about spas in a new and wider light than the classical European model with its primary focus on the waters.

Integrating Spa Cultures and Concepts

The concept of wellness in the holistic sense brought together a number of popular concepts, all of which had self-improvement at their core. It was commonplace to go to a salon to become more beautiful, a vacation resort to relax, and a gym to work out.

In Europe, the governments were reducing and canceling subsidies for spas as locations where traditional healing practices were sanctioned. These spa towns and their spa properties were turning to a greater degree than before toward tourism to attract visitors. They offered a rich history of water treatments and spa traditions that were gradually noticed and incorporated into the first contemporary destination spas.

As spas in the United States borrowed from European traditions, European spas were learning from the American tourism industry. A new image of spa was developing on each continent that clearly had the potential to transform the way people thought about relaxation and personal growth. This period saw the emergence of three of the major modern categories of spa that exist today: destination spas, day spas, and resort spas.

Profile

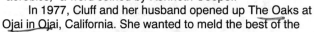

Sheila Cluff

The "grandmother of aerobics" is the title Sheila Cluff, a former professional ice skater, fitness expert, and the founder of The Oaks at Ojai and the Palms in Palm Springs, earned as one of the first to start teaching what she then called cardiovascular dance. It was her way of getting young women interested in physical education classes in the late 1950s. She'd bring in a piano and show her students how to do skating moves to music—only without the skates. She even had the woodworking teacher build wooden boxes for the students to step on in time to the music. It was this cardiovascular dance that would many years later become "aerobics," a word coined by Kenneth Cooper.

In 1977, Cluff and her husband opened up The Oaks at Ojai in Ojai, California. She wanted to meld the best of the European spas with the American interest in exercise and nutrition. She also very consciously targeted her spa at women. "I would like to be remembered for helping women tap their full potential," she said.

It's the work she has done throughout her life. She hosted a fitness show called "Shape Up with Sheila" and has written several books on health and fitness. She founded a business called Fitness, Inc. that taught cardiovascular dance.

"As a child, I watched her create tools and motivate people toward a healthier lifestyle," said her daughter Cathy Cluff, managing director of The Oaks at Ojai. "She has always said you must walk your talk and she does this in spades. I have met many people both at The Oaks and in social settings that have told me my mom helped change their lives, that she was such an inspiration to them. Another attribute to her as a mentor is that she has never let her success go to her head; she remains very genuine and generous with her time and thoughtfulness."

Most importantly, she's continued to keep The Oaks an affordable place for women to attend a spa. "The spa experience should not be the exclusive domain of the trophy wife or the very wealthy woman," she said. "That young schoolteacher, mom, or lawyer needs the spa vacation even more than the woman who doesn't have any financial pressure. We've been able to hold to our mission statement."

Included in the spa's philosophy was that The Oaks was a spa, not a fat farm where people would go to starve themselves or punish themselves through exercise. Rather, Cluff wanted to encourage people to make healthy choices.

"We started as … a belief that I had that if you can keep people from dieting and over-exercise that you could help them to have a higher quality life, they would be healthy," said Sheila Cluff.

From Fitness to Wellness

During the 1970s as the baby boomers started to reach their 20s and 30s, they began to flex their muscles. The "fitness craze" of the 1970s had a profound effect on the social psyche, but a relatively small effect on the hospitality industry. Resorts and hotels added gyms and workout rooms to accommodate guest demand, but they amounted to non-revenue generating amenities comparable to the hotel swimming

Bonnie Prudden: Sounding the Fitness Alarm

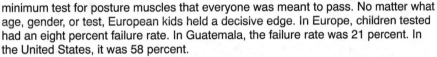

In December 1953, Bonnie Prudden, a fitness pioneer and researcher, and Dr. Hans Kraus, M.D., associate professor of physical medicine and rehabilitation at New York University, both top mountain climbers, sounded an alarm. They published an article, "Muscular Fitness and Health," in the *Journal of the American Association for Health, Physical Education, and Recreation,* claiming that the nation was becoming soft. The affluent lifestyle of twentieth century America was making life so easy and effortless that American adults and children were rapidly losing muscle tone. To compensate, the authors warned, Americans would have to engage in regular exercise to attain a state of physical fitness comparable to that of an earlier era, when Americans walked for transportation, worked on farms, and accomplished most activities of daily living and work through manual labor.

Prudden used a test devised by Kraus and Sonja Weber and began testing children in Europe, Central America, and the United States. The test involved six simple movements and took 90 seconds to administer. It was a minimum test for posture muscles that everyone was meant to pass. No matter what age, gender, or test, European kids held a decisive edge. In Europe, children tested had an eight percent failure rate. In Guatemala, the failure rate was 21 percent. In the United States, it was 58 percent.

Europeans relied less on automobiles, school buses, and elevators. European children walked miles to school, rode bicycles, hiked, and chopped and hauled wood for home heating. In contrast, American children were largely driven in cars by their parents, confined to their own neighborhoods, and obligated to perform only easy chores such as making their own beds and setting the table, nothing more strenuous than walking the dog or mowing the lawn.

On July 11, 1955, Prudden and Kraus hand delivered their test results to President Dwight D. Eisenhower at a White House luncheon. This led to the founding of the President's Council on Youth Fitness. For three years, Prudden served on the council, until she became frustrated with its ineffectiveness.

"I resigned in the Times. I was a regular on the Today show on NBC. I told everyone that would read or listen that they (the Council) weren't doing anything and that I was going to leave it because if you don't get results, you're wasting your time," Prudden said. "No kids got thinner, believe me. No one got any better movement on the floor. No one increased their breath control."

So Prudden found other ways to spread her message. She went on to write books on physical fitness, create exercise albums, host exercise spots on television, and create hundreds of exercise and fitness programs in places from schools, hospitals, camps, factories, prisons, mental institutions, and social clubs. She also established pre- and post-natal exercise classes and developed the Prudden Way of teaching babies to swim, launching baby swim classes at YMCAs across the country.

(continued)

Profile *(continued)*

Ruth Stricker, owner of The Marsh, A Center for Balance and Fitness, worked with Prudden in the early 1960s. "I followed her around. She worked with babies in the water and with children. We went to what we then called old people's homes. She worked with every population and it was a combination of gymnastics and stretching. It was the first holistic glance that I had at wellness and fitness."

It was also an eye-opener for Enid Whittaker, a physical education teacher who now works in Prudden's clinic. "I was never taught that a baby needed to be exercised or that an older person did. All of my training was for people between the age of 6 and 18. It wasn't until I met Bonnie in 1970 that the light went on. I was so amazed and not only was I amazed, I was amazed that after spending a weekend with her I could do all the things that needed to be done. It was incredible."

Prudden working out on equipment she designed.

In 2008, at age 94, she continues doing daily strength and flexibility exercises in her pool and preaching the message of fitness. In mid-2008, she was writing an article for massage therapists in Florida.

"The first thing I say is that the massage therapist should bring to the school a strong, flexible, and resilient body with good breath control," Prudden said. "Then you can be a massage therapist without getting a backache."

She also sees the need for wellness as greater than ever before.

"All of the things that Bonnie and Hans Kraus predicted would happen if America didn't get moving—like low back pain, diabetes, obesity, and coronary heart disease—all of those things are now epidemic," said Whitaker.

---

pool, both of which were generally poorly equipped and unsupervised. Fitness facilities were a must-have component, but they did not add much to the bottom line.

Some of today's spa pioneers recognized that the fitness movement was focused too exclusively on physical fitness, encouraging a superficial narcissism that ignored the deeper needs of the mind and spirit. They realized as Ruth Stricker, founder of The Marsh: A Center for Balance and Fitness, would say, "We'll all have tight abs and pecs, but vacant hearts and minds." This inspired some to begin the search for something deeper.

The "something deeper" was the desire for a fit mind and spirit to match a fit body. Fitness was important, but only insofar as it was one part of a greater goal. As people like Jane Fonda turned Kenneth Cooper's aerobics into a household word with fitness videos, Cooper himself was incorporating spiritual welfare into his spas and fitness centers.

It was during the 1970s and 1980s that something revolutionary began happening with spas in America. People caught on to the earlier concept pioneered at the original **destination spas** like Rancho La Puerta, The Oaks, and the Golden Door. The answer could be found in wellness. These spas drew upon traditions ancient and modern to develop holistic philosophies that healed the entire person.

"Wellness has evolved substantially in the past 20 to 30 years," explained Jeremy McCarthy, director of spa operations for Starwood Hotels & Resorts Worldwide. "What we thought about as wellness in the 1980s was aerobics. If you were talking about wellness, you were thinking about leg warmers and leotards and step aerobics. That has evolved somewhat to go from being more of a physical experience to much more mind-body-spirit. It's hard to say how much spas were an output of that evolution or whether spas were a driving force in this evolution, but one way or another, it's evolved to be much more mind-body-spirit."

The wellness vacation took hold as an alternative means of getting away. A guest could come home looking fitter and feeling better, and having learned something about wellness in the bargain. The idea of somehow tempering and balancing the vacation experience to some degree with wellness and relaxation has influenced the travel and hospitality industry ever since. Fitness was fine, but wellness was wonderful—and clearly, as fitness became wellness, there was much to explore.

Spas have become places where people can go to find spiritual renewal and mindful exercise.

Destination Spas

Early destination spas often didn't call themselves spas at all. With the word "spa" yet to be rekindled, most establishments were referred to as ranches or health farms, places where the lifestyle was a healthy departure from everyday life. They focused on helping people find ways to live healthier lifestyles.

The origins of the contemporary spa movement sprang from a small health camp that slowly evolved over several decades into what is known as a world class spa: Rancho La Puerta. Here, just south of the U.S.–Mexico border near Tecate in Baja California on June 6, 1940, Professor Edmond Bordeaux Szekely, a Hungarian scholar, agriculturalist, and natural philosopher and Deborah, his bride of six months, established their first spa in a one-room adobe hut (still standing) in the middle of a now much enlarged vineyard. Along with health lectures, deep breathing classes, seawater, herbal and mud baths, and long walks in the mountains, the principal policy was that of "absolute simplicity."

Rancho La Puerta is considered the first destination spa, and it launched a movement that continues to grow and evolve today. Rancho La Puerta combined a philosophy of natural foods, exercise, fitness, and spiritual practice that later became the foundation of the contemporary spa experience.

In those days, a guest could experience the first modern spa experience for "$17.50 per week; bring your own tent; no running water; no electricity; neither gym nor swimming pool; but a great mountain (Mount Kuchumaa or Tecate Peak) for climbing, plus a river for swimming; goats for milk and cheese; an organic vegetable garden—the West Coast's first, yielding a generous harvest."[1]

Deborah Szekely also opened The Golden Door in 1958, following the model of Rancho La Puerta. It offered a week-long experience that combined personal health and fitness training and Japanese-inspired hospitality. Guests learned and practiced healthy lifestyle habits and many testified to the life-changing experiences they had at the spa. The Golden Door became an iconic symbol of spa as a combination of luxury, personal growth, education, and fitness.[2]

Profile

Deborah Szekely

There are few names as revered in the spa industry as Deborah Szekely. For more than 65 years, she has embodied the heart and soul of spa, leading the way with the founding of the world class health spas Rancho La Puerta and the Golden Door.

"Deborah Szekely's sincere passion for the spa industry, as well as her many contributions to its growth, are an inspiration to us all," said the 2005 ISPA Chairman Kate Mearns.

Known as the godmother of the mind/body/fitness movement, Szekely and her husband Edmond opened Rancho La Puerta in 1940. Edmond's teachings on the Essenes included a focus on the interconnectedness of mind, body, and spirit.

Their teachings would help to launch the tremendous growth spas have experienced over the past six decades.

"Deborah Szekely is an industry pioneer," said Sean Handler, of Solace Spa at Boyne USA. "Her words, smile, humor, and wisdom are an inspiration to us all. We are very lucky as an industry to have such a loving and talented lady as Deborah Szekely as one of our founders."

"She embodies spa and is a bridge between the spa of the past and to the present," said Loren Stone, the CEO of Sovereign Hospitality. "She volunteers and gives back to the community with a dedication to always being better and influencing positive change in individuals."

The health spas were just one manifestation of a life committed to service. Her accomplishments are myriad:

- She served as a U.S. delegate to the UNESCO Conference on Fitness in 1977.
- In 1978, she founded an arts and education council which has raised more than $25 million to support 221 cultural organizations in San Diego County.
- She was the president and CEO of the Inter-American Foundation.
- She was a U.S. diplomat, working throughout Latin America and the Caribbean.
- In 1991, she founded Eureka Communities, a leadership training program for CEOs of nonprofit organizations.
- She founded the New Americans Immigration Museum and Learning Center.
- In 2005, she was awarded the ISPA 2005 Alex Szekely Humanitarian Award, an award named for her late son. She had previously been named an honorary lifetime chair of ISPA.

"Giving, sharing, easing pain and suffering is what people who work in spas do all the time," she wrote to a guest who had asked about whether spas have a philanthropic obligation to their communities. "Just as the benefits of massage do not stop at the neck, a truly giving person, the term that describes a good therapist, does not stop healing people just because they are not paid in the coin of the realm."[3]

Deborah Szekely is someone who, in her more than eight decades of life, has never stopped giving and healing.

"Making healthy people healthier is a joyous profession," she says. "It's a helping profession. It's a giving, caring profession."

reflections

John and Ginny Lopis: Knowing What's Good For You

Years ago, (destination) spas exercised greater control over the guest. Upon arrival, guests were counseled and given programs with guidelines for what to eat, what classes and activities to take, what treatments to include, etc. We remember talking with a guest who had just been to a spa in Florida and she was not happy with the practice there of knocking on guests' doors in the morning to be sure they were up for the morning walk.

At one of the country's largest and most successful destination spas, the spa felt the need to control guests and impose a "health eating" experience. They gave out information on many things that were considered unhealthy to eat and why the spa program DID NOT ALLOW them: salt, sugar, ketchup, coffee, alcohol, chocolate, butter, maple syrup, cream, etc. (the list goes on). However, behind the scenes, we staff would often go out together after work and enjoy most of the ingredients not allowed at the spa. Yet, we were all very fit and healthy and had healthy lifestyles. In the back-of-house space where the employees ate at the spa, except for the alcohol, all of these items were readily available. Return guests who knew "the routine," would get staff to sneak them some "real coffee." As for the alcohol, the clinking suitcases at check-in were a dead giveaway.

In contrast, today's spa programs are much more geared to healthy living through moderation rather than abstinence and guests are encouraged to apply moderation during their stay.

Pioneers of contemporary spa, like the Szekelys, enveloped the fitness concept into a more holistic approach to well-being. Emphasis was placed on a rigorous fitness regimen, accompanied by a natural, spartan culinary program. Much emphasis was given to weight loss and lifestyle change.

Early destination spas guided and nurtured not only their spa guests, but the entire notion of spa as an entity unto itself. Viewed by many in the 1980s as a fad, destination spas held firm in their belief that spa was much more, that it would continue to define and redefine what it meant to be proactively healthy. Spa, the movement, the way of thinking about health and wellness as practiced in daily life, was the seedling that was watered and grown by the destination spas from the post-war period through the 1980s.

As spas gained popularity in the 1980s, resorts and many destination spas began to reward the demands of the spa regimen with relaxing treatments like massages, facials, and alternative healing and personal growth modalities.

Day Spas

Day spas source their roots to Florence Nightingale Graham, better known as Elizabeth Arden, who brought the concept of makeup, spa, and beauty treatments to the United States in 1910. Her business was called The Red Door. In 1922, she opened a salon in France. In 1934, Arden turned her Maine summer home into a spa called Maine Chance Beauty Spa, a franchise that would expand internationally. By

Noel de Caprio

Noel de Caprio, the acclaimed mother of the day spa industry, lived a life that embodied her motto of "Never quit!"

Noel opened Noelle the Day Spa in the early 1970s, featuring a day of beauty—a package of spa services and lunch available in a small room at the salon. It was a success with clients and inspired others throughout the country to follow her lead.

"If I had a mentor in the spa industry, it was Noel, because she had a passion for it," said Pam McNair, owner of the Gadabout SalonSpas in Tucson, Arizona. "She also had a vision of the future."

When in 1979, she met the cabinet-maker and carpenter who would become her husband, Peter de Caprio, her spa was already generating $3 million a year in gross revenue.

"I was always fascinated by this sort of larger stage that she was playing on," Peter said. "One of the things as a cabinet maker, when you met another cabinet maker they wouldn't tell you what kind of sandpaper they used. Nothing was ever shared. I started getting into this world and everyone talked about business. The openness of the industry was really, really fascinating to me."

In 1984, Noel was diagnosed with breast cancer and given three months to live. It was a sentence the de Caprios weren't prepared to accept. Instead, they decided that she would fight it.

"I credit her with my life and who I am and who I've become," Peter said. "I credit her with teaching whoever was listening her philosophy of never quitting, which is a lesson that you've got a whole lifetime to work on."

Two years after her cancer diagnosis, she took in a 12-year-old boy, Jason, who is now following in her footsteps at the spa.

On a Saturday morning in 1995, the day spa, which was then 10,000 square feet and employed 75 people, caught fire during a February blizzard. The spa was destroyed. Noel quickly went looking for a new home and 12 hours after the firefighters left, she had opened a temporary spa in a vacant storefront a short distance away—even managing to get a building permit on a Saturday.

"Otherwise," she told a New York Times reporter in 1998, "75 people would have been out of work."

"Now, we brought in $700 that day as opposed to normal business where you're making about $12,000," said Peter. "The sign we painted that day said, 'Noelle: Hotter than Ever.' We all took photographs with fireman's hats on and had T-shirts that said, 'Fire? What fire?'"

Jason said the fire forced them to recreate themselves. When it burned down, he said she went to one of her mentors, who very calmly said, "Don't worry, Noel, fires are very cleansing." His mother responded with "What? Are you kidding me? I just lost my salon!"

The mentor's words were prescient, "If it wasn't for that fire, we wouldn't be in this beautiful space," Jason said. "It shifted from being a day spa to being a wellness

Profile *(continued)*

center. That was one of my mother's last visions—wellness, one step above a day spa. It looks at the inner beauty as opposed to the outer beauty only."

Together, the de Caprios created Spa University and Hair Academy and the Noelle Salon and Spa Consulting Group—which, among other things, helped establish the first day spa in Japan.

In 1998, fourteen years after she was diagnosed with cancer, Noel died.

"We laughed as much as we cried that entire 14 years," her husband said. "It's been an amazing life."

"I really can't get through one of my days cutting hair without hearing someone say how she impacted them, which is truly amazing," Jason said. "The most random people say 'I knew your mother.' 'Your mother touched me.' 'Your mother wrote me a card.' 'Your mother helped me when I was going through cancer.' So it's pretty nice. For me, it's like she's still here."

"Her ability to size up a situation and make you feel comfortable inside was unparalleled, absolutely unparalleled," Peter said. "I will still meet people on the street who will say, 'Noel. She was my best friend.' Was she to that person? Absolutely. How did Noel do that? She had that particular magic and built a business on it."

Nor will the industry that she helped launch soon forget her.

---

the 1960s, it was a fully realized day spa brand (before the phrase "day spa" was coined) with more than 50 locations worldwide.

However, at this point it was still the salon that was the industry, not day spa. The Red Door began as large salons with skin care because skin care was the specialty of Elizabeth Arden and her company.

The term 'day spa' would not flourish as a business until Noel de Caprio opened her day spa in 1972, offering European-style massages, body wraps, water therapy treatments, and facials. These were services that she added to her beauty salon, a concept that would prove to be popular and copied by many around the country. She served as a model for the day spas that were to come and she is credited with being the founder of the day spa industry.

In the late 1970s, Gillette did an intensive study of destination group spas and the beauty industry. One of the conclusions was that the general population was "time poor." Americans had a difficult time slowing down and wanted to, as one airport outlet offering spa services advertised, "Relax in a hurry!"

It was out of this time poverty that day spas arose to fill a niche. They took the best elements of the destination spa market and made it more accessible to people who couldn't spend a week or more away from home. They offered spa services that could be received in a single day. The presence of day spas has increased both the number of people who can have spa experiences and the frequency of their visits.

Day spas offered many of the same treatments as destination and resort spas—facials, massages, and water treatments, but did so without providing overnight facilities. Guests would come for one or two treatments rather than an entire

reflections

Pam McNair: Growing a Day Spa

Pam McNair, the founder of Gadabout SalonSpas is a visionary and one of the early day spa pioneers. She owns seven spas in the Tucson, Arizona area and one in Italy.

(Growing Gadabout) has been a process that has taken about 27 years. I've had a lot of help, a lot of energy, and a desire to help make this industry better. Twenty-seven years ago, when I opened my first location here, we had a nail technician and a skincare technician who worked in a small area like a closet behind the front desk. But I always felt that it was a necessary part of the total picture of a salon—which was quite different at that time. They were very lonely for a while until we started educating and training other people in their departments.

It was 1984 when we started putting spa treatments of some kind into our mix of services. We went through a lot of transition in order to get where we are now. Anything that was high touch, I always felt would have a future in our industry, at least in Gadabout's future, and it hasn't proved to be wrong. There are a lot of services that are available—and have been for years—that are mechanical. They're technologically on the cutting edge, but they don't put a feeling or relationship with a client together. That is what has always been important to us.

Within the first seven years we had five locations. I had the momentum and the passion and the energy, so we just kept going.

I was very fortunate to be in the same community with Canyon Ranch. For 15 years, we had the salon at Canyon Ranch. I was aware of some of the things that Canyon Ranch was developing. It was very beneficial to take what the resorts and destination spas were developing and ask how our clients could benefit from them. But we had a huge learning curve. There were a lot of things that the resort and destination spas were doing for our clients that we said, "yeah, let me do that." For instance: hydrotherapy tubs. The first time I saw them at ISPA, I was thrilled. I bought one. I bought two. I had people come in and train staff members. I put them in our facility and they were beautiful and they made beautiful noise, but we couldn't get clients to use them. They were so unsuccessful that about six years later I realized they were never going to be a commodity for us, so we removed them.

I think one of the things we failed to do was ask our clients. And maybe we were ahead of the curve; maybe we were five years too early. Because now I have friends who have hydrotherapy tubs who are very successful with them. But it took for the consumer to want these services because they had used them at resort and destination spas to request them from us. We've gone through a lot of things like that: Vichy showers, soft pack beds, a lot of things that probably today if we were to purchase them and go through the marketing, we would have tremendously different results.

I have to understand my market, I have to understand my clients. Then I understand what services are reasonable for us as a day spa to have. Granted there are a lot of places that call themselves day spas. There will always be people who tag on: dental spas, pet spas, but it is up to us to keep integrity. When a client comes in knowing that you are a spa, you have to create an environment that lets them know that this is what a spa is meant to be.

La Costa Resort and Spa

La Costa Resort and Spa in Carlsbad, California, represents the original U.S. resort spa of the modern era, opening in 1965 with a resident doctor, wellness programming, salon, and spa.

Jeremy McCarthy

Sean Handler served as the spa's director during the final years of the historic original facility and the opening of the new La Costa. It was a meaningful experience that he says continues to impact him, "The old walls did speak—and the stories of history and charm will forever be a guiding light for me from the innovative beginnings of La Costa."

The new La Costa has a 42,000 square foot spa and an 8,000 square foot fitness center—called the Athletic Club, each far removed from the other.

"There is always this debate that happens with properties: should spa and fitness be separate?" said Jeremy McCarthy, former spa manager for La Costa, explaining the separation. "The fitness center is more of a high energy environment and people are pumped up and wanting to go to work. The energy is at a different level than at the spa where people are going to relax and calm down. If you put these two different clients in the same environment, they might distract each other from what they are there to accomplish."

At La Costa, they knew they were going to have two different types of guests that would use the facilities, arriving with different mindsets and different goals. However, they also recognized that there would be people going to the spa who wanted a fitness component to their wellness retreat.

The solution? La Costa built a small fitness studio in the spa.

"In one sense, spa and fitness are two very different activities and two very different experiences that don't necessarily have much to do with each other, but where they overlap is that they are both parts of a wellness life cycle," McCarthy said. "If you're going on a trip where wellness is going to be an important part of your trip, you are going to want to have spa and fitness. They're two distinct activities and experiences, but they're all part of that wellness lifestyle."

regimen of treatments. Day spas often followed the working model established by salons and were operated in similar fashion.

By 2006, there were nearly 11,000 day spas, making up 79 percent of the total industry.

Resort Spas

Resort spas trace their beginnings to La Costa Resort and Spa, which opened in 1965 in Carlsbad, California. It was the first U.S. resort of the modern era to offer a full-service spa, thus launching the resort spa concept, which has become a guiding force in resort development throughout the 1990s and into the twenty-first century.

In the early 1980s, a few resorts added luxury spa treatments and facilities. The resort spa was first positioned as a hotel amenity that could be enjoyed by women while the men were golfing. They were built from the platform of other recently added, must-have amenities like fitness facilities and pools. This would provide the development impetus for making spas accessible to a much wider market: the general resort-going public. Many people who had never had a massage or tried a spa, did so at a mainstream resorts in the 1980s. The contemporary spa had arrived.

In 1986, the Claremont Resort & Spa opened as one of the first urban resort spas to offer full spa programming with the focus on lifestyle and wellness. The spa partnered with Dr. Dean Ornish and Dr. Ken Dychtwald, authors of *Age Wave*, to provide a true lifestyle program. Claremont wanted the public to get away from the perception of spa as an indulgence and began a campaign to educate consumers. Their message was that going to the spa was the same as a tune-up for a car.

Historically, health resorts, spas, and the travel industry have shared a mutually supportive relationship. In 1989, this relationship was reinforced with the publication of Bernard Burt's list of health resorts in the first edition of *Fodor's Health and Fitness Vacations*.[4] Taking a vacation for health reasons was not a new concept, nor was it new to have a list of resorts and spas telling travelers where they could find the needed health resources. What was new and important about Burt's guide was its listing of health resort and spa resources, not only by region, but also by the types of fitness programs and health spa treatments. He listed 12 categories of programs including: luxury pampering, life enhancement, weight management, nutrition and diet, stress control, holistic health, spiritual awareness, preventive medicine, taking the waters, sports conditioning, youth camps for weight loss, and non-program resort facilities. This list was useful for health-seekers looking for wellness and fitness.

By 2006, there were 1,345 U.S. resort/hotel spa properties.[5]

Medical Spas

The fastest-growing category of spas in recent years in terms of locations is the medical spa, which has grown at an average rate of 19 percent annually between 2004 to 2006, according to the 2007 Spa Industry Study commissioned by ISPA. A medical spa is defined as a facility that operates under the full-time, on-site supervision of a licensed health care professional whose primary purpose is to provide comprehensive medical and wellness care in an environment that integrates spa services, as well as traditional, complementary and/or alternative therapies and treatments. The facility operates within the scope of practice of its staff, which can include both esthetic/cosmetic and prevention/wellness procedures and services.

There are two typical scenarios for medical spas. The most common is for spa services to be an expansion of a health professional's practice, such as a dermatologist's office or plastic surgeon's practice where services such as Botox, chemical peels, microdermabrasion, photofacials, and soft tissue fillers including collagen, Restylane, and Perlane. With plastic surgical procedures, physicians know that including manual lymphatic drainage massage will speed the patient's recovery process and reduce swelling and bruising, thus many have added this spa service to their pre- and post-surgical protocols. Others will conduct a series of facials, for example, to treat specific skin conditions such as acne. There are dental "spas" that

Profile

Karen Korpi

In the world of resort spas, Karen Korpi is known as <u>Spa Mama</u>.

It's a title she's earned through 20 years in the industry and by giving birth to the spa corporate leadership model at <u>Ritz-Carlton</u>, a model that has been emulated by other resorts throughout the industry.

"The Ritz-Carlton was the first luxury brand with the vision to hire corporate leadership so early in the spa industry development," said Korpi, vice president, spa division, Ritz-Carlton Hotel Company.

The winner of two Malcolm Baldrige awards, Ritz-Carlton hired Korpi in 1999 as the vice president of the spa division. At that time, there was only one Ritz-Carlton spa. Over the next ten years, she added 45 spas to their portfolio.

"I started with Ritz-Carlton's gold standards and our quality service. That became the foundation for the spas," said Korpi. From there, she found herself involved in developing every spa from scratch—every floor plan, design, treatment menu, product, and hiring.

"The spa organizational structure was being developed that we see in all the full service spas nationwide," said Korpi. "The top focus in the early stages (as it is today) was hiring and training to ensure satisfaction and retention of employees. We are in the business of delivering an experience, one that is also part of the guest's overall hotel visit. When the Ritz-Carlton designs a spa, it is not just about treatment rooms, it is the total spa experience with great attention to experiential elements that set the stage for a lasting benefit."

In selecting Korpi to turn this vision into a reality, The Ritz-Carlton chose a spa expert who had vast experience in the industry. She had helped to open the first urban spa with the Claremont Resort & Spa in Berkeley, California. She had collaborated with Howard Murad when he opened his medical day spa. She had worked at PGA when they were just building their spa.

"Spas were looked at as an amenity in the hotels at that time," she recalled. "It started out they were being built because you had to have it to play the game. As spas started turning profits, there was a whole different view to them. That was where there was a major drive to take the money to the bottom line. That's another reason why the industry just exploded—because there is money to be made."

Korpi also owned her own spa consulting company, which is what she was doing when Ritz-Carlton came to call. They courted her for more than a year while she was consulting with a day spa in Sun Valley.

"Consumers are looking for more than luxury pampering," she said. "They seek out a sense of community within a secure environment. These are the guiding principles of The Ritz-Carlton and a natural for the world of spa."

The Ritz-Carlton has committed to having spas in all of their new hotels, clubs, and residences, ensuring that the future growth of their spas will be vibrant, providing their guests with a lifestyle experience.

(continued)

$\mathcal{P}$rofile *(continued)*

"In the early years of the industry, there was great need of education to the hotel operators to understand the business of spa in order to optimize the financial contribution the spa delivers," Korpi said. "It is a delicate balance to create the standards and structure that honors not only the heart and soul of spa, but the true business acumen to lead the business."

Korpi said even today some hoteliers shy away from learning about spas because they don't understand the territory. She says she's been able to reach them by equating spa to rooms and food and beverage operations. You can compare a spa to a small hotel, only the guests check in and out every hour, not every night. Spa is the umbrella of many specific businesses that operate as standalones across the world from salon, massage, skin care, retail, to fitness.

"When they start looking at it like that, it changes," she said. "They go, 'Oh! I get it.' It's not frightening, it just has some of its own intricacies."

will perform teeth whitening and may use a spa therapist to help the guest relieve anxiety during dental procedures, or the chiropractic spa where massage therapists are included in the program to help the patient relieve pain. In all of these cases, the business is really the medical practice, and while the licensed health care professional may hire a spa manager to supervise the spa therapist staff, the spa treatment revenue is a component of the health practice business itself.

The second typical scenario would be where a medical practice has leased space from the spa, or there is a clinic built adjacent to the spa facility itself and the medical practice is completely independent from the spa. While there may be a revenue-sharing agreement, the medical service's space is a tenant of the spa business and the spa revenue derived would be rental income. Some spas do hire doctors and other medical professionals as part of the spa staff, where complete medical evaluations are conducted as part of a spa program, but they are generally limited to significant destination spas such as Canyon Ranch, the Cooper Center in Texas, The Marsh, and some others. In the European spas, it is much more common to have a health professional on staff with whom the spa's guests meet upon arrival for a brief health evaluation. The doctor would then 'prescribe' a treatment schedule and what 'taking of the waters' program the spa guest should follow.

The Contemporary Spa Movement Gathers Steam

By the mid-1980s, the spa industry, a relatively fragmented group of day spa/salons, weight-loss retreats, and health and wellness resorts, was poised for the dynamic growth period that would continue through the early part of the twenty-first century. This growth was characterized by the convergence of a number of trends that would transform the way people regard themselves and their potential for growth and self-realization.

The founders and leaders of the first ground-breaking contemporary spa organizations were driven by their personal visions for wellness and growth. Many who experienced their vision were inspired to continue as spa goers and

reflections

Celeste Hilling: Defining Medical Spas

Celeste Hilling is the co-founder and CEO of Skin Authority, a leading provider of medical-grade skin care services and products. She and her team have built a nationwide network of authorized skin wellness centers operating within medical practices, destination and resort spas, and large, regional day spa chains. She is a highly sought-after speaker on the topic of medical skin care. She is also a committee member on the Foundation Committee of Scripps Health Organization, Chair of the Advisory Board of Scripps Memorial Hospital, board member of ISPA, Board Chair of the Development Committee of the New Children's Museum in San Diego, and a founding board member of DOCS (Doctors Offering Charitable Services).

The challenge in defining what constitutes a medical spa is that the concept varies widely, not only within the United States, but also from country to country globally. The diverse structure of medical spas is reflective of a wide variation in laws and governing bodies which dictate the way spas can operate within medical environments, as well as the terms for compliance of insurance liability and treatment protocols.

Complementary and integrative medicine are very similar. While there are distinct definitions of both, the consumer perspective is that the concepts are similar. In many cases, a practice will integrate complementary treatments as well as cross disciplines of expertise (integrative) because it allows the practice to treat a much broader spectrum of patients as well as offer a more comprehensive service per individual patient.

Integrative medicine combines various but related disciplines or modalities of medicine and healing under one roof as a comprehensive, preventive program offering to patients. Complementary treatments are alternative medicine approaches that can be added to traditional Western medical care. Allopathic is more reactive, rooted in diagnosis of disease and prescription as opposed to homeopathic, which is more focused on the overall well being of the body.

The differentiation comes down to philosophy toward prevention or treatment, the level of involvement of the physician(s) in the spa implementation, and the specific discipline of the physician. When you look at integrative medicine, you have someone who is bringing together all the traditions with an eye to total well-being. Diagnostic and other assessments are used, but then alternative medicine components are integrated to deal with the spiritual and emotional well-being: a nutritionist and a sleep therapist, the mind-body connection, the diagnostic, the effectiveness of diet, stress reduction, mindfulness training, and yoga. It's almost like a one-stop shop for a lot of those things.

Complementary or alternative medicine is about complementing traditional medical services. It is an alternative to traditional medicine—which is going to be different based on where you are. In North America, we would consider Chinese herbal medicine as a complement to treating allergies with a prescription. It's not a core treatment philosophy in the West. The West is very diagnostic driven. We have to do a test in order to diagnose you. In Europe, on the other hand, the

(continued)

reflections

(continued)

diagnostic tool of imaging might be considered complementary to their traditional practice. In France, the first thing they'll do for a cold or allergy is aromatherapy. Here, we'll give you Claritin.

A complementary spa is providing the services that aren't part of core medical practice in that area. They are all components that add to standard medical treatment. In North America, that would be things like acupuncture, mindfulness, yoga, and herbal treatments.

In today's world, many medical practices have added alternative offerings because many of these cosmetic or alternative offerings are elective or cash-based transactions versus limited insurance reimbursements, so they are more profitable.

In North America, many medical spas are day spas that have a doctor come once a week or twice a month to do treatments there. There are a lot of day spas and destination spas who bring a doctor in to do treatments for their guests. It's important to really educate people that, for liability purposes, that is not a place to have a medical treatment. There are not appropriate emergency facilities or supervision to handle a medical emergency in case of error.

In North America, you also have a lot of retail medical service venues that use the term medical spa but are singularly focused: laser centers, for example. You go in and get laser treatments or Botox. In many cases, a supervising doctor is not on site. Although it is a retail medical service, it is not a medical practice or spa. It's very targeted at a singular or series of treatment, but they're not meant to be long-term treatment centers. Consumers need to identify what is important to them in terms of guidance, supervision, and long-term treatment to choose the appropriate format of medical spa offering.

---

to advance those concepts into new businesses. The subsequent growth of the industry was essentially an outgrowth and application of these original concepts to other industries and communities.

Yoga studios sprang up in many communities. Salons began adding treatment rooms and converting slowly to what are now known as day spa operations. Health food stores were selling natural foods and "new age" lifestyle accessories. Eating healthy food was no longer considered fringe behavior. Maintaining a healthy image and a healthy body was becoming part of mainstream thinking.

In the early 1990s, there were plenty of mechanisms in place to measure hospitality growth, but there were none to measure the growth of the brand new spa industry. Spa industry leaders recognized the need to measure and catalog this movement, but they had no means to do so. Of primary concern was their struggle to categorize and define what it was they were doing. The spa industry needed an identity.

The word spa was being used in the early 1990s primarily to describe whirlpool tubs, as well as any kind of business that involved massage treatments, personal growth, and water treatments. As hotels added spas by converting sleeping rooms or old workout facilities, the term was rather loosely defined. The early years of the International Spa and Fitness Association (later known as ISPA) were spent focusing on the challenge of defining a very fragmented, diverse, and free-thinking

Spa Snapshot: How did the spa industry grow so fast?

To delve into what has contributed to the growth of the spa industry, an understanding of what led up to this growth is necessary. In 1990, the salon and spa industry began a revolutionary change. Why? Albert Einstein said that for every action there is an equal and opposite reaction. The pendulum began to swing the other way. The "coffee achievers" of the 1980s, the "you can have it all" attitude, began to take its toll, and we began to turn inward. We realized we cannot grow, we cannot succeed, we cannot nurture our careers or our families if we are not nurturing ourselves. And we sought out those places to nurture us.

Spas could not be built fast enough in the 1990s. Out of this interconnectedness of need for balance, an entirely new way of thinking about wellness is beginning to emerge. How did the spa industry come so far and so fast in 15 years? People demanded wellness, respite, rejuvenation. And those people of passion and compassion—the spa owners—delivered. They pioneered, they created, they failed, they succeeded—they persevered in developing a $12 billion industry [in the United States] that for the most part did not exist 25 years ago.

Our world is changing; it's in a constant state of flux. The one constant is the need for balance. I, for one, am happy to know that there are places all over the world that I can seek out to nurture me and make me whole again.

—*Alison Howland, Spa Development, Aveda*

group of individuals and businesses. The work of the organization in defining spa was aided by the palpable desire of the general public to learn more about themselves and the opportunities they had for self-care. This public thirst for knowledge about personal health and wellness fueled the business community's ability to grow the industry at a very rapid rate. Today the concept of spa, as defined by ISPA, is:

> Spas are places devoted to enhancing overall well-being through a variety of professional services that encourage the renewal of mind, body, and spirit.

Today's Spa Industry

An increasingly hectic daily life with ever increasing pressure to earn more and more money has spurred the growth of the spa industry. Specifically for women, pressure was at a zenith in the 1980s with baby boomer women breaking out of traditional roles in droves and pursuing careers as well as family life. The "I can have it all" attitude of the time, which persists today, was a lot to sustain, and

reflections

John and Ginny Lopis: What About Stress?

The spa experience was so focused on weight loss and heart disease, that there wasn't much room for anything else. About the same time "the spa diet" became better known, there was a parallel preoccupation with heart disease in the media. What emerged was the awareness that a heart-healthy diet was very close to the same diet being promoted at spas for weight loss. However, although there was quite a bit of interest in relaxation, there still wasn't a strong connection between stress and chronic illness.

We were running a special spa program teaching highly successful people to attend to their lifestyles to improve their health and wellbeing. In addition to learning about diet and nutrition, and taking part in an extensive exercise program, program guests met each evening with their executive peer group to discuss stress and how to handle challenging situations in their lives. The night before we launched the first program, the vice president of training for a major corporation happened to be in house and when he found out about the program, he went to the owner and suggested that "the last thing these busy people need to do is sit round and talk about work and stressful situations." The owner came personally to the evening session a few nights later and shared this concern with the group. The participants responded that discussing their personal stress with a group who could understand and relate to their challenges was one of the most valuable things they were doing. This was in 1984.

Prior to this time, there wasn't much emphasis placed on the psychological or emotional side of wellness. There was a change happening then, with the emphasis on the physical body making room for a more holistic perspective.

---

combined with the information overload of the 1990s, created a "perfect storm" of stress in the daily lives of millions. The antidote: Spa.

Relaxation and stress reduction always have been and continue to be the primary drivers of spa visits. As technology grew exponentially, and people became constantly accessible and available, stress and the need for relaxation increased. People began feeling less human and more like numbers or bytes of data. The high-tech world needed to be balanced with high-touch. This remains the foundation for the relevance of spa today and into the future.

While the rest of the world is increasingly hooking up to one broadband after another, spas are creating places where people can truly unplug. Many spas have instituted an unplugged atmosphere where they help guests check their stress at the door by also checking their cell phones, personal handheld devices, and other electronic devices.

Beyond the elemental need for people to relax, there were and are many elements of contemporary spa that warrant close examination. The first need for data on the spa industry came from the industry professionals themselves, in part to justify spa as a bona fide movement.

The first controlled studies of the modern spa industry were conducted by Dr. Mary Tabacchi, Professor at the Cornell University School of Hospitality Management. Tabacchi, whose background was in food science and nutrition, was a founding member of the International SPA Association. She had been mentored by Deborah Szekely in the mid-1980s. In the early 1990s, Dr. Tabacchi was asked by the early ISPA boards to do research for the industry. Much of this was funded by Deborah and Alex Szekely through the ISPA Board, of which Alex Szekely was then president. Dr. Tabacchi's first ISPA work was, "The Non-Spa Goer" written in 1994, soon followed by an industry analysis written in 1995. She then conducted a meta-analysis of complementary medical treatments.

Dr. Tabacchi reports that the early research was challenging, "as few individuals from either the academic side or the spa community understood spa research."[6]

She researched whether there was a market for health-related travel, conducting her research at the Haaga Institute in Helsinki, Finland. Over the next several years, she studied such spa-related topics as the structure of the spa industry, marketing to the international spa consumer, the efficacies of spa treatments, integrating spas into hotels, the future of the spa industry, and the growth of the spa industry, publishing numerous papers and legitimizing spas as a recognized part of the hospitality industry in both academic and financial circles. She has also given papers, seminars, and certificate programs throughout Hong Kong, Thailand, Japan, Malaysia, and Indonesia.

By the mid-1990s, consumers were expecting a quality spa as part of a resort experience, and they even began selecting destinations based on the availability of a superior spa component. The demand for spa data was very concrete: investors required statistical studies to justify investments of millions of dollars in these new projects called spas. In 2000, ISPA commissioned PriceWaterhouseCoopers to conduct the first of many detailed surveys and studies of the spa industry.

Since 2000, ISPA has been releasing statistics biannually on the following key measures for the U.S. spa industry: the number of spas, industry revenues, number of spa visits, employment, and square footage.

The evidence has shown that the spa industry continues to thrive even after years of rapid expansion. As the spa sector continues to evolve, it is fast becoming mainstream—an accepted way of life that is far more than just pampering. With its increased focus on health and wellness, the spa concept has evolved into a lifestyle choice that many people are now buying into.

Growth

In 2004, some predicted that spas were growing too fast. The cautious industry watchers said that spas were over-saturating the market and that there would be a costly meltdown for spa owners. As of 2008, this has not occurred. There are spas, particularly in the day spa sector, that no longer exist, but new spas are opening at a faster pace than spas are closing.

As of 2006, the spa growth had slowed to a steady pace. It is still growing, but not in leaps and bounds that characterized it for many years. The day spa sector in particular has experienced some saturation and has had the most difficulty in growing.

In the meantime, more resorts and hotels than ever are recognizing the need to have a spa on property. Spas rank with environmental concerns as the leading issue at many industry gatherings. This has led to new challenges for hotel operators.

Spa Snapshot: What has been the oddest or most unusual use of the word "spa" that you've seen?

Dental spa, never tried one, but I might like to!

—*Darlene Fiske, Owner, The Fiske Group: Public Relations & Marketing Strategies*

I'm always annoyed when I hear the word "spa" used interchangeably with "hot tub." A hotel will boast a 'spa'—when all they have is a hot tub. However, with the origin of spa being "solus par aqua"—health through water, there's not much to be done! With the growing popularity of spas, it's only natural the word is extended into other uses: pet spa, dental spa, spa water, spa bathroom design, spa cuisine items on restaurant menus, etc.

—*Wanda Love, Director of Sales & Marketing, Santé Spa*

I recently read about a scrapbooking spa.

—*Angela Cortright, Owner, Spa Gregorie's*

Resorts without a spa are no longer perceived as luxury destinations. Their guests are demanding that a spa be on the property, but there isn't always enough demand to keep them profitable. This is forcing resort and hotel spa managers to spend more time marketing to grow their customer base beyond the hotel guests. Many properties are developing programs for local residents.

It is difficult to explain exactly why the spa industry is growing so quickly, but there are several possible explanations. One is that the spa concept has been integrated into mainstream North American culture. Spa has come to mean more than just pampering and is considered part of an individual's way of life.

In an era where issues like obesity, stress, and environmental toxins have become serious concerns, spa-goers are looking beyond treatment-based spa concepts and calling upon spas in their more ancient sense—a place where they can learn lifestyle habits including fitness, diet, and overall health. The term spa is also being incorporated into a diverse number of products and services. Linking itself to everything from "spa cuisine" to "spa friendly" skin care and cosmetics, "spa" is becoming a household word.

While spas have grown more popular, the industry has become increasingly aware of the fact that the growth curve for the number of spas is outstripping the growth curve in consumer demand. This will be one of the largest challenges facing the industry in the next ten years. Spa focus will likely need to shift away from building new spas toward creating awareness and growing the consumer base for the spas that exist.

Spa Snapshot: With everything from air freshener to detergent using "spa" in their names, do you feel the word has become tainted, or is the industry actually benefiting from increased awareness?

As we move into a reality where people from all walks of life are producing more, buying more, and becoming technologically advanced to the "nth" degree, the exponential growth of the spa industry offers a balance to the stresses of the everyday rat race. The word "spa" is signature for relaxation. I believe the word "spa" has not yet passed its heyday; on the contrary, the mainstreaming of "spa" into mass market products denotes the positive aspects of a spa treatment. If clients and consumers can bring this experience home, then they can take a moment to relax and balance their lives. Products and consumables that have jumped on the bandwagon of incorporating spa into the names have helped our industry by increasing awareness of the positive benefits of going to a spa. Our industry as a whole benefits from increased exposure, by guiding consumers back to basics. Self-care at home, and creating a serene space or block of time to recharge our mind and body, simply makes for happier, well-adjusted people. The restoration of a balanced lifestyle, even if it's because you got a free CD of relaxing music with your air freshener at the supermarket, still helps to remind us to take some time for ourselves.

—*Luanne Sauer, President, Luna Mesa Day Spa, Inc.*

Corporate America's newfound fondness for the word "spa" has greatly benefited the health and spa industry by opening the eyes of the public to the healthful, relaxing, and glamorous aspects of spas! From Fiji Water's "Salus Per Aquam" (*health by water*) SPA advertisements to Trim Spa weight-control pills, businesses are bringing the sensation of a spa to everyday Americans and piquing interest in the ever-growing world of health and beauty. These spa-associated campaigns motivate the public to nurture and care for their bodies, which in turn boosts business and awareness of what exists in the classic spa industry. Similarly, these marketing techniques help businesses in the spa industry build relationships and establish firm foundations for joint ventures.

—*Jackie Allder, Marketing Director, Blinc, Inc.*

I believe that the increasing use of the term "spa" is having a deleterious and trivializing effect—much in the same way that "aromatherapy" has caught the public interest and subsequently applied by Madison

(continued)

(continued)

Avenue to hawk everything from bathroom cleaners to automobile air fresheners. This is especially the case for us where we see ourselves as a spa in the larger definition of health and wellness promotion, more akin to how the term is used in Europe. Our entire building is our spa, from the training center, Pilates studio, health education center, studios, restaurant, shop, overnight rooms, and finally, also, our "spa" in the smaller context of the word. The ISPA decision to create a definition of spa is something that needs to be out in the public's eye to help us educate and inform, as well as differentiate, what we see spa to be.

—*Hilmar Wagner, Spa Director, The Marsh, a Center for Balance and Fitness*

I recently drove around the Las Vegas area and saw a sign that read "Car Spa," then my sister called me the same day and mentioned that she was having a "spa" installed in her house. I believe that the word "spa" has been so misused and applied to so many different things that instead of helping create an increased awareness it is actually creating confusion. Those who are already spa savvy customers will not be affected by it, but those who are just beginning to consider it might have a hard time understanding the differences and become frustrated in the process. We need to figure out how to change this to help us increase the percent of spa-goers and make it easier for them to be educated about the different kinds of spas and the differences in how the word is used.

—*Zahira J. Coll, CEO, Resources & Development, Inc.*

I don't believe the overuse of the word "spa" has tainted the industry, but I do believe it has confused the consumer. If there are "spas" in strip shopping centers and malls and if products are sold promising a "spa experience," people may begin to understand the word to mean something different from what we offer. That creates a challenge to those of us in the destination spa industry. It puts the burden on us to clearly define the services we offer and differentiate them from the pop culture definition.

—*Dr. Deborah Kern, Executive Director of Lifestyle Enrichment, Lake Austin Spa Resort*

Proliferation of Spa

As the twenty-first century dawned, the term spa was more clearly understood than ever, the spa lifestyle was more incorporated into the mainstream culture and the idea that the word "spa" could add value to nearly any business concept resulted in a proliferation of the word "spa" in many unlikely applications.

Spa had come to connote luxury, enhanced value, pampering, nurturing, and health. The term spa began to show up in surprising places. Legitimately, dental practices, airports, hospitals, malls, residential communities, private clubs, and other businesses all began to incorporate elements of the spa experience into their business models.

Spa services became a point of differentiation for beauty salons and fitness clubs. Incorporating spa services into the business mix had the effect of elevating the market position of the business as well as increasing the revenue collected per guest visit. Salon owners were especially interested in a day spa component because not only did it give their clients more reasons to visit, but it also encouraged customer loyalty to the salon. These businesses were plagued by stylists leaving and taking clients with them to their independent business. With the addition of spa services, the day spa/salon became the reason for visiting, not necessarily the stylist alone. Guests would be more inclined to return for the experience, which might or might not include the particular stylist or treatment provider.

In other places, the word "spa" was applied to businesses not closely associated with the core values of spa. For many people, "spa" was synonymous with "hot tub." In the hotel industry, the definition of spa is one that widely varies. In some properties, a hotel might claim to have a spa if it has a single massage room and a whirlpool, while others work to bring in truly authentic spa services. The result is that guests don't always know what they are getting when a hotel says that it has a spa.

The World of Spa

As the variety of spas grew wider and their numbers increased dramatically, ancillary businesses were launched to support spas and provide them with cutting-edge products and specialized business-to-business services. Academic communities scrambled to learn about the spa phenomenon and provide management and technical training for these new businesses. Along with the properties themselves, the popularity and proliferation of the spa experience spawned another world of businesses and opportunities to participate in the spa phenomenon.

Spa Education. One of the first deficiencies in the marketplace when the spa boom began was that of high quality technical education. There was a large and increasing demand for massage therapists, estheticians, cosmetologists, and spa managers, but schools that existed either did not offer courses (spa management) or were tailored mostly to independent practitioners (massage and esthetics). In the early 1980s, The Swedish Institute in New York City and a handful of other prominent massage schools taught manual therapies to students who typically made careers as independent massage therapists.

Dr. Mary Tabacchi at Cornell University began teaching three courses regarding spas in 1986. They were electives requiring business education as a prerequisite. The classes were Spa Management and Development, Wellness in Business, and Healthy Cuisine Development, Production, Marketing, and Sales.

By the 1990s, spas were beginning to demand greater numbers of qualified graduates. They began looking for therapists who also had skills in spa-related therapies, were able to perform various modalities, and were trained as much as possible in the art of customer service.

Gradually, experienced spa therapists saw education as a natural evolution of their careers, and several founded schools that added spa education to the curriculum and gave their graduates the option to study spa-specific practices and therapies. CIDESCO, a European training program that covers a wide range of spa services and certifications, acted as a model for beauty and esthetics programs in the United States, many of which were founded by CIDESCO graduates. These schools began teaching and educating a new tide of therapists to feed the growing demand for spa treatments. Today, there are thousands of schools teaching technical spa skills, and as spa treatments become more and more mainstream, this trend is expected to continue.

In 1995, the American Spa Therapy and Education Certification Council was founded to enable spa therapists to become spa professionals—empowering therapists with the physiology and science of spa therapies, beyond traditional teaching requirements. ASTECC was developed to take education out of the hands of vendors and into a more objective teaching situation. Designed to meet the growing demands of the luxury global spa market, ASTECC features a comprehensive 271-hour post-graduate spa education curriculum composed of 12 individually certified components. Widely regarded as a benchmark for spa therapy education excellence, ASTECC-certified therapists are among the best trained in the industry. In North America, the standards that CIDESCO, ASTECC, and others set are not compulsory. There remains a divide between industry, government, and education.

In recent years, four-year universities have begun adding spa classes and programs to their hospitality curriculum. These programs have included education on the management of spas as an alternative or supplement to the technical spa skills offered by other institutes. Two-year community colleges have also developed programs and associate degrees around spa management.

Spa Publications. *Spa Management Journal*, founded in 1991, was one of the earliest official industry trade publications of the contemporary era. It documents spa trends worldwide. The editorial content of *Spa Management Journal* supports professional advancement, focusing on practical approaches to enhancing both business and professional career success in spa operations, and sustainable practices. The Journal was the first publication to document the need for standards to cover spa services.

ISPA's first edition of *PULSE,* then a monthly newsletter, was created about the same time as *Spa Management Journal,* both publishing in 1991. Bernard Burt, a spa pioneer journalist and the editor of that first issue, was taking an aerobics class at the Watergate Hotel in Washington, D.C., when the instructor shouted, "Feel the pulse!" and the name of the newsletter was realized. Now an award-winning publication, *Pulse* continues to monitor trends and events in the industry.

Spa Finder, founded in 1986, had pioneered the consumer publication on spas, with its reviews and descriptions of various spa vacations. In the early days, most spa press was to be found in already existing fitness or health publications like *Self* and *Shape* magazines. As the industry grew and public interest tuned in, publishers responded with material specifically geared toward spas. *SPA Magazine, Healing Retreats & Spas,* and others, focused entirely on spas, and many consumer publications had spa or spa-related columns and content.

Bernard Burt

It is impossible to talk about spa publications without the name Bernard (Bernie) Burt coming up. When the founders of ISPA, including Burt himself, gathered at New Age Health Spa in September 1990 to consider the future of the spa industry, Guy Jonkman and Bernard Burt were there, the only journalists invited by co-hosts Jeffrey Joseph, founding owner of Spa Finder travel agency in New York, and Werner Mendel, ISPA's first president.

Burt had been covering fitness fads in the 1980s for *American Health* magazine. When he became involved in spas in the early 1990s, he predicted that the industry would grow, and staged annual conferences for the spa industry. He co-chaired the first international summit meeting of industry leaders in Baden-Baden, Germany, in 1996.

Burt writes a column for the *MEDIcal SPAS: The Healthy Aging Business Review*, tracking international trends and news of new products. He also maintains his SpaGoer website filled with industry news from around the world.

Burt co-authored *100 Best Spas of the World* with Pamela Price and created *Fodor's Healthy Escapes*, a North American guide to spas, health resorts, and spiritual retreats.

In 1994, ISPA honored him with a service award and, in 2000, a Dedicated Contributor Award.

Spa and Health Resort Organizations/Associations

Just as the focus on fitness preceded the current emphasis on wellness, so too did fitness associations pave the way for spa associations. The International Health, Racquet and Sportsclub Association held its first conference in 1981. They formed to serve the health and fitness club industry. Their members are for-profit businesses that operate in the health, racquet, and sports club industry. They have 8,500 members in 74 different countries as well as 604 industry supplier members. Included in their membership are both fitness club spas and fitness clubs that offer à la carte spa services, such as facials and massages. Fitness clubs have also been expanding to offer comprehensive in-club day spas that provide the full range of services, including medical spa services like microdermabrasion, peels, and Botox injections.

In 1982, Peter and Kathie Davis founded IDEA, a membership organization of health and fitness professionals. Their membership includes personal trainers, program and fitness directors, business owners and managers, and group fitness instructors.

During the 1980s and 1990s, several influential American health spa owners and managers, travel agents and writers, and marketing and public relations consultants met to establish an organization for the "spa and fitness industry." In 1991, the International Spa and Fitness Association organized its first International Conference and Trade Exposition hailed as "The Ultimate Workout." In attendance were 91 delegates from 20 states and 10 countries. They included spa owners, managers, marketing and public relations directors, nutritionists, chefs, massage therapists, aestheticians, trainers, consultants, travel agents, government officials, airlines, and equipment and supply vendors. A significant event at the 1991 ISPA conference was Deborah Szekely's keynote address. Szekely spoke about her late husband Edmond Szekely's trials and successes with **Essene** health camps in Mexico and her own successful spa program in California.

The Day Spa Association was founded in 1991 by Hannelore Leavy to address the specific needs of day spas. Leavy was involved during the formative years of Spa Finder as vice president of sales and marketing and associate publisher. Her early research into day spas in the early 1990s resulted in the publication of the first day spa directory, and she later launched the Day Spa Association to support day spa professionals with business resources, increase consumer awareness, and elevate the professional standing of day spas. The group launched a sister association in 2002, the International Medical Spa Association, to cater to the increasingly specific needs of that segment.

Paralleling the founding of ISPA in the health resort, fitness, spa, and travel industry, other organizations have emerged. In the fall of 1997, a group of spa owners united to establish Destination Spa Group (DSG). Over the years, DSG has grown into a participatory marketing, networking, and advocacy group consisting of the top destination spas in the world. The DSG's stated mission is to "encourage healthier lifestyles by educating the public about the unique wellness and self-improvement opportunities of Destination Spas and to unify the Destination Spa Industry."

See Exhibit 1 for other associations with close ties to the spa industry.

Branding the Spa Experience

Branding is the natural hallmark of a maturing industry. The spa industry is no exception. As it developed and grew, certain brands naturally evolved. There was also increasing interest on the part of investors and owners to brand the spa experience to increase market share and profitability. The first recognized spa brand was The Red Door, which evolved from the original concept Elizabeth Arden established in the early 1900s. Other brands, such as Canyon Ranch SpaClub and The Golden Door, grew out of the strong name recognition they had earned as popular trendsetters.

Deborah Szekely's Golden Door had become an iconic symbol of spa as a combination of luxury, personal growth, education, and fitness. Not surprisingly, others wanted to copy this model. Resort developers in the mid-1990s wanted to associate with Golden Door to enhance their own properties. They felt that having Golden Door spas in their properties would elevate their quality perception in the marketplace and create added value to each resort with a Golden Door spa. Golden Door expanded by taking over existing properties and bringing their management styles and philosophies into the resort properties. There are now Golden Door spas in a number of locations. All of them offer spa cuisine, a high staff-to-guest ratio with specialized personnel, and individualized programs that include both up-to-date fitness therapies and ancient techniques. This represented the first of many initiatives which sought to marry a particular spa experience with a brand name.

Exhibit 1   Spa Associations

In addition to the associations listed in the text, other associations that serve some aspect of the spa industry include:

- Aerobics and Fitness Association of America
- Allied Health Association
- American Alliance of Aromatherapy
- American Association for Esthetics
- American Association of Cosmetology Schools
- American Beauty Association
- American Council on Exercise
- American CranioSacral Therapy Association
- American Massage Therapy Association
- American Oriental Bodywork Therapy Association
- American Reiki Masters Association
- Associated Bodywork and Massage Professionals
- Association of Massage Therapists and Wholistic Practitioners
- Cosmetology Advancement Foundation
- Independent Cosmetic Manufacturers and Distributors, Inc.
- International Council of Reflexologists
- International Estheticians Association
- International Massage Association
- Nail Manufacturers Council
- National Association for Health and Fitness
- National Association of Nurse Massage Therapists
- National Center for Complementary and Alternative Medicine
- National Coalition of Estheticians, Manufacturers, Distributors, and Associations
- National Cosmetology Association
- Personal Care Products Council
- Professional Beauty Association
- Society of Cosmetic Chemists
- SPATEC: Spa, Wellness, and Beauty
- The Salon Association
- The Salon and Spa Association
- World International Nail and Beauty Association

While Golden Door expanded its brand through acquisition, Canyon Ranch expanded its brand internally, opening its second location in Lenox, Massachusetts, in 1990. In 2000, their first resort spa opened as the Canyon Ranch Spa Club in the new Venetian Resort Hotel in Las Vegas. In 2005, the brand expanded again, this time to the open sea onboard Cunard's Queen Elizabeth II. The company continues to expand into a new concept, Canyon Ranch Lifestyle Communities, which takes the brand and the concept of spa into a new realm of spa communities.

As more spas expanded, they struggled with how to keep their founding principles—often based around the philosophies of individuals—alive. Up to this point, spa programming centered around the founder's philosophy and the experience was built by those who ran them. When the visionary behind the brand left—either due to retirement or death—spas began struggling with how to keep the founding principles when the actual person behind that vision was no longer there. In many cases, there was a family member who would carry on the dream. In other instances, the founding principles were so deeply ingrained that when a corporation would take over the spa, they could enhance what already existed.

Elizabeth Arden's spas were owned by three major companies after her death, yet they still managed to have a thread of what she stood for. There are service providers today within the brand who worked for Elizabeth Arden when she was alive. This has kept the tradition alive. While the spa has had to modernize in order to survive and be sustainable, the foundation retains the Elizabeth Arden principles.

Likewise, many hotel spas have a strong thread of legacy. Many hotels began developing their own brands of spa. Fairmont built Willow Stream, Hyatt built Still Water, Shangri-La built Chi, and Starwood developed Heavenly Spas. Other companies, such as Mandarin Oriental, Ritz-Carlton, and Four Seasons, developed spas associated with their already strong luxury branding.

New and Emerging Spa Concepts

As the number of spa locations has increased dramatically over the past two decades, a flurry of classifications have become necessary to categorize the array of spa experiences being offered in the market. It also became necessary to distinguish spas from those businesses that simply offered one or two spa services as an adjunct to their main business.

This was especially true for the medical spa industry. The term "medical spa" covered a broad range of establishments from those that were total wellness centers to those that were retail outlets offering medically supervised services. There were those medical spas that focused on complementary and alternative medicine, as well as those that were purely focused on cosmetic treatments, such as microdermabrasion and Botox injections.

In addition to the major types of spas, other concepts have begun to grow within the industry.

The Spa Lifestyle Concept. As spas become mainstream, more product line manufacturers and service companies, such as American Express and Splenda,

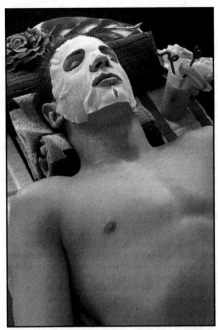

The modern trend is toward a reawakening of male grooming, something men are turning to spas for.

to name a few, are looking to cross-market their brands with the "spa lifestyle" concept, so that by association, they are considered to be products that healthy, forward-thinking people will embrace. This effort by loosely related businesses to associate themselves with spas in the mind of the consumer is actually a testimony to the longevity of the spa movement itself, since big business has obviously recognized the emotional value of spa in the mind of the consumer.

One example of this is United Airlines, which recently formed a partnership with Westin Hotels to create "Renewal Lounges" in their airports using concepts from Westin hotels and spas.

Men's Spas. Men have always participated in the spa world. Fitness resorts have attracted men interested in athletic pursuits. Executive men have had their nails done and hair cut and groomed by professionals. More and more urban, professional men are adopting grooming regimens once viewed as feminine in their intensity and sense of detail. This includes greater attention to hair style, hair appearance throughout the day, and the look of the facial skin, hands, and nails. The driving factors here are, in part, increased inner-directed cosmetic vanity among men, as well as the fact that more men over the age of 30 are dating.

Reality makeover television shows have helped convince some men that women actually are impressed when they take care of themselves. More men have become aware, for instance, that women pay attention to the quality of facial skin, hands, and fingernails, not just a man's choice of shirt, pants, and shoes. All these

Douglas J: Men

In 2007, Douglas J, a day spa with several locations throughout mid-Michigan, opened a men's spa. The second floor men's salon was remodeled, turning it into a more private space with a spa-like feel.

The atmosphere was built to make men feel comfortable, complete with sports playing on flat-screen televisions. The spa also offers complimentary shoe shines, shirt steaming, real barber chairs, and complimentary neck trims between visits.

Spa offerings are from the Aveda men's grooming line. Their marketing states: "Imagine starting your day with a warm neck shave, hot towel facial, and stress-relieving scalp and shoulder massage before your haircut. Our specialized team, including a licensed barber, will ensure you receive an exceptional Douglas J experience."

Among their list of spa packages, they offer a men's retreat that includes a 60-minute Swedish and deep tissue massage using Aveda aromas, a scalp massage, and haircut.

aspects of grooming were once governed by strict conventions of formal dress for all men. Though they were abandoned in the 1960s and 1970s, the trend is towards a reinvention of male grooming.

In June 2006, *DAYSPA* magazine reported that the following statements were myths when it comes to men enjoying spas:

- To connect with men, you must use macho language.

- Men represent a single-niche market.

- Spa wear is unisex.

- When communicating with men about skin care, keep it simple.[7]

Teen Spas and Kid Packages. There is strong evidence that teenagers are now highly predisposed to go to day spas for services they once went exclusively to nail and beauty salons to receive. The services they care about when visiting spas are still those related to on-stage body regions (those parts of the body that are visible to others). Even facials are attracting teen audiences, because they feel like more "powerful" ways to deal with date-ruining nightmares such as acne, break-outs, etc.

The estimated number of spa-goers who are teenagers is nearly four million in the United States and more than half a million in Canada. In both countries, the most common treatments received by teenagers are the most popular treatments of spa-goers overall: manicures, pedicures, full-body massage, and facials.

In late 2007, Florida's Disney World opened up a spa boutique for young children called the Bibbidi Bobbidi Boutique. Children must be at least age 3. Girls are greeted by a Fairy Godmother-in-Training and can choose from makeover packages that include Diva, Pop Princess, or Fairytale Princess. The makeover includes a hairstyle, shimmering makeup, and nails. Girls can also choose from costumes

reflections

Bill Chrismer: Personalizing Spas for Men

Bill Chrismer is the owner of Gentleman's Quarters, day spas for men in Colorado. Opened in 1996, their motto is "Feel Like a Man Again."

There was really a market for men's services. Men have traditionally been uncomfortable going to men's salons. They don't like the perm smell, they don't like to sit in the chairs and have women walking around in capes. What they want is a place that's all their own. We were designed to fill that void about 12 years ago. We have two properties, and despite increased competition, we're growing every year.

I really think there is increased personalization in spas. What people want—and men especially—are services and products geared toward them. They don't want to order off a menu. They want something that is specific for them—personalized. We see that as a big trend.

Also, I think people want things that work. They don't want to be sold to, they don't want hype, they're looking for products and services that truly, authentically produce results.

---

that include Tinker Bell, Belle, Snow White, Ariel, Cinderella, or Sleeping Beauty. Nor have they left out the boys, who can get a "Cool Dude" makeover that includes colored gels and confetti in a special hairstyle.[8]

Not everyone, though, thinks that teen spas are a trend that is going to last. Cathy Cluff, managing director of The Oaks at Ojai, said she thinks having kids at the spa is more of a fad. She likens it to Las Vegas' attempt to market to families by opening up such properties as Treasure Island and Circus Circus.

"I think it is a little bit trendy in the sense of the kiddie spa day pampering parties," she said. "I think what would be wonderful was if it could go beyond that. With our obesity levels at an all-time high, we could take it from the educational aspect of what spas can offer. If the message could come from the spa of health and wellness and proper eating and then trickle down to the kids—then maybe the concept of kids and spas wouldn't, in my opinion, die out."

Residential Spas. Real estate developers are getting into the spa game by building "residential spas" in residential properties, gated communities, and high-end condominiums. Residential spas are enjoying considerable success, particularly in the high-end condo and gated community markets. As the opportunity becomes more widely understood and embraced by real estate developers, there is expected to be a significant increase in the number of spas that are being incorporated into new housing projects. This is an area growing in both North America and Europe.

Private Club Spas. Spas in private membership clubs have traditionally been housed in the locker room area and were part of either the locker room or fitness operation. The explosive growth in spa operations around the world is leading to a change in the scale and style of spa operations in clubs. A traditional private club spa had a massage room, sauna, steam room, and whirlpool. These amenities were designed to complement the members' physical activities in the fitness center with soothing, relaxing experiences.

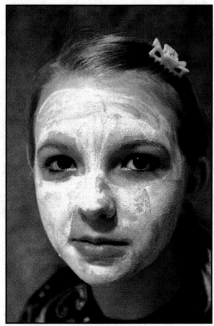

Spas are offering services for teens and kids. That segment is particularly interested in facials.

New, purpose-designed spas can be stand-alone facilities, separate from the fitness center, that may include a number of different treatment rooms, areas focused on beauty- and health-oriented treatments and services, and a variety of food and beverage options, classrooms, and other facilities.

A major challenge for club managers and members has been to find a design compromise that provides desired spa facilities and services, but does not duplicate too many existing facilities. For example, a club may already have a fitness center, whirlpools and steam rooms in both the men's and women's locker rooms, another whirlpool by the pool, and a massage room adjacent to the fitness center or one each in the two locker rooms. Managers have had to determine whether the members' desire for a full-service spa is sufficient to justify the cost of duplicating existing facilities in a coordinated spa building or area. They also have to determine whether dispersed facilities can continue to provide the experience and services that members want.[9]

The Influence of Spa

As the spa industry has grown and evolved, its ideals and influences have spread outside the walls of the spa itself. The concepts that have evolved inside the spa, nurtured by spa professionals and devoted spa advocates, have begun to permeate

The Spa at Pinehurst

The Spa at Pinehurst in North Carolina has created spa space for both teenagers and kids.

For teenagers, there is a Teen Spa Lounge that lets teenagers ages 12 to 17 and their friends sample health and beauty products, drink smoothies, and read health magazines. They also offer a number of services specifically for teens from a total facial in which the staff helps to teach about home care routines, make-up application and lesson, and a teen tune-up with a certified personal trainer. Packages are titled "Teen Time Out Spa Package" with a massage, facial, and makeup application; a "Mother and Daughter Teen Re-TREAT Package" with spa pampering for mom and daughter; and "Friends Always and Forever" for a group of teens to enjoy the spa together for a day.

A parent or guardian is required at all massages for teenagers under the age of 16. Teens must wear a bathing suit or underwear and therapists are always the same gender as the guest.

They also offer limited treatments for children ages 6 to 11. These children must always be accompanied by a parent or guardian and they are not allowed to use the private lounge areas, wet areas, fitness room, or pool. Services offered to kids are massages, facials, "cutesy cuts," and "twinkle toes and fancy fingers"—their younger version of a spa manicure and pedicure.

the culture at large, affecting a wide variety of other industries, personal habits, and beliefs.

The spa experience is weaving its way into every walk of day-to-day life, resulting in an increased array of traditional and non-traditional partnerships.

Spa Culture and the Service Ethic

To characterize excellent service before the proliferation of spa, one might use words like professional, detached, smiling, gracious, and polite. Many of these words can still be used to characterize excellent service today, however, consumers might add: caring, personable, engaged, empathetic, and genuine to that list.

When spas became a part of hospitality, the service ethic changed as a result of shepherding guests through a variety of intensely personal experiences. It had the effect of closing the distance between the server and the served. Spa technicians were more than specialists, they were entering a gray area that was part servant, but also part therapist, part healer, part hand holder, part confidante. Spa therapists learn things about the people they work with, and being known opens people up to a different experience of service, and different expectations of being served.

Spa culture continually challenges the service ethic to be more aware, more empathetic, and more sensitive to the core components of leisure: reconnection and total well being.

Spa cuisine is food that is both healthy and tasty.

Spa Culture and Spa Cuisine

One of the major influences that spa has had on culture has been in the growth in popularity of spa cuisine. Even frozen food aisles contain microwave dinners that advertise themselves as "spa cuisine" choices.

Spa cuisine is based on food that is fresh, healthy, local, organic, clean, and lovingly and consciously prepared. It is food that is well-thought out and balanced. Spa professionals carefully research the science of food and nutrition as they prepare the recipe. They look into how many times it is healthy to eat different foods and food preparations.

Spa programs began educating their guests on such things as how to eat healthy, how to have more calcium in the diet, how to balance minerals in the diet, how to eat fewer processed foods, why organic food is important and what it means for their body, how to get food that is as fresh as possible. They taught their guests to be mindful of how their food was prepared and to adopt principles to truly enjoy food. They placed emphasis on portion control, mindful eating, pacing oneself, and concentrating on the food and its texture, color, consistency, and taste.

The phrase spa food was first coined in the late 1970s and evolved to spa cuisine in the 1980s. It represented a marriage between professional chefs and dieticians working together to create food that was both healthy and tasty.

Cheryl Hartsough, spa director for Gurney's International Health and Beauty Spa and one of the pioneers of spa cuisine, described chefs and dieticians as being oil and vinegar with conflicting interests when spa cuisine was first getting started. Chefs were taught to be pleasers, to create the best dish possible. Dieticians were taught the science behind food and were about cutting out such things as salt and fat, adding more of other things. Now, she says, they're an emulsion that has come together to create healthy foods in moderation.

"We were always about moderation on the plate," she said. "We were about filling the plate with more fruits and vegetables so you weren't missing the salts and fats and excess oils. We believe in the spa world that you are what you eat. We know our blood cells regenerate every three months. We can make our body healthier. We've seen the reversal in the aging process, we've seen the difference in people with their blood pressure coming down and their cholesterol lowering. It's through diet and exercise, the combination of energy in and energy out."

Rules for spa cuisine included no more than 30 percent fat (with most spa food being closer to 20 percent), only healthy oils (olive oil and flaxseed, for example), foods that were high in antioxidants, and foods that contain fiber. Spa cuisine became a collaboration of two mindsets that came together to make healthy dishes and then taught people how to snack between meals to keep their blood sugar and metabolism up. "It's about food and the mindfulness of your selections," Hartsough said. "It all comes to loving yourself, taking care of yourself, and nourishing yourself body, mind, and spirit."

When it came to food and nutrition, early spas were primarily engaged in educating people about diet. People were starving themselves, suffering from bulimia, and practicing the wrong kinds of diets. The spa educated people on exercise and nutrition, guiding people on how to pamper themselves, relax, eat well, and be joyful—not to simply deprive themselves or follow the latest fad diet. In the early 1990s, much of the spa cuisine movement at resorts and destination spas was about weight loss for the rich and famous.

Now, Hartsough says, spas have moved on to the third generation, where the people spas educated are now going out and educating the general populace about healthy eating. Throughout the 1980s and 1990s, spas were constantly in the media. Whenever there was an article about food or food preparation, spas would be mentioned. People were constantly turning to spas as the experts in clean food, organic food, and food that was good for the body and soul. Spas made it glamorous to eat healthy. This spread the spa message to the masses.

Spa Culture and the Medical Community

The spa world's emphasis on wellness has not escaped notice of those who have traditionally been charged with maintaining health and curing illnesses. While early spas were considered medical treatments, and Europe has always recognized their medical benefits, they fell out of favor among American doctors in the early part of the twentieth century.

It has only been as the contemporary spa has flourished that the medical community began turning once again to its more traditional roots. Increasingly, hospitals are incorporating treatments such as massages and doctors are prescribing acupuncture. The influence of spa is even being found in the décor of medical centers.

reflections

Steven Bernstein: Making Spa Cuisine Work

Steven Bernstein is the executive chef at the Enchantment Resort and Mii Amo Spa in Sedona, Arizona. He oversees food preparation and production at the resort's three restaurants. Before that, he was executive sous chef at Miraval Life in Balance, a Tucson, Arizona, spa. He has received international attention for his modern approach to spa cuisine.

Spa cuisine is becoming so popular. When I first started out, it was very intimidating.

My approach is fresh ingredients. I know where my ingredients come from. I know where my fish is from, where my meat is from, where my vegetables are from, where those mushrooms that I used yesterday are from. That's the first thing. Everything has to be really, really fresh. Of course, where you source it from is important so that you know what's not in it and whether it is sustainable, organic, and so on.

What I try to do is look at it as regular cuisine and not approach it as foreign spa cuisine. So you look at a traditional dish, for example, then you modify it. You keep it very interesting by using buffalo, lamb, any ingredients you want to; keep the portions a little smaller; be conscious of the amount of fat and content that you're putting into the dish. Really, it's all about the cooking technique. Use high quality ingredients that have better flavor so you can use less of it. Just let your imagination go.

If you look at it from a traditional standpoint and modify it to a spa standpoint, it's a little easier to create and be a little more flexible with everything. That's really how we approach it. Before I was, "this much protein, this much starch, this much fat." Now what we're trying to do is get it a little more intricate, a little more exquisite with bolder flavors and more excitement.

Guests at the spa don't believe the low calories and the fat content in our meals. They come to the cooking classes and are amazed at the approach to it. We explain to them that without that added fat, they can eat something that's really good. They think they're going to be eating tofu when they can really eat filet mignon, rack of lamb and it's only 400 calories for that entrée instead of the traditional 700 or 800 calories. We give them recipes to take home. I always tell them, "Here's my phone number, give me a call if you have questions. If you have anything at home you're interested in doing, give us a call." It's very personal. We encourage it and get great feedback.

The medical industry has moved more toward integrative medicine and incorporating treatments that spas have promoted for years. Spa historian Jonathan Paul de Vierville wrote that:

> Historically, what is important to know is this recent emergence and development is not being guided by, or driven from within, the spa industry. Rather, the new medical interests in spa are coming from medical and healthcare professionals and institutions seeking to redefine, rediscover and reinvent themselves within a wider and more comprehensive spa industry that is still defining and redefining itself. The consequences of this medicine and spa courtship, engagement and marriage are still being

worked out in unknown family dynamics. Caution is warranted, especially given the sad state of affairs with our current public healthcare systems, health maintenance organizations and private medical practices. On the other hand, here and now is a great challenge and opportunity for the spa industry to facilitate helpful transitions and corrective transformations. Good spa medicine will require a fully-integrated, interdisciplinary and multidisciplinary explanation with authentic knowledge and comprehensive understanding above and beyond the current marketplace fads and forces.[10]

Spa Culture and the Fitness and Health Club Industry

Fitness continues to play an important role in spas. The 2006 ISPA Consumer Report found that spa consumers want customized spa experiences that provide real solutions with long-term results. It's a need that spas and the health club industry are increasingly partnering up to provide.

On the flip side, spas have also come to play an important role in health and fitness clubs. Their message of wellness and total mind, body, and spirit health has made its way into clubs, which used to be focused only on the body. Spas and fitness/health clubs have enjoyed a symbiotic relationship where it is often difficult to tell who has influenced whom as both have had tremendous impact on the other.

Fitness clubs and companies like Sports Club LA and Equinox are increasingly incorporating spa components and services into their offerings.

When the American Council for Exercise released its health and fitness predictions in 2007, many of them were describing conditions and trends that spas have been addressing for years. They talked about specialized fitness programming for older adults, healthcare providers teaming up to address health-related trends, and connecting the mind and body for a complete health experience (including offering such things as yoga, Pilates, and tai chi as alternatives to high-impact activities).

In an October 2007 *Club Industry Fitness Business Pro* Jasmine Jafferali, a fitness and wellness manager at a Chicago health club, quoted ISPA spa trends and talked about how fitness and health clubs need to better understand them to meet the demands of their guests. She said that the days were gone when their members want to leave the club in pain. Instead, they want a total wellness solution that focuses on relieving stress and practicing good nutrition. Her recommendation was that health and fitness clubs need to either start offering spa treatments and packages or partnering with a neighboring spa to offer joint packages.[11]

Where spas and fitness clubs experience the greatest symbiotic relationship is in the arena of wellness. It is here that they converge in clients and offerings. The people who are interested in a health club or fitness club are those who are interested in their physical well-being—a trait shared with those who attend spas.

Jeremy McCarthy, director of spa operations and development for Starwood Hotels & Resorts Worldwide, points to spinning as an example of how the fitness movement began to move toward wellness. Spinning is a stationary bike program that simulates riding outdoors. While it is a very physical activity, it is also about visualizing the ride and imagining the outdoor scenery that would be seen on a ride. It also incorporates music that is meant to have a spiritual effect on participants.

reflections

Brent Bauer: Spas and the Medical Community

Brent Bauer, M.D., is the director of the Complementary and Integrative Medicine Program at Mayo Clinic in Rochester, Minnesota. He is also an associate professor of medicine at Mayo Medical School and a graduate of Mayo Medical School. He is the medical editor-in-chief of the Mayo Clinic Book of Alternative Medicine *and host of the Mayo Clinic* Wellness Solutions *DVD series. He is also a board member of the ISPA Foundation.*

Fixing Broken Things

We don't currently have a medical system in our country. We have a largely government-financed approach that rewards providers mainly for fixing broken things. If we do a bypass surgery and charge a large amount—let's say $50,000, Medicare will cover most, if not all of that. But if we spend an hour talking to a patient about diet, mind-body issues, or try to get them into meditative practice or adopt wellness and lifestyle activities that could prevent the heart disease in the first place, our current system often values that at less than $50 an hour. By not valuing the power of simply talking to patients and focusing on preventive care, we set ourselves up for failure. To focus only on treating diseases and conditions, rather than on wellness and prevention, is a short-sighted approach.

Fortunately, more and more people are recognizing it makes a lot more sense to try to prevent problems in the first place. These days, at a large busy hospital, you're quite likely to hear about things like acupuncture, massage, and mind-body therapies. We teach much of that here at Mayo Clinic. In a three to four day hospital stay, we might introduce patients to several of those concepts. Then they're going to go back to their own community, where the spa industry has a wonderful opportunity to teach the mind-body approaches and how to take better care of ourselves. This can be done through yoga, tai chi, movement meditations, etc. Lots of spas have cooking classes and classes on good nutrition, too.

Thus, medicine and the spa community have a great opportunity to jointly build the culture of wellness that seems critical for our nation's health. Mayo Clinic has massage therapists on staff and we have a number of people trained in mind-body therapies and guided imagery. If we consider patients with high blood pressure, we recognize that many of them need medication. But some can get by with less medication if we can also apply lifestyle changes and use guided imagery, for example. Some of those patients can even get by without medication by incorporating such therapies on a routine basis. The goal is not to have them keep coming back to a medical center, but to find these treatments in their community close to home. It's a great opportunity for medicine and the spa industry to work together to value those things like yoga that can be delivered in a place like a spa or whatever venue is going to be closest to the patient's home.

Knowing What Will Work

When it comes to research on spa-like treatments, most of the research is on acupuncture, specifically around pain, lower back pain, pain after surgery, and

reflections

(continued)

headaches. The medical community has considerable data. Mayo Clinic has been using acupuncture since 1974. Many of our patients report feeling that it works.

We're exploring acupuncture for other things like smoking cessation and other applications that are less proven. Massage is close behind acupuncture in the amount of research and data available in the last 15 years. We know massage makes us feel better, but research shows that massage actually lowers blood pressure, improves heart rate, and improve the nervous system. These facts are really hard to ignore.

The whole realm of mind-body therapies is now receiving more attention. Much of the research on mind-body therapies is overwhelmingly positive, and there is very little risk involved with most of the mind body therapies.

Most therapies are things you do for yourself. The old paradigm is the doctor doing things to fix problems —a paradigm where there's not a lot of self-care and self-practice. As we start to look at our lives and become more mindful, mindful-ness-based practices can have a huge impact on our health. It puts you in charge of your health care instead of having the mindset "I'm broke and someone else needs to fix me."

Get off life's treadmill for a moment, slow down, and focus. People can start to learn to do that at a spa and then translate it to a daily practice at home. Spa can introduce a whole other generation to the concept of mind-body.

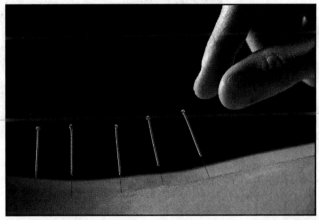

The medical community has considerable data on the effectiveness of acupuncture—one of the many places where medicine and spa have intersected.

Mind-body physical activities like this led to the inclusion of such activities as yoga, tai chi, and other classes being offered at health and fitness clubs. "A lot of the gyms are now offering yoga classes and movement classes that are more mind-body-spirit. It's not so much anymore that you have to go to the gym to lift weights and then a yoga studio to do yoga," said McCarthy. "People are more and more realizing that wellness is not just going and lifting weights and eating a certain diet. It's how you feel, it's how you think, it's how you use your mind, and it's how your attitude is."

Spa Culture and the Tourism and Hospitality Industry

Two of the hottest issues in the hospitality industry today are spas and going green. When PriceWaterhouseCoopers reported that spas were a greater determining factor for meeting planners choosing a resort than golf courses were, this spurred hotel executive interest and activity. It would not be overstating it to say that spa had essentially taken over the high ground of the peak luxury experience, at least for women, and studies have shown that women are the primary determiner in families of vacation destinations. Hospitality listened.

There is recent evidence from Smith Travel Research, the leading hospitality resource for statistical revenue analysis, that suggests that a property's average rate is dramatically affected by the presence of a spa at the hotel or resort. Luxury properties that have a spa charge an average daily rate of $317, while the average daily rate (ADR) for luxury hotels without spas (but other similar amenities) was $250. The average occupancy tends to stay the same, but the revenue is much higher.[12]

Most resorts now have spas, and many have world class spa facilities and programs. Many use the spa as a lynchpin of their marketing efforts. The spa is the sizzle that sells the resort by exemplifying the resort's dedication to total luxury, relaxation, and rejuvenation. Spas have become profit drivers of the highest order, both by selling the spa experience and by enhancing the image of the property and helping to sell rooms.

Spas have introduced a whole new species of employees to the resort and hospitality industry. Managing spa employees has trained hospitality leaders to anticipate trends in human resource management and encouraged non-spa employees to learn about the spa and the spa experience. Spas have raised guest expectations about room and bed comfort, bathroom and vanity design, quality of in-room amenities, personalization of the guest experience, inclusion of healthy cuisine, and myriad other finer points of service.

In Europe, spas used to be subsidized by national health systems, spa guests were often referred by physicians, and spa visits were largely reimbursed. With the removal of government funding in the 1980s, European spas have had to reinvent themselves and their destinations, repositioning the spas and spa towns as tourism drivers and following the American model of spa marketing.

Spas have changed how resorts and hotels serve, operate, and market themselves. These are changes that do not figure to be reversed any time soon, as the influence of the spa movement on hospitality and tourism appears to be here to stay.

Conclusion

Spa professionals are healers for people and society. They are also business people. While spas continue to embrace their origins and roots as places of healing and spiritual renewal, spas are maturing as a business, industry, and profession. Increasingly sophisticated and profit-focused organizations are entering the market, influencing the others in the market to think more about the financial bottom line and how to generate a sustainable profit. Manufacturers and product distributors have become more creative and innovative in their marketing and branding. Investors are more aware of spas and why they are worthy of investment.

Spas are now a part of contemporary culture. A plethora of newspaper, magazine, and other print and electronic media are teeming with spa-related topics. Spas have become as emblematic to relaxation as champagne is to celebration. But the role of spa in contemporary culture must be associated first and foremost with a sense of rejuvenation and redefining oneself for oneself. The act of visiting a spa is an act of self devotion, of giving back to self and learning from self. It can be an indulgence, a reward, or a ritual of self preservation. At face value, it is a respite, a relaxation break, or a feel-good gift to oneself. On a deeper level, it is the modern day equivalent of the ancient vision quest, a journey of self-discovery and personal realization.

The rise of much new technology can be correlated with the collapse of many long-cherished values: the integral family, personal connections, and relaxation. Ironically, the proliferation of time-saving devices and the availability and accessibility of luxury goods have left people with no time for anything and made time into the last luxury.

As the human species continues to evolve and create more and more "bells and whistles" in every facet of life, it will undoubtedly get carried away and distracted with all the fanfare and noise. The fundamental function of spa is to remind people to experience a deeper peace and genuine quiet as a way to rejuvenate, regenerate, and return to what is most real, authentic, and sustainable.

Spas are here to remind people that there is more content and meaning in a personal connection than in a gigaload of bandwidth. That "memory" means more than just storage capacity, and that although connectivity is valuable, human connectedness is priceless. Spas connect us: to ourselves, with others, with experiences, to the world, and most of all, to nature and spirit. Spas will continue to play this vital role of human connectivity, especially in the key role of transforming the culture into one that renews and sustains all people.

Endnotes

1. www.rancholapuerta.com/home/history-vision/early-days.html, Retrieved June 23, 2008.

2. Deborah Szekely, *Secrets of the Golden Door*, William Morrow and Company, Inc., New York, 1977.

3. Nan Sterman, "A Woman of the World: Deborah Szekely Proves That Age is Just a Number," *San Diego Jewish Journal*, May 2006.

4. Bernard Burt, *Fodor's Health and Fitness Vacations*, Fodor's Travel Publications, Inc., New York, 1989.

5. "The ISPA 2007 Spa Industry Study," International Spa Association, 2007, p. 6.

6. Information contributed by Mary Tabacchi, Ph.D., Cornell University.

7. J. Elaine Spear, "Manning the Spa," *DAYSPA*, June 2006.

8. "Disney Creates Fairytale Treatments," *Spa Business*, June 23, 2008.

9. "Spa-Goer Study," International Spa Association, 2006, p. 82.

10. Joe Perdue, ed. "Contemporary Club Management," American Hotel & Lodging Educational Institute: Lansing, Mich., 2007.

11. Jonathan Paul deVierville, "Spa Industry, Culture and Evolution," *Massage & Bodywork*, Aug./Sept. 2003.

12. Jasmine Jafferali, "Joining Forces with the Spa Industry," *Club Industry's Fitness Business Pro*, Oct. 5, 2007.

13. Jan D. Freitag, "To Spa or Not to Spa: The Impact of Spas on Hotels," *Lodging Magazine*, April 2007, pp. 21–22.

 Key Terms ────────────────────────────

day spas—Spas offering professionally administered spa services on a day use basis.

destination spas—Facilities with the primary purpose of guiding individual spa-goers to develop healthy habits.

Essene—A mystical, ascetic Jewish group thought to be the authors of the Dead Sea Scrolls. They taught the value of simplicity and a simple life, among other things.

European model—A model whereby the government supported trips to spas as an important part of a person's health. European spas encouraged stays lasting several weeks so that people's bodies could heal themselves.

resort spas—A spa within a resort or hotel that provides spa services.

 Review Questions ────────────────────────

1. How did spas evolve from fitness to wellness?

2. What were the beginnings of the day spa industry in the United States?

3. What were some of the early destination spas and who founded them?

4. What are some of the major spa and health associations?

5. How were the initial spa brands developed?

6. What are some of the new and emerging spa concepts?

7. How has spa culture influenced the service ethic? Cuisine? The medical community? The hospitality industry?

 Internet Sites ──────────────────────────

For more information, visit the following Internet sites. Remember that Internet addresses can change without notice. If the site is no longer there, you can use a search engine to look for additional sites.

American Spa Therapy and Education
Certification Council
www.astecc.com

CIDESCO
www.cidesco.com

Cornell University School of
Hospitality Management
www.hotelschool.cornell.edu

Destination Spa Group
www.destinationspagroup.com

Douglas J Men's Spa
www.douglasj.com/men/index.html

Elmcrest College
www.elmcrestcollege.com

Enchantment Resort and Mii Amo Spa
www.miiamo.com

Equinox
www.equinoxfitness.com

Fairmont Willow Stream
www.willowstream.com

Four Seasons
www.fourseasons.com/spa

Gentleman's Quarters
www.gquarters.com

Golden Door
www.goldendoor.com

Hyatt Still Water
www.hyatt.com/gallery/stillwater/
home.html?icamp=stillwatersparedirect

International Health, Racquet and
Sportsclub Association
www.ihrsa.org

La Costa Resort and Spa
www.lacosta.com

Mandarin Oriental
www.mandarinoriental.com

Mayo Clinic Complementary and
Alternative Medicine
www.mayoclinic.com/health/
alternative-medicine/CM99999

PULSE
www.experienceispa.
com/ISPA/Magazines/Pulse

Rancho La Puerto
www.rancholapuerta.com

Ritz Carlton
www.ritzcarlton.com/en/Default.htm

Shangri-La Chi
www.shangri-la.com/en/property/
chengdu/shangrila/health/chispa/intro

Skin Authority
shopping.netsuite.com/skinauthority

Spa Finder
www.spafinder.com/index.jsp

Spa Management Journal
www.spamanagement.com

Starwood Heavenly Spas
www.starwoodspacollection.com

The Day Spa Association
www.dayspaassociation.com

The Marsh—a Center for Balance and
Fitness
www.themarsh.com/Marsh.htm

The Oaks at Ojai
www.oaksspa.com

The Red Door
www.reddoorspas.com

The Spa at Pinehurst
www.pinehurst.com/spa_resort.asp

Chapter 4 Outline

Understanding Trends
    Know What the Customer Knows
    Talk Less, Listen More
Key Market Trends
    Staffing
    Standards
    Competition in the Marketplace
Social Trends
    General Population Trends
    Attitudes/Habits by Generation
    Men
    Social Spa Visits/Groups
    Healthy Lifestyle
    Loneliness
    Body Image
    Techno-Stress
Market Trends
    Mini-Mass Markets
    Medical Treatments and Spas
    Residential Spas
    Spa on Vacation
    At-Home Spas
    Mobile Spas
    Corporate Wellness
Technology Trends
    Revenue Management
    Centralized Call Centers
    Check-in Kiosks
    Treatment Room Computers
    Music
    Cross-Selling
    High-Tech Equipment
    Spa Design
    The Internet
    Social Networking
Treatment Trends
    Customization
    Authenticity
    Indigenous Treatments
Industry Trends
    Ownership Structure
    Investors
    Mergers and Cross-Marketing
Environmental Trends
    Triple Bottom Line
    Sustainable Spas
    Local Food
Developing a Future Orientation
    Managing the Future

Competencies

1. Explain how key market and social trends affect the spa world. (pp. 113–132)

2. List emerging markets and trends that are likely to affect the future of the spa world. (pp. 132–141)

3. Describe technology and treatment trends that are changing how spas do business. (pp. 141–155)

4. Explain the ways in which ownership structure, investor interest, and mergers are affecting the spa world. (pp. 155–157)

5. Describe how spas are changing the way they operate to ensure future sustainability and environmental responsibility. (pp. 157–165)

6. Explain how developing a future orientation can help spa professionals manage change and prepare for the future. (pp. 165–166)

4

Trend Analysis: Predictions and Possibilities

FROM ALMOST THE BEGINNING OF TIME, spas have provided renewal, regeneration, and rejuvenation. They have been special places where people go to find themselves. They go to rest, reflect, and rediscover themselves so they can later re-enter the world with a refreshed body, mind, and spirit. Over the centuries, spas have evolved, experiencing sometimes rapid proliferation into mainstream culture. During the past two decades, spas have witnessed a rapid growth and expansion around the world.

The future is always uncertain, but if spa professionals are to foresee the future direction of spas, it will be necessary to examine thoroughly the current ups and downs of market trends as well as to review and remember the historical legacy of spas.

Looking away from the starlight of the past and the mirror of the present, it is time to peer into the waters of the future to divine what may be held there. Within these waters, spa professionals can attempt to discern where the dreams of today will take the spa of tomorrow. The future of spas will not only be a direct result of future short-term market trends, but also serve as a cause for spas to become active cultural institutions that play vital roles in the ongoing services and activities for individual renewal and social regeneration. The actions taken today by spa professionals worldwide will help determine whether spas will be able to sustain their present growth rate while continuing to fulfill their mission of uplifting the health and well-being of the world, both inside and outside of the spa.

While making predictions is a difficult business, it is possible to take a look at current directions in the spa world to see where spa is traveling. In order to envision tomorrow, it is necessary to look at the way the spa world is acting today and in the recent past. It is also worth noting that the further anyone tries to see into the future, the greater the risk of inaccuracy.

Understanding Trends

The growth and changes in the spa world over the past decade have created a highly competitive environment for spas and resource partners (vendors). The internal infrastructure has often been unable to keep up, causing labor shortages, a lack of standards, and other challenges. Many of these challenges will be addressed in this chapter along with discussions about how each of these challenges affects the spa world. There are also bounteous opportunities. The world needs spa like never before, and spas are poised to do great good. This chapter will explore:

- Key market trends

- Social trends

- Market trends

- Technology trends

- Treatment trends

- Industry trends

- Environmental trends

This chapter will also explore how to develop a future orientation that will help spas survive.

While trends help spa professionals prepare for the short-term future, professionals must also be concerned with the broader significance of spa that goes beyond the market economy. Spas have existed and served their purpose in all types and conditions of market economies: supply and demand and capitalist economies as well as socialist, nationalist, and communist-controlled societies. Spas are now part of the global market. Understanding this broad purpose of spa will help professionals support a sustainable and responsible future of spa.

Spa professionals might consider both short-term trends and long-term traditions for the future. Trends can make significant differences as they develop and unfold. Trends may be local or global, micro or macro, natural or fashionable, but regardless, trends introduce a measure of change which, when it happens, means more of some things and less of others. But market trends are not fundamental changes like those of cultural traditions and legacies. Trends are more like the seasonal weather patterns while cultural traditions and legacies are more like the long-term climates between the ice ages.

A trend typically has four stages that can last for varying lengths of time:

- Introduction: The trend becomes a buzzword and its images begin cropping up in the media and on the streets.

- Growth: The message spreads and there is an increased awareness that this trend exists.

- Maturity: Variations on the trend can be seen, including copies and "knock-offs," and the trend is commonly known.

- Decline: The trend begins to lose its luster, is viewed as somewhat outdated, and is replaced by a new trend.

Knowing what stage a trend is in helps spa professionals plan for its life cycle. Fads are trends that sweep in and out quickly, generating a large amount of attention in a relatively short amount of time. It is critical for spa professionals, as they examine fads and trends, to use the information to choose the more enduring path to sustainability.

Major social trends are typically of the most help to spa professionals as they plan. Highly successful trend spotters look for those trends that have a deep and lasting effect on society. They then identify which trends they can either take advantage of or test.

Spa Snapshot: How will spas look different ten years from now?

I believe spas will have a more boutique look as the spa categories are more clearly defined.

—*Wendy Clark, President, I-Bella*

Spas will continue to evolve but may begin to address health on a more serious level. Sleep deprivation clinics, allergy, and detox offer mechanisms to cope with depression and grief – not "medical" but receiving "health care" on another level.

—*Darlene Fiske, Owner, The Fiske Group: Public Relations & Marketing Strategies*

I believe the wellness focus will only become stronger and spas will continue to adopt and adapt the health component to their location. (There will be) more partnerships between day spas and fitness facilities, etc. Efforts to improve sustainability and decrease ecological footprints will continue. Organic treatments will become more popular, with soy, bamboo, and sustainable fabrics being used. (There will be) reduced packaging for spa products.

—*Wanda Love, Director of Sales & Marketing, Santé Spa*

The perception of a "fluff" experience will soften as people begin to view spa treatments as necessary and more mainstream. Also, I think the medical field will begin to recommend spas as places to recuperate from health issues more.

—*Debra Koerner, Chief Operating Officer, imassage, Inc.*

I think there will be more mid-stream 'spas'—places for people to relax and receive treatment that aren't so exclusive and expensive. I also hope that they are perceived as sources of healing rather than pampering.

—*Angela Cortright, Owner, Spa Gregorie's*

I believe that there will be a trend in services that can be performed outside of the room in order to increase retail sales and educate guests on stress reduction, service benefits, and retail. I believe this trend will create an increase in "service bars" and "consultation stations" in the retail areas of spas.

—*Sara Cruncleton, Ihloff Salon & Spa*

Know What the Customer Knows

To the customer, spa professionals are the industry experts. Customers may come in with questions about certain trends, trusting that if anyone would have an educated opinion on the subject, it would be the spa professional. As professionals, spa staff members have access to the best industry data and information. They can attend trade shows, subscribe to industry-related websites and e-newsletters, read magazines, and network with other spa professionals. All of these activities keep them abreast of trends that the average consumer may not be privy to yet.

Like everyone else, spa customers are flooded with messages through magazines, television, and Internet channels on a daily basis. Spa professionals reassure their customers by being able to talk about trends and other opinions. Doing so establishes the spa professional as the expert and spa customers come to trust his or her opinions when they are offered.

Talk Less, Listen More

The importance of listening is huge when addressing spa planning and trends. Listening to the media is obviously important, as the media is the ultimate reporter of trends. But even more importantly, spa professionals listen to the messages that their staff, peers, and customers give them.

If a spa professional keeps getting calls from customers about whether a particular treatment is offered, he or she pays attention. The callers are giving valuable tips about what interests them. If the staff is buzzing about a new trend, spa managers take their opinions into account. The spa staff is a great resource when it comes to deciding which trends to follow and which to pass up.

Key Market Trends

Spas are deeply affected by the world around them and by the same market conditions that affect any other business. Three primary market issues shaping the world of spa are human resources and staffing, the uneven application of standards for the industry, and increased competition from both within and outside the industry.

Staffing

Spas often succeed or fail based on the quality of employees they have on their staff. Since 2000, staffing and human resources issues have been raised in every spa industry study conducted in the U.S. and Canada. If the International SPA Association (ISPA) industry research had headlines over the last several years, here's what they might have said:

2000 "The spa industry needs to recruit qualified resources."

2002 "Labor market is a key industry concern."

2004 "Human resource availability is still a huge problem for the industry."

Spa Snapshot: During the past 15 years, which trends have helped shape the future of spa?

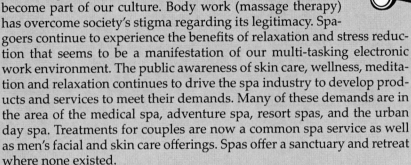

Over the past 15 years, we have seen the spa environment become part of our culture. Body work (massage therapy) has overcome society's stigma regarding its legitimacy. Spa-goers continue to experience the benefits of relaxation and stress reduction that seems to be a manifestation of our multi-tasking electronic work environment. The public awareness of skin care, wellness, meditation and relaxation continues to drive the spa industry to develop products and services to meet their demands. Many of these demands are in the area of the medical spa, adventure spa, resort spas, and the urban day spa. Treatments for couples are now a common spa service as well as men's facial and skin care offerings. Spas offer a sanctuary and retreat where none existed.

—Bruce A. Taylor, Director of Spa Operations, Desert Springs, J.W. Marriott Resort & Spa

The rapid growth of the industry over the past 15 years had demanded the need to put a line item in the budget for education, a significant change for the way spas previously operated. Investing in a beautiful physical facility is not enough for a spa to be successful if the staff's consistency and professionalism doesn't back up the money the client perceives has been invested in the spa itself. To address this need, spas have sought independent educators, in addition to vendor educators, to enhance the staff's understanding and knowledge about treatments, treatment benefits, and how to better serve the client's needs.

—Ann Brown, Spa Director, Spa Shiki at the Lodge of Four Seasons

I personally feel that the quest for wellness, beauty, and health evolved a long time ago with the discovery of "the healing powers of water." The heart of the modern spa, just as the ancient spa, is water and the rituals that evolve around it. History has made a complete circle, and we are back loving this elixir of life: The water! In recent years spas have been strongly teaching the proper sequence of the typical spa ritual, which is to cleanse, heat, cold, treatment, and rest. The teaching of the healing properties of the water has had a profound impact on our industry; it has been more than a trend ... these practices have revived an "old way of life."

—Cecilia I. Hercik, Director of Spa Sales & Operations, Grand Wailea Resort Hotel & Spa Wailea

Source: *Pulse*, Nov./Dec. 2005

Spa Snapshot: What trends do you think spas should tap into?

I believe spas should look to outside partnerships to add value to the customer experience. For example, partnerships with a bookstore like Borders. Adding a boutique book store that is a lease-hold partnership would benefit the customer and both business partners by offering books, DVDs, etc. on healthy life style topics.

—*Wendy Clark, President, I-Bella*

Continue to customize the experience as much as possible; green change as a trend is here to stay.

—*Loren Stone, CEO, Sovereign Hospitality*

Addressing the aging population which would include the child as caregiver—who is giving back to them? Also, address the childhood obesity problems. Parents need help raising children on a healthy life-style—spas are an obvious resource.

—*Darlene Fiske, Owner, The Fiske Group: Public Relations & Marketing Strategies*

Eating healthier—the 100-mile diet concept which promotes sustainable, organic choices with natural immunity boosters because food comes from local sources.

—*Wanda Love, Director of Sales & Marketing, Santé Spa*

This is solidified through the ISPA member surveys. In 2005, 87 percent of members stated the top issue facing the industry is the number and quality of workers entering the industry. The key human resources challenges are the lack of qualified labor pool, hiring and retaining staff, compensation, training, lack of business skills, cost of labor and benefits, and the lack of training standards.

The challenges for spas in the coming years include:

- Management turnover
- Labor shortages

Management Turnover. The ISPA 2007 Spa Industry Study identified that the average spa employs 17 people. Nearly one-third of those spas surveyed had made some sort of change in their management staff, either hiring management staff to new positions (24 percent), losing management staff (16 percent), or replacing management staff (18 percent). The exact reason for this turnover isn't known, but it is theorized that it could be the result of spas not being able to find properly qualified people

Exhibit 1 Management Turnover in the Past 12 Months

	Management Turnover by Spa Type				
	Club Spa*	Day Spa	Medical Spa*	Resort/Hotel Spa	Other*†
Hired Management Staff to New Positions	25%	21%	27%	44%	49%
Lost Management Staff	12%	13%	15%	39%	21%
Replaced Management Staff	21%	16%	15%	36%	31%
None of the Above	66%	70%	67%	50%	42%

Notes: * Interpret results with caution due to small sample sizes.
†Other type of spa includes mineral springs spas and destination spas.
Responses sum to more than 100% due to multiple responses.

Source: ISPA 2007 Spa Industry Study

for management or simply a human resources retention issue where spas are losing staff to competitors. The issue is most pressing for resort/hotel spas. See Exhibit 1.

Labor Shortages. Labor shortages are affecting spas and other service industries throughout the world. Spas require very specific skill sets and there are not enough trained people available to meet the burgeoning demand. The industry's growth has outstripped the rate at which professionals are being trained in the skills needed for spa. In the U.S. spa industry, 72 percent of spas report that they have at least one open position.

Research conducted by ISPA indicated that there were a large number of job openings in the industry at each spa, particularly among the massage therapist positions. There is a shortage of almost 24,000 massage therapists in the United States and 6,600 openings for spa directors and managers.

Many spas reported that they are experiencing a significant shortage of people who have the proper skills qualifications to do the jobs needed in a spa. This was particularly true for the top management positions.

Some of the shortage can be attributed to the significant growth that has taken place in the industry—growth that has far outstripped the ability to train the necessary personnel. Responses to the labor shortage can include:

- Certification initiatives
- Educational programs in technical schools, colleges, and universities
- More in-house training at spas
- Clever recruiting that draws from other industries for non-therapist positions
- Public awareness campaigns aimed at promoting spa careers

The industry has done an excellent job of promoting spa as a healthy lifestyle that benefits its guests. Where it has fallen short has been in promoting the career opportunities and career paths available within spa.

Standards

The modern spa industry operates relatively free of any regulatory standards. In the United States, it is almost a completely unregulated industry while other countries have light regulations. Those regulations that do exist range from sanitation to legal, with such rules as nudity being prohibited during any service that includes hypnosis in Michigan to requiring all massage rooms in Malaysia to have a window so that police or government agents can look in if necessary.

The industry has expressed a desire to self-regulate so that the government won't get involved, but currently there is still a struggle with exactly what that regulation should look like. While spa is ancient, the modern industry in its current form is still fairly young and in the early stages of determining what is healthy, appropriate, and should be made into a standard.

There are three major types of standards that affect the spa world:

- Training protocols and licensing
- Service and quality
- Facilities

Training Protocols and Licensing. It can be difficult to establish standards for training protocols when every country, state, and municipality has different requirements and standards for licensing. There is little agreement among governing bodies about what is required for licensing spa technicians, service providers, and even the spas themselves.

In the United States, spas may have to apply for a license from either a local health board or a local cosmetology board. The requirements for the technicians also vary. An esthetician may be allowed to work only on the face and neck while in other states they are permitted to do extensive body work. They also need to have manufacturer training in the application of the skin care products that they use. Most massage therapists must be licensed in order to practice. Some places require therapists to get ongoing training; others do not.

Service and Quality. There is a move in some areas to require therapists to increase the number of hours they practice before they can become licensed.

Some in the industry have called for an increase in health regulation as the decreased number of health inspections in some areas have led to poor health and sanitation practices by some spas. These few spas that endanger their guests' health tarnish the reputation of more reputable, health-conscious spas.

One of the biggest challenges in determining how to create standards is the risk of lawsuits. If someone develops a Staph infection because the cleaning standard for the manicure equipment was wrong, or a massage is given inappropriately to a pregnant woman, who is responsible—the standard, the spa, or the individual therapist?

There is a move toward creating quality standards. *Mobil Travel Guide* has started rating spas. It has established more than 450 service standards and criteria that it uses to rank a spa. *Mobil Travel Guide* inspectors make unannounced visits to spas in the United States and Canada. Spas are now paying careful attention to these indicators.

Mobil isn't alone in establishing independent standards by which to judge individual spas. Another organization working on standards for the industry is Visit Britain. They have created a spa accreditation for spas in Great Britain that meet minimum standards for cleanliness, health, safety, service, and quality. The accreditation attempts to define and maintain standards for the spa industry. Accredited spas undergo an assessment and are given written and oral feedback. They are listed on VisitBritain.com and Enjoyengland.com and are allowed to use the accreditation on their marketing materials.

"Spa Quality—Excellence in Spas" has extremely stringent, comprehensive, and detailed quality requirements. They can be found at www.spaquality.com. In Canada, Leading Spas of Canada (Canada's national spa association) has standards and practice requirements as a condition of membership. It is currently finalizing an agreement with Canada Select, a rating organization like *Mobil*, to conduct mandatory member inspections.

Facilities. Some locales have standards for facilities and maintenance issues, but there is not a single clearinghouse that a spa can consult to learn what is required and what is not. Instead, there are several sets of standards that may apply. In the United States, spas may have to meet facility standards from local health and sanitation boards as well as being in compliance with the Americans with Disabilities Act. Some spas are attempting to have their facilities meet Leadership in Energy and Environmental Design (LEED) standards as established by the U.S. Green Building Council.

Competition in the Marketplace

According to the ISPA 2007 Spa Industry Study there are 14,600 spa locations owned and operated by about 12,800 different businesses in the United States. Most spas are single-location operations, all in competition with each other and with several different yet similar sectors. New spas have been opening at the average rate of 1,600 per year; 1,700 new locations opened in 2006.

However, even as new spas open, surveys have found that a substantial number of spas go out of business each year, often succumbing to pressure from competition, and lack of ability to operate in a profitable manner. Others have stopped offering spa services, so while they are still in business, they are not a spa. This could mean that the cream is rising to the top with those businesses that offer a quality product and consumer experience surviving and excelling.

Other segments that are providing competition to spas include massage therapy centers, massage schools that offer services to the public, and beauty salons and hair salons that offer massages or facials. Also, as more people are becoming familiar with and demanding spa services, more professionals are adding those services to their offerings. Medical and dental offices have begun hiring nurses trained in pre- and post-op esthetic treatments and medical massage.

There has also been significant competition over retail sales. While the number of spas is growing, consumers aren't increasing their visits at the same rapid pace. There are more spas and more products, however, there aren't immediately more consumers. While the industry is working at expanding the market, it is not happening at the same speed at which new spas are being developed.

While so far the competition issue has been primarily a U.S. concern, many parts of Asia are feeling similar pressure with growth spurts in development that are faster than the growth in demand from consumers.

Social Trends

Future spa guests will be more informed, knowledgeable, sophisticated, demanding, secure, aware, worldly, and better traveled than ever before. Vast amounts of information about spa alternatives will be at their fingertips. They will be able to quickly evaluate the array of spa offerings and judge which ones best suit them. Their purchases will be better attuned to their expectations, resulting in enhanced satisfaction.

Understanding future guest behavior will mean understanding the dynamics of guest life cycles and the accompanying guest transitioning process. Guests are always on the road to becoming "something else" as they marry, divorce, move back in with parents, change jobs, are laid off, embark on new careers, return to school, start a family, adjust to widowhood, establish a home, retire, and so on. In the process, their lifestyles are altered and their need for spa services changes. Taking account of these transitions means embracing the future needs of guests and recognizing that they are harder to identify and categorize and more challenging to understand and service effectively than was the case previously.

Spas have always been and will always be about touch. No matter what technological breakthroughs occur, there will always be a need for spa service providers to touch their guests. Even hotels and the more commercial members of the hospitality industry have realized that the watchwords are no longer "location, location, location," but "service, service, service." Service, as an all-encompassing determinant of future guest value, will continue to dominate as the "thing" that differentiates spas from their competition (whether it is other spas or other industries).

Along with the heightened importance of experience and personal service, a significant future countertrend will continue to emerge. "Self-service" will continue to evolve. Spas will increasingly rely on equipment and technology that allow guests to provide themselves with some of the services that have typically been provided by staff, primarily in the reservation, registration, and check-out areas. The driving force of the do-it-yourself trend is reducing costs, saving time, increasing efficiency, eliminating personnel, and maintaining lower prices. However, equipment and technology treatments are not cheap and investors typically want to get their investment back within one to three years, so spa professionals need to proceed carefully. Self-service also has a non-business side to it. Guests often come to a spa in search of themselves and a place to renew their spirit. Much of this work has to be done alone, alone in the environment that the spa provides and creates. Younger spa-goers are also more likely to want to have some of the registration and reservation functions automated.

Technology will supplement—but will not replace—the human element in spa services. Guests, by and large, will still expect and want to deal with people. Spas will have to find the appropriate mix of technology and touch to best meet the needs of their guests. This will involve experimentation, adjustment, and

Spa Snapshot: What social issues do you think will most affect how and why people use spas?

I feel that economic factors that cause us to work long hours and experience stress in managing finances will actually have a positive effect on the spa industry. A customer who may not be able to take a long vacation can visit the spa to relax and rejuvenate. Competition in the workplace can also be a contributing factor in the need to look young and fit no matter what your age.

—*Wendy Clark, President, I-Bella*

Health, obesity, and balance in one's life. The social issues out of their control with business demands and increased stress levels, peer pressure from individuals realizing the benefits of the spa lifestyle to combat the various needs.

—*Loren Stone, CEO, Sovereign Hospitality*

Technology issues. There will be greater demands on the body, on the length of our workdays, on our inability to "disconnect" on vacations or anywhere else. Where can we turn it all off? Almost nowhere anymore. A massage table is truly the one sacred place where we can literally turn it all off. (ok, maybe the shower…)

—*Darlene Fiske, Owner, The Fiske Group: Public Relations & Marketing Strategies*

Obesity, heart health, diabetes, super bugs, more allergies—many of the challenges which are facing us today are being exacerbated by unhealthy lifestyle patterns. There is growing support and acceptance for natural solutions, and spas are helping guide guests in their quest for natural health/wellness solutions.

—*Wanda Love, Director of Sales & Marketing, Santé Spa*

judgment, with staff members performing certain activities in conjunction with various machines at different stages of the service chain.

General Population Trends

Demographics deal with the changing composition of our population with regard to age and income distributions, number and types of households, wealth, expenditures, occupations, employment, and so on. They provide valuable insights into future consumer lifestyles and spa markets. Such sources as the Census Bureau's website and its publications can be extremely helpful to spas as can the ISPA Spa-Goer studies.

The U.S. population in 2000 (the year of the most recent census) totaled 281.4 million and grew by 32.7 million from 1990 to 2000. The world population has reached 6.5 billion. The 45 to 54 and 55 to 64 age groups (at which most consumers realize their highest incomes) are projected to increase substantially. In 2000, the 45 to 54 age category totaled more than 37 million and it is projected to grow to about 45 million by 2010. The 55–64 age group, also a high-income group, totaled more than 24 million in 2000 and is expected to grow to more than 36 million in 2010.[1] These increases augur well for growing profitable future spa markets.

Attitudes/Habits by Generation

The emphasis for spa-goers is increasingly that of keeping their physical bodies in good shape. Baby boomers and their children will pay to look young and healthy. Spa-goers have been increasingly looking for healthy aging treatments, exercise, and products that deliver results. Some guests view these products and treatments as a more attractive alternative to injections and surgery. Additionally, guests are also looking for personal care programs that can be used at home.

Graying Segments. The population of most industrialized countries is rapidly aging and graying. Today's seniors tend to see themselves as much younger than their chronological age. In the future, they will be healthier, more active, better informed, live longer, and expect more from life during their retirement years than did their predecessors. They will be more concerned with health and fitness and will be more knowledgeable, informed, and demanding consumers. They will expect spas to meet their needs and cater to their desires. Moreover, they will be wealthier and able to afford an array of spa services.

Seniors have been more exposed to the outside world than at any time in the past. They have grown up eating out regularly, dining in fine restaurants, taking cruises, traveling extensively, and enjoying spas around the world. They will have higher expectations and exhibit more sophisticated and cosmopolitan tastes than their predecessors. For many of them, a scarcity of time rather than of money will be a major factor governing their consumption of spa offerings.

In the future, guests who are 65 or older will defy the oft-held caricature of poor, uninformed, doddering consumers with plebian and antiquated tastes. By and large, they will represent large, growing, attractive, active, and relatively well-off spa markets. They will be unusually well-informed and have worldly exposure, with the flexibility of time and money to take advantage of special offerings like off-season travel and spa specials. As one senior explained so insightfully, "Every day is Saturday and Sunday for us."

How can spas cater to older guests? Some seniors develop health problems. Many become more concerned with food preparation. Many guests over 80 have physical limitations and consequently may need special attention such as wheelchairs, easy access, and home delivery. That said, spas can play a major role in helping reduce these needs through lifelong prevention. They can also learn more about elderly diseases and how to mitigate them, as well as offering pain and cancer relief treatments.

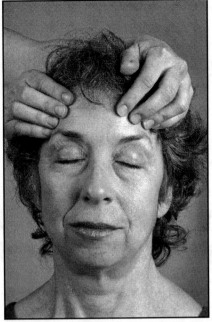

Seniors are a growing market segment for spas as they are active longer and looking to engage in activities that promote their health and wellness.

Seniors also make up an increasingly experienced labor pool for spas, as many of them assume second and third careers. As full-time or part-time employees, they bring maturity, people skills, experience, and knowledge to their new jobs.

Baby Boomers. Baby boomers, those born between 1946 and 1964, are now starting to enter their senior years and have brought with them various lifestyle and market changes. As consumers, baby boomers have experienced the larger world, having traveled more extensively than their predecessors. They are used to, and will continue to expect, convenience, pampering, service, and accessibility. Some research findings suggest that to appeal to baby boomers, future offerings might emphasize such aspects as affordable luxuries, distinctive products and services, guarantees, and discount packages. Advertising and promotional messages might feature themes like fitness, safety, family values, and community involvement. Distribution methods will include greater emphasis on technology like data mining, the Internet, wireless networks, flash drives, DVDs, and remote access computer-based self-service.

The boomers have also had an increased focus on healthy aging. This is the generation that began the worship of youth and it has been reluctant to let go of youthfulness in appearance, ability, or mindset. Spas have filled many of their needs to continue looking and feeling young and healthy. More importantly, spas have been able to introduce a concept of aging mindfully in mind, body, and spirit.

As of late 2006, adults age 50 and older controlled 77 percent of all the assets in the United States. They are active participants in the healthy aging market. A

December 2006 *Pulse* article pointed out that spas can help people get out of the anti-aging game and into "appreciating who they have become today and what they can be in the future. The spa industry provides the perfect environment for people to do just that."

In *Organic Spa* magazine, Jeremy McCarthy wrote, "Visiting spas offering these anti-aging treatments is one of our ways of struggling mightily against the ravages of time—digging our heels in as deep as we can while we continue to slide forward towards some distant but gloomy horizon." He goes on to say that while he has used the anti-aging theme in the past, that by doing so, spas are contributing to a form of denial.

"Aging is a function of time, and until a spa treatment is capable of warping the very fabric of our universe, the aging shall continue. Our attempt to manipulate how we move through this process is a struggle against the laws of physics themselves. …In recent years, I am happy to say, there has been a movement away from 'anti-aging' towards the concept of 'active aging.' This slight change in semantics has a vast impact on the psychology of the process. The idea is not to fight against aging but to accept and embrace it. By focusing on aging actively we do not push to reverse the aging process but rather to remain an active participant, and to suck all that we can out of this life."

He then suggested yet another approach that spas can take. "The idea is not anti-aging, not active aging, but happy aging. Isn't that really what we should all be striving for? Not reversing aging, but aging joyfully. Not active aging, but enjoying each moment regardless of your level of activity. I'll take wrinkled, slow, and happy over smooth, spry, and miserable any day! The idea of 'happy aging' overthrows the harsh philosophies of those who would decry that happiness and aging are mutually exclusive. There are those who choose to bemoan each passing year and spend their birthdays in a fit of depression. I say celebrate life and eat cake. Laugh in the face of Father Time, knowing that smiling and laughing are two activities you will never be too old to perform."

What spas do now will affect their ability to respond to how the aging of the boomers may contribute to a growing labor shortage. They can begin by surveying their current position. What are the demographics of the spa's employees? What are their retirement policies? Do they encourage early retirement or discourage it? Given that spas teach healthy aging, employees who practice what the spa teaches can be encouraged to work past the traditional retirement age of 65 to 67. Indeed, a University of Michigan survey reported that 57 percent of boomer men and 45 percent of older boomer women expect to work past normal retirement age.

The spa also needs to figure out how to capture critical work knowledge and skills of the employees who will be retiring. Those who have been with the spa for a long time have helped create the spa's culture in the minds of the guests and other employees. Spas must also be prepared to customize their training for learners of all ages and life experience levels.

Generation X. Generation X includes those born between 1964 and 1982. As they have matured, they have shown an increasing desire for personalized experiences while still exhibiting extreme brand loyalty. This has fueled the growth of boutique hotels and the demand for spa services—services which are intimately personal and unique.

As a generation that was raised with electronics, their expectations about connectivity and involvement differ from their elders. They demand instant connections and expect to be a participant in the services they receive. They don't simply want to be passive receptors of the service, they want to participate in an experience that will be memorable and lasting.

They are also a generation that is increasingly looking for mini-escapes from the technology that dominates their lives. They turn to spas as a way of taking time out and engaging in self-reflection away from the constant beeping and buzzing of their many electronic devices.

Generation Xers are also serving as midwives to boomers who resisted the earlier spa and fitness movement to become new spa-goers. Adult children are introducing their parents to the rituals and benefits of spas through gift certificates for special occasions. They are sending their parents on expense-paid visits to a day or destination spa. They are stripping away some of the 1950s taboos of spa-going (i.e., luxury, unnecessary indulgence, parlor experience, etc.) and teaching their parents the value of taking care of themselves from the inside out. This trend also finds parents joining one another for their first spa experience and often continuing this pattern, making a trip to the spa into a couples outing.

Generation Y/Millennials. While there is not yet consensus on the name for those born between 1980 and 1990, they have begun to influence the workplace with their very specific needs and culture. In Peter Sheahan's book, *"Thriving and Surviving with Generation Y at Work,"* he writes that it will take more than money to motivate these workers. "They're after a sense of purpose, work-life balance, fun, variety, respect, and the opportunity to do 'real' work that makes a difference. Arguably everyone wants these things from a job but the difference with Generation Y is that they'll talk with their feet when their needs are not fulfilled."

This could be good news for spas—both for their labor needs and for future guest growth. Spas are able to provide a place where people can find a sense of purpose and balance.

Teenagers. There is strong evidence that teenagers are now highly predisposed to go to day spas for services that they once went exclusively to nail and beauty salons to receive. In fact, in 2007, there were nearly four million teens going to spas. The services they care about are most often those related to what other people can see—their hair, face, and hands. Even facials are attracting teen audiences, because they feel like powerful ways to deal with date-ruining nightmares such as break-outs, acne, etc.

Teens are also more likely to value a social visit to a day spa for these kinds of services. Many spas have responded with teen services and opened their spas to teen parties and social get-togethers.

Several spas have also begun tapping into the teen market with their health awareness and wellness classes. However, they have had to modify their programs to reach the younger audience. Heather Schwartz in the July 2006 *Pulse* wrote that programs for the younger set need to:

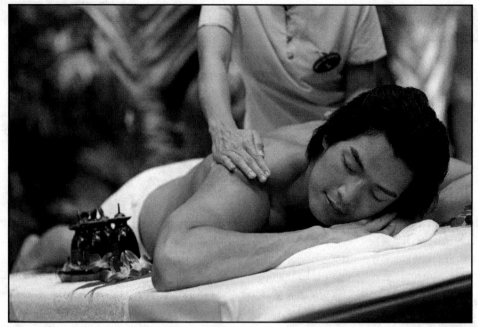

Men will continue to increase their spa usage as spas find ways to create experiences and décor that appeal to them.

- Be relevant and fun.
- Empower teens with an understanding of how healthy behavior can be incorporated into their everyday life.
- Be aware of their self-consciousness and not embarrass them.
- Get their parents involved so that they'll have support for their new healthy lifestyle choices.

In Europe, there is a great deal of effort put into healthful eating, exercise, and good health in general. For European teens, spa is more about building healthy bodies through good nutrition, exercise, and sleeping than it is about skin, nails, and hair.

Men

While women are the spa's most comfortable consumers, men are catching on that spas have a lot to offer them. Spas are also learning that the needs of their male guests are different from those of their female guests.

The most popular treatments among women are manicures, pedicures, and facials. Among men in the United States, Swedish massage, deep tissue massage, and sauna/steam baths are at the top of the list. They're less interested in spa services for cosmetic purposes and more interested in treatments that can assist them with physical ailments they're experiencing.

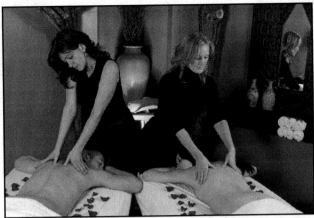

Many spas now offer services that couples can experience together, putting together attractive packages that create a joint escape.

Even the language that spas use to attract men is different than the words they use to appeal to women. Men are interested in results and in undoing damage done to their bodies by age and the environment. The language used in marketing reflects that and downplays the pampering angle that appeals to women. Spas have traditionally used the same words when marketing to women and men. However, while things such as "the soothing scent of lavender" doesn't resonate with a man, men will respond to terms such as "going in for a tune-up" or "detailing yourself just as you would your car."

To appeal to men, some spas are creating more masculine entry points for spas and separating their male and female guests. While some spas tried gender-neutral approaches in design, others found that it was better to have separate areas with specific appeals to each gender. They can then vary treatment menus, spa products, and décor.

Social Spa Visits/Groups

Group spa experiences are becoming more common, with the term "togethering" being used to describe group spa visits for such things as bridal showers, bachelorette parties, couple visits, parent-child spa visits, or teen birthday parties. Larger spas are also welcoming corporate bonding groups that combine a meeting and spa agenda.

Friends are bonding at spas while receiving the kind of pampering they can't get at home or in a restaurant. First-time spa-goers may find group trips a popular way to test the waters as they can get feedback from their friends and have others with whom to share the experience. Even if they are all first-timers, the burden of anxiety is shared across the group. It can also relax new spa guests to be with their friends while experiencing something new.

Spas that do not have the facilities to offer services to groups are sometimes offering open houses and seminars to fill a group need. Others are hosting wine parties that discuss the healthy benefits of moderate wine drinking.

Healthy Lifestyles

While hardly a new trend, the desire for a healthy lifestyle will continue to drive spas and their offerings the way it has since the beginnings of spa history. Guests turn to spas as the experts in teaching ways to eat, live, and exercise in a healthy manner.

Food plays a huge role in people's search for a healthy lifestyle and spas have long specialized in cuisine that is both tasty and healthy. In recent years, families have begun organizing vacations around food in a trend that has been dubbed gastro-travel. It's ideal for spas, and many are offering cooking experiences from week-long schools with celebrity chefs to private lessons on cooking healthy at home.

Spas are also teaching the basic principles of eating nutritious food, exercising, and relieving stress. It is becoming common to find spas offering educational programs and nutritional consultations, healthy eating classes, educational offerings on obesity or weight gain issues, and exercise programs for children and teens. These are numbers that are expected to grow as people learn more about what can keep them healthy and help them live longer, fuller lives.

Loneliness

As traditional connections between neighbors start to fade among a populace that is always on the move, life can be an isolating experience. Connections such as family and church that were once major parts of the fabric of society have been replaced with a society that is mobile and electronically connected, but increasingly disconnected emotionally and physically.

The *Los Angeles Times* reported in 2006 that Americans have fewer close friends than they did 19 years ago. Using data from the General Social Survey, researchers compared responses from 1985 and 2004 and found that the number of people with whom Americans can discuss important matters dropped from 2.94 in 1985 to 2.08 in 2004.

Because spas create connections, they have the potential to be part of the answer to restoring connectedness in society. Spas have been stepping forward to help fill the gap left in in the lives of people who feel increasingly isolated from others. While many spas are a place of retreat where guests get away from others, some guests are turning to spas as part of their social network where they can go and form new, healthy relationships.

Body Image

Body image refers to people's perceptions of their own physical appearance. It can have little to do with what people actually look like and everything to do with how they feel about their appearance. Negative feelings toward one's own body can sometimes lead to mental disorders such as depression and eating disorders—two disorders that have been on the increase in recent years.

Both men and women suffer from negative body image, with men often worried about muscularity while women tend to worry about weight. The latter has become a cultural obsession, as people equate obesity with a danger equivalent to smoking.

Spas offer people a place where they can learn to cultivate a healthy body image that is focused on wellness, acceptance, and attention to what the body is

reflections

Tinka Hrounpas, MD: Responding to Body Image Issues and Loneliness

A spa guest who has been attending spas for approximately 40 years, Dr. Tinka Hrounpas is active in Greet the Day, a non-profit organization that trains massage therapists in oncology massage. While she was undergoing six months of chemotherapy for breast cancer, she had a massage therapist come to her home once a week, an experience she describes as "integral to my healing."

I had no hesitancy with receiving a massage. I think for my friends some issues have always been undressing during a massage or modesty at being partially covered during a massage. I think with my medical training background I'm a little more comfortable with being disrobed.

What has been an issue since my breast cancer and my double mastectomy are those new body issues of not being like I used to be. There are a lot of breast cancer survivors who have surgical scars or are in the process of breast reconstruction. They are embarrassed that they look so different than they used to. There are some issues for breast cancer survivors—specifically in terms of disrobing in a locker room—body issues about having people see scars and breast reconstruction. It takes just a little bit more mindfulness on the part of the spa personnel to make people feel more comfortable.

Spa treatments have had a huge impact on my life. It has been a very healing process with my breast cancer. It made me really appreciate the benefits of massage with a medical condition. Spa treatments offer not only the physical comfort of massage, but also an emotional benefit of relaxation.

As our communities have expanded, they've become more impersonal and people have experienced more alienation. On a daily basis for most people, touch has become less and less practiced. This is especially true for the patients who are isolated because of their treatments. Their family members withdraw from them because they're afraid that they're going to hurt them if they touch them, so the patients feel more and more isolated. The touch that they do receive is the touch of procedures and treatments: IVs being started, blood draws, scans, biopsies. So very quickly patients develop the association of touch being hurtful, touch being impersonal, and touch being poked and prodded. Many patients develop a form of post-traumatic stress disorder because of the association of touch being hurtful. So massage and other touch modalities are very important to desensitize that negative experience. Patients can realize once again that touch is nurturing and it helps them reestablish a feeling of community with people, especially when the massage therapist is being intentional and mindful.

---

saying. Spas can continue to educate their guests on eating habits, health, and physical fitness while offering treatments that help their guests feel beautiful inside and out.

Techno-Stress

Technology has sped up people's lives. BlackBerries, iPhones, Palms, and cell phones keep people constantly connected to others. The electronic revolution

Exhibit 2   Hyatt's Blackberry Balm

> Hyatt developed a massage treatment called Blackberry Balm for overstressed BlackBerry users.
>
> For $80, the guest receives a 30-minute massage that warms the hand with a warm stone and hot towel. The therapist then uses a combination of acupressure and traditional Swedish massage strokes, focusing on the thumb. It also uses warm oil and a balm containing blackberry powder, fruit acid, cajuput, camphor oil, cinnamon, clove, and peppermint. At the end of the treatment, an aroma hot towel is wrapped around each hand and the guest is given a small blackberry balm to take home.
>
> (Please note: Spas do need to be careful about the use of registered trademarks in their spa menus. It is one thing to use blackberry powder as a way of identifying it closely with the BlackBerry brand. It is a clever way to mimic a trademarked name without having to get a trademark release. However, spas are not free to use branded trademarks as they see fit and they need to be cautious and creative—two traits the Hyatt treatment and its marketing demonstrate.)

means people are working more and getting much less sleep. Doctors are prescribing more and more sleep aids and people are spending more and more on coffee.

Spas can play a role in helping people unplug from techno-stress whether it be through simply providing an environment in which cell phones and PDAs are left behind or through sleep awareness classes and one-on-one advice. Several spas are responding to techno-stress by offering specific treatments that respond to technology-related stresses (also known as **techno-stress**). The BlackBerry-specific hand and neck massage is growing in popularity. Some spas are using **myofascial massage** as an alternative medical technique to help ease repetitive stress injuries caused by using handheld devices. Myofascial massage stretches the fascia, or connective tissue, to increase the range of motion of the muscle. See Exhibit 2.

"Low tech will exceed high tech in the sense that people have techno-stress and are experiencing an overload of information and technology," said Cathy Cluff, managing director for The Oaks at Ojai. "When they are coming to the spa, the idea of having that human touch is just going to become more and more of a factor. Things like a machine that works along with a facial technician are going to become less important. The client is going to want all the time with the human being and that personal touch. People are needing to get away from all the stresses of the wonderful technology we have."

Market Trends

While no one knows for certain which trends will continue to have a widespread effect on the industry, it is possible to identify some that seem to have a lifespan that transports them beyond a fad. They are the trends that are shaping today's industry and are likely in one form or another to sculpt aspects of the future.

For example, in recent years, the fashion industry has begun proposing collaborations between spa and fashion. Some fashion lines are designed specifically to be sold in spas. Spas will sometimes host fashion shows for their guests. On a broader basis, fashion superstar Giorgio Armani recently opened his first spa in Tokyo and is planning to expand with more spas.

What will the important trends be? Some trends worth reflecting upon include:

- Mini-mass markets
- Medical treatments and spas
- Residential spas
- Spa on vacation
- At-home spas
- Mobile spas
- Corporate wellness

Mini-Mass Markets

Hospitality marketing has already begun the shift away from mass marketing approaches to ones more familiar to most spas—the mini-mass, niche, and individual guest emphases.

In 2003, Chris Anderson coined the phrase "the long tail," referring to the long tail of a demand curve. He said the long tail would affect the future of business which would be selling less of more. In an article published in *Wired* and later in a book, he put forth the thesis that products and services that are in low demand can together make a larger market share than those top-sellers and blockbusters if the store or distribution channel is large enough. While not every company could fit the Long Tail model, such companies as Amazon, Netflix, and eBay have established expectations among consumers that they can find what they want somewhere—even if they are demanding a product or service that is not in high demand.

The result of such expectations means that spa markets will be more fragmented, with market offerings and marketing programs tailored for specific groups of guests. For the most part, spas do not fit the model of having large warehouses or huge distribution channels, though such organizations as Spa Finder and Expedia do serve as distribution systems. However, what many will find is that all spas do not have to look alike, nor do they have to try to capture the same homogenous market.

The one-size-fits-all approach of the past will give way to customizing and tailoring spa offerings to meet more precisely the needs of guests in niche markets. Doing so will require pertinent, timely guest information and heightened sensitivity to and understanding of the guest preferences of different cultures, social classes, age groups, lifestyles, and similar demographic segments. The challenge will be to develop tailored offerings without incurring a high price tag. It is a matter of achieving the productivity associated with standardized spa offerings while delivering a level of guest satisfaction associated with individualization.

As spa professionals increasingly reach out to niche markets, they are changing not only their marketing and services but also the entire spa. The various

Spa Snapshot: What do you think will be the next area of growth for the spa industry?

Although community spas and teen treatments are rapidly increasing in number, I personally feel that spas for men will be the next area of major growth in the spa industry. This is because there is so much potential in terms of revenue if you offer other services in order to complement the spa services—these add-ons include a barber shop, shoeshine station, and business lounge. One could even go as far as to locate these services near a golf course and really cash in. All these combined with the fact that more and more men are now booking spa treatments for themselves makes me sure that spas for men will be the next area of major growth in our industry.

—*Sheila Otieno Osanya, Spa Manager, Arabella Sheraton Grand Hotel Cape Town*

As people's views about spas and wellness evolve, the opportunity to reach out to these "newbies" greatly increases. An area of growth I see is the "Do It Yourself" spa experience. Without having to spend a lot of money or endure the anxiety attached to being undressed in front of a therapist, the spa guest can pay a small fee to use, for example, a water circuit or enjoy body treatments such as scrubs and mud applications. Guests will feel empowered by their ability to make themselves feel good and begin to cater to larger parties, opening the spa to be viewed as more of a social scene.

—*Kristin Shaw, Director of Spa Services, Plus One*

In our spa, we offer daylong packages, but typically, clients want the results and relaxation a full day can offer but in a shorter period of time. Busy parents and professionals sometimes can only really relax for so long without feeling like they need to be doing something else.

In response to the demands of our clients, we have made changes to our menu. Some of our most popular treatments include two therapists. A foot fantasy is a foot and lower leg reflexology treatment with hot stones that is performed with a facial treatment. The experience of a massage of the feet and lower body while simultaneously receiving a facial and upper body massage is truly blissful.

We will also often customize treatments for people who want their results and relaxation in a hurry. For example, we can offer a body firming treatment with a microdermabrasion of the face and neck. Or, a hand treatment while an anti-aging facial procedure is being performed.

(continued)

In just one hour, or perhaps even less time, our clients can see visible changes in their skin and receive much-needed relaxation and stress-relief. It is very satisfying to be able to provide all the results our clients are looking for, even when they have time limitations.

—*Kile Law, President, Bluewater Spa, A Plastic Surgery Medical Spa*

Spas are places of celebration and connection: Spas will need to include more "comfort zones" or lounges where people can gather together and have access to certain treatment rooms that, when combined with the lounge area, become a "private spa within a spa." Some of these spa suites or "cluster spas" (because of the cluster of rooms) can also have private bathrooms, showers, eating areas, sleeping areas, indoor as well as outdoor space, etc. When properly planned, these cluster spas can be for children or adults, couples or singles, men or women. Versatility and flexibility in design and location will be critical in order to meet the needs and interests of the various markets while still providing a sense of privacy and intimacy.

—*Judith L. Singer, Owner, Health Fitness Dynamics, Inc.*

I believe that in the next few years the big development is going to be in teen spas. They already pop up in some cities, and when we study the potential in that market, it is quite grand. With 76 million Gen Y's in the United States between the ages of 5 and 22, they are a lot of potential.

Teens have grown up in the era of almost uninterrupted prosperity and they are spending in the areas that their parents would have thought [un]necessary at their age. The teen eats out at least once a week with their friends and buys the latest gadgets. Teen girls take their moms to a spa and educate them in services and products. Teens are seeing the spa industry as a fun way to spend time with their friends and family. An average American teen spends more than $104 a week and receives daily allowance of $10 a day.

Many spas are adding treatments for teens as we speak, but we will see more spas gathering to the teen-only type of spa.

—*Fabienne Guichon-Lindholm, Director of Communication, Decleor USA, Inc.*

I believe that dental spas will be a huge growth area for the industry. One of the early indicators is a recent study that shows more and more dental practices identifying themselves as dental spas. In addition, there will be a rise in the demand for take-home spa treatments. We are seeing more spas looking for easy ways to pamper their patients in between spa visits.

—*Bonnie Koch, Partner, Taking the Waters/Thera:Vie*

(continued)

(continued)

The trend we're seeing at Krystyna's European Spa is a strong interest in anti-aging treatments for the face and body. Forty is the new 30, and our clients want to look as youthful and fresh as they feel. Many of our clients want visible results without the risks of Botox or surgery and at a fraction of the cost. We've done extensive research to find leading-edge anti-aging treatments to fulfill our clients' needs, and they have reacted enthusiastically to our unique offering.

—*Krystyna Ejsmont, Owner, Krystyna's European Spa*

I think that the majority of consumers are too busy and simply too smart to buy into any far-fetched spa marketing. The greatest area for growth in the industry overall is professional skin care, which really thrives best in a small, intimate setting. But speaking of the spa phenomenon as a whole, I think that there is great untapped potential in how men use the spa experience. They're not looking at it as a health or grooming experience, but as a business venue. We're all so over the metrosexual thing, but the spa will replace the squash court and the golf course as a place for executives to bond, negotiate, possibly let down their guard a bit, and perfect the art of the deal while wearing towels and flip-flops. This has been the case in Japan and much of Asia for decades.

—*Jane Wurwand, Founder/CEO, Dermalogica*

Source: *Pulse*, Sept./Oct. 2006

different spa types that have been emerging over the past several years are one way that spas are appealing to niche markets. Such things as oxygen bars, residential spas, and mobile spas target their services to very specific customers with specific desires and needs.

Spas may find that relatively small markets that were in the past too unprofitable to pursue will become more attractive. This trend will be heightened as incomes rise around the world, allowing spas to reach global market niches rather than just the ones in their neighborhood.

Medical Treatments and Spas

Percentage-wise, one of the fastest growing segments of the spa industry is medical spas—between 2004 and 2006 they had an average yearly growth of 19 percent, according to ISPA 2007 Spa Industry research. As of 2007, 14 percent of spas in the United States indicated that they offer medical treatments either through partnership with a doctor or medical practice (59 percent) or with an onsite doctor (22 percent).

People continue to expect more from their spa visits than simply being pampered. They want results. More than one in ten spa-goers treats spa-going as part of a larger health and wellness lifestyle. The American Massage Therapy Association found that 30 percent of Americans who integrate massage therapy into their routines do so for medical reasons such as injury recovery, pain reduction, headache control, and overall health and wellness.

The most popular medical treatments are chemical peels, microdermabrasion, and natural weight loss measures such as body wraps. Additionally, the medical industry in general, and the plastic surgery sector in particular, are incorporating spa treatments such as naturotherapy and acupuncture into their service structure.

From dentists to dermatologists, the partnership between spas and doctors is due to requests from guests. People are savvier about the spa experience and they are busier than ever before. There is great appeal to being able to combine such things as an annual physical or medical procedure—something that often has increased stress associated with it—with relaxing spa treatments. Medical spas offer guests the opportunity to focus on complete health and wellness by offering stress reduction and other treatments alongside their diagnostic services.

It should be noted that medical treatments aren't limited to medical spas. Destination, resort, and day spas are also starting to embrace treatments that have medical outcomes. These treatments include such things as teeth whitening procedures, chromatherapy lighting, microdermabrasion, chemical peels, Botox, photo-facial/Intense Pulsed Light (IPL) therapy, laser hair removal, collagen injections, laser skin rejuvenation, medical consultation with a licensed physician, and insomnia.

Residential Spas

It sounds like a dream, but a pretty realistic one for many: living at the spa. Major spa players are adding residential apartments and condominiums to their spa property and real estate developers are adding spas to their gated communities and condominium developments.

Location continues to be a big factor for spas. Spas are in health clubs, resorts, and hotels, doctors are adding spa elements to their practices, and treatments are even being offered in airports, malls, and on cruise ships. It has been a natural transition then to add spas to residential communities and to create rental and ownership programs at destination and resort/hotel spas.

The concept behind **residential spas** is taking the wellness and spa lifestyle choices that a spa teaches and transforming it from a vacation experience to a balanced daily way of living. Residential spas help the real estate company to express its philosophy and to help them to command a premium price. Some residential spas have been launched by such spas as Canyon Ranch, Sundara Spas, Miraval, Silverleaf, Greenbrier, Red Mountain Spa, La Costa Resort and Spa, Montage Resort and Spa, and Kingsmill Resort and Spa, to name just a handful. At these communities, the spa mission comes first, with the residents being the next step in making their mission a reality in the lives of guests.

Other spa communities are being added as a perk to developments. The developers are adding spas as an amenity the way they once added golf courses. These communities are ones in which the residents will subsidize the spa and have to support it with dues so that they can be sustainable after the developers have pulled out.

Residential spas are particularly visible in the coastal areas of Florida, although they are also emerging in urban areas, including New York City and Las Vegas.

reflections

Tinka Hrounpas, MD: Teaching Oncology Massage

Greet the Day is a non-profit organization that has developed over the past three or four years, which currently teaches oncology massage. Oncology massage is specifically for cancer patients and cancer survivors.

The class at this point is focused on educating massage therapists. If we are successful in the next few years, we will expand that program to teach registered nurses and other clinical personnel and then eventually hospice workers and family care givers so that they can be educated on what is important about massage for specialized clients. They'll be able to have the knowledge that they aren't harming or jeopardizing the patients in any way. The goal is to perform massage for these patients that have become disenfranchised with mainstream spa experiences.

Spa Gregorie's was the instigator in helping us develop a spa day package which consists of yoga and meditation and a spa treatment, either a massage or facial, followed by lunch. There are groups of six to ten cancer survivors (who receive these treatments) all free of charge. This has been an absolutely wonderful experience for both the clients/patients as well as the massage therapists.

Greet the Day currently has a course that we teach three or four times a year to massage therapists on oncology massage. Once those massage therapists are certified in oncology massage, they participate in an internship experience, where they go to the infusion centers and do head, hand, and neck massages while patients are receiving their chemotherapy infusions. It has been a remarkable experience. We're having chemo patients who are rescheduling their treatments to be there the day that the massage therapists are there.

Once we get more infrastructure for our non-profit organization and more funding, it's my hope we can participate in clinical research so we can have documented benefits of massage for cancer survivors and eventually other medical conditions. I think this program can be greatly expanded to other medical conditions: To children's cancer, to patients with neurological diseases, to patients with Alzheimer's disease. The benefits to cancer patients are that there immediately is an increase in their sense of well-being, an increase in their quality of life, a decrease in the amount of pain medication they need to take, and an increase in their immune system performance. I am very confident that we just need to do the research. We will definitely show the benefits. It's not a matter of whether or not it is helpful.

I think 10 to 20 years ago the medical community may have had more of an attitude of misunderstanding of what massage therapy is. (They looked at it as) more of the fluff and buff. I think most medical personnel are very appreciative that there are other modalities that can offer improvement in quality of life and easing pain and suffering. From our Western medical perspective, really all we can do are prescriptions and we all know that narcotics are not the cure for pain, they're just masking the pain. I think physicians are mindful that we need other modalities such as massage and acupuncture and yoga and meditation.

Spa on Vacation

As spas have matured and grown, they've become more pervasive in the lives of their guests. More than ever before, spa-goers are including spas in their vacation plans, often as a central part of where they plan to go and what they plan to do.

This is especially true of resort and hotel spas, which guests find convenient to incorporate into their travel plans.

Sixty-three percent of U.S. spa-goers have visited a spa while traveling from home, according to ISPA's 2006 Spa-Goer Study. Apart from budgetary considerations, trips to spas are shaped by desires to visit particular places and have specific types of vacations. Women are more likely than men to be spa-goers, though spa traveling reduces the gender gap considerably as 36 percent of spa travelers are male.

In Canada, studies done through the Canadian Tourism Commission and the Leading Spas of Canada have revealed that people are using the spa as a primary destination and motivator for a vacation as opposed to simply getting treatments on vacation.

Travelers are particularly drawn to indigenous treatments and products. New textures, aromas, and sounds with meaningful storytelling help forge connections to people, places, and traditions. It also creates a memorable vacation experience that fulfills their need to experience more fully the place they are visiting.

When on vacation, most people are predisposed to experiment with all sorts of things, even more so when they're abroad. Spas offer a memorable way to combine fun, experimentation, and indulgence into a "story to tell people when I get back."

At-Home Spas

A growing trend among spa-goers is to make spa more than just a visit to the building where they can receive treatments. Spa is becoming a lifestyle—a true success in the mission of spas to encourage healthier living.

From cooking classes to lessons on balance and managing stress, lifestyle classes at spas teach guests how to take the healthy lessons of the spa home with them. Additionally, spa décor—including tubs, showers, products, and massage tables, as well as clothing and candles—is mainstream. Home spa parties are popular for bridal and baby showers, as well as for birthday celebrations.

Spa retail is one of the key areas that make at-home spa experiences a success. Evenings, weekends, and the end of the day are moments when people often feel a need to get away from the demands of their immediate social networks and from social interaction itself. These social time-outs aren't likely to drive spa visits because the focus is on immediate relaxation and on avoiding people temporarily. There is also a sense that completely unwinding at a spa, where strangers abound and where being seen in various states of undress by other spa-goers and therapists, is not nearly as likely as it would be in a spa ritual conducted at home.

Elements of the self-guided services of at-home spa experiences include mood music, aromatherapy, bathing and soaking, exfoliation, facial treatments, massage bath tubs, small tools and equipment, foot rubs and pedicures, and manicures. These at-home spa rituals rely on the existing infrastructure of the home but receive their magic and energy from body care products purchased through retail channels. Most of these products focus on affecting the feel and look of consumers' skin and/or nails and use either manufactured scents or aromatherapy. Consumers who often engage in spa-like rituals like this are often fairly discriminating purchasers of bath salts, foam bath agents, skin moisturizers, exfoliating scrubs, scented candles, etc.

As the spa culture spreads throughout society, luxury homes are being built with exercise rooms, hydrotherapy showers, and saunas and steam rooms.

Nor does the at-home spa experience end with spa retail products. Luxury homes are now being built with spas in mind. They contain exercise rooms, spacious bathrooms with all the newest shower features along with amenities like saunas and even massage rooms being included off the master bedroom.

Mobile Spas

A variation of the at-home spas are "spas" provided away from the traditional spa setting. **Mobile spas** are used to describe spa companies or individuals who travel to provide spa services at a location of the guest's choosing. They put on parties or offer services at conventions or meetings. Spa parties can be for either small or large groups.

Corporate Wellness

Corporate wellness has been around for a long time. The Japanese used a model in which all of the employees in a factory would perform morning exercises. However, until recently, corporate wellness focused primarily on fitness. Today, it has a far wider emphasis that includes total wellness, a need which spas are able to service.

William M. Kier, the founding chairman of the Wellness Councils of America, said, "For small business owners who often measure profits in thousands—not

Spa Chicks On-the-Go

In 2003, Marie Scalogna-Watkinson decided to create Spa Chicks On-the-Go.

She definitely had the background for it. She was a licensed massage therapist who had worked as a massage director at day spas in New York and as the company massage therapist for the show, Saturday Night Fever, on Broadway. In 1997, she'd owned her own medical massage practice that specialized in prenatal massage. She was also the founder of Mama Spa, a prenatal mobile massage company.

Spa Chicks On-the-Go bills itself as a "spa event marketing company that creates customized spa experiences for private and corporate clients." They'll create a spa event at any location. They also offer private label spa events in which companies can sponsor an interactive branded spa experience with customized spa treatments.

Their business has created a lot of buzz. They've made appearances on such television shows as The Apprentice 3, Queer Eye for the Straight Guy, and Party Girl. They have put on private spa parties for celebrities and given massages to performers in their dressing rooms.

Their corporate clients include eBay, Smith Barney, Trend Micro, and Yellow Book. They've provided pampering services for the Tony Awards and its presenters. Magazines such as *Allure, Bon Appétit, Family Circle*, and *InStyle* have hired them to put on parties for their clients or as prizes in promotions.

millions—of dollars, the net effect of an employee wellness program could mean the difference between profit and loss."

The corporate world is starting to catch on to what athletes learned long ago: Massages have many healthy benefits. Massage has led the interest in spa services partly because it directly treats those issues that office workers often struggle with. Massage therapy can reduce headaches, create more flexible muscles that resist repetitive stress injuries, reduce back pain, and relieve fatigue. Large companies that have incorporated massage therapy as part of their benefits packages have experienced a decline in turnover rates, an increase in problem-solving aptitude and happier employees.

In 2007, Google was selected as *Fortune's* top company to work for. It's not a coincidence that Google offers on-site massages to its employees. Its first massage technician has now retired with millions from the stock options she earned with them.

According to the *American Journal of Health Promotions*, for every $1 spent on wellness programs, employers can expect a return of up to $10 through lower medical claims, reduced absenteeism, improved productivity, and other factors. Spa experiences in the workplace demonstrate that the business cares about the health and total well-being of the employee.

Spas have begun offering special packages for corporate wellness—either chair massages at corporate events or group treatments for specific businesses. Exhibit 3 shows what a few spas are doing for corporate wellness.

Exhibit 3   Corporate Wellness Programs at Spas

Qui Si Bella Luxury Eco-Wellness Spa

Companies may select individual or group wellness/ educational packages for their employees through Qui Si Bella. These programs which include relaxing spa therapies help individuals reduce stress which positively impacts the work environment, team morale, and increases productivity. Our on-site experts offer injury prevention education, therapeutic treatments, chiropractic care, acupuncture, naturopathic care, and wellness coaching.

Go Relax Wellness Spa
Corporate Wellness

Job related stress can be in relation to corporate shifts, growth within the company, projects with strict deadlines, or even the normal competition that occurs in the company. Ailments such as fatigue, the flu or common cold, and even more serious physical conditions such as carpel tunnel or arthritis can take place at work. Natural wellness and massage therapy are proven methods of reducing or even eliminating these conditions as well as building immunity and overall well-being. Companies that offer packages like this to employees not only have healthier employees but employees that are happy and feel appreciated, allowing them to willingly apply themselves to succeed.

We also can work at your events! If you are sponsoring a company get-together, or even a large event, we can set up a booth and offer chair massages!

Rejuve MedSpa & Wellness

We help companies implement customized holistic wellness programs to improve productivity, reduce sick leave, maximize healthcare cost savings, and improve the bottom line. Our programs keep staying healthy interactive and enjoyable! Call us for more information about our corporate programs.

Sources: Websites of individual spas

Technology Trends

To say that technology is changing things in a pervasive manner is almost cliché. Even in the spa world—a place that offers its guests a temporary escape from the tether of technology in their lives—technology has created new ways of doing things, from administrative tasks to retail sales to treatments both medical and traditional.

The future will see technology shaping the way that spas maintain their relationship with guests. Technology like databases, smart cards, virtual reality, and other applications have already begun appearing in the spa world and will continue to expand.

Spas will interact with their guests and collect valuable information on a real-time basis. Spas will be able to track who is using what service, build a one-to-one relationship with guests, and run continuing reports of spa activity. Services and spa time will be customized to increase guest value, benefits, and satisfaction while enhancing opportunities to create loyal guests.

While people want to take a time out, they also want to stay plugged in. Spas have been finding creative ways to do this, including incorporating Wi-Fi in relaxation rooms, offering cyber treatments that combine biofeedback technology with guidance from wellness professionals, and light therapy to help those suffering from depression, Seasonal Affective Disorder, and insomnia.

The important thing with any technology in a spa is in how the spa uses and introduces that technology. A spa shouldn't try to automate everything. Technology will not replace the human service and connection that spas are known for. However, spas can and should use technology in strategic and transparent ways that can improve their customer service and make the spa visit a smooth experience for the guest.

Revenue Management

Spas are beginning to adopt the technology that has been used by hotels and airlines for years: revenue management software. As they have grown, spas have looked at ways that they can maximize their resources and revenue potential. The answer is often **revenue (yield) management**. Typically, revenue management manages demand through either prices or availability.

Price management has spas change their rates so that services are more expensive during periods of high demand and lower during periods of low demand. This can sometimes be seen in spas that have weekend and weekday rates or that offer "discounts" off the premium prices during slow times to generate more business during those days.

More common in the spa industry is managing availability. Spa software is able to help spas ensure that they are providing their highest margin services during peak times while attempting to reschedule their lower margin services during slower times. This allows the therapist to generate the most revenue while still providing excellent service to guests. If, for example, 11 A.M. to 2 P.M. on Saturdays is a peak time, once the spa passes a set level of occupancy, such as 65 percent, the software can close out lower-margin services, so that receptionists schedule only higher margin services.

Revenue management becomes important for spas because they deal with perishable inventories—the treatment rooms. If an hour goes by that the room is not scheduled, that hour cannot be resold later. Once a spa gets to 100 percent occupancy for its treatment rooms, the only way it can increase its revenue is to make sure that higher margin services are not turned away in favor of lower margin ones. Revenue management is further complicated for spas in that they must take into account the availability of therapists and what treatments they are licensed in and trained to perform.

For revenue management to be conducted effectively, spas need both good interactive software and good data about historical trends and past business. The software has to be able to handle spa-specific needs, while the data has to be useful and extensive enough to make good predictions.

Centralized Call Centers

Among larger branded spa chains, there is a trend toward hiring centralized call centers to handle scheduling and basic information distribution about their various spa locations. The agents at these centers often go through intensive training so that they can be knowledgeable on treatments and can be a regular resource for guests who may visit several spas.

The danger to centralized call centers is that they have the potential to destroy a sense of local community within each spa location. There is no chance for relationship-forming between guest and the reception staff, who they will meet on the day of their visit. Guests who are committed to the ideals of spa will be turned off by call centers and are likely to go elsewhere. Call centers also need to be prepared to accommodate guest requests for specific therapists.

Check-in Kiosks

Another innovation that has met with mixed results has been check-in kiosks. While hotels and airlines have experienced success with them, spa guests typically want personal contact and personal relationships. There have been a few uses, however, where check-in kiosks have met with success. The first is at club-style spas where the members come on a regular basis. They can swipe a card that gives them access to the spa and to their own personal locker. The second use is when large groups are checking in for lifestyle classes that are offered on a weekly basis. The ability to check in at a kiosk or with the swipe of a card lets class attendees avoid long lines.

Treatment Room Computers

Some spas are starting to have computers in the treatment room. These computers allow the therapist to record preference information for guest histories, place retail orders, and provide additional educational information for guests. The spas that offer this have found unobtrusive ways to have the computer in the room without the technology jarring the guests out of their spa state of mine. At Elmwood Spa, a large day spa in Toronto, Canada, computer tablets are placed in drawers in the treatment room. When the guest's face is covered in a towel or cucumbers are over their eyes, therapists can quietly open the drawer and enter anything they have learned about the guest (e.g., the guest prefers firm pressure during a massage or is allergic to milk products). Their tablet system is a unique proprietary part of a paperless system that allows electronic storage of client data and also allows for recommendations to be transferred unobtrusively from the treatment room to the front desk where these products can be gathered and readied for presentation to the client when they checkout. In one spa in the Ukraine, therapists have computers in the treatment room that allow the therapist to place any orders for products guests have expressed interest in. The item is then pulled from inventory, bagged, and is waiting for the guest at check-out time.

"The strongest spa operators," said Frank Pitsikalis, president of Enablez, which supplies ResortSuite Spa management software, "will be the ones who use technology in very strategic ways."

Music

Music has always been a part of the spa experience. Technology has given spas even greater control over the music that is played throughout the spa and allowed them to innovatively manage their spa's music. With the popularity of MP3 players, spas are able to increasingly select individual pieces out of an ever-growing range of music created for spas and spa-like situations.

Any music that helps the guest to be calm and relaxed can be useful in a spa setting. One thing for spa professionals to remember is that the music is primarily for the clients to listen to, not necessarily for massage therapists or estheticians to match their movements to.

Some spas are creating customized CDs that spa-goers can take home that feature the music that was played during their treatments. Some spas are using private-label music designed specifically for their spa, and the CDs carry their logo and add personality to their brand. Other spas are allowing their customers to download digital music collections from their website directly to their music player.

Other spas are recording guest preferences and starting to customize the music experience based on individual guest desires. Spa software has the potential to interface with the sound management system. The specific music or genre preferences of guests can be recorded on their profile and then the music can be piped into the treatment room. It increases the ability to customize a guest experience.

The popularity of iPods and MP3 players has led manufacturers to design such equipment as tanning beds and fitness equipment with docking centers. Guests can then listen to their own music while working out or participating in other spa services.

Cross-Selling

The resort spa market is increasingly integrating the spa experience with other parts of the resort. Most hotels and resorts are already selling packages that include rooms, meals, and spa treatments, and are looking for ways to increase the average spent across all their outlets. Right now, however, spa guests often feel like they are going to a different business when they visit a spa while staying at a resort. As resort spa software becomes more sophisticated, the lines between the businesses will blur. Eventually, resorts will be able to do such things as confirm guests' spa appointments when they check into the hotel, book appointments directly from the concierge desk, and integrate spa cuisine into the food and beverage options for spa guests. If a guest mentions in the spa that he or she has an allergy to nuts, that alert is noted and sent over to the food and beverage department. The marketing department will also be able to capture guest information and package specials that include spa services or wellness classes, depending on the individual preferences of the guests.

High-Tech Equipment

In many ways, such technology as hot tubs and Vichy showers changed the way water treatments were delivered in spas. Throughout the modern spa period, high-tech equipment has had a hand in spa services and hydrotherapy treatments. As medical spas continue to be the fastest growing segment of the industry, the equipment is becoming even more high-tech.

Many medical spas use technology for such things as microdermabrasion, laser treatments, teeth whitening, etc. In the future, technology is likely to become

Music at Spa Avania

Spa Avania at the Hyatt Regency Scottsdale Resort and Spa in Scottsdale, Arizona planned its music from the spa's conception. Gordon Tareta, vice president of spa operations for Hyatt Hotels Corporation, and a music styling company created a customized music program for the spa, which was built with a design and treatment philosophy based on the science of time. "Everything is geared around the time of day and our body's natural rhythms and requirements as we go throughout the day," said Ann Lane, senior director of advertising and public relations for the spa. "And music is a key factor."

According to Lane, the spa provides holistic, total immersion spa experiences based on the seven elements deemed most essential to the body's natural cycles during three specific periods of the day: morning (awakening and revitalization); mid-day (restoration and balance), and evening (relaxation and repair). "Music was not designed as an afterthought, rather a main attraction," said Lane. "From the moment you reach the front doors to the moment you leave, the music has been carefully calibrated to not only enhance your experience, but to actually contribute to your body's ability to heal, restore, and replenish itself."

The spa features 14 different music zones designed to progressively ease spa guests into their spa experience, from arrival (zone one) to treatment (zone 14) to departure (back to zone one). Other zones include the area from the reception area to the locker room, the locker room itself, French Celtic mineral pool, salon, yoga studio, and fitness center. "As you progress, the music will shift accordingly," Lane said, "bringing you to a spot that is going to make you better able to relax and reap the benefits of the treatment you are having." Lane explained that the music has a cyclical mission, designed to take guests from the high-energy pulse of the lobby and reception area, "where energetic sounds are meant to mirror the outside world," to the rich, reflective rhythms of the relaxation spaces deep inside the spa.

Each treatment room in the spa has its own Apple iPod, which features 10 play-lists guests can choose from, including three time-of-day choices, as well as desert, Indian, Mediterranean, Oriental, classical, rehydration, and relaxation-themed selections; guests can also bring their own iPod to play. According to spa director Dzeneta Arslanovic, this has been a big hit with the guests, especially for her repeat clients. "That was really taking it to the next level," she said. "I can remember all of the other spas I was with in the past, having to manage and change the music. A lot of times it was not uncommon to have the same music playing across the month. Just to have this for our repeat guests is great." And to ensure new music is always being heard, the spa uploads new songs every six months.

Music is also used to wake spa-goers back up after a treatment. "After you have the treatment, you then have to go out and face the world," said Lane. "So that music will have the reverse effect. It will ready the body again subconsciously to face the world, so you're not walking out exhausted. It really works with the body. It's amazing."

Source: Rachel Zawila, "Tune In, Turn On: How Music Enhances the Spa Experience," *Pulse,* December 2007.

more sophisticated, especially as personal monitoring technology improves. Monitors are also being sold on an individual basis that track a person's heart rate and breathing patterns. If a person starts to get too stressed out, he or she is reminded to do breathing exercises or something else that will bring him or her back to normal. These monitors are fairly simple and low cost. Other examples include a heat cuff or a vest that monitors more than 30 vital signs. A guest wears it every couple of months, and the data is sent to his or her regular physician to provide them with better information on the person's health.

Spa Design

Technology is helping to enhance the spa's overall ambience with colored lighting, LCD screens, iPod docking stations, and more water features and nature-related décor. Technology is also helping spas to be more environmentally conscious by creating sophisticated energy management, geothermal heating systems, and water reclamation systems. It is also allowing spas to develop paperless management systems that reduce their carbon footprint.

The Internet

It's no longer innovative to have an Internet presence—it's expected. Today's spa guests are Internet savvy and often begin their spa experience by researching spas on the Internet. What they encounter on a spa's website will set their expectations for what they will encounter once they walk through the doors.

First-time spa-goers also frequently turn to the Internet to learn more about a spa before making a reservation. It is essential that the spa website be well designed and in harmony with the spa's mission. Many of the same principles that are used for designing the retail space and treatment rooms can and should also be applied to the spa website.

Spas can also partner with their product providers to sell professional products online. Many vendors will arrange to have their products sold directly from the spa's website, with the spa receiving a percentage or a referral commission.

Spa users now make reservations for appointments online in much the same manner that they make airline or hotel reservations. This will become especially essential for spas that market to a younger demographic, accustomed to booking services for themselves. They don't want to sit on the phone and wait for availability. By not having someone hand-holding the guest through the reservation process, it doesn't mean the spa isn't giving good customer service. Rather, the spa is using technology in a manner that many of their technologically savvy guests will prefer. However, nearly 80 percent of the country's wealth is being held by the over-50 crowd. There will be a transitional period where a large part of the spa-goer population will prefer to talk to a live person, while another segment prefers to go the electronic route. There will likely be the need to offer both means of communication and booking to capture both groups.

Spas might also consider sending customized treatment thank you messages and follow-ups to their guests via e-mail—either from the spa or from their individual therapist, as well as reminders of future appointments.

Spa Snapshot: How have you successfully used the web to market to your clients?

At Glen Ivy, we use our website to promote services and products as a resource of information for guests visiting our spas and as an online store. Glen Ivy strives to keep services and products accessible to guests from a wide range of income and lifestyle groups versus catering to only well-to-do clientele. Many of our guests are first-time spa-goers and by providing information on how to plan [their] day, what to expect, and where to go, we help make them feel more at ease. This sensory preview of Glen Ivy and all we have to offer also builds anticipation for the experience that awaits.

Our recent website redesign has allowed us the added capability to manage promotions, e-commerce, and content updates in-house and in real-time, keeping the information fresh and exciting. A monthly e-mail blast supports marketing initiatives by highlighting featured treatments and products, new locations, and upcoming events. We are also working toward adding features to our Web site that encourage integrating "spa" into daily lifestyle with professional advice ranging from personal care to diet.

—*Karen Fojas, Marketing & Design Specialist, Glen Ivy Hot Springs, Inc.*

TerraNova does this in several ways:

- Changing our home page frequently to let our customers know what's new at TerraNova. Every time we have a product launch, we change the homepage to reflect the feel and colors of this new collection. We provide a link for customers to read all about our new products.

- Having a "Shop Online" page for customers to find links to sites that sell our products online. This also pleases our wholesale customers with e-commerce capabilities since it drives traffic to their site.

- Reviewing our keywords and metatags on a timely basis, to ensure their relevance and aid in search engine optimization.

—*Mrs. Laurence Diaco, Marketing/Press Relations, TerraNova*

We've made our website a true resource for both our clients and consumers. Consumers can use the site to learn more about our line, see what's hot for the season, learn about ingredients, etc. Most importantly, they can type in their zip code or area code and find the nearest spa, salon, or medical practice that carries the line; this really helps to drive

(continued)

(continued)

consumers into the doors of our professional accounts. We also have a professional section on our site that is only available to our accounts. This site provides a treasure trove of information for the esthetician or makeup artist, such as Jane's newsletters, educational offerings, promotions, and new products.

—*Theresa Robison, Director of Business Development, Iredale Mineral Cosmetics Ltd.*

Over the past five years, we have grown and changed our website to accommodate our clients and, in the most universally compliant ways, make our website user-friendly, esthetically pleasing, and full of information. We offer an interactive website that allows clients to give us their feedback and ask an expert questions about hair, skin, nails, and body. We continued throughout the changing process to monitor each step of the way where people were going and what was important to them. Two years ago, we added the option to print our gift cards at home with the ability to add a personal message. This has been a huge success! [Also], in looking at our demographic and in honor of our Hispanic population, last year we made our website bilingual. Our clients now have the opportunity to view our website in both English and Spanish! Our website has been a valuable investment and a great tool for communication through e-mailers to our clients.

—*Dawn Burruel, Director of Advertising, Marketing and gadabout.com, Gadabout SalonSpas*

At Sonya Dakar Skin Care, we capitalize on our very strong, not to mention large, consumer cult following. Because of this, the web has been an unbelievably lucrative source for our spa partners. It allows us to market our existing clients and promote spa partners, pushing new business and foot traffic through their front doors. We use web tools to send our existing Sonya Dakar clients through the doors of local spas that carry our products. All in all, our business and the business of our spa partners would not be what it is today without the advantage of genius web marketing.

—*Mimi Dakar, V.P Public Relations & Marketing, SONYA DAKAR*

Source: *Pulse*, May/June 2006

Spas need to be strategic in e-mailing clients. Spas don't want to spam their clients with an overload of announcements, reminders, thank you's, product or services specials, seasonal packages, gift certificate promotions, surveys, newsletters and the like, or they could end up turning off the client even though the intent was to turn them on. There always needs to be an easy, secure way for the client to unsubscribe.

Social Networking

Savvy spas can use the Internet to strengthen the bond between the spa and the guest. The Internet is a wonderful communication tool. Spas can send out monthly e-newsletters and write blogs with helpful educational and wellness information. Both tools keep the spa in the forefront of spa guest minds and help to integrate the spa into their regular routine.

Social networking is growing in popularity in almost all business sectors. It first became popular amongst the 15 to 24 age group as purely social technology. It has slowly been adopted by businesses who have witnessed the power of review and social connection sites. Some of the more common social networking technologies include message boards where people communicate on numerous topics and trade information on events, notices, and broadcasts; blogging with contributions by individuals, departments, or an entire spa; online video, social networking sites such as Facebook and MySpace, Wikis that allow anyone to post information; and podcasting.

Treatment Trends

At the heart of every spa are the treatments that are offered to guests. It is the treatment itself that guests come to the spa for. Three major trends affecting treatments include:

- Customization
- Authenticity
- Indigenous treatments

There are also minor trends that affect the industry such as the growing popularity of paramedical treatments, oncology massage, and skin rejuvenation techniques that use LED technology.

Customization

One size no longer fits all when it comes to the spa experience. Spa-goers desire experiences that are customized to their personal needs and desires. From booking time instead of a treatment, to selecting the background music, lighting, room temperature, and massage oils; being a spa-goer is not a passive spectator sport.

Demand for gender-specific experiences is rising. While initially spas tended to be "everything to everyone," consumers are now looking for more tailored experiences. With 31 percent of spa-goers being men, the demand for products and services designed specifically with men in mind is at an all-time high.

The increase in male grooming has contributed to the rise in men going to spas. With such shows as Queer Eye for the Straight Guy promoting spa use, metrosexual men (and even those who would not define themselves as metrosexual) are crossing over into areas that were traditionally female-dominated. There remain differences of opinion in the spa world about how to cater to men. Some argue that men want the same relaxing and calming experience that women do and not the high-impact environment with flat-screen televisions everywhere. Others point out that men do like the very gender-specific environment. They want it to be like a boy's club, not frilly and soft like traditional spa environments.

Another trend that has recently begun is the desire for skin care to evolve from a product-based service to an experience-based service. New facial treatments are focusing on creating an experience for the consumer based on how the product is put on and taken off the skin by incorporating elements like massage into the service. As one individual testifies in the ISPA 2007 Spa Industry Study, "when guests receive the total treatment, they love it." Also, the retail price of the product is included as a component of the overall cost of the experience. In China, some spas are setting up membership programs. Clients purchase a membership that includes treatments and products.

The future is likely to see more spas creating customized options for every service session. They might do such things as provide a simple menu with massages of various lengths listed. The guest and therapist can then discuss the guest needs and the therapist can customize a healing regimen for each client. When it comes to customizing spa treatments, the therapist should be the one driving the offerings to meet the guests' needs. Spas do not want to get into offering a sampler plate of services where a guest requests (for example) 15 minutes of Shiatsu, 25 minutes of Swedish massage, five minutes of Thai massage, and then an 11-minute body polish.

Also, it can be stressful for guests who do not possess the training to know which services will most benefit them for their specific needs. Customization needs to provide some choice and consumer control, but not force them to make all of the decisions. Rather the emphasis is on making them feel special and adding a layer of mysterious richness to a minimalist spa menu. However, the mysteriousness cannot add to or create stress for spa neophytes who may be nervous of doing or saying the wrong thing or on edge about what is going to happen next. The spa needs to offer clients the option of having a detailed walk-through about exactly what is going to happen and what the client should expect.

Some spas have responded by allowing guests to book blocks of times instead of specific services. This allows them to create a treatment that is all their own from the music to the products to the room temperature. It also allows them to present the outcomes they would like to experience and let the therapist come up with the treatments that will help them reach that outcome. The challenging part for spas is how to manage therapist scheduling when it is unknown what treatments the guest will be getting.

Therapist-driven customization can make all guests feel like they are being treated specially and individually, while retaining an ability to maintain a coherent experience that all guests can share in common. The shared ritual drives word-of-mouth marketing in places where spa goers gather. Spa goers still want the ritual even while wanting to customize it to their needs.

Authenticity

With massages being offered at street corners and "spa treatments" being sold off the shelves of discount stores, spas are increasingly looking for ways to distinguish themselves as true spa experiences. This has increased the focus on **authenticity.** It

reflections

Annika Jackson: Customizing Every Guest Stay

Annika Jackson is the vice president and managing director of Enchantment Resort in Boynton Canyon, Arizona. Prior to that she was the first general manager of the resort's destination spa, Mii amo, a position she held for seven years. The 24,000-square-foot spa was named "world's best destination spa" by the readers of Travel + Leisure during her tenure. Jackson was born in Stockholm and has worked in the hotel and travel industry in Europe, the Caribbean, and the United States.

We wanted to create something a little bit different when we first opened, so we came up with a particular intake process for our destination spa. The moment guests book their stay, we start working on preparing for their stay. Between booking the stay and their arriving, we work very closely with them. There's a couple different ways they can do it: filling out some forms online and working with one of our spa coordinators to create the perfect opportunity for them.

We have some pre-set programs or journeys—since Mii amo means journey. We put together some general ideas of what people can do with their time here. But when it comes down to the nitty gritty, to the details, we work with each individual. Even if two sisters come and they have picked the same journey, their stay will look slightly different because it will be tailored down to the little details that's going to make it special for them. That might be pairing them with the perfect service provider for particular treatments or scheduling their fitness or meditation classes around their needs and what they want to obtain from their stay.

We know people don't have enough time in today's world. So when they're here, they don't have to spend any time at the front desk trying to book or juggle around treatments or services or fitness classes. It's all done. It's already laid out, they already have an itinerary done when they arrive. We think it's nice and it also saves on our part because we really know what they want when they come and we can then tailor their stay according to that.

---

is a concept that matters to increasingly knowledgeable guests who are skeptical of exclamation point-laden marketing messages that oversell a product or service.

Spa professionals have become increasingly concerned about false claims, integrity issues, reliability, and scams that they see at spas and in products. They are concerned for the consumer and their perceptions of spa in the long term, as well as the profitability of their own businesses in the short term.

One response has been to educate guests about the spa lifestyle and benefits of spa-going and spa products, while addressing guest perceptions. Most professionals want their guests to know and demand high quality and authentic spa experiences.

But what is an authentic experience? There are no industry-wide standards for what is authentic or high quality. Nor is there even a global definition for spa or the varying types of spa. For now, authenticity is defined by individual spas and by the perception of their guests.

Discerning spa guests are skeptical of whether services and products can live up to their claims. Today's spa guests are highly educated and informed and expect their spas to deliver what they promise. Many of them will turn off if a spa

reflections

Mary Bemis: Authenticity, Healing, Wellness, and Anti-Aging

Mary Bemis, founder and editor-in-chief of Organic Spa, has been a spa trend-watcher for many years. She has written about the spa industry for more than 20 years, launching American Spa in 1997, New Beauty magazine in 2004, and Organic Spa in 2007. She's also written for Spa, Allure, Self, Shape, Luxury SpaFinder, Spa Asia, and many other magazines.

Trend is a trick word. I've been reporting on spa trends for a long time and I keep coming back to the same four trends.

As cliché or as old as it sounds to those in the industry, authenticity is still major. It's key. People are still looking for authentic experiences in every aspect of their lives, especially with their spa experiences. People bandy about that word a lot these days, but I do think that the consumer is looking for authenticity when they are looking to the spa. That brings up the whole craving or desire for indigenous treatments. We started years ago with this whole looking toward different cultures and the spa used the word "inspired" rather than "taking from" other cultures. The consumers will expect the spa now like never before to really walk their talk. They are demanding more than ever, especially green and organic. So all these things: green and indigenous and authenticity is all combined in one big trend.

Spas are wonderful places to heal, to renew, and for introspection. We're a healing center and we're going full circle to that. One hopes that every spa is a healing center and I mean nurturing and teaching certain lifestyles. It's very hard for everyone to have one cohesive message and to live up to it. There is a lot of consumer confusion in the marketplace. Ultimately, it is the spa's responsibility to really teach and I think that consumers are looking for that as well: for the spa to teach someone how to live a better lifestyle, to better themselves internally and externally. There is a consumer demand for finding alternatives to heal oneself. To live. The medical community is finally taking that side more seriously, partly because of the consumer demand. The rise of yoga, Pilates, and gentle exercise forms over the years and the more esoteric treatments speak to that demand. Things that have been off the spa menus for years—craniosacral work, energy work—are returning to the menus. We've been seeing a rise in that all across the country.

Years ago, I preached wellness. It was wellness, wellness, wellness that was going to be the big thing. We see more spas calling themselves wellness centers. That is still a trend: being a holistic center for someone seeking wellness services.

The fourth trend is all of the anti-aging and longevity concerns. How does one live better and longer? This is big, big, big. I don't want to say it is a trend, but it is a major category that is growing.

---

promises to reverse the aging process or to make them look 30 years younger after a one-hour service.

"The concept of spa has become very homogenized. We need to make sure that what was created doesn't become so diluted that it really loses the essence,"

Sea salt with bentonite clay and the collection of spring aromatherapy products are examples of special ingredients used by spas to create a unique experience.

said Cathy Cluff, managing director at The Oaks at Ojai. "I think the consumer will recognize that. The consumers drive what is successful and what is not successful. The more properties that don't have a certain level of authenticity, the more damaging it is to the overall concept. To the consumers, it becomes a confusing point and they get turned off to the whole concept before they've actually been able to embrace what is so wonderful about the spa industry.

Authenticity encompasses a variety of factors. Spa-goers associate authenticity with earth-friendly products, services that are natural or organic, and services that have a local flavor or even a story to tell.

Indigenous Treatments

Spas help connect people to nature to celebrate the earth. It's part of the reason that **indigenous** treatments have gained such resonance with spas and spa goers. It offers a way for people to connect with nature in a way that is unique to a specific time and a specific place.

Indigenous treatments mean different things in different parts of the world. In Asia, the Western spa model was used for many years as they modernized their spa offerings. However, they soon learned that Western research and statistics were often meaningless for their guests and their culture. They now are returning to their own rich history of indigenous treatments that are unique to their area and their guests. By embracing rituals and rites arising from the traditions and cultures of their countries, they have been able to offer unique experiences that have begun to spread throughout the spa world.

The consumer interest in all things local and indigenous will likely continue unabated in the years to come. Consumers seeking the most distinctive products or experiences generally rely on authenticity as the ultimate justification for their distinctions. Place or geography and tradition (indigenous ways of life) have a way of lending authenticity to a practice. The appeal of a local, authentic, indigenous ritual treatment is particularly attractive to tourists and other travelers. It represents something they cannot get at home. It sends them home with not just a great unique experience but with a story to tell. It gives them bragging rights with their friends and colleagues who have never been there.

Those spas that are able to leverage local places and indigenous traditions will provide more distinctive, compelling spa experiences. These can be seen in body treatments featuring local ingredients and the practice of employing local traditions. However, it must be noted that the treatments must be authentically indigenous and not merely an important treatment with no connection to the spa's locale. When it comes to indigenous treatments and offerings, place matters. Not every place is going to have something that is interesting or appropriate. See Exhibit 4.

This logic is especially powerful as a point of distinction in destination spas. It is here that guests more easily embrace the magic of the local, the indigenous, and the exotic. Integrating contact with a destination's natural and cultural elements through spa services is a growing interest among consumers.

Equally important to ingredients is the need for a captivating story that weaves the local indigenous products, ritual, protocol, music, and all means of ambience together into a powerful spiritual journey. Even if guests forget the name of the place or the name of the product, they will always be anchored by the story. So it is very important that spa staff who are involved in this journey have excellent, captivating story-telling skills.

Industry Trends

Some of the major changes in the spa industry have had to do with ownership structure, investor attractiveness, and spa mergers and consolidations. All three are indicators of a maturing industry. Spas are facing many of the challenges that more traditional businesses face while still keeping their focus on the mission that makes spas unique.

Ownership Structure

The contemporary spa era saw the birth of spa brands and the inching away from sole proprietorships to corporate ownership. It's a move that continues to take place as the increasingly competitive spa market requires greater investment and sophistication to attract savvy spa goers.

While chains are likely to continue to grow in popularity with spas building on the success that comes with a thriving brand, franchising—popular in many other segments of the hospitality industry—simply isn't happening. As of 2007, 95 percent of all spas were not affiliated with a franchise—down only two percent

Exhibit 4   Products with Indigenous Active Ingredients

Products with Indigenous Active Ingredients

One particular area of authenticity that the spa world can leverage is to sell products based on indigenous active ingredients. This involves leveraging the qualities of substances naturally occurring within some easily understandable geographical/cultural locale.

To do this, however, requires a significant origin narrative that explains how an active ingredient is both unique and native to some local natural world.

The following represents a rough hierarchy of authenticity when making the indigenous active ingredient claim:

- **Indigenous to the spa's local environment:** Spa-goers find the most authenticity in active ingredients derived from natural sources from the spa's local ecological environs.

- **Indigenous to Europe**: Spa-goers attribute high quality to products imported from Europe. Spa-goers perceive the spa industry's European origins and the locus of cosmetic innovation as ultimately European, and products from there as inherently authentic, of superior quality, and maximally effective.

- **Indigenous to a non-European 'somewhere else'**: This strategy works less well when the theme of indigenous ingredients pertains to a truly natural, but ultimately foreign/distant, world. For example, marketing indigenous active ingredients from rural Tibet in a Chicago spa comes off more as a marketing gimmick than truly authentic. Spa-goers who encounter this kind of ingredient marketing may easily decide that they can get this "Tibetan" item elsewhere for less, since it is clearly available outside of Tibet.

Hypothetical product examples:

- Dead sea salt
- Vancouver Island sea kelp exfoliate
- Flagstaff mud
- South Indian flower/botanical essences
- Javanese mango fruit extract

Source: ISPA 2006 Consumer Report

from 2004. Medical spas are the most likely type to be a franchisee—but even that number accounts for only six percent of all medical spas.

What is more common than franchising is for large spa companies to open up multiple locations while retaining ownership of all properties.

Investors

With spas increasing their business savvy and becoming more profitable, they have attracted more notice from investors. It has become easier for start-up spas to attract financial backers. Investors are also becoming more attracted to spas because spas have become more integrated into lifestyles with increased popularity in spa cuisine and spa lifestyles.

Mergers and Cross-Marketing

Major players in the spa industry have been growing by purchasing other spas and making them a part of their brand. This has created some consolidation in the industry.

Spas are also partnering with other organizations to cross-market products that make sense together. Karen Korpi, Vice President, Spa Division, Ritz-Carlton Hotel Company, says the Ritz-Carlton makes agreements with corporations to use their names and products in a couple of their locations. However, she said that while partnering with a star to build interest in a spa's offering is currently trendy, she sees spas more often turning their own employees into celebrities.

"As we're moving forward, our celebrities are the gurus we have within our spa," Korpi said. "It's identifying them and promoting them as our vehicle to the consumer providing education and knowledge."

Other trends that have created new alliances that extend the spa industry into non-traditional areas:

- Product line manufacturers such as American Express, Coca Cola/Dasani Water, and Splenda, have begun cross-marketing their brands with the spa lifestyle concept.

- The medical industry in general and the plastic surgery sector in particular are beginning to incorporate spa treatments such as naturotherapy and acupuncture into their service structure.

- There is increased cooperation between the spa sector and the skin care industry with some skin care brands allowing hotels and spas to market their products using their own brands.

- Real estate developers are building residential spas in gated communities and high-end condominiums.

- Some businesses are starting to merge the spa concept with entertainment. Examples include a New York spa that doubles as a night club, along with other spas that are starting to use their facilities for various after-hours social activities.

Environmental Trends

Spa professionals are focusing more and more on activities extending well beyond the walls of their spa and the typical business goals. There is a continued return to the roots of spa, the roots where people see the spa as serving social purposes and improving the quality of life. This stems partly from more stringent government and legal requirements and partly from a feeling of social responsibility.

Spa professionals have become quite concerned with being good corporate citizens who behave in an ethical and socially-sanctioned manner. More attention

Spa Snapshot: What "green" measures is your company taking to become environmentally friendly?

Erbaviva uses recyclable packaging, (mainly glass, with 1 PET bottle). Erbaviva also offers some fabric packaged items. The fabric pouches are made by a Hill Tribe in Thailand; it is part of a project set up with ecological roots, whereby helping provide this Hill Tribe with income (from making our pouches and also gift baskets) we are able to give them income which is what leads them to stay away from practicing harmful "slash and burn" agriculture. Instead, with the income, they build reusable rice paddy farms, whereas when they practiced their former methods of Hill Farming they would have to slash and burn a new area of forest every year.

—*Robin Brown, Co-founder, Erbaviva*

Hosteria Las Quintas ECO Spa (note the word "Eco") has been on the leading edge of the ecological front for many years. Almost eight years ago we installed a "green" water treatment plant on property to process all of our "white" waste waters. Our water treatment plant is based on live micro-organisms that consume the bacteria found in the waste water, which is then re-used for watering our grounds. Due to the fact that the treatment plant contains live micro-organisms, we do not use any products that are non-biodegradable, as products such as chlorine bleach can destroy the balance of the treatment plant and kill the live micro-organisms. Due to this, all of our cleaning products are biodegradable as well as our fumigation products, which are all natural pesticides.

Finally, all of the lighting at Hosteria Las Quintas, including grounds, guestrooms, etc., is special low voltage, low wattage (nine watts), reducing the consumption of electricity and therefore helping the environment in the long run.

—*Orlando Hidalgo, Spa Director/Owner, Hosteria Las Quintas Eco Spa*

ResortSuite SPA, a fully integrated software system designed specifically for the spa industry, generates more than 250 comprehensive management, operations, sales, marketing, staff and product reports that could potentially consume heaps of paper. Instead, we created an export and e-mail function within ResortSuite SPA that completely eliminates the need to print these reports to paper. We also included a scheduling function that assembles any report (i.e., management or operations) and automatically e-mails it to a distribution list; again, paper-free.

—*Frank Pitsikalis, President, Enablez Inc., makers of ResortSuite*

(continued)

Ten Thousand Waves has operated in a water-restricted environment ever since we opened in 1981. Because of that, we've taken extreme measures to save water. When we expand, we plan to garner 100 percent of our landscape irrigation needs from hot tub runoff, grey water recycling, and active rainwater harvesting, instead of the present 50 percent. We also build with materials that don't outgas, such as cement, adobe, and planks instead of plywood as much as possible. Our main building was designed to face south, with a two-story glass greenhouse, which is a passive solar heat collector. The heated air is harvested from the greenhouse and circulated in the spa.

—*Duke Klauck, President, Ten Thousand Waves*

Red Mountain practices and teaches Leave No Trace and conscious outdoor recreation in its sensitive desert environment. All outdoor recreation staff are Leave No Trace guides. They also removed nine acres of grass and replaced it with indigenous desert plants that require less water. In addition, the gardens and lawns are organic, with no synthetic fertilizers or sprays. Finally, the laundry is done with phosphorus-free enzymes.

—*Marjory Hawkins, Public Relations, Red Mountain Spa*

Lake Austin Spa Resort is a member of the Green Hotels Association and a Certified Habitat with the National Wildlife Federation. Because we are on the water, and a lot of our programs, spa treatments, and architecture are influenced by nature, we are respectful of Mother Earth and incorporate the following items into our everyday operations:

- We manage pests organically.
- We compost all plant materials on property.
- We recycle toner cartridges.
- We recycle Styrofoam, office paper, newsprint, and cardboard.
- We buy recycled paper and office supplies.
- We have a towel recycling program.

—*Darlene Fiske, Director of Sales and Marketing, Lake Austin Spa Resort*

Colorescience understands the importance of keeping our environment safe and is dedicated to giving consumers a natural and eco-friendly option to traditional makeup. This mineral makeup line depends on nature to find all of its ingredients, and it gives back to nature in return. Colorescience uses super-goat bristle in all of its brushes—the highest quality bristles that can be obtained without causing any harm to animals. All Colorescience packaging is totally ecological, refillable, recyclable and reusable. In addition, Colorescience is tested on humans, never animals.

—*Diane Ranger, President, Colorescience*

Source: *Pulse*, March/April 2004

is being directed at such considerations as the role of marketing decisions and actions in increasing the standards of living, overcoming poverty, providing jobs, training and educating employees, advancing ethical practices, and providing for the health, safety, and security of employees and guests.

Spas are being challenged to deal directly with such issues as litter, waste, sewage, air pollution, water, and energy conservation, and other psycho-social issues. Even though all of these issues go beyond the bottom line, they will become increasingly important considerations for spas.

Triple Bottom Line

Sustainability is the ability of this generation to meet its needs while not impeding the ability of the next generation to meet its needs. The triple bottom line refers to our use, production, and conservation of people, profit, and the planet. Loma Alexander, a member of ISPA's Sustainability Task Force, and Larry Dean in a 2005 *Pulse* article defined it as:

People: How does a business impact people, not only its customers, but the people who contribute to the business. From service to products, as well as how those products are made.

Planet: The natural world: air, water, earth, as well as the entire eco-balance of all living creatures.

Profit: The economy, making a profit while contributing to the planet and people.

Spas have never been strangers to environmentalism, with their emphasis on waters and their closeness to the earth and its benefits. At some point, though, environmentalism passed from a "fad" in the greater culture to a compelling issue that no business is able to ignore. Not surprisingly, 76 percent of U.S. spas apply environmentally sustainable practices to their business, whether it is on-site organic gardens; products made from locally-grown fruits, vegetables, herbs, and plants; mineral makeup; or green building and energy practices.

Far more than just a passing trend, **sustainability** and the **triple bottom line** became watchwords of responsible businesses in the 1990s and the new century. Spa businesses in particular realized they needed to be good stewards of the resources that they use.

The focus on how to sustain a business through the triple bottom line necessitates a change in the way businesses have traditionally looked at nature. It isn't merely a pool of resources to be drawn upon until it runs dry, but rather a dynamic system in which we contribute and pull out. The role of the modern spa is to find a way for the business, the people, and the earth to thrive through the way the spa does its work. See Exhibit 5.

Some of the things that spas can do to be more ecologically conscious include:

- Using energy-efficient light bulbs such as compact fluorescent lights
- Creating a compost site to process consumer food waste
- Recycling candles by melting them down and making new ones
- Shredding paper and using it as mulch on garden paths

Exhibit 5 The Triple Bottom Line

There is a triple bottom line of benefits to be reaped from going green.

Enacting environmentally sound polices increases the economic health of a property. Properties that have enacted green policies have reaped millions of dollars in cost reductions. Economic benefits have included:

- Energy savings

- Waste reduction and lower disposal costs

- Eligibility for government incentives

- Reduced labor costs

- Reduced employee absenteeism

- Increased productivity

Environmental benefits include the conservation of limited resources. The actions a spa takes to conserve water, save energy, reduce waste, and purify the air are making the world a healthier place to live. They reduce pollution and help preserve natural habitats. They ensure the long-term success of a spa by helping to make tomorrow's world a sustainable environment.

Social benefits are also plentiful. Publicizing a spa's environmental activities make it more attractive to eco-conscious guests and to groups calling for greater environmental accountability. Spas can reap the benefits of environmentally friendly philosophies by:

- Creating a sense of pride in the community

- Increasing the morale and health of employees

- Enhancing a spa's image

- Providing a competitive edge in the industry

- Establishing the property as an environmental leader

- Creating a deeper level of trust in guests, suppliers, and partners

- Offering education to staff and guests

Source: *Managing Hospitality Housekeeping Operations,* 3rd edition, American Hotel & Lodging Educational Institute, 2008.

- Adjusting Vichy water treatments to use less water by covering the bather with warm, wet towels and using a Vichy shower that allows individual showerhead flow

- Using recycled construction materials during a remodel

- Buying recycled products whenever possible

- Using biodegradable soaps for laundry

- Installing tasteful recycling bins for guest use throughout the spa

- Removing the spa's name from junk mail lists at the Direct Marketing Association to reduce waste

- Offering guests refillable water containers and glasses instead of plastic, disposable bottles
- Refilling room amenities rather than replacing them with disposable bottles
- Avoiding paper or Styrofoam cups
- Buying in bulk whenever possible
- Refilling toner and ink cartridges
- Minimizing the use of plastics
- Using e-mail to replace many traditional paper communications
- Offering a cloth shopping bag for use in the spa's retail areas. Offering discounts when guests bring the shopping bag back to use again.
- Buying locally grown and manufactured products
- Using renewable resources such as cork floors, bamboo walls, recycled carpet, and non-toxic paint and materials
- Increasing natural ventilation and daylight
- Installing solar-heated hot-water and low-flow fixtures in showers and washrooms

In 2006, ISPA partnered with LOHAS (Lifestyles of Health and Sustainability) to bring environmentally sound ideas and conferences to the spa industry. Some of the LOHAS-initiatives include:

- Participating in community-oriented programs such as Race for the Cure, free treatments for military families, Earth Day
- Educating staff on sustainability
- Recycling programs
- Using organic and natural products in the spa and in the back-of-house areas
- Providing organic, vegan, and vegetarian menu choices

Exhibit 6 shows the characteristics of a green spa as laid out by the Green Spa Network.

Sustainable Spas

Spas have found ways both large and small to green their facilities and live an authentically sustainable example. Here are just a few of the initiatives spas have undertaken:

- Fairmont Hotels & Resorts has a strict environmental policy for all of its properties—many of which have spas. It has a stewardship program that is committed to minimizing the company's impact on the environment and respecting and valuing the local, indigenous culture. Its policy states that each property will "comply with all applicable environmental legislation,

Exhibit 6   What Is A Green Spa?

A *green spa* is a center for healing, aesthetics, and wellness where reducing the spa's environmental footprint is a top priority.

Some Characteristics of a Green Spa:

- Strives to conserve energy and water resources.
- Is committed to using materials that can be recycled, follows recycling practices, and is always looking for ways to minimize waste.
- Utilizes natural and organic skin care products.
- Believes that it has a responsibility to guests and to the planet to reduce exposure to toxic substances and to minimize hazardous waste generation.
- Is open to learning and adopting new environmentally friendly strategies and techniques.
- Shares its concern for the Earth's well-being with guests.

Source: Green Spa Network, www.greenspanetwork.org

build local practices, consider the opinions and feedback of our guests... regarding environmental programs ... and identify areas for improvement and innovation at the property level and support the efforts of Green Teams at all properties."

- Sundara Spa, Wisconsin Dells, Wisconsin, was committed to sustainability as it built its new lifestyle villas. It protected open spaces, indigenous pine trees, and local plants to minimize site disturbance. It collected rainwater and used it during the construction process. It took efforts to conserve water and laundered linens less frequently with guest permission.

- In Wexford, Ireland, the Solas Croi Eco Spa was built to provide customers with natural and spiritual beauty that didn't expose them to harsh chemicals or invasive procedures. Instead, it offers meditation and yoga classes along with a range of body treatments. It strives to use ecologically sound treatment methods. The spa is also dedicated to creating and promoting environmentally sound business practices. It uses geo-thermal heating and its hot water comes from renewable wood chip technology.

- The California Wellbeing Institute at the Four Seasons Westlake Village is a complex that includes a diagnostic medical center, a luxury hotel, and a 28-treatment room spa. It encourages its guests to conserve electricity and re-use linens and towels. It also built a hothouse that includes orchids and planted 100 cypress and sequoia trees on its grounds. The noise of a nearby freeway was reduced by the establishment of a man-made waterfall that cascades over boulders.

- The Mohonk Mountain Spa in New York had an eye toward eco-consciousness when it was built. They selected and built a geo-thermal heating and cooling system that controls the spa temperature using the earth's constant temperature. It provides an emission-free, noise-free alternative to traditional heating

Guests have increasingly high expectations that a spa will operate in harmony with nature, sustaining and healing the world as well as individuals.

and cooling methods. It also installed an easy-to-maintain green roof that helps to insulate the building while reducing water-run-off and providing a habitat for birds and butterflies.

- The Sheraton Wild Horse Pass Resort in Arizona has gardens on site. The gardens are tended by school children, who learn about their Native American ancestral heritage while working. The fruits and vegetables grown there are used in recipes throughout the resort's restaurants.

- The Lake House Spa at Lake Austin Spa Resort was built with native Austin limestone, cedar, and terra cotta. Herbs from their own garden are used to create customized spa products that guests can select according to their individual needs.

- The El Monte Sagrado Living Resort and Spa in Taos, New Mexico, designed its spa to be in harmony with its surroundings. It built a Living Machine, which is a water-recycling system that filters wastewater through pools rich with fish, plants, and other natural filters. The reclaimed water is then used to irrigate botanical gardens and landscaping. The harvests from the gardens are served in its restaurants. The water system is also used to help cool and heat its buildings.

- Nusta Spa, a day spa in Washington, D.C., is certified by the U.S. Green Building Council's Leadership in Energy and Environmental Design (LEED) program. It has a gold certificate in interior design for using woods taken from an abandoned barn, an old sawmill, renewable forests, and bamboo. It enhances its air quality with MERV 8 air filters. For its walls, the spa used paints that are at low or zero VOC (volatile organic compounds). It also used recycled carpet to reduce the amount of off-gassing from chemical fumes. It has a carbon dioxide sensor that automatically adjusts the fresh air exchange so that there are proper oxygen levels.[2]

Local Food

Local food is a term used to describe an increasingly popular movement within the sustainability movement. It emphasizes locally produced goods and services. This reduces the **ecological footprint** necessary to package the food and move it around the world. It also encourages the local region to be healthier environmentally, economically, and socially.

From the early days of Rancho La Puerta and Canyon Ranch, which had their own organic gardens, spas have believed in local foods and acted upon those beliefs. Organic food helps to ensure the safety and cleanliness of the food. In 2007, Rancho La Puerta opened a cooking school, La Cocina Que Canta, in its six-acre organic garden.

Developing a Future Orientation

Part of survival—whether personal, spiritual, or business—is planning for what comes next and ensuring that one's actions today are providing for the future. Today's spas are flourishing and successful and in a perfect position to prepare for even greater things ahead. This is true both on the aggregate level of the spa world and the individual spa.

Why do some spas succeed on a grand scale while others flounder and fail? Why do some spas reach new creative heights while others barely keep their heads above water? Charles Darwin, in commenting on the survival of the species, noted that, "It is not the strongest of the species that survives, nor the most intelligent; it is the one that is most adaptable to change." So it is with spas. Spas that can adapt to change and adjust to new guest needs and market conditions are the ones that survive and thrive. Spas that refuse to change and continue only those tested approaches that they've "always" used find themselves becoming irrelevant.

The trends and issues discussed in this chapter can provide a foundation of information that can help spas to manage change. It can help spas to look around the corner at the future. However, there is a constant influx of new information that spa professionals will have to monitor.

Successful spas won't simply react to changing guest wants, they'll anticipate what needs are and create the demand. Spas have always focused on delivering what people need, and moved ahead with the faith and determination that they will be able to communicate their message to the betterment of their guests. Successful spas will watch trends and analyze what those trends mean for the future and what they will be able to teach and provide, based on those trends.

Spas also need to make sure that they're not simply following trends, but that they are also meeting the needs of their clients by evaluating and measuring their current situation. They should adjust their spa according to the culture and needs of their customers and areas. Trends and forecasts can help spa professionals make sure that they are aware of what is going on in the market so that they can make better judgments about which trends will affect them and their spa.

In developing a future orientation and assessing future opportunities, spas must consider the likely effect of a host of external factors.

Managing the Future

Who is in charge of the future? Who is responsible for monitoring demographic, economic, sociological, technological, and other trends, discerning their implications, and assessing likely opportunities they offer? When the response is "everyone," as it so often is, the implication is that no one really is. The result is that a future orientation is neglected, often at great cost.

It can often be easier to deal with the past and present than with the future. The past and present are where all the hard data is. Spa managers can put their hands on data about treatments offered, treatment room occupancy, retail sales, return visits, and so on. It is much harder to predict the future. Yet, spa managers have no alternative but to try to peer around the corner and develop a feel for what will likely emerge. Just the act of doing so, regardless of any inaccuracies, furnishes valuable insights and helps spas to be more prepared for what is coming.

When imagining what the future holds, making straight-line projections about spa futures can be disastrous. The future is not a mere continuation of past trends, and for every trend, there may be a countertrend. The trend of eating more fish and poultry is accompanied by the success of steak houses. Spa cuisine featuring low-fat foods like fat-free yogurt and desserts are offset by the success of fat-laden Ben & Jerry's and Haagen-Dazs ice creams. The growth of ethnic foods is paralleled by the growth of regional American cuisine, and so on.

Four points should be kept in mind when dealing with future trends. First, expect the unexpected, because unanticipated events will occur. Second, beware of the countertrends that are embedded in trends. Third, realize that competent and informed forecasters may arrive at vastly different conclusions when assessing the same landscape. Fourth, remember that looking to the future highlights obsolete experience and underscores the importance of continuous learning and training.

Managing the future means:

- Gathering information and intelligence.
- Scanning spa environments and discerning trends and tendencies.
- Developing and assessing future market scenarios.
- Assessing emerging opportunities.
- Developing contingency plans.
- Adjusting offerings.
- Assessing competitors.

Spa professionals who become skilled in all of these tasks will find themselves well prepared for whatever the future brings.

Endnote

1. U.S. Census Bureau, *Population Change and Distribution*, 1990 to 2000, Census 2000 Special Brief, April 2001.

2. Naomi Serviss, "Reaching (and Keeping) the Conscious Consumer" *Pulse*, March/April 2007; J. Elaine Spear, "The New Prophets of Bloom," *Pulse*, August 2005.

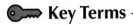 **Key Terms**

authenticity—Being honest in claims, treatments, and offerings.

body image—A person's perception of their own physical appearance.

corporate wellness—Corporations that provide health and wellness services to their employees as a way of reducing turnover, time off, and health care costs.

ecological footprint—The total effect on the environment that an item has. This effect includes fuel used to transport something and materials used to package it.

indigenous—Treatments, rituals, rites, or ingredients that are native to a particular area.

local food—Eating food that is produced within a near radius, often 100 miles.

mobile spas—Spas that travel to wherever the client is.

myofascial massage—A form of massage that stretches the fascia, or connective tissue, to increase the range of motion of the muscle.

residential spas—Spa communities where people can live.

revenue management—Maximizing revenue by changing prices and reservations according to supply and demand.

social networking—A form of online technology that connects people through sites such as Facebook, MySpace, and wikis.

sustainability—The ability of this generation to meet its needs while not compromising the ability of the next generation to meet its needs.

techno stress—Increased tension caused by technology.

triple bottom line—The use, production, and conservation of people, profit, and the planet.

yield management—Maximizing revenue by changing prices and reservations according to supply and demand.

 Review Questions

1. What is a trend and what are the four stages of its life cycle?
2. What are the two major staffing challenges that spas will face in the future?
3. What type of standards affect the spa industry?
4. What are some of the major social trends that will mold the future of the spa industry?
5. What are some emerging spa markets?
6. How can spas use revenue management?
7. What are three major trends connected to spa treatments?
8. What is sustainability and the triple bottom line?
9. What can spa professionals do to help manage the future?

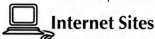

Internet Sites

For more information, visit the following Internet sites. Remember that Internet addresses can change without notice. If the site is no longer there, you can use a search engine to look for additional sites.

Enablez/ResortSuite
www.enablez.com

Green Spa Network
www.greenspanetwork.org

Greet the Day
www.greettheday.com

Leadership in Energy and
 Environmental Design (LEED)
www.usgbc.org/
DisplayPage.aspx?CategoryID=19

Leading Spas of Canada
www.leadingspasofcanada.com

Mobil Travel Guide
mobiltravelguide.howstuffworks.com/
spas-channel.htm

National Corporate Wellness
www.nationalcorporatewellness.com/
index.php?option=com_content&task=
blogcategory&id=41&Itemid=67

Organic Spa Magazine
www.organicspamagazine.com

Spa Avania
scottsdale.hyatt.com/hyatt/pure/spas/
index.jsp

Spa Chicks On-the-Go
www.spachicksonthego.com

Spa Quality—Excellence in Spas
www.spaquality.com

Visit Britain
www.visitbritain.com/en/
things-to-see-and-do/itineraries/
spas-and-pampering

Chapter 5 Outline

Competencies

1. Explain the differences between a business that manufactures a product and one that delivers a service. (pp. 171–186)

2. Explain how to achieve superior service by creating memorable experiences. (pp. 186–191)

3. List the realms of experience. (pp. 191–195)

4. Describe the importance of delivering on the service promise. (pp. 196–209)

5

The Spa Service Experience

SERVICE IS SO INTEGRAL to what a spa does that many menus list treatments as services. A spa delivering poor service risks not staying in business for long. Even though spa treatments are often called services, it isn't service alone that brings people into the spa and entices them to return time after time. Rather, the service is part of something larger. It is part of the overall *experience*. By creating a sensory experience, a spa business is able to successfully nurture the heart and mind of the spa consumer. To do this, attention to the smallest detail should be considered in creating a seamless experience that can be felt, seen, tasted, touched, and heard by the spa-goer. Common threads should be woven into every aspect of the spa business—from architectural design to marketing collateral to spa menus to spa interiors and employee appearance.

For guests, the experience isn't just about how the spa staff treats them, it's about the entire sensory journey that they take while at the spa. It is the ritual of the spa experience and every component of that ritual. It's the relaxing music that soothes their ears. It's the soft lighting that relaxes their eyes. It's the beautiful aromas of essential oils that tantalize their noses. It's the relaxing caress on their bodies of the water in a wet lounge's whirlpool or the warming sensation of the sauna or steam room. It's the warm greeting upon arrival with a personal tour of the spa. It's the euphoria after a good workout in a spinning class or the sense of total calm after a guided meditation class. All of these, plus the treatments provided by the staff, are elements of the total experience.

The spa experience also goes beyond the physical. Spas are able to provide a holistic experience that nurtures the body, mind, and spirit. Spa professionals frequently emphasize the importance of **mindfulness**—whether it is mindful exercise, mindful massage, or mindful treatments. A spa experience is one that will offer guests a place to heal their bodies, expand their minds, and nurture their souls. It offers them a place where they can come together with others and connect through reflection, touch, and renewal.

The spa helps guests transition from the hectic pace of everyday life to an immersion in the total peace of a spa experience. Guests can curl up with a glass of herbal tea on a comfortable sofa while waiting for their appointments in the spa relaxation lounge. Perhaps the experience starts with a 15-minute workout on an elliptical trainer followed by a soothing shower in one of the multi-head showers in the locker area followed by a few minutes in the steam room before their appointment. Perhaps the guest pops into a spa for a quick pedicure to break up a hectic day. Or perhaps the guest will follow a massage with a few laps in the spa pool and relax on one of the ample chaise lounges around the pool with a glass of water infused with cucumber.

Whatever the series of activities surrounding or integrated into a spa treatment, it should always be an experience.

Service and the Spa Experience

Service is generally defined as "work done for others." However, most people in the industry would impose a quality factor into that definition. There is an expectation that the service is done well and appropriately and even beyond that, quality service means exceeding the guests' expectations.

Spa guests arrive with unarticulated needs or expectations. According to the International SPA Association 2006 Spa-Goer Study, approximately one-quarter of the total U.S. population has been to a spa and spa-goers have become more savvy and far more discerning about what they expect from a spa and its services.

"People are becoming much more educated," said Jason de Caprio, hair stylist and manager at Noelle Spa for Beauty and Wellness in Stamford, Connecticut. "I don't know if it is because of the computer age or they're more fickle with where they spend their money, but before they spend their money, they really look into things. They Google it or check it out on the web or talk with their friends a little bit more."

The elements of good service at a spa include everything from the first impression made during a website preview, the initial phone contact, or just driving by the spa itself:

- Is the website easy to navigate and designed in a way that is in harmony with the spa's environment?

- How do people at the spa answer the phone?

- Are receptionists able to explain the services and help guests select the proper experience for their needs?

- Is there a quiet relaxation area where guests can unwind and simply exhale while preparing for their service?

- Are the treatment rooms peaceful and impeccably clean?

- Do the therapists and technicians deliver the service in a competent and warm manner?

- Are spa policies explained?

- Is billing done accurately and proficiently with no surprises?

- Are retail products suggested that can help a guest continue the benefits of the spa experience at home?

These are just some of the standards guests use to form opinions about the spa. If all of the parts of this process are performed better than expected—that is, if reality exceeds expectations—then guests subconsciously rate each element of their experience as better than average or high. If reality matches expectations—the guests get what they expected, no more and no less—then service is satisfactory and they may or may not return. But if reality is less than what is expected, the service is considered poor and not only will that guest not return, but he or she will surely tell others about the poor experience.

Spa Snapshot: How does your company measure or define "quality?"

My first and only thought was "The quality of our company is only as good as the staff representing the company." I decided to show (this question) to our staff and asked them to respond, as I wanted it straight from them. Ten minutes later I get a two-page letter. It was obvious to me this was straight from their hearts. Here is what they wrote in the letter:

Define Quality:

- Pure excellence
- Friendly hardworking people
- Building friendships
- Making our surrounding an easy work place
- Fresh-made products made with extra care and support by quality workers

Company:

- Get along well and acknowledge each other
- Knowing our part in the company
- Make customers satisfied
- Always take in everyone's ideas
- Love to listen to customer responses
- Take our time to do things perfectly
- Create products for our customers to enjoy

Service:

- Reliable
- Responsive
- Assurance
- Empathize
- We love to be there for our customers and would like them to benefit from our products.

All I can add is you cannot have a true quality company without a united vision of pride in your product and your company.

—*Kelly Rose, Owner, Spa Blends*

(continued)

(continued)

Quality is measured by customer satisfaction. The price ticket on the service or treatment and the hard cost of the treatment do not dictate the quality of the treatment. I have been to the most expensive spas for treatments and some smaller, lower-cost spas. I measured the quality of the experience by how personable and friendly the staff was, how well the technician performed and explained the procedures, how much effort was made to make me feel "special" and the level of expertise the technician showed me.

— *Andy R. Jones, President, JOQ Day Spa for Men*

We measure quality two-fold. First, and most obvious, is the quality of our products. All of our products are carefully manufactured using high-grade botanicals and ingredients. Each product goes through intensive quality assurance tests before being released from production. We also measure quality in terms of our customer satisfaction. A great product is only a part of the equation. Providing our customers with superior customer service before and after they receive our products is the other part of Get Fresh quality equation.

— *Jacquelyn Overcash, President, Get Fresh*

Source: *Pulse*, Jan./Feb. 2005

Spas in the United States have grown tremendously over the past ten years. From 1999 to 2006, the spa industry grew by an average of 1,600 locations per year, according to the ISPA 2007 Spa Industry Study. However, that spa growth should not give a spa operator a false sense of insulation from the laws of supply and demand. Spas that fail to provide consistently engaging experiences or overprice the experience relative to the perceived value by the spa-goer will ultimately lose market share to other spa facilities entering the market. Of course, price also plays an important part in how a spa experience is evaluated, because spa treatments can be expensive and thus amplify guest expectations. When guests pay more for a service, they expect more in return. The amenities and environment must support the prices paid.

The expectation for service at a spa is tied to the expectation of the experience. From the beginning, spas existed for purposes other than providing a service in exchange for money. Spas were and are about health and wellness. Spa staff in quality spas are committed to providing an experience that promotes the health and welfare of the guest in mind, body, and spirit. Spa service providers carry an extra layer of responsibility when it comes to service. Not only must they create memorable experiences, but they must also care for guests and help enrich their lives.

One approach to the service experience is to look at it as *a performance directed at satisfying the needs of guests.* Compare what guests experience in a spa to what they experience in a theater. In a theater, the audience or theater guest sees only what happens on stage. In this way, spa employees can be compared to actors on a stage who are expected to perform according to the standards of the script in a way

Guests often come with unarticulated expectations about what a spa experience will be. This can make the provision of good service a challenge.

that the audience—or guests—expect them to act, not the way they may feel like acting. In live theater, audience members play an active role in that the energy they bring to the theater can affect the quality of the performance. So too, the spa guest's active participation in the spa service means that the quality of the physical and emotional response will be deeply affected by their participation in the service.

While good service is often defined as "meeting guest needs in the way that they want and expect them to be met," spa guests often do not know what they want or what to expect. This is particularly true of first-time or new spa-goers who have had their expectations set by magazine articles, friends, or television feature stories. The expectations they have might be for an experience very different than what a particular spa typically provides. This can make the provision of good service a challenge. Some spas now book time instead of specific treatments so that the therapist can consult with the guest on what treatments would be best to help the guest reach his or her goals. The treatments would then be chosen together to help meet those goals.

While spas can stage guest experiences and manage all the details the way a director would a show, they must be wary of some of the same traps that theatrical directors fight against. How does an acting troupe ensure that each performance is as fresh and compelling for each audience as it was the first time they read and spoke the words? How do they keep it from losing its passion? Likewise, spa experiences that are carefully scripted run the risk that they will lack authenticity. If the actors and spa employees don't believe in the words that they are speaking, it

Exhibit 1   Maslow's Hierarchy of Needs

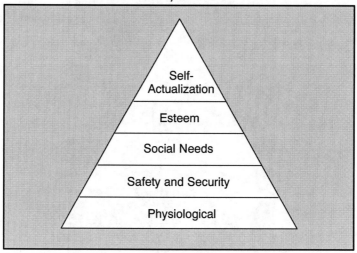

becomes an immediate turn-off. Think of the greeting in a restaurant when a server arrives at the table saying, "Good evening, my name is Justin and I will be your server this evening." It can come across as authentic or as stilted and rehearsed; it all depends on the delivery.

Also, just as a room full of people all experience the same play, it is inevitable that some will say it was outstanding while others will say it was poor. In a spa, individuals have their own expectations and each comes with unique baggage. Likewise, an individual's chemistry with spa staff varies. Some people may offer feedback with praises for a particular staff member while another guest may complain that the same staff member is intrusive or too bubbly. Providing the best experience is seldom a one-size-fits-all undertaking and it emphasizes the importance of finding out what the client needs at the particular time of the visit—which can also vary from visit to visit for the same client.

Today's experienced spa-goer is well traveled and savvy and will instantly see through artificial communication and experiences. They will greet with skepticism a claim that a jar of night cream will take years off their appearance—they simply know better. If the therapist asks the same old question, "Is there anything specific you want me to work on today?" the experience may seem staged. The goal is for the guest to experience authentic communication with the employees of the spa in a way that distinguishes one experience from another and that develops a sense of genuine care and a long-term relationship.

How guests feel when they have a spa experience also makes a difference in whether they will return and in whether a spa is successfully fulfilling its purpose. Spas can help provide healing and regeneration, but to do so, guests must have transformative experiences that take them to the peak of Maslow's Hierarchy of Needs (see Exhibit 1).

There are several critical **touchpoints** in the spa experience. Each stage is experienced slightly differently depending on whether the spa-goer is a **periphery**

reflections

Jana Westerbeke: Being Committed to Extraordinary Service

Jana Westerbeke is the vice president of operations and director of guest relations at Gad-about SalonSpas. In June 2008, she won a Global Entrepreneurial Excellence Award for Salon Leadership at the 2008 Global Salon Business Awards. She and her husband, Frank, were selected for "rising above expectations, delivering exceptional service and an impeccable product to guests, exhibiting integrity to both staff and guests, and sustaining a loyal following and a prosperous business."

Extraordinary service is what we're always trying to reach for. There are very few times in my life that I have experienced extraordinary service.

As a team, we are constantly trying to find what is going to propel us and take us to the next place. We look for how our guests are going to feel like they are enveloped in extraordinary service from the time they walk in to the door until the time they leave.

I think extraordinary service is absolutely a work in progress—at least in our company in our industry at this time, when you're dealing with so many different types of employees and teammates and technicians from attendants to guest service representatives. Each person has to evolve to their own level of exceptional service. The hardest thing is to get everyone to understand what that vision is. Every day we keep adding to what that looks like for us. Are we there? Absolutely not. Do we strive for it? Absolutely.

---

spa-goer (someone who is a first-timer or an infrequent user of spas), **mid-level spa-goer** (someone who uses spa services occasionally but for whom spas are not a part of their regular lifestyle), or a **core spa-goer** who embraces the spa lifestyle and is an advocate for spas.

Pre-Visit. Savvy spa professionals know that the consumer experience begins the moment a potential guest learns about the spa opportunity. It could be when the guest calls the spa to set up an appointment. It is critical for all spas to make new and repeat guests feel special. Guests don't expect or desire the kind of phone reception they get at a car dealership. The reservation call should reflect the mood expected by guests in their spa experiences: calm, soothing, and peaceful, because these emotional cues symbolize the indulgence guests expect at the spa. The spa professionals who take reservations must be knowledgeable, accurate, and polite. They should not leave people on hold, drop their calls, or be unable to answer guest questions—these create a stressful situation for the guest, not the calm, soothing one that a spa should be providing. Spa professionals should also treat e-mail reservations as if the person were standing in front of them. It is very helpful if the staff member who is taking reservations and phone calls has personally experienced a full range of spa treatments so that he or she is able to speak to guests from experience.

Spa guests will judge their experience by many touchpoints, including whether a spa is pleasing to the eye, clean, and well-organized.

Arrival and intake. Once guests get beyond the periphery of the spa world, assessing the operational smoothness and efficiency of the arrival process becomes important. The sheer, indulgent fun of being at a spa has worn off and the focus becomes more and more on work or escape. Although there is always room for personality variation, core spa-goers are much more likely than periphery spa-goers to write off a spa based on a poor arrival experience alone. Combined with a poor transition experience, these guests may never return and begin to spread negative buzz in their social network. When possible, first-time guests should be given a tour of the facility after they have been greeted and had a chance to consult with a service staff member.

Transitional moments. Guests will be more comfortable if they are accompanied from the registration desk to the men's or ladies' lounge and then greeted by an attendant. The area needs to be clean, with a place for guests to store their clothes. Donning the ritual costume—robes and slippers—becomes an important identifying factor for spas. Robes and slippers are often associated with the spa world in general and offering them can fulfill common expectations of the spa as a luxurious and indulgent experience. Mid-level and core guests also usually expect a sauna, steam room, or whirlpool and perhaps a cold plunge as an essential part of any body experience at a resort or destination spa. Whirlpools and mineral waters are desired prior to most spa treatments as they warm the body. At a day spa, guests may experience a foot bath before their treatment or be served water or tea.

The lounge area also says a lot to guests about what kind of spa they are in. It is a place where guests want to have a quiet, secluded feeling as they prepare for their spa treatment. It is also in this area that many spas will offer perks that are becoming increasingly expected by core guests. These include teas and herbal elixirs, foot soaks, foot massages, chaise lounge chairs for total recline and relaxation, and hot towels for the face.

It is often difficult for day spas to provide lounge areas. Many day spas rent the building that they are in and are under pressure to have as much space as possible generating revenue. Space at a day spa is often very tight. In these cases, spas must plan for how they can overcome these obstacles without compromising the spa experience.

Treatment. Truly experienced therapists have a knack for figuring out what is driving a particular consumer on a given occasion. Knowing what is bringing a guest to a spa on a particular day can help therapists customize their language and their treatment. Most spa-goers prefer the treatment room to be extremely quiet and secluded. Most prefer discussions on product to take place after the treatment. The treatment is the heart of the service experience. Therapists need to be focused on the guest and providing them with the best experience possible. Ideally when guests leave, they are feeling that they've just received the best treatment they've ever had.

Exiting. The more spa-goers seek transformation within the spa experience, the more valuable they find an exit transition that allows them to savor what has just happened. Abrupt return to street clothes and everyday life can easily kill the emotional benefits of treatments before they have had time to sink in. Many guests say they wish for a return to the lounge or to the sauna as a way to feel like they're not being dumped at the register. Who wants to think about money a few minutes after a glorious massage? Some spas have responded to this concern by either having guests sign the ticket before the service or signing their credit card slip before entering the treatment room. Retail sales are also part of the exiting experience and can be used to encourage guests to extend their experience into their daily home life.

Intangible Services Versus Tangible Products

Management experts long ago learned that there are fundamental differences between the way that service businesses manage and market their services and the way that manufacturing businesses manage and market their products. Spas, which deal in **intangibles** such as comfort, rejuvenation, renewal, and restoration, have very different management and marketing challenges than do businesses that create tangible products such as automobiles or laptop computers.

Management expert Christopher H. Lovelock identified these differences:

- The nature of the product is different.
- Guests are more involved in the production process.
- People are part of the product.
- It's harder to maintain quality control standards.
- The services provided can't be inventoried.
- The time factor is more important.
- Distribution channels are different.

The next few sections will look at each of these differences in detail and what they mean in a spa setting. It will then take a look at how spas can respond to the differences between tangible products and intangible services to get the best results.[1]

The Nature of the Product

Manufactured goods are tangible products. We can pick them up, look at them, study them, carry them around, or in some other way physically handle them. A service is a performance or process. Marketing a spa service, which may involve the use of physical objects and goods such as skin care and body treatment products, is quite a different thing from marketing the manufactured goods themselves.

In the 2006 ISPA Spa-Goer Study, respondents said the essential elements to their enjoyment of a spa experience were the following customer service aspects (see Exhibit 2):

- Availability of convenient treatment times
- Hospitality extended by the staff
- Appointment starting on time
- Expertise or credentials of the staff
- Gender of therapists available for the requested service
- Staff's ability to recognize their knowledge about spa treatments
- Tipping policy

When asked what products—amenities and features—were most essential to their enjoyment of the spa, the number one answer was the atmosphere and ambience in the spa, followed by the ability to stay after the treatment and continue to relax. See Exhibit 3 for a complete breakdown.

Guests aren't purchasing the service/treatment room as they would purchase a hotel room and they aren't necessarily purchasing the products that are used on them during the service/treatment. They are purchasing the performance of service, the experience, and its benefits, something qualitative and intangible. However, what they are really purchasing is the experience and the benefits they get from that experience, whether it is a massage, a facial, or a nail service. Spas must manage the production of these services as well as the professional products used during the service, and must guide potential guests to select these intangible things (services) that best suit them—things that the spa may not be able to show them a picture of or even, in some cases, adequately describe. What can help is having front desk staff and web programmers who know the benefits and results of spa treatments on a firsthand basis and who can communicate their own enthusiasm to prospective guests.

The Guest's Role in Production

Guests have little involvement in the production of manufactured goods. A cell phone is produced and packaged at a factory and purchased by a consumer at an electronics store or distributor. The people who make the cell phone never see those who use it, and the ones who use it don't go to the factory when they want

Exhibit 2   Which Aspects of Customer Service Are Essential to Your Enjoyment of a Spa Experience (At the Type of Spa You Last Visited)?

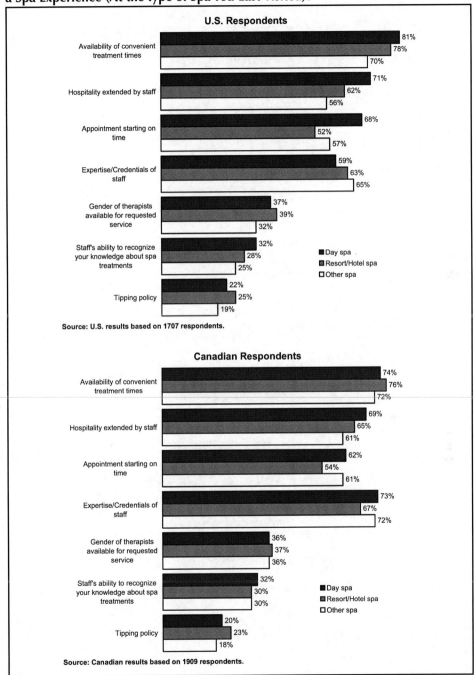

U.S. Respondents

Availability of convenient treatment times — 81% / 78% / 70%

Hospitality extended by staff — 71% / 62% / 56%

Appointment starting on time — 68% / 52% / 57%

Expertise/Credentials of staff — 59% / 63% / 65%

Gender of therapists available for requested service — 37% / 39% / 32%

Staff's ability to recognize your knowledge about spa treatments — 32% / 28% / 25%

Tipping policy — 22% / 25% / 19%

■ Day spa
▨ Resort/Hotel spa
☐ Other spa

Source: U.S. results based on 1707 respondents.

Canadian Respondents

Availability of convenient treatment times — 74% / 76% / 72%

Hospitality extended by staff — 69% / 65% / 61%

Appointment starting on time — 62% / 54% / 61%

Expertise/Credentials of staff — 73% / 67% / 72%

Gender of therapists available for requested service — 36% / 37% / 36%

Staff's ability to recognize your knowledge about spa treatments — 32% / 30% / 30%

Tipping policy — 20% / 23% / 18%

■ Day spa
▨ Resort/Hotel spa
☐ Other spa

Source: Canadian results based on 1909 respondents.

Source: ISPA 2006 Spa-Goer Survey

Exhibit 3 Which Amenities and Features Are Essential to Your Enjoyment of a Spa Experience (At the Type of Spa You Last Visited)?

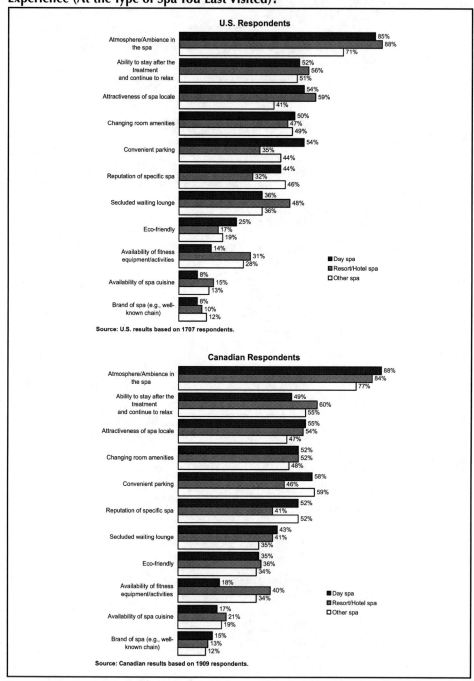

Source: ISPA 2006 Spa-Goer Survey

to make a phone call. The two activities of production and consumption are completely separate. This is not true in a service-based business. In a spa, the guest participates in the creation of the product ('the service') and there is considerable interaction between the consumer and the provider—a task that a manager of manufactured goods never has to face.

Therapists can immediately change a service based on the needs of the client—product producers can't. For example, a therapist may give two separate clients a Swedish massage with the same amount of pressure for each guest. The first guest may have loved the treatment and felt the pressure was just right. The second guest may have felt the pressure was too light and wanted something deeper to work out the knots in his back. If you purchase a mop at the store, it is yours and if you don't like it, you can return it or buy another one. You can't tell the mop you want more scrubbing power on the floor and expect it to respond. Nor is it likely you would get much of a response if you went to the manufacturer and said that you want more pressure. In the case of a massage, you can tell the therapist, "I'd like more pressure, please." Or you can say nothing and leave feeling you didn't get your money's worth—and you can't "return" an experience the way you can a mop.

It is worth noting that service businesses have begun to influence manufacturing businesses. Customization has started to occur even in mass production environments. Dell will build computers to their customers' specific needs. There is even a blue jean company where customers get measured and custom jeans are sent to them. However, these are exceptions—exceptions built around the service business model.

People Are Part of the Product

In a service business like a spa, guests not only come in contact with staff members but with other guests. That makes the other guests a part of the experience and often defines the quality of the service. Have you ever been to a movie or play where the people around you wouldn't keep quiet or had their cell phone go off and spoiled some of your enjoyment? What about a restaurant where you went for a quiet romantic evening and there was a party of 12 loud people at the next table celebrating someone's birthday? A spa guest who is looking for a quiet, rejuvenating experience may get annoyed with a group of bridal party members chattering excitedly with each other in the relaxation room. A guest sitting with her feet in warm water while looking at a magazine in the relaxation room might have her peace shattered by someone else's cell phone conversation. Another guest might be starting to enjoy a facial when the hair dryer in the adjoining salon starts up and the stylist and guest start speaking loudly over it.

Spa professionals must be prepared to respond to guests who disturb the experiences of others. When such things are anticipated, they can come up with possible solutions that will mitigate the effects one guest can have on another. Good management will ensure that such things are planned for and not left to chance.

In short, all of the people with whom a guest comes in contact, both other guests and employees, are an integral part of the service product and the overall experience. They often are the main difference in the quality of the experience one spa provides over another.

reflections

John Lopis: Spa Experiences Are Personal

John Lopis is the co-founder of JGL, a spa design, development, and management team in the United States. He has held top management positions at several of the finest resorts in the country. He and his wife, Ginny, launched the Doral Saturnia International Spa Resort in Miami and were directors at Canyon Ranch Vacation/Fitness Resort in Arizona.

Being involved in spas is an invitation to make what we do with our lives professionally an expression of what we do with our lives personally.

We find on a day-to-day basis when we try to create program experiences and when we talk with our guests, that it is a very authentic connection. The reason people come to the spa, especially a destination spa, is to ask questions and to have insight into their answers. That's the reason that I come to the spa every day. Our guests are so often my teachers, because they express themselves so openly. They do it because they're looking for support and nurturing, so we share that.

When you come as an individual for a healing moment and you are in the company of others who share that, you see the real power of the spa. There is a collective healing that happens. I get very passionate about the idea of spa and its opportunity of bringing us together and creating a healing environment where each of us embraces the other.

There's a very interesting paradox with appropriate selfishness. We go around and meet all of our guests each day. We are receiving so much of the reward because they are so thankful they have a place where they can come and step out of the intensity of their daily life. Immediately they are thanking you. It's a very appropriate selfishness that we go around and get nurtured by our guests.

There's a shift in spas toward higher consciousness, to a connectedness and an identity with our being. The awakening opportunity is to take a moment when you slow down and in that stillness and in the quiet you discover things about yourself and others that are shared. We felt that is important to do in a very natural way because it is a very personal thing. What we have done for many years—and what spa does really well—is to create opportunity. Many people go through the same experience and opportunity and take different things with them and discover different things because their readiness for what is important for them to learn is personal.

We had a gentleman who stayed in his robe for three days. When does he get to do that? We had another guy extend his stay because he wanted to read two more chapters in his book. He knew if he went home, he'd never finish the book. He said, "I have a book by my nightstand, I read a few pages, get sleepy, fall asleep, and I realize I don't really know what the book is all about." He said he was loving the spa experience because it was such a gift to be able to sit and read a book.

To add another layer of complexity, the individual guests are also a key contributor to what type of experiences they have. Not only can other guests distract them, but they are also capable of distracting themselves. In order to receive the benefits of many services—in particular energy work, movement work, and meditation—guests must be receptive and open to the experience. They have to be able to set aside their own distractions to reach a meditative state.

Maintaining Quality Control

When a factory produces a product, the product can be inspected for quality before it goes out the door. As long as proper quality control procedures and inspections are in place, defective products are not delivered. But services, like other live performances, take place in real time. That means that expectations are not always going to be met.

There is also the challenge that quality is subjective and unique for each person and for each moment in time. A guest may schedule a massage in January and arrive feeling exhausted and needing a relaxing, out-of-this-world escape. In February, the same guest may go to the same therapist, but this time have gotten off work early after getting news that she's just gotten a raise. This time she is arriving ready to celebrate and reward herself with a massage. She is the same guest at the same spa with the same therapist but with two mindsets. She's expecting two different things. She wants to relax or sleep in January and in February, she wants to rejoice and keep that feeling of "I can conquer the world." If the therapist is not in tune with that, then the quality and the guest's expectations may not be met.

Also, most services in spas are provided to guests in privacy where there can be little to no direct supervision of the people providing the service. It is rarely possible to inspect the work done by spa staff. Managers who want to maintain quality control often have to rely on guest comment cards and feedback in order to "inspect" the quality of work. This is another reason why spas need to offer continuing education and training.

Perishable Inventories

Manufacturers can inventory their products in warehouses until they are needed. But because services are live performances, they cannot be made in advance or stored for future use. That means that at 5 o'clock on a Friday afternoon, a spa cannot sell the use of a treatment room that was empty at 3 P.M.. The inventory of treatment rooms, like the inventory of hotel rooms or airplane seats, vanishes every hour in the case of a spa and every day in the case of a hotel. Spas also need a trained therapist or technician to make it happen. Few spas can afford to keep a pool of therapists in the back waiting for customers to come—it is too expensive to pay the therapists to sit around and wait. Guests must be turned away from spas that are fully booked or that don't have enough technicians scheduled to fully utilize every treatment room.

Many service businesses, such as hotels and airlines, use revenue and yield management techniques as a way of capturing income that would otherwise be lost to perishable inventories. This is still a fairly new concept for spas, but one that many are adopting, especially as the technology becomes available to facilitate it. Spas are finding that they can change the price of a service at a higher demand time or close off services that have a lower margin.

The Importance of Time

Because spa services are delivered where they are created, guests have to be present to receive them. When guests are present, they expect the service to be performed "on time," which in their minds means "when they want it."

Time becomes an especially important element in spas because of the emphasis on renewal and relaxing. Guests are often seeking the experience of being taken out of time. They want to be able to leave behind the cares of the outside world and relieve the stresses that accompany it. This doesn't mean that they are willing to sit in a waiting room unattended. They still want to be greeted and escorted to a spot where they can begin their spa experience. Spa staff must devise strategies to keep guests from feeling that during their pre-treatment time they are being ignored or that they are not important, while balancing the need to give them their privacy and alone time.

Time, space, and rhythms are elements of the spa experience (along with waters, nourishment, movement, touch, integration, esthetics, environment, cultural expression, and social contribution). Spas facilitate the perception of space and time and their relationships to the natural cycles and rhythms of life. Historically, people would spend weeks at a spa, concentrating on their health. Spas set the stage for the body to do its own healing. Some treatments can't be rushed because they are about getting in tune with the body's natural rhythms.

Spas have a role in sensitizing people about time, emphasizing that healthy living does not involve simply packing more things into less time, but in taking time to breathe, to live, and to connect with self, nature, and community.

Different Distribution Channels

Companies that manufacture goods move their products from the factory by trucks, trains, or airplanes to wholesalers, distributors, or retailers, who then resell them to the ultimate consumer. This is not the case with service companies, where guests come right into the spa or contact it directly. For instance, spa guests may make reservations via the Internet, by phone, or by walking up to the reception desk. Spas must train their employees to handle the marketing function of dealing with guests. Employees who manufacture goods do not for the most part require those skills. Even when intermediaries are involved (such as a concierge for a hotel with a spa), transferring a service to a guest requires more people skills than transferring a physical product from factory to warehouse to retail store.

Creating an Experience

While spas are a service business by classic definition, consumers today want more than just services. Now, consumers are looking for an experience that is memorable and lasting.

In *The Experience Economy* by Joseph Pine and James Gilmore, the authors call upon the economics of coffee as an illustration of how customer demands have evolved. At first, consumers wanted to purchase the product of a coffee bean. They would go to a supermarket or grocery store and buy a can of coffee beans. This evolved to where they wanted to go into a donut shop or a local restaurant and be

Spa Snapshot: How do you adapt your spa's business hours to accommodate the needs of your clientele?

The Spa at Laguna Cliffs constantly changes our 12-hour service day to accommodate any guest or group that may wish to use our facility. We recognize that there are many places out there that our guests can choose from and the fact that they wish to spend their time with us makes us feel honored, so we will flex and bend any way we can. We have performed treatments as early as 6 A.M. and as late as 9 P.M. before and have noticed that these guests will generally come back to us as they feel that we are more accommodating to their needs than other spas in the area, which is a huge benefit.

—*Jane Lohmann, Spa Director, The Spa at Laguna Cliffs Marriott Resort*

Mission Hills has a wide range of visitors—the golf club members, property owners and residents, hotel guests, corporate retreats, etc. Since all have different activities and schedules during the daytime, Mission Hills Spa is running flexible hours from 10 A.M. to 1 A.M., which are appropriate to the demand and needs of our visitors. We see this more as a benefit than a challenge. Long operating hours guarantee good accessibility of our services, and it has been proven that it brings convenience to our visitors, too.

—*Peggy Liong, General Manager, Mission Hills Spa, Shenzhen, China*

As a resort, our guest business is 60 percent leisure and 40 percent group. Many of the groups that visit are traveling from the East and are on an East/Midwest time clock. Hence, we receive many requests for opening as early as 5 A.M. We have found that we have been able to increase our revenue by opening early at their request; the activity is not only in spa services but also in the salon and retail shop as well. These groups are planned well in advance, sometimes one to three years lead time, so internally, scheduling staff is not so difficult. As a rule, we are delighted to alter our operational hours for a group with advance notice. I believe that in the hospitality industry, the customer is expecting the flexibility to accommodate them and provide them an exceptional experience. It goes a long way in creating a reputation as a world-class spa.

—*Bruce A. Taylor, CHA, Director of Spa Operations, Marriott Desert Springs, a JW Resort Spa*

At the Ocean Tides Spa located in The Hilton Oceanfront Resort, our hours are 9 A.M. until 5 P.M., seven days a week. Since we receive a lot of

(continued)

(continued)

executive travel and tourists who drive in, we offer in-room massage after business hours. This enables business guests and late-arriving travelers to receive a massage in the evenings. It is a great way to satisfy the hotel guests' needs while increasing revenue with no extra expense to us.

—Brandi Byrd-Lavertu, Spa Director, The Hilton Oceanfront Resort

Every aspect of SenSpa's services is geared toward busy, career-minded urbanites that are on the go and want to make the most of their time. While SenSpa is closed on Mondays, we decided to expand our reservation desk hours to this day when we noticed how many of our guests like to kick off their week by making appointments. We have also extended weekday hours until 9 P.M. and weekend hours starting at 9 A.M. to accommodate the active lifestyles of people who live in the Bay Area. The strategy has paid off with a consistently full calendar of bookings during these time slots.

—Randy Schreck, President & General Manager, SenSpa

Source: *Pulse*, Jan./Feb. 2007

served a cup of coffee. Now they were purchasing not just the coffee bean itself, but the service of receiving the cup of coffee. Then came the wave of coffee shops that sold not just coffee or the service, but an entire experience in which the barista had artistic leeway and a particular mood was created in the shop.

Similar evolutions from goods to service to experiences are happening all over and are of particular importance for the spa world.

A spa creates an experience that completely involves the guest. What distinguishes a service from an experience? When a person purchases a service, he or she buys a set of intangible activities carried out on his or her behalf. With an experience, the person is immersed in memorable events that engage the guest in a personal way.

Consider again the coffee bean. The people who harvest the beans and sell them to the market are providing a **commodity** and contribute a few pennies to a cup of coffee. The company that roasts, grinds, packages the beans, and sells them to a grocery store turns the commodity into a **good**. This increases the price anywhere from five to 20 cents per cup. Then a local diner or small-town coffee shop brews and serves the coffee, where it now costs a dollar or two. But when that same cup of coffee is surrounded by a five-star dining experience or served by a barista at a local coffee house, that cup of coffee may cost five dollars or more.

A massage should not be a commodity. A facial should not be a commodity. The very core of these spa services is the experience that they provide to guests. Guests want not only a service that produces a benefit, but an experience that they will remember and that can perhaps have a positive effect on their lifestyle.

The concept of creating an experience isn't unique to spas. It's an idea adopted by many service businesses that understand that their **unique selling**

Customer perception of coffee and what they are willing to pay for it varies greatly on whether it is the commodity of the bean, the roasted beans that are a good, the delivery of a hot cup of coffee as a service, or the experience of a barista in a coffee house.

proposition comes from creating memorable experiences more than from providing a service alone.

Restaurants such as Hard Rock Café and the House of Blues are a perfect example of a business that capitalized on the experience it provided with its service. They decorate around a theme and create an environment and service styles that are about more than just consuming food.

In spas, the idea of an experience is often taken a step further. Many of the core spa-goers who are savvy about the experiences that they can receive at a spa, don't just want an experience. They want a *unique* experience. They want an experience that they cannot get anywhere else. They want to be able to tell their friends and acquaintances a story about their experience that is different from what anyone else has experienced.

The pioneer and classic example of an "experience economy" is the Walt Disney Company. It delivers superior service consistently. It is the attention to each and every small detail that creates a memorable experience for its guests. It is built around Disney's four basic service priorities: *safety, courtesy, show,* and *efficiency.*

However, the service that Disney provides—like the service that any business provides—disappears as soon as it is performed. What lasts is the guest's memory of the experience. Families do not experience Disney World just for the event of being there for the day. They experience it because they are able to tell stories and share the experience with one another for as long the memories linger. Likewise,

Guests want unique experiences such as this six-handed massage on a beach in Bali, Indonesia.

people who visit a spa hope that the spa experience will lift their spirit and that the uplifting will linger in their memories until their next visit.

The orchestration of the complete spa experience is as important for each individual spa as it is for the entire Disney conglomerate. An engaging environment must be created to alter guests' sense of reality and move them from the mundane stresses of everyday life to something extraordinary. The spa assists guests on a journey to a place suffused with tranquility and harmony, aiding them in forming indelible impressions that are the point of distinction for the spa experience.

While all businesses, including spas, are measured by the revenue they generate and the payroll and cost controls that are in place to maximize profitability, a spa is not a place where a commodity or good is simply pulled from the shelf and sold to the customer. In a spa, the guest **experience** is the product. Each sale is personalized for the specific needs of the guest and guests will immerse themselves in the experience. ISPA defines the spa experience as "your time to relax, reflect, revitalize, and rejoice." The key words in that definition are "your time"—meaning it is unique to each person.

A danger arises when the focus of a spa is only on the business of spa, increasing revenue by price increases and measuring success on retail sales per treatment or on reducing payroll and operating expenses. That spa is traveling down the road of *commoditization* of the spa experience, leaving the spa able to compete based only on price and eliminating those distinctions that create a loyal guest following.

While advertising is essential to creating awareness and sampling in the marketplace, it is also worth noting that one of the strongest brands today, Starbucks, spent only $10 million in advertising between 1987 and 1998. Howard Schultz recognized early on that great experiences are worth much more than an extensive marketing campaign. In his autobiography, *Pour Your Heart Into It*, he writes, "What we've done is we've said that the most important component in our brand is the employee. The people have created the magic. The people have created the experiences."

reflections

Pam McNair: Creating an Experience

Pam McNair, the founder of Gadabout SalonSpas, is a visionary and one of the early day spa pioneers. She owns seven spas in the Tucson, Arizona area and one in Italy.

When I came to this market, I recognized two things that were not happening that were primary for me. One, no one was advertising or marketing in the community visually, and two, no one was educating their staff.

People were very grateful to their clients, but they weren't exuding that kind of gratitude. For the first three months we were open, we delivered a rose to each of our clients. If they didn't want to give us their address, we hand-delivered it to them in the spa. Otherwise, we would drive in our automobile to their address and deliver a rose to them within a two-day period. I had such a response from people who had never had a facility or a business give them a flower.

That was the beginning of showing gratitude to our clients, because without them, anything we wanted to do was moot. On the first anniversary (of the men's spa), we gave out 23,000 roses to clients. When we had our 25th anniversary (of Gadabout), we did it through the whole company. In the first six-week period of the year—six weeks is the cycle that most of our clients use—we gave them a rose. We've kept that tradition going because of the response we got from the initial clients.

If ever there was an industry that relies extensively on its employees, it would be the spa industry. Each and every treatment commits a minimum of one employee to every single customer, plus all of the support staff at the reception desk, locker attendants, and so on. Even in a small day spa and salon, each guest receives the full attention of a service provider working on his or her specific needs.

The Spa at the Montage Resort in Laguna, California, offers evidence of the importance of the spa staff. The *Mobil Travel Guide* began inspecting spas in 2004 as an addition to its long-standing rating of hotels and resorts. In 2005, the Montage was the first spa awarded the Mobil Five Star rating. While the property is blessed with an idyllic setting on a bluff overlooking the Pacific Ocean, it was the extraordinary service delivered by the therapists and staff that distinguished the spa as the best in America.

Realms of Experience

In *Experience Economy* by B. Joseph Pine and James H. Gilmore, the authors explain that an experience can engage guests in a number of dimensions. An experience might be passive where guests do not directly affect or influence the experience, such as attending a movie or any pre-recorded experience. The experience can also be one in which the guest personally affects the experience, such as kayaking through white water rapids on the Colorado river or attending a live performance where the performers are affected by the audience response. Additionally, the

---

Changing People's Lives

Spas aren't just about a moment's pampering or a temporary escape. Spas have the power and ability to change people's lives in real and permanent ways.

Several years ago, a guest arrived at the PGA National Resort and Spa in Florida. He was a writer for *Golf Digest* but had not been able to play a round of golf for several years. He had so much back pain that he wore a belt that provided electronic stimulation on his back.

Pete Egoscue, one of the spa's professionals who ran a postural clinic, was an advocate for the belief that most people are out of alignment because of their lifestyles—whether it is sitting at a computer, driving a car, or working at a desk. Based on his research and his own injuries suffered during the Vietnam War, he developed a treatment to realign people's bodies.

The guest arrived interested in the treatment and whether it could help him. He'd already seen chiropractors, acupuncturists, and numerous doctors, many of whom had recommended surgery.

Egoscue set up pictures around the person and then said, "I bet that if your pain is more intense, it is on your lower left side."

"How did you know that?" the guest responded. For Egoscue, it was a matter of listening to what the guest's body was saying and looking at his alignment. For three days, Egoscue worked with the guest every day on a series of stretching and alignment exercises. At the end of the three days, not only did the guest play a round of golf, but he played 18 holes of golf without his belt and then went out and played the next day as well.

That's the power of spa. That's the purposeful side that elevates a spa from having a mission of selling massages, facials, and retail products to one where it has an opportunity to make a difference in people's lives. That's the real future of spa.

---

experience spectrum can be shallow where the guest absorbs an event happening before them to the other end of the spectrum where the guest is immersed and becomes physically a part of the experience itself.

These continuums—passive to active, and shallow to full immersion—yield the four realms of an experience:

- Entertainment

- Education

- Escape

- Estheticism

A successful spa professional can orchestrate each of these four realms to achieve a memorable spa experience.

Entertainment

Not all entertainment experiences are things like laughing at a joke while at a comedy club or listening to a symphony concert. The *Oxford English Dictionary* defines entertainment as "the action of occupying a person's attention agreeably."

In a spa experience, the entertainment is accomplished by such things as:

- Carefully designing the ambience of the spa with peaceful soothing music playing in the background throughout the experience
- Possibly incorporating music that changes as guests move between areas, with the treatment rooms having music the guest has personally selected
- Beautiful aromas from candles or essential oil diffusers creating a delicious olfactory sense of well-being
- Carefully planned soft lighting
- Water features with streams of water gently moving down their surfaces
- Soft and embracing colors used throughout the décor

These elements can create a sense of calm and individual tranquility as the guest begins the spa experience.

Education

Education isn't simply a teacher lecturing in a classroom. As people continue to research educational theory, education has increasingly been focused on engaging the student or learner in the process as an active participant. This is true in the spa as well as the classroom.

How does a spa educate its guests? Consider a personal training session in a spa fitness facility where the personal trainer observes the guest while working out and discusses his or her current workout program. The trainer might participate with the guest in suggesting improvements to his or her regimen or recommending a new fitness activity such as yoga or Pilates.

Destination spas and some resort spas include education as a core value, whether it is a medical or nutritional evaluation or an evening class on subjects ranging from stress reduction techniques to art classes, from meditation to spa cuisine cooking.

However, a spa does not have to be a destination spa to include education as part of the experience. A hairdresser discusses the guest's hairstyle or color and gives the guest a fresh new look and tips on how to style it at home. An esthetician informs guests about the products he or she used during the facial. The discussion may go beyond that to a discussion about the guests' skin type and issues observed during the facial. He or she might recommend modifications and products for the guest's daily skin care program. Education happens when a spa offers a session with a lifestyle counselor to review issues in the guest's life and make suggestions to improve the overall well-being of the guest.

It is important to capitalize on the various opportunities for education within a spa as it increases the value for the price paid and engages the guest with the spa experience.

Escape

A spa is often marketed as an escape from the hectic world. It's a place where guests leave their cell phones, BlackBerries, and iPhones in their lockers, take off

reflections

Ginny Lopis: Creating a Place Where Everyone Learns Together

Ginny Lopis is the co-founder of JGL, a spa design, development, and management team in the United States. She has held top management positions at several of the finest resorts in the country. She and her husband, John, launched the Doral Saturnia International Spa Resort in Miami and were directors at Canyon Ranch Vacation/Fitness Resort in Arizona.

I see spas as nurturing environments—very gentle, caring, and sensitive environments—that offer a collection of life-enhancing, inspiring, and educational experiences that can improve people's lives. I think we're going to see the word spa expand into the personal growth and self-awareness domain even further as we go forward into the next couple of decades.

It comes from ownership and management. It comes from a place of authentic desire to grow personally in ownership and management. The most powerful spa experiences will always be driven by people who created them so they could themselves grow and expand and be part of that experience. That is a really critical reason why John and I wanted to create a place for ourselves to grow and to learn and to have access to these resources. The original intent was that we wanted to share it with other people. To this day, we see ourselves as sharing the journey, rather than presenting it or teaching it or providing it. It's really about sharing it ourselves. I think that is the path to authenticity: Caring personally about it so that it comes from your heart, not just a business model.

---

their clothes, and wrap themselves in a luxurious robe to move from everyday life to a sanctuary of tranquility where the only person who matters is themselves. Guests subconsciously wash the cares of life away while soaking in a whirlpool or sweat away life's challenges while sitting in a sauna or steam room. They then might curl up on a soft sofa or chaise lounge with a glass of herbal tea, closing their eyes and transporting themselves to 'the spa world' where they have broken contact with constant interruptions. They escape into a world where they become the center of the universe within themselves. Then the guests are personally escorted by their therapist to the inner sanctum of the spa where the treatment focuses only on them.

At a day spa, guests may not be able to escape in as complete a manner, but they are still exiting the daily bustle of the world and entering a place where they can focus on themselves and their needs, whether for an hour, two hours, or an entire day. They enter a building that is designed to be peaceful, relaxing, and harmonious.

Escape is a key element of the spa experience for most spa-goers who are not using spa services as an end to therapeutic goals. Spas provide one of the few service venues in modern American life where a sense of escape from the social and other demands of everyday life becomes possible.

Modern media are filled with examples of escape experiences. Commercials promote the person strolling down the pavement absorbed in the music from her iPod. They depict people riding a virtual tour of another planet in a theme park attraction. But none of these experiences compares with the spa escape, where the guest is transported to a warm, embracing, aromatic experience where he or she is the feature of the event.

Many experienced spa-goers are looking for as complete a separation from the rest of the world as possible. This means no interruptions, no pager beeps or cell phone ring tones, no chatter from the therapist, no noises in the hallways or waiting rooms, no sounds from adjacent treatment rooms, etc.

The treatment room, in particular, is where spas create this rare sense of escape and where guests feel it most powerfully. Even when accompanying friends or family to a spa, the treatment room still separates consumers out for a private, hidden journey, guided by their therapist. It also is responsible for the most primal feeling of vulnerability among first timers. Although first time guests don't want hand-holding or excessive chattiness in order to make them feel less vulnerable, they do most likely want some acknowledgement of empathy and concern for their comfort. Other spa-goers increasingly want their therapists to do their work unobtrusively, allowing them to feel holistic escape from the everyday. Others want a truly calm environment in which to allow for emotional healing. Chatty conversation only threatens to bring the everyday back into the treatment room. Communication should always be minimized to the necessary in order to make the treatment effective and comfortable.

Esthetics

Many experiences are memorable because of esthetic appeal. These can include standing on the observation deck at Niagara Falls or on the rim of the Grand Canyon or visiting the Metropolitan Museum of Art. The observer is immersed in the environment and leaves with memories.

Some spas have awe-inspiring settings. The spa guest at the Ritz-Carlton Laguna Nigel can walk on a treadmill in front of a two-story glass wall overlooking the Pacific Ocean. Guests at the Mii Amo Spa can sit on the pool deck and gaze at the beauty of the rocks of Boynton Canyon near Sedona, Arizona.

Other spas manage to create an oasis of peace and harmony in the midst of an urban asphalt jungle. A guest can step in off a busy metropolitan street and be transported to a quiet place of beauty to receive a massage, a facial, a manicure, or a hair style.

For the most part, spa design connects the building with surrounding nature, but often without having the advantage of such awe-inspiring views. For this reason, the interior architecture and the overall esthetic design of the spa facility is critical to enhancing the spa experience. Design elements such as water features, gardens, artwork, and natural finishes can transport the guest from the everyday visual and allow them to reconnect with nature within the spa environment.

There will always be pressure by spa developers to "value engineer" (i.e., eliminate from the project in order to reduce construction costs) out of the design those "non-revenue-generating" spaces such as large, welcoming lobbies, generous relaxation spaces or expensive water features, but it is exactly those elements of a spa that will create the esthetic experience for the guest.

The setting in which a treatment takes place can have a huge effect on the type of experience a guest has. Having a massage on the beach with the sound of waves rolling in can be an esthetically pleasing experience for some guests.

Delivering on the Service Promise

The bottom line for spas is delivering on the promise that a spa makes to its owners, employees, and guests. It is easy enough to write a mission statement that says, "We intend to be a premier and progressive spa" or "Our goal is to deliver the most relaxing, uplifting experience of any spa in our class"—but how does each spa do it? What makes it really happen?

Guest Loyalty

It's a truism that the most profitable customers are the loyal customers. They purchase more, cost less to serve, refer others, and are willing to pay for receiving exactly the experience they want. Despite widespread knowledge of this truism, most companies invest more in acquiring new customers than they do in retaining the customers they have.

Investing in guest loyalty is an investment in profits. There is an oft-quoted business axiom that it costs six times more to acquire a new customer than it does to keep an existing customer. By investing a small percentage of revenue into strengthening the loyalty of existing customers, a spa can sustain profitability and in some cases make dramatic increases in revenue. However, some loyalty programs have not achieved the desired outcome. Grocery store loyalty cards have become so commonplace that they act today as price promotions and incentives

reflections

Thad Hyland: Delivering the Best Service Every Day

Thad Hyland is the managing director of the Ojai Valley Inn and Spa in Ojai, California. He led the property to earning the five diamond designation from the American Automobile Association (AAA).

We set the goal to give the best service. We wanted to be the best. We all signed a two-page commitment dedicating ourselves to the property regaining the (AAA) five diamond and dedicating ourselves to each other. You have to have a commitment to dedicating yourself to your weakest link: your trainees, your new folks.

We have a lot of employees who have been here 20 years. They have a lot to do with the culture. You have to have a strong culture and a strong sense of self and family in order to get a five diamond. There are 89 properties in the world with five diamonds out of 39,000 properties. That's a small percentage of excellence. There has to be a total commitment and a lot of heart and character goes into being a five diamond.

Every guest who comes in is new. They don't know you and you don't know them. Sometimes you have 48 hours to make them love you. You have to be impatient about the outcomes with the guests. We have great patience with our associates, but as far as our guest experiences, our guests need it and they need it now.

My advice to my associates is that it is a business of servitude and I say that in only the finest way. I tell my employees that I am proud to be a servant and those are some words they don't hear much nowadays. I am a servant in the best way. I've been one for 35 years and there is no more gratifying thing than serving other people, seven days a week, 24 hours a day at a hotel. There is no better calling than to take someone who is stressed out and calm them down and bring their life around to a whole different level. We treat them better than they've ever been treated anywhere else before. The outcomes for you as a business are absolutely amazing.

The repetition of doing something well is what makes you good. If you can't repeat a perfect performance every day, then you're not the maestro you thought you were. We're never perfect, but we're excellent here.

---

for customers to spend their grocery budget with whoever has the best price offerings. They do little to build loyalty. Airline frequent flier programs started off as loyalty programs, but now all major airlines have them. The generally uninspired service delivered along with the miles for many airlines is not achieving the mission of building loyalty.

Spas recognize the importance of repeat guests. Many will track their retention rate, which is determined by the percentage of a given day's or month's guests who have been to the spa before versus how many are first-time users. In *Customer Loyalty: How to Earn it, How to Keep it,* author Jill Griffin suggests a ladder of customer relationships that moves from prospect to a first-time customer to a repeat customer, but continues to two additional levels of loyalty: the client and the advocate.

In the spa world, the **prospect** is the consumer who is either unaware of the spa and its offerings or has yet to make up his or her mind about whether to purchase spa services. The spa is in the courting stage with prospects and must convince them that there is a reason to partake of spa services.

The **client** is a guest who buys everything the spa has to sell that he or she can possibly use. The client purchases regularly and over time the business builds a strong, ongoing relationship that makes the client immune to the pull of the competition.

The **advocate** is like a client in that he or she buys everything the spa has to sell that they can use. However, advocates also encourage others to buy from the spa. They talk about the spa, defend it when others raise objections, and bring new customers to experience it.

Only 15 to 20 years ago, a major metropolitan city might have had only one or two spas. Customers had few choices and repeat customers were probably assumed to be loyal clients. Today, however, there are many more choices. When clients find a spa that delivers a better experience, they are likely to become former clients instead of advocates. Even within the resort and destination spa markets, a specific spa's competition is not simply those properties that are in a close geographic proximity.

With the affluence of the average spa-goer (44 percent of U.S. spa-goers have a household income of $100,000 or higher with an additional 41 percent making between $50,000 and $99,000), each spa is now competing with the world of spas. It is no longer good enough to be the best spa in a served market. With the convenience of air travel, a guest can simply choose to get on a plane and fly over one resort at 30,000 feet and check into a spa that is delivering a better guest experience.

When asked how many spa visits they anticipate taking in the next 12 months, nearly two thirds of Canadian and U.S. spa-goers said they intend to take one or more trips to a spa. See Exhibit 4. The figures suggest that once a prospect is turned into a client, they are increasingly likely to make the journey from client to advocate.

Clearly, advocacy is not an event but a process. The relationship with the guest grows over time and must be built systematically. All spas conduct training and establish service standards and protocols. They must also design the experience to consistently deliver on the spa's brand promise. There are several assumptions that can be made before designing a spa experience:

Develop a brand promise. The brand promise needs to be well-developed and deeply ingrained in the spa's culture so that it cannot be separated from how the spa experience manifests itself. The brand promise is not simply a marketing slogan, but a core value or mission that is synonymous with the spa itself and cannot be torn apart by any competitor.

Recruit the right employees. Spas need to recruit and hire employees who have an attitude consistent with the spa's promise.

Provide the right resources. Employees need to have all the tools, knowledge, and skills required to deliver the promise day in and day out over time.

Exhibit 5 shows what sources of information spa-goers trust the most to help them decide which spas to visit.

Exhibit 4   Number of Visits Made to Spas in Past 12 Months and Expected to Make in Next 12 Months

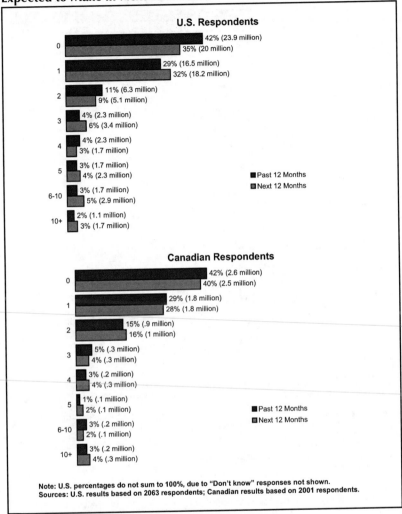

Note: U.S. percentages do not sum to 100%, due to "Don't know" responses not shown.
Sources: U.S. results based on 2063 respondents; Canadian results based on 2001 respondents.

Source: ISPA 2006 Spa-Goer Survey

With those assumptions, the spa is now ready to design the guest experience. It is not simply the massage itself or the haircut that defines the experience. As guests journey through an individual spa experience, they are constantly and probably subconsciously creating a report card of each element of the spa experience. It begins when they form their first impression of the spa as they pull into the parking lot or approach the building and continues through their final impression as they check out and pay for their experience. As they pay, they make that final judgment about whether the experience was equal to the value that they are paying. The guest will subconsciously evaluate each and every encounter with spa

Exhibit 5 Which of These Information Sources Do You Trust the Most to Help You Decide Which Spas to Visit?

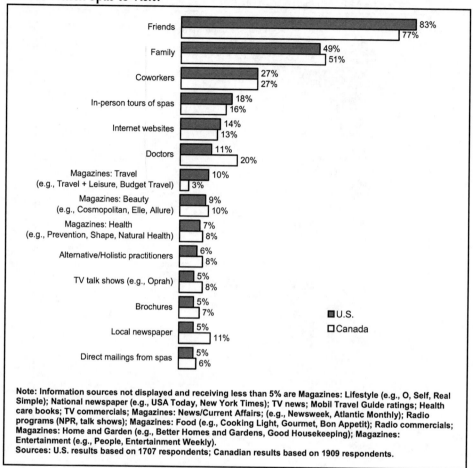

Note: Information sources not displayed and receiving less than 5% are Magazines: Lifestyle (e.g., O, Self, Real Simple); National newspaper (e.g., USA Today, New York Times); TV news; Mobil Travel Guide ratings; Health care books; TV commercials; Magazines: News/Current Affairs; (e.g., Newsweek, Atlantic Monthly); Radio programs (NPR, talk shows); Magazines: Food (e.g., Cooking Light, Gourmet, Bon Appetit); Radio commercials; Magazines: Home and Garden (e.g., Better Homes and Gardens, Good Housekeeping); Magazines: Entertainment (e.g., People, Entertainment Weekly).
Sources: U.S. results based on 1707 respondents; Canadian results based on 1909 respondents.

Source: ISPA 2006 Spa-Goer Survey

staff and will be comparing memories such as "the check-in at this spa was better than X or was not as professional as at spa Y", "the locker room attendant was just great", or "why didn't I get a foot bath in the relaxation room like I did at spa Y?"

Every guest in every spa in the world today is constantly conducting this evaluation process whether the spa has designed their experience or not. So it makes sense for a spa to carefully construct the guest journey to build advocates rather than leave the outcome to chance.

Touchpoints

The concept of **moments of truth** was popularized by Jan Carlzon, the CEO of Scandinavian Airlines System (SAS) in the early 1980s. "Each of our 10 million customers came in contact with approximately five SAS employees, and this contact

reflections

John Lopis: Letting the Staff Be Authentic

Our staff has for the most part never seen a facility like what we've built. There's nothing like this in this area of the country. When they come in, I ask that they maintain a small-town orientation. They're very genuine. They're very friendly. They're very helpful. But they don't have scripted service.

I say there are certain etiquettes in service that are expected and our guests will feel disappointed to not see those, but the style with which you deliver it is yours. I can't tell you how praised our staff is that they're so caring. I always say to the guests that when staff say, "May I help you?" I want the guest to look in their eyes, because they mean it. They just do. We get very high comments from our guests about our staff.

If I tried to make these people be what I think they should be rather than helping them to be what they are, I know they wouldn't be that way.

---

lasted an average of 15 seconds each time. Thus SAS is 'created' in the minds of the customers 50 million times a year, 15 seconds at a time. These 50 million 'moments of truth' are the moments that ultimately determine whether SAS will succeed or fail as a company. They are the moments when we must prove to our customers that SAS is their best alternative," Carlzon explained.[2]

Unfortunately, it is also all too easy to create a memorable experience by delivering particularly poor service during those moments of truth. Everyone has stories of a horrible restaurant experience or an unknowledgeable, unhelpful clerk at a retail store, or the frustration generated by calling a help desk where the goal is to minimize staff and time spent per call to reduce fixed costs and overhead, resulting in limited time being spent with customers. The customer then becomes not an advocate, but a vocal critic of the business.

Touchpoints have been defined as all of the communication—human and physical—that spa guests experience during their relationship lifecycle with a spa. This includes ads, the website, employees, and the spa treatment rooms.

Touchpoints are important because customers form perceptions of a spa based on their cumulative experiences. The average spa has numerous touchpoints. Some of the basics include:

- **Website:** Often a guest's first communication from a spa is with its website. A spa needs to ask whether the website articulates the spa's experience promise and engages the prospective guest.

- **Local or national ad:** Does the marketing align with the spa's brand promise and engage guests in the experience that awaits them at the spa?

- **The information call:** In many cases, the prospective guest will call first to learn more and to ask questions generated while browsing the spa's website.

- **The reservation call:** Does the reservations employee make the guest feel that the spa is concerned with his or her individual needs or is he or she just there to book a massage or facial? Did the reservationist offer a true suggestion or recommendation according to the individual's concerns?

- **Cleanliness:** The cleanliness of a spa will have a major effect on the experience that guests have. Has the equipment been sanitized? How inviting and clean is the spa area? Are the towels crisp and fresh? A physical plant that is worn—worn furnishings, chipped paint, mold in corners or on ceilings of wet areas, dirty carpets, or broken equipment—has a significant impact on the overall experience. How healthy is the physical plant?

- **The sense of arrival:** Guests form impressions even as they walk or drive up to the spa facility. Is the signage easy to spot and read? Does the outside landscaping and storefront represent a pride of ownership or is it unkempt?

- **The welcome:** How does the spa staff greet the guest? Is it easy for guests to determine just where they are supposed to go? Is there a collection of sensory impressions greeting guests? Do employees give an attentive and personal greeting or is a guest treated like just one more person to check in?

- **Entering treatment areas:** Are guests escorted to the ladies' or men's locker rooms or is the door simply pointed out? Does an employee nicely direct and guide the guest?

- **Locker room:** Does the locker area have an attendant? If so, does he or she extend a warm welcome? Is there a locker room orientation tour for first-time guests? How is the tour designed? As the guests open lockers, are they impeccably clean? Are they well-stocked with slippers that are the right size and a fresh robe that is large enough? Is the area well-organized?

- **Wet lounge:** Is the guest shown how to use the sauna, steam room, and whirlpool? Is there a plentiful supply of clean towels? Are there easy-to-understand instructions for use, safety, and enjoyment? Does the locker room attendant routinely check on the guests in the wet lounge or showers? Do they refer to the guest by name? Is there a sign for temperature and how to use the equipment?

- **Relaxation lounge:** Is the guest shown the relaxation areas and told what to expect next? If there is a hospitality station in the relaxation lounge, what does it communicate? Are there skimpy or diminished offerings or an ample offering of fresh, well-stocked refreshments and interesting things to read? How are guests received when the therapist collects them and escorts them to the treatment room?

- **Pre-treatment interview:** Is the therapist engaging and personal? Does the guest end up feeling like the interview is a somewhat mechanical rote process all therapists conduct? Is there a consultation with the guest?

- **Treatment room:** How does it speak to the guests? Is it calming and full of sensory aids that allow the guest to deepen the relaxation experience?

- **Treatments:** The ultimate spa experience is the treatment itself. Does it include the spa's attention to points of distinction? Is it professionally administered with technical skill and evident training? What are the therapist's behaviors during the treatment? Do they enhance the relaxation process or distract from it? Does the treatment meet the spa's experience promise? What is the therapist's intent? The greatest number of touchpoints can be found during treatments—and the most crucial ones. They will vary depending on what type of treatment is being received.

- **Post-treatment protocols:** Do they reinforce the experience or is the guest simply left with the impression that they are to get up and leave the room with an "it must be over" feeling?

- **Product suggestions:** How is the product suggestion process handled? Does the guest perceive it as a pushy attempt to sell spa products or is it seen as an educational experience?

- **Transfers:** How does the spa transfer a guest from one therapist to another for those having several treatments? How is the experience handled when guests who are having a treatment in one area are taken to another, for example, from the spa to the salon?

- **Exit process:** Is the guest escorted back to the relaxation lounge or perhaps outside by the spa pool and encouraged to continue the relaxation process or are they made to feel that it is time to take a quick shower, get dressed, and leave? Once back in the relaxation lounge or locker room, does the attendant inquire as to the quality of the guest's experience and perhaps ask if the guest would like to add an additional treatment to extend the experience?

- **Complaint resolution:** If guests have a problem during their spa experiences, how are conflicts resolved?

- **Retail area:** If guests wander through the retail area, are they traveling alone or is there someone available to assist and enhance the shopping experience? Is there someone with product knowledge available to assist?

- **Check-out:** When the guest checks out at the reception desk, what things are done to continue building a relationship with the guest? The departure memory may be the most important element of the spa experience to design correctly, as it is that last perception the guest has. This perception will imprint the memory of the value of their experience. When the guest is leaving, are they simply offered a thank you for coming or is there a design to stay in contact with the guest and continue building the relationship?

- **Post-visit:** Through the use of technology, does the spa maintain communication with the guest to strengthen the relationship, which can lead to creating a new advocate for the spa?

This is just a basic list. Spas will have additional touchpoints depending on whether they have accommodations, fitness facilities, food service, classes, outdoor activities, or educational programs. Spas must examine each of their touchpoints and determine whether what is being offered deepens the delivery of the spa's service promise. Destination and resort spas have touchpoints that last 24 hours a day.

reflections

Thad Hyland: Encouraging Individualism

There is nothing cramped in our verbiage when we talk to guests. We don't say the same thing to you at the front desk as we do in the spa.

We encourage individualism, we encourage people to use their personality. People have wonderful personalities around here. We encourage them not to say hello every day the same exact way. We have a little structure, but during our orientation we tell staff members that it is style, substance, and structure, in that order.

Style is everything at a hotel. You have to have the substance to back it up, and structure is third. We're not all about rules, we're about the individual acting.

The spa must dissect the guest experience and identify each touchpoint. Once those touchpoints are identified, they must align each and every communication with the guest to support the brand experience promise.

Successful spas focus a good deal of management attention on establishing quality standards for each touchpoint, communicating these standards to employees through training programs, and measuring performance. Quality standards can include how long a guest has to wait, how guests are approached, or what techniques are used for each service.

Providing consistent services is extremely complex where guest contact is involved. This is especially true with therapists and technicians who deliver services that are highly personalized and artistic in nature. Spa leaders must convince highly independent providers to give service that meets the same standards across the board. However, they must not try to take the variations of personality out of individual staff members. In many ways, it is the differences among staff members that can keep the spa experience unique and interesting through multiple, repeat visits.

Uncertainty and Concerns

Since guests cannot evaluate and experience the services they are considering purchasing in the same way that they can products, they often feel more hesitant, anxious, and unsure of their decisions. Not being able to experience offerings increases perceived risks and presents barriers for spas. This is especially true with more exotic treatments such as Thai massage or Shiatsu. To overcome their feelings of uncertainty, guests often rely on the experiences and advice of "knowers"—their peers and friends, reviews, testimonial letters, and comments on the Internet. Spa professionals should also be prepared to recommend treatments for the first-time spa-goer, treatments that will help guests to relax and appreciate the spa experience.

There are several common sources of anxiety among infrequent spa-goers:

- Getting there early enough—not coming early enough to unwind before the treatment.

- Clothing removal—not knowing how much they have to remove relative to their comfort level

- Pain during massage—knowing how to ask a therapist to change the pressure

- Temperature—worrying that the temperature of some body treatments, such as wraps and scrubs, will be too extreme

- Skin rashes or breakouts—guests who are about to try a body wrap, facial, or skin treatment for the first time want to be assured that they won't break out or develop a rash.

Some spas will now introduce their services by providing a mini treatment for free—such as a chair massage or an add-on aromatherapy element to a massage.

Fluctuating Demand

Spa services are perishable and cannot be stored, which means that widely fluctuating demand can create challenges. During peak seasons and busy periods, the spa's capacity may be taxed to the limit. In off seasons and hours, excess capacity may exist. Delivering excellent service to guests during periods of peak demand is a continuing challenge. It can be just as difficult for guests to obtain outstanding service during lulls when employees have nothing to do and are standing around talking to each other. Yield management, promotion strategies, and pricing strategies are used to iron out and reduce the amplitude of swings in demand.

Making sure the appropriate number of staff members are on hand to service customers during fluctuating demand times is also critical. Many spas use a mix of fixed and variable staff positions, with fixed positions being covered by permanent full-time workers or permanent part-time workers. Variable positions typically include therapists and technicians.

The scheduling of variable staff positions becomes much easier when the spa is run by appointment-only. However, one of the issues that spa-goers have is that when they want a spa service, they often need it with little advance notice. Some will preschedule or call ahead, but others have had a bad day and decide that they need a massage. Or they have an important meeting and realize that their nails look terrible and want a quick fix. If the spa doesn't have an open appointment, they'll go somewhere else—sometimes for good.

Spas can manage demand through promotions and creative scheduling. Some spas use day of the week pricing—offering discounts on a slow day or increasing the price during peak times. Some are even implementing time-of-day pricing where a morning massage is less costly than one received during peak demand (such as late afternoon). Another way to manage demand is to encourage the front desk staff to always offer alternative appointment times or different treatments, if what the guest wants at first isn't available. They can also offer a wait list or try to figure out how to get the guest in with an alternative plan. Promotions during non-peak times help to fill the books. For example, an e-mail blast can advertise a special offer for an upcoming weekend. Giving special discounts on specific days to identified VIPs works to make the most of a spa's top clientele.

Evaluation

After a spa plans and delivers an experience, it needs to ensure that the experience is delivered consistently and over time. It is one thing to have carefully crafted an experience promise and for the staff to be passionate about that promise. However,

Spa Snapshot: What resources does your spa use to make sure your guest is getting the best experience?

I use a Secret Shopper checklist. I give it to friends and community people. I also call on some of my regular clients to complete one on occasion. We are located in the Sheraton Steamboat Resort, and I also ask the general manager to do walk-throughs for me. I am an absentee owner and have found this to be a very useful tool for me. I have the client pay for the service and then I reimburse them. I have also installed Web-cams in my retail areas so that I can see the store at all times—wherever I am.

—Crystal Cook, Owner, Sol Day Spa

Our company has secret shoppers that enjoy a multitude of resort services and report back to management. These can be families or single guests so we see the entire view of the resort and spa from the perspective of our guest profile. We also have a strong customer comment system. We use a formula to determine the percent of satisfaction in several key areas. We report this feedback to our staff. Lastly, we have an employee service program so not only do we allow our staff to experience our services, we receive feedback from them on how we can enhance our service levels and improve consistency. They are really involved (and relaxed).

—Kate Mearns, Director, Sports Operations, Kingsmill Resort

The first day for new employees is a full day at the spa. Our current staff members do not know the new employee yet. This serves two purposes: 1) The new employee gets to experience the treatments, ambience, and customer service as would any guest and 2) They evaluate the experience with a professional, fresh eye. After services, we then debrief and compile notes. At our next staff meeting, I break the staff into groups and hand each group a note card with a situation that was experienced by the new staff member. Then each group has five to ten minutes to come up with a solution. Whatever the group decides, a vote comes to order. Whatever the vote, we incorporate it as policy. I have found that when the team makes the rules, they abide and execute ideas better. If you can get to the core of the dissatisfaction, there is usually a simple solution. Most solutions are just awareness of the problem.

—Marylyn Alexander, Owner, Bergamos Spa Retreat

We accept "Spa Wish" gift certificates and appear on their website. They started a new program a few years ago, and here's how it works: For a fee, they send in a secret shopper who evaluates everything from the first phone call to make the appointment to the check out at the end

(continued)

of their appointment. They use a number system [to do their ratings], which includes the reservationist and whether he/she recommended anything other than the service they requested, to the client check-in experience, the way the spa looked, whether there were refreshments, and much more, and then finally how the actual service was. They then calculate this rating and enter a "Gold Seal" on their website indicating they came for a service and [the score] we received.

—*Lisa Hills, Retail Director, Giuliano Day Spa*

Tracking customer satisfaction has been key to our goal of building guest loyalty from the moment the doors opened. We wanted to get meaningful feedback from guests and knew a standard evaluation form would not meet our needs. So we developed a survey that generates honest feedback in a creative way. In addition to general satisfaction questions (how would you rate your suite, your spa services, the facility, etc.), we ask guests to choose the top 10 words that best describe their visit to Sundara, selecting from a list of 33 words such as: energizing, stress-relieving, romantic, valuable, healthy, therapeutic, necessary, environmentally friendly, personalized, indulgent. We've learned much more about guest satisfaction using this method than we would have by simply sticking to straightforward questions. The survey goes on to ask guests to "be imaginative" and suggest services or special amenities they'd like to see added at Sundara.

—*Kelli Trumble, CEO, Sundara Inn & Spa*

Tea Garden Springs initiated a "Staff Wellness Program" that is a true win-win situation for Tea Garden Springs employees and their spa clients. For every 25 days that an employee works, they receive one complimentary spa service, and the program is managed so that each staff member will receive a different treatment each time. The staff/client is encouraged to act as a client and critique the entire experience from start to finish, including the telephone booking, front-desk greeting, tea service, practitioner connection, facilities, the treatment itself, follow-up, and check-out.

—*Roy Nee, Spa Director, Tea Garden Springs*

Here in Orange County, California, we have formed a Spa Directors Roundtable, which currently consists of about a dozen of the top spas in the area. Our mission is to share ideas and solve problems to provide a higher standard of service to spa-goers in our communities. One of the things we do is a secret shopper program. The shoppers are spa owners or directors who know what to look for. We can use either a common form we have developed or a form unique to the property. We're just getting it rolling, and I think it is going to be very effective.

—*Angela Cortright, Owner, Spa Gregorie's*

Source: *Pulse*, May/June 2004

the verbal commitment and passion is only the launching pad for what the staff actually does day in and day out.

If a spa really wants to deliver a consistent, superior experience over the long term, then it has to inspect and evaluate. Customer and employee feedback systems are the most common form of ensuring that the experience promise is being delivered. It also provides the spa with information about changing guest expectations. An experience that exceeds guest expectations today may fall short when those guests desire change. Feedback systems can help create lines of communication between the spa and the guest. However, feedback should not be reserved for after the guest has left the spa. Spas need to talk to and listen to their guests each and every time they arrive at the spa. They need to evaluate the guest and try to understand what the best experience is for that person's needs at that moment.

A guest feedback system should attempt to measure how well the spa's experience is meeting guest expectations and whether the guest perceptions are what the spa has designed them to be.

This feedback system usually takes the form of a report card. The spa will set goals for each touchpoint and then collect data—usually in the form of guest and employee comment cards—on how that area is doing. So, for example, a spa might establish a five-point scale for each department. If the spa reception desk is averaging 4.2, it might set a goal for the front desk to raise that rating to 4.5 over a specific period of time.

Such a feedback system also lets a spa monitor which areas might need additional attention if the numbers start dropping, or let the spa know what area is doing something particularly well that could be adapted for other areas.

Another suggestion that spas use frequently are secret shoppers. They are firms spas can hire to come in and evaluate the spa and the experience, then provide management with a full report and consultation afterwards.

One of the challenges with a guest comment card process is that it reports only on how the spa is currently doing. It doesn't ascertain what the guest wants that the spa is not doing. Dave Power III of J.D. Power & Associates says, "When we measure satisfaction, what we're really measuring is the difference between what a customer *expects* and what the customer *perceives* he gets."

So how does a spa identify just what it is that the customer really wants? There are several techniques that might include:

- Guest surveys.

- Paying attention to what the guest is buying and not buying. When a treatment doesn't sell, a spa should investigate why. Is it just not wanted? Is it priced too high?

- Industry surveys.

- Phone calls to follow up on the spa visit. Spas can give a personal contact to find out what worked and what didn't work.

Another issue is that most guest comment card surveys are designed for the 'average' guest, but the goal of designing the spa experience is to create advocates. How does the spa communicate with its most loyal guests? One way is to design special surveys sent by e-mail to those potential advocates. Another might be to invite those guests to the spa to meet with the leadership team for an open focus group discussion.

The Spa Experience

Every spa will offer its own unique experience to its guests just as every guest will participate in a unique experience at every visit. Spas will offer services that center around their missions: providing experiences and rituals that renew, refresh, and regenerate a guest's heart, spirit, and mind.

While there is no magic formula to creating an experience that will wow every guest every time, consistent commitment to high quality service at every touch-point demonstrates that a spa cares about its guests and the experiences that they have. Spas that succeed create a strategy for providing a superior experience and stick to it. They make certain that everyone who works at the spa understands both its philosophy and its mission. They promise only what they can deliver and then deliver everything they promise. By doing this, they not only create memories, but they help their guests achieve a healthier and happier lifestyle.

Endnotes

1. Portions of the sections on services versus products were adapted from Rocco M. Angelo and Andy N. Vladimir, *Hospitality Today: An Introduction*, 6th ed. (Lansing, Mich.: American Hotel & Lodging Educational Institute, 2007).

2. Jan Carlzon, *Moments of Truth* (Cambridge, Mass.: Ballinger, 1987), pp. 21–29.

Additional Reading

Pine II, Joseph, and James H. Gilmore, *The Experience Economy: Work is Theatre & Every Business a Stage*, (Boston, Mass.: Harvard Business School Press, 1999).

Smith, Shaun, and Joe Wheeler, *Managing the Customer Experience*, (London: Prentice Hall, 2002).

Key Terms

advocate—A client who encourages others to buy from the spa and who brings new customers to the spa.

client—A guest who buys everything the spa has to sell that they can use.

commodity—A product that investors buy or sell, usually traded solely on the basis of price.

core spa-goer—Someone who embraces the spa lifestyle and is an advocate for spas.

experience—The actual product sold to guests by a spa. It is everything the guest sees, hears, smells, tastes, and touches while at the spa. It is an event which creates a memory for the guest.

good—A physical or tangible product that can be purchased by consumers.

intangible products—Those offerings by a business that cannot be touched or held in one's hand.

mid-level spa-goer—Someone who uses spa services occasionally, but for whom spas are not a part of their regular lifestyle.

mindfulness—Performing a task with a purpose and a focused intention.

moments of truth—The moments in which a spa must prove to its customers that it is their best alternative.

periphery spa-goer—Someone who is a first-timer or an infrequent user of spas.

prospect—The consumer who is not yet aware of the spa or who has not yet made the decision to become a guest.

service—Usually defined as "work done for others."

touchpoints—All of the communication, human and physical, that spa guests experience during their relationship lifecycle with a spa.

unique selling proposition—A marketing concept that identifies the one thing that makes a product or a service different than any other. It is the reason that consumers will purchase the service instead of others that seem just like it.

 Review Questions

1. How does the delivery of intangible services differ from the sale of tangible products?

2. What are the differences between a commodity, a good, a service, and an experience?

3. What are the four realms of experience?

4. Why is the investment in guest loyalty considered an investment in profits?

5. What is the difference between a prospect, a client, and an advocate?

6. What are some of the major touchpoints in a spa experience?

7. What techniques can a spa use to identify what the guest wants?

Chapter 6 Outline

Traditions
    Ayurveda
    Traditional Chinese Medicine
    Folk and Native Traditions
    Aromatherapy
    Complementary and Alternative
        Medicine
    Allopathic Medicine
Massage Therapy
    Massage Techniques
Types of Massage Therapies
    Western-Based Massage Therapies
    Asian Bodywork Therapy and Energy
        Work
    Other Massage Techniques
Movement Education and Mind-Body
    Fitness
    Pilates
    Yoga
    Tai Chi
    Qigong
    Feldenkrais Method
    Rolfing
    Alexander Technique
    Trager Technique
Hydrotherapy
    Balneotherapy
    Thalassotherapy
    Hydrotherapy Treatments
Body Treatments
Skin Care/Facials
    By Therapeutic Goals/Skin Profile
    By Ingredient
    By Technique
Conclusion

Competencies

1. Describe some of the traditions from which current spa therapies have emerged. (pp. 213–219)

2. Describe the different strokes used in massage therapy and how various types of massage are classified based on technique, purpose, or therapeutic goal. (pp. 219–223)

3. Explain the concept of energy work and how it relates to Asian massage styles. (pp. 223–227)

4. Identify some of the pioneers in mind-body fitness and movement education. (pp. 227–235)

5. Distinguish between the types of hydrotherapy and hydrotherapy treatments. (pp. 235–240)

6. Explain the purpose of various body treatments. (pp. 240–242)

7. Identify skin care/facial treatments by therapeutic goals, ingredients, and technique. (pp. 242–245)

■■■■ = she went over in class

▭▭ = competency questions

6

Traditions, Treatments, and Terms

$\mathbf{A}$ MENU OF spa services can be confusing to anyone unfamiliar with the terminology used to describe the array of treatments available. However, a look into the traditions from which the treatments come, their countries of origin, or the people who developed techniques can shed light on the unique language found within a spa.

Learning more about the history and background of spa treatments is an important part of the professional development process for all spa professionals, not just the therapists who perform the treatments. By learning more about traditions, treatments, and terminology, spa professionals can more effectively research new treatments and products with a greater insight into their therapeutic effects and claims and whether they accurately represent the philosophy and goals of that spa. They will know whether a particular treatment has an established history and proven therapeutic value or if it is a passing fad.

Additionally, those who are educated about many therapies and knowledgeable about spa terminology—who speak the language of spa fluently—will be more confident with training, handling performance evaluations, and communicating with therapists and treatment supervisors. They will also be able to explain these treatments to their guests, to help them make informed decisions about the types of treatments that will best meet their wellness needs.

Traditions

Spa treatments come from all over the world and have been developed over the centuries by people from many cultures, religions, and medical perspectives. Many modern spa therapies have their origins in one or more of the long-standing traditions described below.

Ayurveda

Ayurveda is considered one of the world's oldest medical systems. There is evidence that the Indian tradition of Ayurveda dates back to the third century B.C.E., but the first writings describing Ayurveda come from 1200 B.C.E. The Sanskrit word means "the knowledge of life." This holistic theory of wellness includes practices of vegetarianism, yoga, breathing exercises, meditation, and massage. In India, where Ayurveda is a recognized medical system of health care, practitioners go through five-and-a-half years of medical training plus a one-year internship, earning a degree in Ayurvedic medicine. The process includes learning traditional

213

Ayurvedic procedures such as oil massage, acupressure, herbal treatments, Vedic chants, cleansing diets, nutrition, yoga, Jyotish (Vedic astrology), Sanskrit, and lifestyle education.[1]

Key components of Ayurveda are:

- Prana—life force or energy
- Chakras—energy centers in the body
- Five elements—earth, water, fire, air, and ether (space)
- Three doshas—vata (air), pitta (fire), kapha (water)

The doshas govern the functions of the body. The predominance of a particular dosha is thought to contribute to different diseases; for instance, people with vata as their main dosha are thought to be susceptible to skin, neurological, and mental disease; those for whom kapha is predominant may be prone to diabetes, stomach ulcers, and asthma; while people with pitta as their primary dosha are thought to be susceptible to heart disease and arthritis.[2] An Ayurvedic practitioner works with a patient to discover his or her primary dosha and achieve balance of doshas to treat and prevent health problems.

Ayurvedic therapies address each of the five senses: herbs and nutrition for taste; massage, yoga, and exercise for touch; aromatherapy for smell; color therapy for sight; and sound therapy for hearing. A sixth sense, spirituality, is addressed through mantra meditation, chanting, and ethical living. All of these practices work together to restore balance to body, mind, and spirit.[3]

Traditional Chinese Medicine

China is the source of many health and wellness practices. Many of them can be found on contemporary spa menus throughout the world, not only in Asia. They come from Traditional Chinese Medicine (TCM), which has been practiced for thousands of years.

TCM is built on three principles known as the Three Treasures. They are:

- **Qi** or chi—Energy or life force
- Jing—The essence of vitality and longevity
- Shen—Mind or spirit[4]

TCM incorporates five elements (wood, fire, earth, metal, water) and four pillars of assessment (looking, touching, listening, asking). These are used by practitioners to discern what types of treatments are best suited to maintaining wellness and preventing or healing physical ailments. TCM identifies 365 acupressure points, which are located along major energy channels, or **meridians**, in the body. These points relate to different areas of the body and can be manipulated as part of healing. Acupuncture, acupressure, reflexology, and massage are used to open blocked channels and enhance the flow of energy.[5]

The focus of TCM is wellness and prevention of illness. Practices within TCM focus on balancing a person's energy to maximize health of body, mind, spirit, and emotions. Yin and yang, the principle of relatedness and connectedness between seemingly different forces, is a key element of TCM.

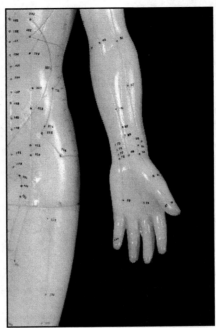

An acupuncture chart shows the body's 365 acupressure points, which are located along meridians, or energy channels in the body. Acupuncture is part of Traditional Chinese Medicine.

TCM began in China, then traveled to Korea. By the sixth century, Chinese medical practices had reached Japan, which adopted and modified them. The Japanese called these traditional Chinese medical practices by the name "kampo," which means "the Chinese way," referring to their origin in that country.[6]

Although elements of TCM were written about by both Marco Polo (in the thirteenth century) and by Jesuit missionaries (in the seventeenth century), it was not widely known in the West until the middle of the twentieth century. George Soulie de Morant, a French diplomat who lived and studied in China from 1901 to 1917, returned to France and taught acupuncture to French medical professionals. In the 1930s, he wrote a 900-page book on Chinese acupuncture that laid the foundation for the modern practice of acupuncture in Europe.

Folk and Native Traditions

Many spa treatments have their roots in folk traditions specific to a particular group of people, a culture, or a region. These techniques are passed down within families, through **apprenticeships**, or through religious or spiritual leaders within the tradition. They may include herbal remedies, social rituals, healing practices, or religious expressions. Examples of native healing practices include Lomi Lomi massage, or the Javanese lulur body treatment traditionally part of an Indonesian bridal ritual.

reflections

Sylvia Sepielli: Embracing and Respecting Traditions in the Spa Environment

Spa consultant Sylvia Sepielli, founder and president of Sylvia Planning and Design, is known for developing spa concepts that embrace and celebrate a variety of cultural traditions with sensitivity and respect. Some of the spas she has designed include Spa Ojai, whose menu reflects the traditions of California's Chumash Indians; Spa Halekulani, which has treatments that honor the healing cultures of Asia, Hawaii, and the South Pacific; and the Spa of Colonial Williamsburg in Virginia, whose menu features modern interpretations of ingredients and practices used by groups in Williamsburg's past, including Native Americans, European colonists, and African American slaves, as well as modern spa therapies of the twentieth and twenty-first centuries.

"Traditions play a role in developing a spa's philosophy and menu," says Sepielli. "But there is a difference between incorporating traditional therapeutic practices of a native healing culture and using indigenous items as ingredients in a spa treatment," and the latter should not attempt to be passed off as the former. For instance, it is fine to create a mango scrub as a signature item at a spa in a locale where mangos are native fruits. It is not acceptable to describe that treatment as part of a native healing tradition.

"I spend more time convincing people not to include native items on their spa menus than I do figuring out ways to add them," says Sepielli. "I don't think every spa needs to or should have indigenous treatments." Avoiding the temptation to make up treatments based on local ingredients leads to more respect than if a spa adds something just for the sake of fitting in or keeping up, she explains.

"There are so many traditions that have a deep, rich history of healing practices; we don't need to make things up," she says. "Spa-goers are savvy. They want efficacy, not fads."

Sepielli cites Ayurveda and Traditional Chinese Medicine as two traditions that have demonstrated their efficacy over time, noting that "they are fully rounded and take in all aspects of body-mind-spirit. They are more than just a body treatment." Even so, she cautions that many traditions, when removed from their cultural context, are not as effective.

"We need to avoid cherry picking a variety of treatments just to create an interesting menu," says Sepielli. "It's important to ask whether a treatment supports the concept of the spa. We always return to that idea."

The Central/South American practice of using a temezcalli (sweat lodge) is another folk tradition that may now be found in contemporary spa settings.

Aromatherapy

Aromatherapy is more than just pleasing scents. It is an ancient practice that uses **essential oils** from plants, leaves, bark, roots, seeds, resins, and flowers as a healing therapy. In modern times, the word aromatherapy was introduced by French

---

A Brief Guide to Essential Oils

Essential oils are used in aromatherapy to achieve desired results for spa guests. Some of the more common aromatherapy oils include:

Lavender: A balancing oil. It is stress relieving and relaxing. In skin care, lavender is good for dry or oily skin, because of its balancing qualities. It is also good for sunburn and skin conditions because it aids cell regeneration.

Orange: A joy oil. All the citrus oils are uplifting and positive, pleasant and refreshing. Orange and grapefruit are good for lymphatic drainage, water retention, and cellulite reduction.

Peppermint: Cooling and refreshing, stimulating. It counters fatigue, increases mental clarity, aids digestion, and calms headaches.

Rosemary: One of the most stimulating oils. Because it stimulates circulation, it is good for muscles and joints. It is also helpful for mental clarity. When used in hair care treatments, it gives the hair a lustrous shine and stimulates circulation on the scalp, promoting healthy hair.

Geranium: A good "female balancer." It is helpful for mood swings and balancing female energy. Its astringent and cell regenerative qualities make it good for mature skin.

Ylang Ylang: Because it slows the heart rate, it is used to alleviate anxiety, nervousness, tension, and fear. It is also used in skin care as a hydrating oil.

Eucalyptus: Classic spa oil for steam rooms. It is used for inhalation therapy for respiratory congestion and bronchial conditions, including asthma. It is also warming to the muscles and joints, so it is classically used as a sports massage oil.

Source: Tara Grodjesk, Founder and President, TARA Spa Therapy.

scientist René Maurice Gattefosse, who studied the uses of essential oils for their healing properties in the 1920s and 1930s. He discovered the healing power of lavender oil by accident when, after burning his arm, he plunged it into lavender oil, discovering an almost-immediate healing effect. Various oils have different properties and can be used alone or with other oils to facilitate a therapeutic result.

In the spa setting, aromatherapy can be applied in many ways. Drops of essential oils can be added to baths, blended with oil for massage, used in a facial, added to water to soak linens for a hot or cold compress, added to a bowl of heated water to be inhaled, or placed in a diffuser to add scent to the air. They can be used in a hair oil or rinse, and a few drops can be placed on a pillow to enhance sleep. Additionally, some therapies use the actual herbs or plants, rather than oils distilled from them, to achieve therapeutic effect.

Complementary and Alternative Medicine

Complementary and Alternative Medicine (CAM) is so-called because it complements or is used as an alternative to conventional Western (allopathic) medical practices. CAM encompasses a variety of treatments that include biofeedback, herbal remedies, homeopathic medicine, acupuncture, chiropractic, nutrition

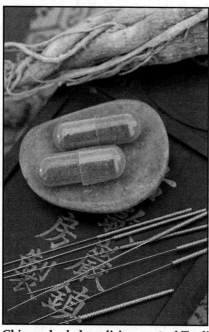

Chinese herbal medicine, part of Traditional Chinese Medicine, is considered comple-mentary or alternative to traditional Western medical practices.

therapy, and naturopathic medicine. The National Center for Complementary and Alternative Medicine of the National Institutes of Health (NCCAM) groups CAM practices into four major domains, as well as whole medical systems, such as homeopathic and naturopathic medicine, Ayurveda, and TCM, which encompass all of the domains.

These four domains are:

- **Mind-body medicine**, which uses techniques designed to enhance the mind's capacity to affect bodily functions and systems.

- **Biologically-based practices**, which use natural substances like herbs, foods, and vitamins.

- **Manipulative and body-based practices**, which are based on movement of one or more parts of the body, such as chiropractic or massage therapy.

- **Energy medicine**, which includes both biofield therapies that are thought to surround and penetrate the human body and bioelectromagnetic therapies, which involve the use of electromagnetic fields.[7]

The term **integrative medicine** is becoming more commonly used today to better describe how wellness practitioners may integrate techniques from various traditions to create a holistic plan for health and wellness. The term integrative is also more respectful than alternative, as many practices included in the term "alternative" are mainstream in the parts of the world where they originated.

Allopathic Medicine

Not all spa treatments have their origins in Eastern, folk, or alternative practices. Many are rooted in conventional Western, or **allopathic**, medicine, which looks at the body's structures and systems and how they function to maintain physical health. Health is defined as the absence of disease, and there is more of a focus on treating illness or injury after it happens, or on diagnosis and treatment, than on preventing problems in the first place. The NCCAM defines conventional medicine as "medicine as practiced by holders of M.D. (medical doctor) or D.O. (doctor of osteopathy) degrees and by their allied health professionals, such as physical therapists, psychologists, and registered nurses." Some people use the term allopathic medicine to refer to the treatment of disease using conventional medical therapies, as distinct from complementary or alternative medicine.

Massage Therapy

Many people associate spa with massage, but may not realize the spectrum of treatments and techniques that term encompasses. Massage is the art of healing through purposeful manipulation of the body's soft tissues. Touch and movement are the key elements of massage therapy. Massage therapists use various techniques to help the body heal itself, depending on the needs of each individual. For instance, an athlete receiving a massage after participating in a sport requires a different style of massage than a person suffering fatigue from prolonged time at a computer. The intention of massage could be for relaxation, improving circulation, balancing energy, or diminishing pain.

Massage Techniques

There are seven basic massage strokes or techniques used by massage therapists.[8] By using or combining these techniques in different ways, therapists achieve varying results to benefit their clients.

Touch. Touch is the act of placing the therapist's hand, fingers, palm, or forearm on the client with no movement. Touch introduces the client to the feel of the massage therapist and reassures the client receiving the massage that the therapist means no harm.

Gliding. In gliding, which can be light or deep, the therapist uses the hand, fingers, or forearm to stroke the skin tissue. This is sometimes called *effleurage*, a French word that means "to touch lightly." Depending on the desired outcome, gliding can be used lightly or with increasing pressure.

Kneading. Also called *petrissage* (from the French for "kneading"), this massage stroke lightly compresses skin tissue between the thumb and fingers or one or two hands, then lifts the skin vertically and squeezes it by rolling it out of the hand. This technique is used to "milk" the fluids and toxins deep inside the muscles.

Friction. Friction helps the therapist to reach underlying tissue. The client's superficial tissue is used to massage deeper by performing traverse or circular movements with the fingers, thumbs, palms, or elbows. This technique is often used

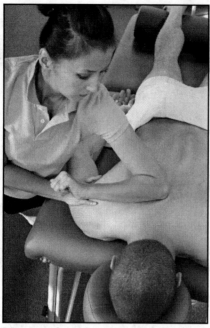 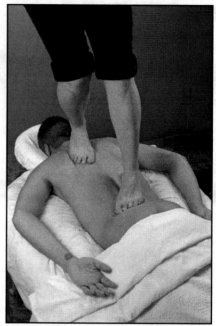

Massage therapists use several different strokes and techniques to manipulate muscles and soft tissues.

to reach the deep area in joint spaces and around bony prominences that have connective tissue buildup and adhesions from overuse. Friction is combined with compression in deep tissue or sports massage.

Vibration. In vibration, therapists place a hand on an area of the body, compress it to a certain depth, then tremble the hand back and forth, vibrating the tissues. It may also be done using the forearm. This can be a tiring stroke for the therapist, but when done correctly, it creates a relaxing, soothing effect on the client's nerves. This can also be done between the fingers and thumb.

Percussion. Also called by the French term *tapotement*, percussion means drumming, patting, or rapping on the body. The therapist uses various hand positions and varying speed and force in downward blows to stimulate the body. Several variations on this technique include hacking, which uses the side of the hand with the little finger striking the tissue; cupping, where the hands form a cup; and tapping, which is a light method often used on the face and scalp or along the spine.

Joint movement. In this technique, the therapist systematically moves a joint through its range of motions. It includes traction and stretching.

Types of Massage Therapies

There are scores of massage therapies, based on different needs, techniques, and materials used. Some of the better-known massage therapies are explained here.

Western-Based Massage Therapies

The following massage techniques are rooted in Western medical thought about the body, its systems, and how they work and interact. These techniques work with muscles, joints, tendons, fascia, and lymph systems to maintain or restore health.

Swedish. This style of massage is what most people think of when they hear the word "massage." This traditional massage technique was developed in the 1800s by Per Henrik Ling, a professor and physiologist at the University of Stockholm. Using information contained in letters written from China by Jesuit missionaries describing massage techniques they witnessed in Asia, Ling created and practiced a system of massage movements. Swedish massage uses five movements or strokes—effleurage, petrissage, friction, vibration, and tapotement. The therapist delivers the strokes in a firm, but gentle manner with the grain of the muscle tissue. This kind of massage is ideal for first-time spa-goers and for people seeking relaxation.

Deep Tissue. While Swedish massage is used for relaxation, deep tissue massage is used for conditions that include chronic pain, limited mobility, recovery from injury, repetitive strain, postural problems, muscle tension or spasms, and fibromyalgia.

Deep tissue massage works to realign deeper layers of muscle tissue. It uses slower massage strokes and deep pressure on affected areas, working across the grain of the muscle tissue. The therapist applies deep pressure with the thumb or fingers, although he or she may also use the palm of the hand and knuckle or elbow. Deep tissue massage is helpful for tense areas such as stiff necks, shoulders, and the lower back. Because it focuses on specific areas, clients experience some discomfort and pain as the therapist works to release tension and toxins from the muscles. The goal of the deep tissue massage is to loosen muscle tissues, release toxins that have built up, and increase blood and oxygen flow through the muscle tissues. Clients usually experience some muscle stiffness or pain after a deep tissue massage, which subsides in a day or two.

Sports Massage. Sports massage has been popular in the United States only since the early 1980s, but it has been practiced in Europe for more than a century. The techniques were developed in Finland around 1900 as an adaptation of Swedish massage. Finnish sports massage received attention in 1924, when Finnish runner Paavo Nurmi won five gold medals at the Olympic games in Paris, including two in one day in events held only 30 minutes apart. Nurmi gave credit to sports massage as one of the key components of his training program.

Also in the 1920s, Dr. I.M. Sarkisov-Sirasini developed the concept for Russian Sports Massage, which he taught at the Central Institute of Physical Therapy in Moscow. In the United States, interest in sports massage was popularized with the 1980 publication of Jack Meagher's book, *Sportsmassage: A Complete Program for Increasing Performance and Endurance in Fifteen Popular Sports.*

The goal of sports massage is to keep athletes injury-free during training. It is typically performed following a workout or athletic event, treating the areas that received the greatest stress during that workout. It may also be performed before a workout or athletic performance to prepare the muscles for the work they are about to do. Sports massage can release built-up lactic acid and waste products in muscles and increase the flow of blood and oxygen to the muscles, helping to repair them.

The benefits of sports massage may include:

- Faster recovery from damage and trauma to muscles from workouts
- Increase in flexibility and range of motion
- Relief from fatigue
- Reduction of repetitive motion strain
- Reduction in healing time from injuries

Myofascial Massage. Fascia is the name for loose connective tissue that surrounds every muscle, nerve, blood vessel, and organ. It holds the body together and gives it shape. **Myofascial** massage releases tension in the fascia to help properly align the body. The massage strokes stretch fascial sheets, break fascial adhesions, and release tensions that are causing the client pain, poor posture, and limited mobility. Developers of various myofascial massage techniques include Elizabeth Dicke, a German whose system of Connective Tissue Massage (CTM) was developed in the 1920s and 1930s, and John Barnes, an American physical therapist who developed myofascial release in the 1980s.[9]

Craniosacral. This therapy was originally part of the body of osteopathic medicine, and is based on work done by William Sutherland, D.O., in the 1940s. Since 1983, Dr. John Upledger has been the chief advocate of this therapy, which requires specialized training to perform correctly. In craniosacral therapy, the therapist assesses the client and performs therapeutic moves by holding the skull and "listening" to the rhythms as the body moves. It is a restful technique for both the client and the therapist, and is noninvasive. The theory behind craniosacral therapy is that restrictions in the craniosacral hydraulic system of the body produce dysfunction in the central nervous system. Practitioners of craniosacral therapy claim that this therapy balances the cranium, spine, and sacrum so that cerebral-spinal fluid flows more freely and improves nervous system function. Some people with autism spectrum disorders have benefited from craniosacral massage.

Manual Lymphatic Drainage. This technique is also called Vodder Lymph Drainage, after Dr. Emil Vodder, the German doctor who developed the practice in Denmark during the 1930s. This gentle massage technique focuses on the body's lymph system, a network of one-way capillaries that collect fluids from tissue spaces and move them into one of two main lymph ducts and ultimately back into the blood. The fluids pass through nodes that are lined with cells that devour bacteria and filter waste products and other foreign substances.

Manual lymphatic drainage encourages the lymphatic system's ability to clear away debris, fat, and unwanted substances and to reduce edema (swelling) resulting from trauma or connective tissue restrictions such as post-surgical scarring. This procedure is particularly useful for cancer patients and cancer survivors who often experience lymphedema, a swelling or increase of lymph fluids.

In this type of massage, the therapist applies gentle massage strokes in the direction of lymph flow to unblock lymph vessels and encourage lymph flow to move more freely to rid the body of wastes. Strokes used include fingertip stationary circles or spirals along the neck and face; a pumping technique in which the therapist makes oval strokes with fingers and thumb; a rotary motion performed with the palms down; and scoop stroke performed with the palms up and fingers outstretched.

Neuro-Muscular Therapy (NMT). Neuro-Muscular Therapy (NMT), also known as **trigger point therapy**, was developed in the 1920s by Stanley Lief, who operated a natural healing resort in Hertfordshire, England. His soft tissue manipulation techniques focus on targeting specific spots, or trigger points, where taut bands of tissue around muscles and tendons cause direct and/or referred pain.

In the United States, trigger point therapy received attention in the 1950s, when it was used by Janet Travell, M.D., to help ease the pain of then-Senator John F. Kennedy, who was injured in World War II. Travell later served as White House physician for both Kennedy and Lyndon Johnson. She used a form of trigger point therapy in which she injected a saline solution into the trigger points.

In the late 1970s, American physical fitness educator Bonnie Prudden developed a systematic approach to trigger point therapy called Myotherapy.[10] The techniques of compressing and stretching muscles at the trigger points of pain are thought to benefit people who experience repetitive stress injuries, such as athletes, musicians, artists, and physical laborers, as well as for those who work at a computer or drive long distances. In addition to their hands, therapists may use elbows, feet, or tools to apply direct pressure to the trigger points.

There are several forms of NMT or trigger point therapy used currently. They include:

- Myofascial trigger point therapy (manual)
- Myotherapy (deep pressure or massage)
- Mechanical vibration
- Pulsed ultrasound
- Electrostimulation
- Ischemic compression
- Injection
- Dry needling
- Spray and stretch
- Stretching techniques

Asian Bodywork Therapy and Energy Work

Several types of massage have their roots in traditional Chinese and Asian medicine. These techniques, whether practiced as they were developed in Asia, or derived from Asian practices with the addition of Western influences, have in common the goal of using massage to balance and enhance the client's flow of qi, or energy, through the body's meridians. The term **energy work** is often used to describe these therapies, because of their focus on balancing and freeing a person's energy flow.

Acupressure. This is a Western adaptation of the branch of Chinese medicine known as acupuncture. In acupuncture, needles are inserted along meridian lines in the body that correspond with body parts and functions to stimulate and control the energy flow through the body. In acupressure, the massage therapist applies pressure and small circular strokes to touch points that correspond to various areas of the body, adding pressure to the point and rubbing it for three to ten seconds. Well-developed muscles might take pressure for up to two minutes. Acupressure is well suited to treating aches and pains, stress, menstrual cramps, asthma, and arthritis.

Shiatsu. Shiatsu is the Japanese method of acupressure, although it is not identical to the Chinese method. In shiatsu, the therapist puts pressure on the points with the pads of the finger or thumb for two to five seconds. Over time, practitioners have developed routines for the whole body designed to reduce common symptoms. Shiatsu is usually done on a floor mat in a treatment room, but many spas offer "table shiatsu," which is performed on a massage table.

Ashiatsu. Not to be confused with shiatsu, ashiatsu, or "foot pressure," is an ancient form of bodywork or massage therapy first practiced by Buddhist monks. Therapists perform an intense massage by manipulating muscles with their feet, while supporting themselves with bars hung from the ceiling. Because the therapist can potentially use his or her full body weight to provide pressure, this therapy may be ideal for athletes or people suffering from chronic pain.

Reflexology. While foot massage is an ancient art practiced in China, India, and Egypt, modern **reflexology** was developed by American Dr. W.H. Fitzgerald in 1915. He identified areas of the feet connected to ten energy zones running from the top of the head to the feet. Putting pressure on a reflex or energy zone is said to affect organs and tissues within that zone. The zones are similar to the energy meridians of Chinese medicine, and reflexology massage keeps energy flowing freely through the zones. Eunice Ingham of New York, another early proponent of reflexology, believed that the practice dissolved crystalline deposits in the feet that were thought to interfere with nerves and blood supply to various parts of the body.

Tuina (or Tui Na). Tuina is a Chinese word that means "push-grasp," and is a massage therapy that dates back to the Shang Dynasty (1700 BCE). By 700 CE, Tuina was offered as a course of study at the Imperial Medical College. In the seventeenth century, Tuina merged with a technique called Anmo to become close to the modern experience of this massage technique. (In Japan, Anmo still refers to this technique, while Tuina is used in China and elsewhere.)

Tuina consists of a series of pressing, tapping, and kneading that stimulates the flow of chi and blood to promote healing and to open the energy flow from the body's meridians. Because the techniques range from light stroking to deep tissue work, this is not considered a recreational massage. It can be quite powerful or even painful, and practitioners often use herbal compresses to assist the healing process.

Jin Shin Do. Translated as "the way of the compassionate spirit," this massage therapy was developed by American Iona Marsaa Teeguarden in the late 1970s.[11]

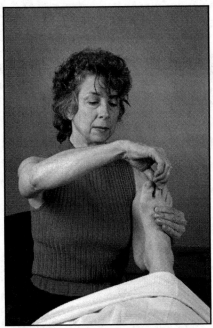
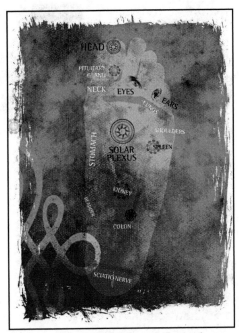

Reflexologists massage energy zones on the foot to affect other areas of the body connected to those zones.

More than just massage, Jin Shin Do combines the theories and techniques of acupressure, acupuncture, breathing exercises, Taoist philosophy, and modern psychology as a way to restore balance to a client's body, mind, and spirit. The therapist uses gentle pressure to release muscle tension and relieve stress. Because there is no movement of the client's body, only the application of pressure, this practice can benefit people who cannot be moved or for whom moving certain body parts is difficult.

Thai. Thai massage, known as Nuad bo-Rarn ("ancient massage" in Thai) works to open the body's meridians to free their energy by using stretches, massage strokes, and body movements. It is done on a floor mat and the client remains clothed. Although associated with Thailand, this style of massage originated in India and was part of the Buddhist religion. A monk named Komparaj, a personal physician to Buddha, is regarded as the first person to develop the technique.[12] As Buddhism spread to Thailand, this massage technique did as well. Along the way, the technique incorporated elements of both Ayurvedic and traditional Chinese medicine.

Originally performed only by Buddhist monks, Thai massage has grown in popularity and is now taught to other practitioners. In Thailand, the Ministry of Education oversees and regulates certification and training programs that teach Thai massage, and many spa owners send their therapists to Thailand for training. While it is considered a healing art in Thailand, most Western spa-goers choose Thai massage for its relaxing effects.

Reiki. Not truly massage, **Reiki** is a healing technique that originated in Tibet more than 2,500 years ago. The word Reiki means "universal life force." This life force or energy is Ki (also written Qi or Chi), the energy that in Japanese and Chinese cultures makes up all living things. Reiki was introduced to the Western world in the 1970s. In Reiki, the practitioner places his or her hands on or slightly above a person with the intent for healing to occur as hand placement enhances the flow of energy. The therapist doesn't actually massage the body at all. In fact, the touch is very light—if at all—as it focuses on the client's aura, the two or three feet of space surrounding a person's body and containing a subtle energy field. Practitioners believe that Reiki can relieve pain, boost the immune system, and relieve physical expressions of pain that are often linked to a person's emotional, mental, and spiritual states.

Other Massage Techniques

The following massage styles are neither Western nor Asian, but unique traditions or combinations of other techniques.

Lomi Lomi. This ancient Polynesian massage is considered to be a Hawaiian massage technique. In 1803, a visitor to Hawaii wrote about his experience of Lomi Lomi, which he found "very lulling and pleasing when gently performed." In 1893, however, the new government of Hawaii outlawed all native spiritual traditions, including the healing art of Lomi Lomi. The tradition continued to be passed down within families until the 1970s, when laws were changed and Hawaiians were again allowed to practice their spiritual traditions publicly. In 1973, Margaret Machado, a respected Hawaiian kupuna (elder) began teaching Lomi Lomi to people outside her family who wanted to learn the art.

The specific techniques of Lomi Lomi massage include circular thumb strokes done in a one-two-three rhythm, knuckle strokes on larger, denser muscles in the same rhythm, followed by forearm strokes delivered in a continuous rhythmic motion. The therapist also performs gentle stretches of the body and gentle rotations of joints to help release tensions and energy flow, returning the client to balance and harmony. Lomi Lomi also includes a spiritual element, in which the therapist begins the massage with a quiet blessing, asking for whatever healing is needed to take place during the massage. The therapist may ask the client to set their intention for any healing they want to receive.

Aromatherapy. In aromatherapy massage, the therapist applies essential oils to the skin, mixed with massage oil or another carrier. The oils are absorbed into the skin in small quantities, resulting in deep relaxation or other effects, such as reduced anxiety, elimination of headaches, or calming asthma. Many massage therapists create their own blends of essential oils and will match the oils they use to the client's purpose for a massage. Aromatherapy can be incorporated into Swedish, Ayurvedic, or other massage techniques.

Hot Stone. While stones have been used in healing arts for centuries, hot stone massage as it is known today was developed in Arizona in the early 1990s, and is now offered on most spa treatment menus. Stones used in this treatment are usually smooth river rock made of basalt. The stones' rich iron content helps them

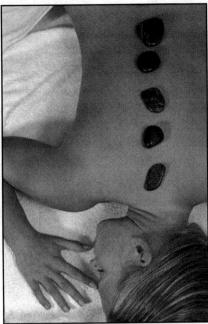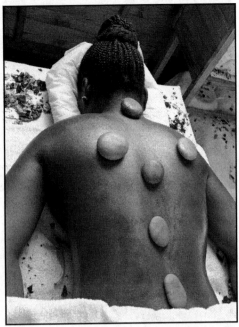

Heated stones relax the muscles, enabling the massage therapist to work more effectively.

retain heat. Stones are sanitized and heated to between 120 to 150 degrees Fahrenheit before the client arrives. The therapist places the warm stones on specific points on the back and on points thought to be energy centers of the body. The goal is to improve energy flow through the body and to warm the muscles. The therapist then uses traditional Swedish massage strokes while holding heated stones. As the stones cool, the therapist replaces them with others. Many people find the hot stones to be soothing. They also relax the muscles, which helps the therapist to work them more effectively without using deep pressure.

Movement Education and Mind-Body Fitness

Part of health and wellness is understanding how one's body works and how the proper functioning of the body contributes to an overall experience of physical, mental, and emotional well-being. In addition to offering traditional fitness activities such as walking/hiking, aerobics, and swimming, many spas offer classes in **movement education** and mind-body-spirit fitness that promote wellness through holistic practices that recognize the interconnectedness of the body and the mind.

A major study conducted by the Exercise Physiology and Nutrition Laboratory at the University of Massachusetts Medical School, the Mind/Body Medical Institute at the Harvard Medical School, and The Marsh: A Center for Balance and Fitness in Minnetonka, Minnesota,[13] found that adding a cognitive strategy to physical exercise resulted in more powerful and positive short- and long-term psychological responses than exercise alone. In other words, the mind-body interaction

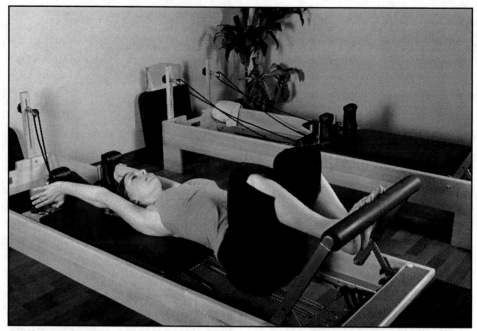

A Pilates reformer provides resistance that assists in the development of core muscles. The machine evolved from Joseph Pilates' first exercise machine, which he created from bed springs.

created psychological and emotional benefits in addition to the physical benefits of exercise.

The fitness and movement education practices described below were designed with a mind-body-spirit component that can offer spa-goers a more complete wellness experience.

Pilates

Pilates may seem like an exercise phenomenon of the late twentieth century, but it was developed in England during World War I and came to the United States during the 1920s. Joseph Pilates developed the exercise regimen to enhance his physical prowess as an acrobat and boxer, focusing on building core strength and flexibility without building bulk.

Pilates uses floor mats and equipment to help participants perform exercises that strengthen deep abdominal and back muscles, known as the "core." Pilates is a mind-body exercise that aims to help people become more in touch with their body—how it feels, where it is in space, and how its movements can be controlled. The system emphasizes proper breathing, good posture, efficient motion, and graceful movement. Most of the exercises are low impact and can be adapted to various levels of ability, for beginning exercisers through advanced athletes. The use of Pilates machines called reformers assists exercisers with proper form and provides resistance to help build and sculpt long, lean core muscles.

reflections

Ruth Stricker: Mind-Body Study at The Marsh

*Ruth Stricker founded The Marsh, a Center for Balance and Fitness.
She is an international spokesperson for the mind-body connection.
She is also an advisor to the Center for Spirituality and Healing at
the University of Minnesota. The President's Council on Physical
Fitness has named her a Healthy American Fitness Leader.*

I became disenchanted with the fitness movement
early on. I said, "We'll all have tight abs and pecs, but vacant
hearts and minds." I saw the narcissism with getting fit. I
also saw a whole decade of people who felt ripped off. They
got fit and it didn't change their lives. So I really started
working on the mind-body thing.

I started the Marsh in about 1983, but I toured Asia and Europe to see what
their idea was in terms of fitness and wellness. I found that Europeans were walking and skiing everywhere. I found out that "fitness" was American. In Europe,
you lived fitness.

I initiated a three-year piece of research. In the health club industry, they were
doing something called "Commit to Get Fit." They were going to invite everyone
into the health club to take a fitness test. I said, "Guess who will line up to do that?
Only the fit." They then asked me what I would do and the research evolved.

I had the firm belief that if people are in their favorite shirt doing their favorite thing that the benefits are much greater than if they're on a treadmill in a white
sterile room gritting their teeth and saying, "This must be good for me."

It was from the research that mindful exercise was born. It was exercise with a
cognitive component. The reason that this is pertinent for spas is that it includes anything with a mindful component. That would include yoga, Pilates, tai chi, qigong,
all of the things that we're doing today for exercise. What we found was that there
was an immediate mood elevation and psychological lift with mindful exercise.

We had four groups: a control group, two walking at different paces, and one
was mindful exercise. The scientists developed a mood assessment to administer
before and after the exercise. Obviously the people who did the mind-body stuff
had the most elevated mood, but we found out that their mood coming in was
elevated just in anticipation of doing some exercise.

The reasons people exercise (in the order mentioned) are:

- It is a stress reliever.
- They enjoy it.
- It makes them feel better about themselves
- It is good for them.
- Improved appearance
- Stay in shape.

I see how this fits into fitness and the spas: Stress relief, enjoyable activity,
making us feel better about ourselves. The research was a turning point from aero-
bic exercise to mind-body exercise.

Profile

Joseph Pilates

Joseph Pilates was a boxer, circus performer, and self-defense instructor. He was born in Germany in 1880 and moved to England in 1912. Because of the physical nature of his work, Pilates developed a system of exercises based on yoga and ancient Greco-Roman fitness regimens. He first taught his method to others when he was placed in an internment camp in Lancaster, England, with other German nationals during World War I. He taught his exercises to help rehabilitate injured and ill camp members. He used bed springs attached to hospital beds to create an exercise machine that would build muscles by providing resistance—a prototype of later Pilates equipment. Pilates called his method "Contrology," because he wanted to stress that the mind, acting on the body, was the key to the success of the exercises.

In 1926, Pilates, with his wife, Clara, moved to New York City, where they opened an exercise studio. The studio was frequented by actors and dancers, including George Balanchine and Martha Graham, who found that Pilates' approach to building strength and flexibility improved their abilities as dancers. Pilates taught his exercise regimen to many members of the New York City Ballet. Pilates taught in New York until his death in 1967, and his wife continued to run his studio. In 1970, Ron Fletcher, a Pilates student, moved to Los Angeles and opened a Pilates studio that attracted many Hollywood stars. Their practice of Pilates propelled the exercise system into the mainstream.

Yoga

Yoga is a spiritual discipline that is part of the Ayurvedic tradition. It includes several areas of practice, including meditation, breathing, abstention from things that tie one to the world, spiritual observances, and practices designed to bring one closer to spiritual enlightenment.

A text called the Yoga Sutras, written more than 2,000 years ago, outlined eight areas or "limbs" of yoga practice. They include:

- Yama (moral behavior)
- Niyama (healthy habits)
- Asana (physical postures)
- Pranayama (breathing exercises)
- Pratyahara (sense withdrawal)
- Dharana (concentration)

Yoga practitioners use asanas, or postures, to focus their meditative practices and create energy flow.

- Dhyana (contemplation)

- Samadhi (higher consciousness)

In modern Western practice, what most people call yoga is hatha yoga, a physical practice that uses asanas, or postures, as a form of exercise and a way to focus one's meditative practices to create desired energy flow. There are many types of yoga. Some of the types more commonly offered in spas include:

- **Hatha yoga:** This yoga uses physical poses called asanas and pranayama—breath control—to achieve mind-body balance, increase relaxation, build strength, and open energy channels. *Most popular*

- **Iyengar yoga:** This type of yoga focuses on precise movements, in which practitioners use props like blocks and straps to help beginners and those who may not be as flexible. This kind of yoga is beneficial for beginners and for people with neck or back pain. It also provides the fundamentals of the basic yoga positions.

- **Ashtanga yoga:** Also known as "power yoga," ashtanga yoga uses powerful, flowing movements, including lunges and push-ups, to build strength and stamina.

- **Bikram yoga:** Performed in a heated room, this "hot yoga" uses high temperatures to help practitioners increase their flexibility. This type of yoga is not recommended for people with cardiovascular problems, because exercising in the heat may place too much strain on the body.

Chinese mind-body exercises, like tai chi and qigong, use forms or movements performed in sequence, such as those shown on this Chinese exercise chart. (Courtesy of Ruth Stricker, The Marsh: A Center for Balance and Fitness)

The health benefits of yoga include improved mood, reduced stress, increased lung capacity, improved strength and flexibility, and lowered blood pressure.

Tai Chi

Tai chi, also called tai chi chuan, is a mind-body exercise that originated in traditional Chinese medicine, where it is a form of martial arts. The practice combines slow, gentle, continuous movements and stretches with deep breathing and meditation. Each movement flows into the next, so the body is always in motion, but in a low-impact way. Technique is emphasized over strength.

The practice of tai chi dates from the twelfth century, when a monk named Chaing San-Feng is said to have created a series of exercises that imitated the movements of animals, such as the crane, snake, and tiger. Many of the moves in tai chi are named for the motions of these animals.

Tai chi can be beneficial for reducing stress, increasing energy and stamina, and enhancing flexibility. Research on the benefits of tai chi suggests that it may also offer other benefits, such as:

- Reducing anxiety and depression
- Improving balance and coordination
- Improving sleep quality
- Slowing bone loss in post-menopausal women
- Lowering blood pressure
- Relieving chronic pain[14]

Qigong

Qigong also comes from traditional Chinese medicine. It is a practice used to balance and enhance one's qi, or energy, through postures or movements, breathing, and focused intentions or mental focus. According to the National Qigong Association, people do qigong "to maintain health, heal their bodies, calm their minds, and reconnect with their spirit." The gentle movements of the practice, combined with focusing one's mind, help reduce stress, increase vitality, and enhance immune function.

There are many forms of qigong. Some styles are gentler and can be performed by people with physical limitations, while others involve challenging physical movements more suited to athletes. While some aspects of qigong make it seem like an exercise program, it is more comprehensive, with aspects of self-development, enriching one's spirituality, and promoting self-healing.

Feldenkrais Method

The Feldenkrais Method is a system of mind-body education that uses gentle movement and self-awareness exercises to increase range of motion, flexibility, and coordination. The method is named for Moshe Feldenkrais, a Russian-born physicist, mechanical engineer, judo expert, and educator, who developed his method in the 1940s after experiencing crippling knee injuries.[15] He taught himself to walk again through a process that integrated his knowledge of biology, physics, biomechanics, and physiology.

The Feldenkrais method teaches people to become more aware of how their bodies work through movement sequences that show clients new ways of moving that will reduce pain and enhance their physical functioning. The method is taught in group classes, called "Awareness Through Movement," and private lessons, called "Functional Integration." In group classes, a trained Feldenkrais teacher verbally leads participants through sequence of movements that involve thinking, sensing, moving, and imagining. In private lessons, the teacher uses non-invasive touching to help the student learn proper movements that enhance functioning.

Rolfing

Rolfing Structural Integration, commonly known as **Rolfing**, is a system of myofascial and soft tissue manipulation and movement education developed by Dr. Ida Pauline Rolf. The basis of Rolfing is a standardized series of ten sessions designed to systematically balance and optimize both the structure and function of the entire body. The "Ten-Series" is a sequence of sessions designed to align the body with each session building upon the last, progressing from the more superficial layers of connective tissue to deeper layers of muscle, and then organizing and integrating the body as a whole. The Rolfing therapist touches the body, feeling for imbalances in tissue texture, quality, and temperature to determine where work needs to be done.

The technique is designed to correct structural misalignment of the body's network of soft tissues, muscles, fascia, tendons, and ligaments. The goal of Rolfing is to effect long-term change and correction of posture and body alignment. This is an intensive therapy. Those for whom Rolfing might be appropriate include athletes, musicians, performers, those engaged in physically-demanding jobs, and people with a history of injury or trauma that interferes with their daily functioning.

Alexander Technique

The Alexander Technique is often used by musicians, singers, and actors to increase awareness of their posture and movements and how those affect their ability to perform effectively. It is a system of movement education that teaches people to

Profile

Ida Pauline Rolf

Ida Pauline Rolf earned her doctorate in biochemistry from the College of Physicians and Surgeons at Columbia University in 1920, at a time when few women pursued advanced scientific degrees. Even though she faced obstacles as a female scientist, she continued her research studies in organic chemistry at the Rockefeller Institute. She studied and experimented with various systems of healing and manipulation as she tried to find solutions to her own health problems and those of her sons.

Rolf's study of homeopathy, osteopathy, chiropractic, and yoga led her to explore ways to achieve correct alignment of the body. She was also influenced by the Feldenkrais and Alexander techniques. For 30 years, Rolf developed a program known as Structural Integration, familiarly called "Rolfing." In the 1960s, Rolf was asked to teach and practice her technique at the Esalen Institute in California. By 1967, she had organized a Guild for Structural Integration to formalize the teaching of her system. Two years before her death in 1979, Rolf wrote *Rolfing: The Integration of Human Structures.*

become more conscious of how they stand and move and teaches proper posture and motion to reduce injury and fatigue and increase comfort and coordination.

The technique is named for Frederick Matthias Alexander, an Australian actor who moved to London in 1904. He developed chronic laryngitis while performing. By watching himself in a mirror, he was able to see that he was tensing the muscles in his neck while speaking, which restricted his voicebox and compressed his spine. He also realized that his body was not doing what he thought it was. He had to think consciously about what he wanted his body to do, and then work to make sure that he was indeed practicing what he intended. He began teaching his technique around 1910, and his students included playwright George Bernard Shaw and educational philosopher John Dewey.

The Alexander Technique focuses on the relationship between the head, neck, and spine and helps people to increase their self-awareness, eliminate bad habits of posture and movement, and regain proper body alignment. It is a system of mind-body movement education because Alexander Technique instructors educate their clients about becoming sensitive to what their bodies are doing and how to control their physical well-being through awareness. The technique can be taught in group classes or one-on-one.

Trager Technique

Dr. Milton Trager spent 50 years developing and refining the bodywork technique that bears his name. During a Trager session, which typically lasts 60 to 90 minutes,

Profile

Milton Trager

Milton Trager was born in Chicago in 1908 and was a sickly child with a congenital spinal deformity. By the time he was 18, he had overcome his disability and become a disciplined athlete.

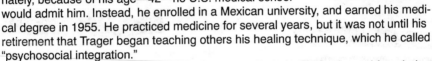

After his family moved to Miami Beach, Trager began training to be a boxer. His trainer usually gave him rubdowns after a training session, but one day, Trager offered to give the trainer a rubdown. The trainer was amazed at the skill and healing he felt coming from Trager's hands and told the young man that he had a special gift. Although not exactly sure what he had done, Trager used his healing touch on his father and healed him from crippling sciatica. He also helped a friend with polio to walk again.

Trager served in the U.S. Navy, then returned to the United States with a desire to become a doctor. Unfortunately, because of his age—42—no U.S. medical school would admit him. Instead, he enrolled in a Mexican university, and earned his medical degree in 1955. He practiced medicine for several years, but it was not until his retirement that Trager began teaching others his healing technique, which he called "psychosocial integration."

In 1975, he began teaching at the Esalen Institute in California, and founded the Trager Institute in 1980. When he died in 1997 at the age of 88, he had trained thousands of practitioners in the Trager method.

the client lies passively on a massage table while the therapist moves him or her in ways they would naturally move. The therapist's touch and movement creates the feeling that the client is moving effortlessly on his or her own. This massage work is supported by "mentas," which are simple, self-directed movements that can be incorporated into one's daily activities.

Hydrotherapy

Virtually everyone has practiced some form of **hydrotherapy** during their lives, even though they may not have realized there was a name for it. Hydrotherapy is the use of water for soothing pain, treating disease, and enhancing health. It includes such practices as using warm, moist compresses to relax sore muscles, putting an ice pack on an injury to reduce swelling, and using steam from a humidifier to soothe a sore throat or stuffy nose. Exercising in a pool, relaxing in a hot tub, and drinking water to stay hydrated also fall under the heading of hydrotherapy—using water in all of its forms, internally or externally, to promote wellness.

Hydrotherapy uses water in its many forms—liquid, steam, and ice—and in various pressures, such as pools, showers, hoses, and jets, to achieve different desired effects. Temperature is also a factor. Warm or hot water raises body temperature, induces sweating, opens pores, increases circulation, and encourages relaxation. Cool or cold water lowers body temperature, closes pores, decreases superficial circulation, and invigorates the person receiving a cold-water treatment. The components included in or added to water, such as minerals, algae, or salts, also achieve various results by introducing trace elements into the body by absorption. Hydrotherapy treatments include at least two broad subcategories: **balneotherapy**, referring to bathing, and **thalassotherapy**, related to using sea water and ingredients from the ocean.

While many people in the United States associate the word "spa" with massage, the origins of spa are in water and "taking the waters," and this is very evident in Europe and Asia, where hydrotherapy—water-based treatments—is the core of the spa experience. Not just a relaxing luxury, hydrotherapy is used as a medical treatment for a variety of ailments from arthritis, joint pain, and muscle pain to heart disease, asthma and other breathing disorders, colds, and skin diseases.

Balneotherapy

Balneotherapy refers to bathing treatments. Baths may be cold or warm (or alternating between temperatures), infused with essential oils, salts, or other additives, immersing the whole body or parts of the body. Bathing relaxes muscles and joints, boosts circulation, stimulates the immune system, and reduces stress. Bathing buoys the client, makes movement easier, and eliminates stress on the joints. Balneotherapy is not limited to plain water. It may also include bathing in mud, milk, or mineral waters.

Thalassotherapy

People have turned to the sea for thousands of years to find healing. Thalassotherapy, from the Greek word for "sea," describes a variety of spa treatments, including body wraps, baths, showers, and scrubs that use seawater, seaweed, algae, and other sea-related materials. The properties of seawater and products from the sea are believed to have beneficial effects upon the body. Trace elements of magnesium, potassium, calcium sulphates, and sodium found in seawater may be absorbed through the skin during thalassotherapy treatments. These elements are important to cellular health. Additionally, the negative ionization of sea air and water is thought to increase serotonin production, which boosts energy and creates a feeling of well-being.

This modern expression of sea-based therapy developed and flourished during the nineteenth century in coastal towns in Brittany, France, and also in other coastal areas, such as Spain and Portugal. In the mid-twentieth century, thalassotherapy resurged in France, where it is highly regulated to ensure the purity of the seawater used in treatments.

Tangentially related to thalossotherapy, **halotherapy** uses salt as a medium for health and healing. According to an article in *Time* magazine, several spas in the Chicago area and throughout the United States have added salt caves and salt rooms where guests can sit and relax while breathing in the salty air. The practice originated in Eastern Europe, where people found that sitting in salt caves relieved allergies, asthma, eczema, high blood pressure, and ulcers. Some spas are importing salt for their salt caves from Poland; others use salt from the Dead Sea.[16]

René Quinton

French biologist, biochemist, and physiologist René Quinton made an important discovery about sea water in 1904, when he found the amazing similarities between nutrient-rich ocean water and human blood plasma.[17] Using a specially-controlled harvesting and processing technique, Quinton bottled what he called "ocean plasma" for use in hospitals to treat a number of diseases. He founded treatment centers in France, Belgium, and Egypt that saved thousands of lives, especially of children, and his plasma was used as a replacement for blood plasma by French military doctors during World War I. However, that war also halted Quinton's research and he died of war injuries in 1925. His work was resurrected in the 1980s, when French doctors and therapists began investigating Quinton's work and using his therapies again. His book *"L'Eau de mer, milieu organique," (Sea Water: Organic Medium)* was reissued in 1995, and the scientific information in that work is still valid and used today.

As an interesting side note, Rene Quinton helped to finance Orville and Wilbur Wright's early efforts with aviation because he thought that airplanes would make it easier for him to deliver ocean plasma treatments to children in Africa who suffered from dysentery, cholera, and dehydration.

Hydrotherapy Treatments

Hydrotherapy treatments vary by the type of bath or shower apparatus employed and by the type of water (hot, cold, mineral, salt, etc.) used to achieve different therapeutic effects.

Scotch hose. Also called a Scottish douche (from the French for "shower"), a douche à jet, or blitz, the Scotch hose uses alternating hot and cold water sprays—often of seawater—to massage a standing client. The high-pressured spray is aimed at specific areas of the body and provides an invigorating experience. The process starts at the feet and works up to the head, with the sprays stimulating each part of the lymphatic system, draining lymph glands, stimulating circulation, and relieving tension and stress.

Vichy Shower. Also called an affusion shower or rain shower, this technique is named for Vichy, a city in central France. In this treatment, a person lies down on a table with pulsating water raining down from multiple jets upon the entire length of his or her body from two to four feet above the table. The water may alternate hot and cold or pulsate in different patterns or may be infused with essential oils and aromatics. It is a gentle technique used for relaxation, to relieve stress, and improve blood circulation. Vichy showers are used to remove products rubbed on the body during wraps and scrubs.

Swiss Shower. This shower features a showerhead directly over the guest's head, as well as multiple shower jets at varying heights surrounding the user. The water can be pulsed at different speeds and may alternate hot and cold water for a soothing or invigorating effect. *The client is standing*

Hydrotherapy baths, such as this whirlpool, were made possible by the work of the Jacuzzi brothers, although not all whirlpool baths are Jacuzzis.

Hydrotherapy Bath. Today's hydrotherapy bath was made possible by the invention of the submersible pump and motor. Used in hot tubs, whirlpools, and jetted tubs (such as the Jacuzzi tub), the hydrotherapy bath uses jets sprayed underwater to soothe and invigorate.

Before jetted tubs, hydrotherapy baths were most often sitz baths or warm baths. For a sitz bath, the client alternated between two adjacent tubs of water, one hot and one cold. This process helped to treat hemorrhoids, pre-menstrual discomfort, and menstrual problems. The warm bath experience consisted of soaking in warm water with various products added to the bath, depending on the client's condition or the desired result. These additives included Epsom salts, mineral-rich mud, aromatherapy oils, milk, seaweed, or Dead Sea salts.

Saunas and Steam Rooms. Saunas and steam rooms have been used since ancient Roman times and have been found in many cultures, including the Finnish sauna, Russian *banya*, Turkish *hammam*, Mayan *temezcalli*, and Native American sweat lodge. All of these cultures realized that sweating is one of the most effective ways to cleanse the body and rid it of toxins. These varieties of saunas and steam rooms were used for religious rituals, purification rites, physical healing, and social purposes. Today, many spas offer their guests some variation on these practices.

Saunas use dry heat to purify and detoxify the body by inducing sweating. While the humidity level in a sauna is very low (six to eight percent), guests can pour water over heated rocks to create steam. They also rinse periodically with

The Jacuzzi Brothers

At the turn of the twentieth century, the seven Jacuzzi brothers came to the United States from Italy. They settled in Berkeley, California, and created an aircraft manufacturing company where they built airplane propellers. After one of the brothers died in an airplane crash in 1921, they left the aircraft business and used their knowledge to manufacture a new deep well agricultural pump.

In 1948, the youngest brother, Candido, developed a portable, submersible bathtub pump to help his son, who had contracted rheumatoid arthritis as an infant. The pump allowed Jacuzzi to recreate at home the hydrotherapy treatments his son received at the hospital.

In the mid-1950s, the Jacuzzi brothers began to market the Jacuzzi whirlpool bath as a therapeutic aid. When it was offered as a prize on the TV show, "Queen for a Day," the Jacuzzi tub became a luxury item rather than a piece of medical equipment. In 1968, Roy Jacuzzi, a third-generation family member, invented the first self-contained, fully-integrated whirlpool bath with jets inset in the sides of the tub.

The company continued to expand, and now, a little more than a century after the Jacuzzi brothers came to America, the Jacuzzi/Sundance assembly plant is an ISO 9001 certified whirlpool production facility, producing up to 300 whirlpool tubs daily for homes and businesses.

cool water to keep from overheating. The treatment ends with a plunge into a cold pool or shower, or, in certain locations, into a snow bank.

A steam room also uses heat to cleanse the body of impurities, but as its name implies, the humidity level is much higher. Guests may also hose themselves down with cool water to regulate their body temperature and to wash away sweat and impurities. Heat and steam help to increase blood circulation, reduce muscle spasms, increase flexibility of collagen tissue, provide relaxation, and produce a sense of well-being through increased negative ionization.

Flotation Tank. A flotation tank provides users with a sensory deprivation experience that allows the body to relax deeply, which promotes cellular reproduction and healing. The tank, which is about the size of a twin bed, is filled with about 10 inches of skin-temperature water into which Epsom salts (magnesium sulphate) have been dissolved, creating a density greater that that of the Dead Sea. Floating in this kind of tank restricts environmental stimulation on the muscles, sensory organs, brain, and nervous system.

Physical benefits of flotation include:

- Reduced muscle tension
- Lowered pulse rate
- Reduced cortisol levels
- Increased release of endorphins
- Increased oxygen and nutrients to cells[18]

Watsu. Harold Dull, director of the Harbin Institute in northern California, developed Watsu in the early 1980s when he began floating his students of Zen Shiatsu in the warm water pool at Harbin. The word is derived by combining "water" and "shiatsu." Watsu combines elements of massage, joint movement, stretching, and dance in a water environment.

The therapist supports the client's head and knees, and the support of the water takes weight off the spine, allowing the client to be moved in ways impossible on a massage table. The therapist uses gentle pulls and twists to relieve spinal pressure on nerves. Watsu is effective for people who have had surgery or who have specific movement restrictions. Others find that Watsu provides an experience of deep relaxation and meditative stillness.

Wassertansen. From the German for "water dancing," this treatment was developed in Germany by Arjana Brunschwiler and Aman Schroter in the late 1980s. Unlike Watsu, where the client floats on top of the water, in Wassertansen, the therapist takes the client into a pool where the whole body is submerged. Freed from gravity, the body can be moved and stretched more easily. The process includes massage elements combined with body rolls, dance, and somersaults. The treatment promotes a deep state of relaxation as well as a physical release of emotions.[19]

Body Treatments

Body treatments include wraps and scrubs that use natural substances to enhance beauty, improve circulation and skin tone, and introduce trace elements into the body through absorption. The first step in these treatments is usually **exfoliation**, which removes dead skin cells through the use of brushes, loofahs, special gloves, or topical ingredients like salts, spices, muds, or seaweed. This step helps to maximize the effects of the treatment on fresh skin.

Body wraps incorporate ingredients that cover the body, plus a wrapping material to retain warmth and enhance penetration of the ingredients and achieve desired effects such as firming, body definition, detoxification, or pain relief. Body masks are similar to wraps except the client is not enveloped in a cocooning material. This is helpful for those who may be claustrophobic. Instead of the heat of a wrap acting on the mask ingredients, the client may spend time in a steam room or sauna, where the heat will help the ingredients to penetrate the skin.

Mud Wraps and Baths. The use of mud in spa therapies is known as **pelotherapy**. The ancient Greek physician Galen wrote about mud treatments for arthritis and rheumatism. The application of mud also has exfoliating properties, increases skin circulation, and helps to remove waste products. There are many types of mud, including coastal mud, clay, loam, peat, and chalk. Each type has specific properties for treating a variety of problems. Mud can be applied to particular areas—knees, shoulders, back, hips—or all over the body, as in a mud bath.[20]

Fango Wrap. In a treatment similar to that described above, fango (Italian for "mud"), a highly-mineralized mud, is used to cleanse, purify, and revitalize the skin. A variant on this, called a parafango wrap, uses a combination of fango mud and paraffin wax.

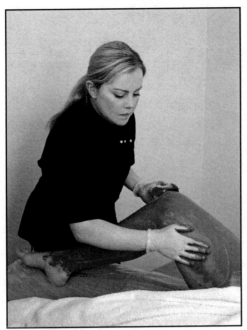 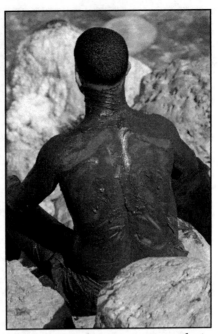

Mud treatments can help to exfoliate skin, increase circulation, and remove waste products. Different types of mud have specific properties useful for treating a variety of conditions.

Herbal Wrap. The guest is wrapped in herb-soaked hot sheets and covered in blankets, with a cool compress on the forehead. Herbal wraps relax the muscles, detoxify the body, and soften the skin. The herbs used will vary depending on the goal of the wrap. For instance, chamomile, lavender, comfrey, and sage are calming and relaxing, while ginger root, rosemary, eucalyptus, and clove have detoxifying properties.

Salt Glow. Also called a salt scrub, this treatment exfoliates and hydrates skin. The therapist rubs a mixture of sea salt, oils, and aromatherapy oils into the guest's skin, then rinses the mixture off with either a hand-held shower or a Vichy shower. The treatment is usually finished with an application of lotion. It can also be the preliminary, exfoliating step in a body wrap.

Seaweed Wrap. There are many types of seaweed: blue, red, brown, green. These provide minerals and trace elements and offer negative ionization. In this treatment, the client is enveloped in warm seaweed and wrapped in a heated blanket. The purpose is to rebalance the body by introducing trace elements that may be missing, as well as to soften the skin.

Loofah Scrub. A loofah is a dried plant used to exfoliate the body. It may be used in combination with salts, essential oils, and water to massage the body and rid the skin of dead cells.

Javanese Lulur. Meaning "coating the skin," this technique has been used in Java since the seventeenth century as a treatment for a bride before her wedding. A

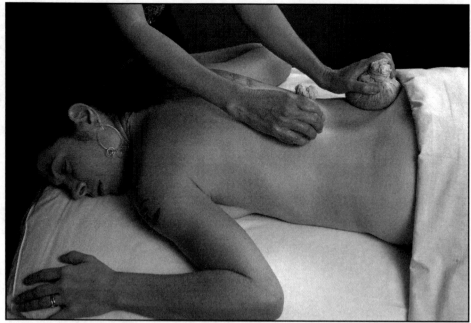

Warm linen bundles filled with marine salts and lavender buds are placed on the body's acupressure points during a Thai bolus treatment.

skin-polishing body scrub is created from finely ground herbs, spices, roots of plants indigenous to India (fenugreek, turmeric, sandalwood), and rice powder. These are mixed into a paste with jasmine oil and applied to the body to dry. The paste is then rubbed off, and yogurt and honey are applied to soften the skin. The final step is a warm bath filled with flowers including jasmine, roses, ylang ylang, and frangipani.

Thai Bolus. This treatment begins with a body polish using marine oil and salts, washed off with a warm Vichy shower. Then, warm linen bundles filled with marine salts and lavender buds are placed on the body's acupressure points to deliver warmth and enhance the flow of energy through the body's channels.

Aromatherapy Wrap. Linen sheets are soaked in water to which essential oils have been added. The oils selected will vary depending on the goal of the treatment.

Skin Care/Facials

A facial is a skin treatment that generally consists of the following steps: cleansing, steaming, exfoliating, extraction, massaging, treating, and moisturizing. Facials vary according to the client's skin type (oily, dry, blemished, sun damaged) or what they hope to achieve (fewer wrinkles, even skin tone, etc.). They can be defined by the goal of the facial, the ingredients used, or the technique employed by the esthetician.

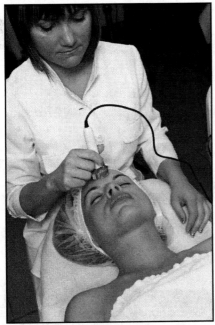 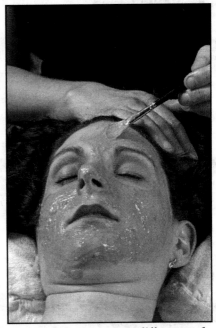

Facials are one of the most popular spa treatments. The esthetician uses different techniques or ingredients to achieve the desired effect for the guest.

By Therapeutic Goals/Skin Profile

Deep Cleansing. A deep-cleansing facial unclogs pores, removes dead skin cells, draws out excess oils, and stimulates circulation. It is particularly good for oily or acne-prone skin.

Purifying. Creams and masks that use free-radical fighting agents like Vitamin A, beta carotene, and Vitamin C work to remove pollution from the skin and deep cleanse it. This facial is beneficial for people who work outdoors or in polluted urban areas.

Anti-Aging. This type of facial uses products with ingredients such as alpha or beta hydroxy acids and Vitamin C to smooth lines and wrinkles, plump up skin, and encourage collagen production to reduce signs of aging.

Hydrating. While hydration is a goal of most facials, a hydrating facial focuses on preparing the skin to accept additional moisture, then provides hydrating ingredients for the skin to "soak up," for longer-lasting hydration. People with dry skin or those in cold, winter climates benefit from this treatment.

Soothing. This facial uses botanicals and other ingredients that soothe sensitive skin or skin prone to redness or irritation, calming the skin and relaxing the client.

Back. This treatment uses the steps of a facial on the back to provide deep cleansing.

By Ingredient

Vitamin. Serums containing vitamins (typically A, C, and E) are used to reduce fine lines and wrinkles, hydrate dry skin, reduce under-eye puffiness, and improve skin texture. The antioxidants in the vitamins combat damage caused by free radicals in the environment.

Aromatherapy. This skin care treatment uses essential oils to penetrate the skin for beauty and health purposes. An aromatherapy facial can improve the skin's function and clear congestion, while also relaxing the client's body and mind. Essential oils may stimulate cell regeneration and provide an uplifting effect.

Peeling (chemical, enzyme, glycolic). Peeling refers to removing damaged outer layers of skin to reveal new, fresh layers of skin. The peeling can be achieved in various ways. A chemical peel uses a chemical solution, such as phenol, trichloroacetic acid (TCA), or alpha-hydroxy acids (AHA) to remove damaged layers of skin. AHAs are derived from flowers or fruits, which are good to use on sensitive skin. A glycolic facial breaks down the "glue" bond that holds dry skin on the face and then rapidly exfoliates it to soften lines and smooth the skin.

Collagen. Freeze-dried collagen, a protein found within the middle layer of the skin, is used to plump the skin to fill in fine lines caused by sun damage, stress, or environmental pollution. The facial includes exfoliation, warm vapor, deep pore cleansing, lymphatic drainage massage, and a mineral or paraffin mask over a freeze-dried collagen sheet to hydrate skin.

By Technique

Oxygen. Oxygen and other nutrients are applied to the face to stimulate and reinforce the collagen level of the skin. The theory behind an oxygen facial is that because of pollution, skin has trouble getting the oxygen that its cells need to operate efficiently and effectively. An oxygen facial targets the skin with medical-grade oxygen to send it to the skin's capillaries. This plumps up the skin, reducing lines and filling in imperfections.

Microdermabrasion. This facial uses tiny particles passed through a vacuum tube to gently abrade the surface of the skin, smoothing it and stimulating new cell growth.

LED. Also called "photo rejuvenation" or a "photo facial," this skin care treatment uses light emitting diodes (LED) and Intense Pulsed Light (IPL) to lift and firm skin with visible red and infrared light. The light stimulates cell growth and increases production of collagen by up to 50 percent. The result is like a mini-face lift with no invasive procedures.

Ayurvedic. This facial incorporates the principles of Ayurveda, including meditation, herbalism, massage, breathing, and diet to balance and restore harmony to the skin and body.

Stone. This facial uses warm stones, or hot and cool stones to relax the muscles of the face and neck, releasing stress. The stones may be basalt, volcanic rock, river stones, marble, or even gemstones. They are arranged on pressure points, either with all warm stones, or alternating warm and cool to rejuvenate the skin.

Conclusion

This chapter is by no means exhaustive in its coverage of the broad spectrum of spa treatments, but it does offer a basic introduction to some of the more common treatments likely to be found on a contemporary resort or day spa menu. Spa professionals may want to explore the origins and histories of other spa treatments not listed here in order to appreciate the depth and richness of all that spas have to offer.

Endnotes

1. Jane Crebbin-Bailey, John Harcup, and John Harrington, *The Spa Book: The Official Guide to Spa Therapy* (London, UK: Thompson Learning, 2005), p. 116.

2. National Center for Complementary and Alternative Medicine, National Institutes of Health website (www.nccam.nih.gov).

3. Crebbin-Bailey et al., p. 117.

4. Crebbin-Bailey et al., p. 31.

5. Patricia J. Benjamin and Frances M. Tappan, *Tappan's Handbook of Healing Massage Techniques*, 4th ed. (Upper Saddle River, N.J.: Pearson Education, 2005), pp. 324–335.

6. Benjamin and Tappan, p. 313.

7. NCCAM, Publication D347, "CAM Basics".

8. Benjamin and Tappan, p. 14.

9. Benjamin and Tappan, p. 246.

10. Benjamin and Tappan, p. 258.

11. Benjamin and Tappan, p. 364.

12. Skin, Inc., magazine, April 2007, "The History of Thai Massage," pp. 119–122.

13. James Rippe, Ruth Stricker, David Brown, Youde Wang, and Ann Ward. *The Acute and Chronic Psychological Responses to Exercise Alone and Exercise Combined with Cognitive Strategies*, (The Exercise Physiology and Nutrition Laboratory, August 1992).

14. www.mayoclinic.com, "Tai Chi: Improved Stress Reduction, Balance, Agility For All," by Mayo Clinic staff.

15. Benjamin and Tappan, p. 437.

16. Jeninne Lee-St. John, "Saline Solutions," *Time Magazine*, March 27, 2008.

17. Crebbin-Bailey et al., p. 12.

18. Crebbin-Bailey et al., p. 62.

19. Crebbin-Bailey et al., p. 58.

20. Crebbin-Bailey et al., p. 123.

Key Terms

allopathic—Treatment of disease using Western medical modalities.

apprenticeship—A system of learning by practical experience under the guidance of a skilled practitioner in a trade, art, or calling.

Ayurveda—A holistic medical system developed in India that includes diet, exercise, massage, meditation, yoga, and spiritual aspects to prevent illness and enhance wellness.

balneotherapy—The therapeutic use of bathing.

CAM—Complementary and alternative medicine, referring to medical practices outside the scope of traditional, Western allopathic medicine.

energy work—Treatment modalities based on the idea that the human body consists of energy fields that can be stimulated and channeled to promote wellness.

essential oils—Aromatic liquid substances extracted from flowers, fruits, leaves, and other plant matter, used for medical or cosmetic purposes.

exfoliation—The removal of dead skin cells through the use of brushes, loofahs, and/or topical ingredients like salt, mud, or spices.

halotherapy—The therapeutic use of salt.

hydrotherapy—The therapeutic use of water to heal and promote wellness.

integrative medicine—A whole-person approach to medicine that combines treatments from allopathic, complementary, and alternative medical practices.

meridians—In Traditional Chinese Medicine, the major channels through which qi (energy) flows.

movement education—The practice of teaching people about the structure of their bodies and how to move in ways that reduce stress and enhance physical and mental well-being.

myofascial—Releasing tension in the loose, connective tissue that surrounds every muscle, nerve, blood vessel, and organ.

peeling—A process that enhances the skin by removing damaged outer layers of skin with chemicals or enzymes to reveal the new layers underneath.

pelotherapy—The therapeutic use of mud.

Pilates—An exercise program developed by Joseph Pilates, designed to strengthen core abdominal and back muscles.

reflexology—A type of energy work massage that focuses on pressure points in the feet that correlate to other parts of the body.

Reiki—Meaning "universal life force," this is a type of energy work in which the therapist focuses on the aura surrounding the body to enhance the flow of qi or ki.

Rolfing—A system of structural integration developed by Dr. Ida Pauline Rolf.

qi—Energy or life force (also written chi or ki).

qigong—A mind-body exercise that combines postures, breathing, meditation, and intentional movements.

tai chi—A form of martial arts characterized by gentle, continuous movements.

thalassotherapy—The therapeutic use of seawater and sea-based products such as mud, seaweed, or algae.

trigger point therapy—Soft tissue manipulation technique focusing on targeting specific spots, or trigger points, where taut bands of tissue around muscles and tendons cause direct and/or referred pain.

watsu—A water-based therapy created by Harold Dull that combines shiatsu massage and gentle body movements performed in the water.

yoga—A spiritual discipline that is part of the Ayurvedic tradition.

 ## Review Questions

1. What practices are included within the scope of Ayurveda?
2. What is the importance of qi to Traditional Chinese Medicine?
3. What are the four domains of complementary and alternative medicine?
4. What are the basic strokes used in massage therapy?
5. What is the purpose and goal of energy work?
6. What are the types of energy work and what do they accomplish?
7. What are the major types of movement education and what do they accomplish?
8. What are the benefits of thalassotherapy?
9. How is each of the following used in a spa environment: Vichy shower, Scotch hose, Swiss shower?
10. What elements are included in the various classifications of facials (goals, ingredients, techniques)?

 ## Internet Sites

For more information, visit the following Internet sites. Remember that Internet addresses can change without notice. If the site is no longer there, you can use a search engine to look for additional sites.

American Association of Integrative Medicine
www.aaimed.com

American Massage Therapy Association
www.amtamassage.com

American Organization of Bodywork Therapies of Asia
www.aobta.org

Associated Bodywork and Massage Professionals
www.abmp.com

Association of Skin Care Professionals
www.ascpskincare.com

Bonnie Prudden Myotherapy
www.bonnieprudden.com

Canadian Massage Therapist Alliance
www.cmta.ca

The Complete Guide to the Alexander
Technique
www.alexandertechnique.com

Craniosacral Therapy Association of
North America
www.craniosacraltherapy.org

Dr. Vodder School of North America
www.vodderschool.com

The Feldenkrais Method of Somatic
Education
www.feldenkrais.com

Home of Reflexology
www.reflexology.org

Institute of Thai Massage
www.thai-massage.org

International Feldenkrais Federation
www.feldenkrais-method.org

International Institute of Reflexology
www.reflexology-usa.net

International Somatic Movement and
Therapy Association
www.ismeta.org

Jin Shin Do Foundation
www.jinshindo.org

Lomi Lomi Massage
www.lomilomi.com

National Association for Holistic
Aromatherapy
www.naha.org

National Center of Complementary
and Alternative Medicine
www.ncca.nih.gov

National Qigong Association
www.nqa.org

Pilates
www.pilates.com

Pilates Method Alliance
www.pilatesmethodalliance.org

Qigong Institute
www.qigonginstitute.org

Rolf Institute of Structural Integration
www.rolf.org

Thalassotherapy Federation
www.thalassofederation.com

Traditional Chinese Medicine
www.amfoundation.com/tcm.htm

Traditional Chinese Medicine
Information Page
www.tcmpage.com

The Trager Approach
www.trager.com

Upledger Institute (Craniosacral
Therapy)
www.upledger.com

The Watsu Institute
www.learnwatsu.com

Triple Bottom
Planet
People
Profit

Chapter 7 Outline

Revenue Centers
    Revenue Center Departments
    Spa Services Revenue Centers
    Additional Revenue Centers
    Contributors to Spa Revenue
Cost Centers
    Labor Costs
    Support Labor
    Indirect Operating Expenses
    Undistributed Operating Expenses
Putting It All Together

Competencies

1. Describe various spa revenue centers. (pp. 251–263)

2. Identify spa cost centers. (pp. 263–275)

3. Indentify a spa's indirect operating expenses and undistributed operating expenses. (pp. 275–278)

4. Explain how revenue and expenses are recorded on financial statements. (pp. 278–280)

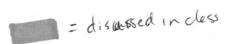 = discussed in class

7

Financial Organization
of Spas

THIS CHAPTER introduces the basic organization and financial realities of operating a spa. It offers knowledge of how a spa is organized financially and how each department functions, either as a revenue or a cost center. There is much more to running a spa business, including writing a business plan, creating financial controls and budgets, strategic planning, forecasting, scheduling staff for optimizing profit, and configuring a software system. These will be addressed in a later text.

To gain perspective on how spas are organized and managed, note these spa characteristics:

- All spas are in the business of providing personal services. These services may vary in nature, e.g., massages, body treatments, facials, manicures, pedicures, hair styling, light therapy, medical treatments, and a number of complementary or alternative therapies.

- Spas vary in type and location; they can be resort spas, destination spas, club spas, cruise ship spas, medical spas near other healthcare facilities, or day spas in hotels, malls, business districts, or even neighborhoods.

- Spas vary in size. According to the *2007 ISPA Spa Industry Study*, day spas averaged 2,969 square feet, while hotel/resort spas averaged 10,830 square feet. Some spas might be as large as 50,000 to 70,000 square feet. The overall size of spas increased 5.9 percent between 2006 and 2007.

- Spas vary in the level of experience they offer. For example, in some small day spas there will be no relaxation area, no water experiences such as whirlpools, steam rooms, saunas, or hydrotherapy treatments, and clients will likely change from their street clothes into a spa robe (if they are even offered a robe) right in the treatment room. Other spas have significant wet lounges and both private men's and ladies' relaxation rooms, along with co-ed relaxation spaces, extensive fitness facilities, a spa swimming pool, and a spa café. Some day spas may even include a medical component, e.g., dermatology, exercise physiology, fitness measurements.

- Day spas typically offer basic services and fewer amenities but see more repeat clients from the local community, whereas many resort/hotel spas are planned as an amenity for the resort guests.

- Resort/hotel spas may allow access only to on-property guests on weekends, and these guests, unlike day spa clients, seldom visit the same resort more than once or twice per year.

251

Clearly, no two spas are alike. Regardless of type, size, or location, a spa must be organized and operated to attract and serve guests while making a reasonable profit.

The stark reality is that spas, like all other businesses, are in the business of providing a return on investment for their owners. A spa's philosophy and its business operations must work in harmony if the spa is to be successful. People who work in the spa industry quickly realize that their passion for purpose must be balanced with equal business passion to operate the spa profitably. Stephen R. Covey expresses it as "no margin, no mission." In his book, *The 8th Habit*, Covey notes, "Unless you run your enterprise in a way that produces consistent profits over time, eventually you lose your opportunity to deliver on your mission. Most businesses, on the other hand, are so focused on margin and meeting the quarterly numbers that they lose sight of the very vision that inspired them to get into business in the first place."

The measure of success for a spa must be more than financial. Success must also include the people who are part of the spa. In a process he calls double bottom-line accounting, Covey urges organizations to move beyond the single bottom line—profit—to create a second bottom line that quantifies the health of the organization by examining how the spa relates to all of its key stakeholders, including customers, suppliers, employees and their families, and the community. "… imagine the power of having a two-page summary of the present and future health of your organization—one page devoted to the financial statement (the present fruits of prior efforts), and the other giving you a leading indicator of your relationships with the stakeholders, which will produce all your future results." A spa may well consider the benefits of developing a performance scorecard with the help of its stakeholders that will reflect how well everyone involved with the spa is aligned with the mission, values, and strategies the spa has established for itself. A spa director must balance both bottom lines and maintain the core purpose of spa in order to be successful. A third bottom line reflects how the spa cares for the planet.

This chapter will discuss the sources of revenue in a spa and the costs that a spa professional must manage to provide a reasonable return on the capital that was required to finance the development and opening of the spa facility. Material in the chapter draws extensively from the *Uniform System of Financial Reporting for Spas* (USFR), published by the International SPA Association Foundation as a reference tool for spa operators.

As noted above, spas vary widely. No matter what category a spa falls into, however, it must be organized in order to (1) coordinate the many specialized services and activities necessary to attract and serve clients, and (2) produce a reasonable profit consistent with the amount of money and time invested in the business.

Revenue Centers

The divisions in a spa are categorized as revenue centers and cost centers. **Revenue centers** generate income for the spa through the sales of services or products to guests/clients. **Cost centers**, also known as support centers, do not generate revenue directly. Instead they support the proper functioning of revenue centers. The USFR provides spa professionals with a wealth of information about both revenue and cost centers. This reference book, created by the ISPA Foundation, in collaboration with the American Hotel & Lodging Educational Institute and Hospitality Financial & Technology Professionals, provides a financial reporting system that allows spas to measure, compare, and report on the financial health of the organization.

An easy way to understand revenue and cost centers is to take a look at some spa organizational charts for day spa, resort/hotel spa, and **boutique spa** facilities.

In the day spa organizational chart (Exhibit 1), the positions listed for each team leader are revenue centers, while the positions listed under the desk manager are support labor/cost centers. In the boutique spa example (Exhibit 2), the estheticians, therapists, salon technicians, fitness staff, and instructors are revenue centers, while the group coordinator, receptionist, and valets are support labor, which is a cost center. The large resort spa (Exhibit 3) has more extensive support/cost centers, including concierges, valets, and attendants, and also has more personnel in each revenue center—not just the technicians, but trainers and leads for each service department.

Revenue Center Departments

Some believe that spas are structured very simply from a revenue perspective; that a spa derives its revenues from selling treatments and retail, but a spa is a much more sophisticated business with several departments under the umbrella of spa. It can be compared to a department store, with its various clothing departments, housewares, jewelry, linens, furniture, electronics, china/glass/silver, shoes, and perhaps even a restaurant.

The USFR presents the organization of a spa in a similar fashion with revenue departments including:

- Massage
- Skin Care
- Nail
- Hair
- Fitness
- Retail
- Membership
- Food and Beverage
- Health and Wellness
- Other Operating Departments, such as:
  a. Art Programs
  b. Adventure Experiences
  c. Pool/Beach Services
  d. Children's Camps
  e. Equestrian
  f. Guided Hiking Programs
  g. Tennis

Exhibit 1   Day Spa—Sample Organizational Chart

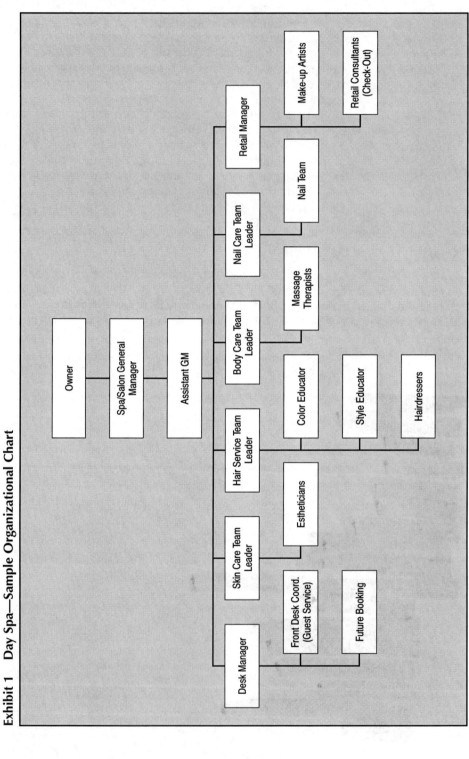

Exhibit 2   Boutique Spa—Sample Organizational Chart

```
                          ┌──────────────┐
                          │ Spa Director │
                          └──────┬───────┘
                                 │
   ┌───────────────────┐         │         ┌───────────────────┐
   │ Group Coordinator │─────────┼─────────│ Receptionists—6   │
   └───────────────────┘         │         └───────────────────┘
                                 │
   ┌─────────────────────────┐   │         ┌─────────────────────────────┐
   │ Estheticians—6 Contractors│─┼─────────│ Valets                      │
   └─────────────────────────┘   │         │ Full-time: 6  Part-time: 1  │
                                 │         └─────────────────────────────┘
   ┌─────────────────────────┐   │         ┌─────────────────────────┐
   │ Therapists—16 Contractors│──┼─────────│ Fitness Instructors—6   │
   └─────────────────────────┘   │         └─────────────────────────┘
                                 │
   ┌─────────────────────────────┐│        ┌─────────────────────────┐
   │ Salon Technicians—6 Contractors│───────│ Tennis Instructors—2   │
   └─────────────────────────────┘         └─────────────────────────┘
```

Spa Services Revenue Centers

The principal source of revenue for all spas is the sale of spa services, although there are some significant variations depending on the type of spa. In accordance with the *Uniform System of Financial Reporting for Spas*, there are four separate departments for spa services: Massage, Skin Care, Hair, and Nail. The mix of these services will vary depending on the type of spa. Exhibits 4, 5, and 6 show hypothetical examples of possible distribution of treatment revenue for the principal categories of spa facilities—a salon/spa, a day spa without hair and nail departments, and a full resort/hotel spa.

There are two principal types of day spas. The first is a business that would be described as a salon/day spa where there is a large hair and nail emphasis with many hair stations and nail stations, but generally a limited number of spa treatment rooms. The second type of day spa is a business that sells only spa services and perhaps nails, but without any hair stations. For day spas, the key consideration is to derive sufficient revenue per square foot to pay the higher rents that their more retail-oriented locations demand. Thus, productivity of the service space must be very high. Service revenue will comprise between 60 percent and 90 percent of the total day spa revenue. Similarly, service providers may be in short supply, and generating strong service revenue while controlling service payroll is vital to financial success.

Destination spas have an entirely different process for recording revenue. Their business model is to sell a package including room, food and beverage, program classes, and some designated number of spa services. Packages may be for a

Exhibit 3   Resort Spa—Sample Organizational Chart

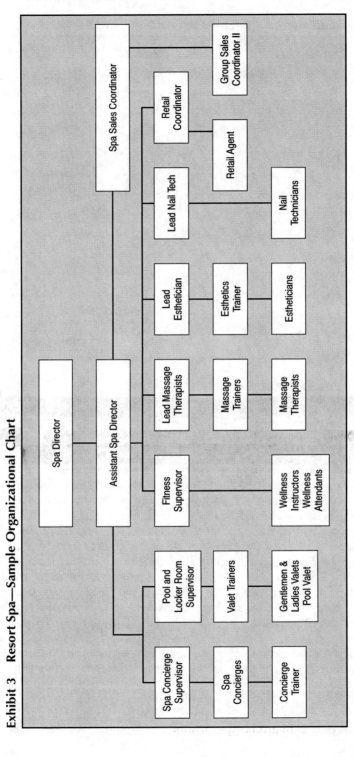

Exhibit 4   Sample Sources of Treatment Revenues for Salon/Day Spa

Massage	18%
Skin Care	20%
Hair	50%
Nails	12%

Exhibit 5   Sample Sources of Treatment Revenues for Day Spa Without Hair and Nail Departments

Massage	45%
Skin Care	55%

Exhibit 6   Sample Full Resort/Hotel Spa With Hair and Nail Departments

Massage	55%
Skin Care	20%
Hair	10%
Nails	15%

stay of three to seven days and are usually quoted for each individual based upon double occupancy of the guestroom. The destination spa then allocates the package revenue among rooms, food and beverage, spa treatments revenue, and fitness and programming (which may include things like fitness classes, guided hikes, and evening lectures). It is also important for destination spas to generate additional revenue beyond the package itself. For example, a destination spa package may include one or two spa services a day or several during the package duration. However, service revenue increases when guests choose to have additional treatments during their stay. Other things like retail merchandise and perhaps a glass of wine with dinner will also bring in additional revenue.

Massage. Massage is the most popular treatment spas offer. The USFR breaks down the types of massages into classifications that include:

- Relaxation and therapeutic, including Swedish, sports, deep tissue, and neck and shoulder massages
- Specialty, including aromatherapy, hot stone, reflexology, Shiatsu, Thai, pre-natal, Reiki, and other **signature massage treatments**.

For financial reporting purposes in accordance with the USFR, this department also includes hydrotherapy treatments like therapeutic baths, Vichy showers,

Scotch hose, hot and cold baths, and other water-based treatments. It also covers wraps and scrubs, such as algae, herbal, muds, loofah scrubs, salt glows, and other exfoliation and body nourishing treatments. Specialty body treatments, such as body bronzing, cellulite treatments, and other signature body treatments, also usually fall under the massage department.

The USFR notes that revenue for body treatments may be included in the massage schedule or the skin care schedule, depending upon which department's service providers perform the treatments. One argument for separating massage revenue from body treatment revenue comes from spa consultant Sylvia Sepielli, who notes that while labor is the same for each, the cost of performing a massage is significantly less expensive than a body treatment. "It makes it much easier for the spa director to see how well body treatments are performing when the two are recorded separately," she said. "If the operator just relies on the spa software system to evaluate the quantity of body treatments, they could be selling a lot but at a reduced margin."

Skin Care. Skin care, or esthetics, continues to grow in popularity as people begin to take better care of their skin to keep the effects of aging at bay and reduce damage caused by sunlight and environmental pollution. The skin care department's revenues may include revenue from offerings like:

- Standard facials, such as deep cleansing, gentleman's, and mini-facials

- Specialty facials, such as collagen, anti-aging, oxygen, ampoules, seaweed, cellular rejuvenation, glycolic, or a spa's signature treatments

- Body hair removal services, such as sugaring; leg, arm, back, and bikini waxing; and specialty services like laser hair removal

- Facial hair removal services, including brow waxing, threading, sugaring, lip waxing, and electrolysis

As noted above, the USFR suggests that spas may choose to include revenue from body treatments, such as body bronzing or cellulite/contouring, under the skin care department if that is where those treatments are performed.

Hair. In a spa with a salon, revenue from hair services may include:

- Hair coloring, such as single process, double process, retouching, glossing, and full or partial highlights

- Chemical treatments, such as partial and full permanents, spirals, relaxers, and straightening

- Hair styling, including haircuts, extensions, updo, formal, thermal, braiding, hair and scalp treatments, and other specialty styling services

Nail. Nail services include both manicures and pedicures. Treatment revenue for this department comes from a variety of services that may include:

- Manicures, including polish changing, classic manicure, hot oil, paraffin, special exfoliation, masks, and custom blending

- Nail enhancements, such as acrylics, gel tips, silk wraps, fill-ins, French nail tips, and nail repair
- Pedicures, including polish changing, classic pedicure, hot oil, seaweed, exfoliation treatments, paraffin, custom blending, and specialty masks

Additional Revenue Centers

In addition to the four main spa services treatment departments that provide revenue to spas, there are several other revenue centers that may or may not be present in a spa. These include retail, fitness, food and beverage, health and wellness, and memberships.

Retail Department. Retail sales are a critical component of a spa's profitability. The retail presence can be as simple as a few shelves displaying products in the lobby of the spa or a dedicated spa retail shop with extensive merchandise offerings. The USFR groups retail merchandise into four categories, which are further subdivided as shown:

Products
    Bath and Body Products
    Hair Products
    Make-up Products
    Nail Products
    Private Label Products — *manufactured for the spa*
    Skin Care Products
Apparel
    Footwear
    Men's/Unisex
    Robes and Terry
    Women's
Gifts and Accessories
    Books and Media
    Fashion Accessories
    Home
Other Retail
    Snacks and Beverages
    Sundries
    Other (includes nutritional supplements, fitness supplies, etc.)

Retail sales enable the spa to sell more to each client, generating additional revenue from each guest who books a treatment. The fact is that when a woman has a facial, she is seeking the clinical analysis of her skin condition and is predisposed to purchasing products to add to or replace her at-home skin care regimen. Guests may find an unstructured sweatshirt that becomes their favorite when they come home after a hectic day that symbolizes the start of the relaxation process and subconsciously takes them back to their wonderful time at the spa. Perhaps it is a spa music CD that guests pop into the CD player to create a peaceful ambience, an

William Randall

Years ago, a sage of hospitality retail, William Randall, developed seven hotel retail stores, an extensive spa retail program, and a major private label bath and body and sunscreen product line for La Costa Resort when it first opened. Within five years following the opening of the resort, the retail revenues were so significant that the retail revenues and departmental profit exceeded that of combined profits from rooms, food and beverage, and golf. Randall used to say, "You may attract 20 percent of the hotel guests into the spa for a treatment and perhaps another 15 percent will play golf, but I guarantee you that 100 percent of all resort guests will shop while they are staying here."

He believed that there could be no better marketing than to have the resort guest go home with a La Costa logo sweatshirt to remind them of the wonderful experience they had while at La Costa Resort and Spa. Better yet, how about that guest who buys a quart of La Costa bath gel with its beautiful fragrance, sitting on the shelf of their shower that will take them back to the wonderful aromas of the La Costa Spa every morning. That kind of thinking drives retail sales in spas.

aromatherapy candle that they light while taking a bath, or a lush robe purchased at the spa that they wrap around themselves before they go to bed.

The percentages of various classifications of retail may vary widely from spa to spa. In day spas, for instance, product sales may be close to 80 or 90 percent of total retail sales, while a hotel/resort spa may see 50 percent of its retail revenue come from products.

From a business perspective, the cost of sales measures the profitability of retail sales. It is the ratio between the cost of the goods sold and the net revenue. A lower cost of sales means a greater profit. Initial markups to retail product have the greatest effect on the cost of sales. Typical industry markup is double the cost of the item (a pricing strategy known as "**keystone**"). Of course, retail pricing can be far more sophisticated than that, as spa retail operators look for opportunities to increase margins and reduce the overall cost of goods sold. The textbook, *Retail Management for Spas*, published by the ISPA Foundation, provides detailed information on pricing strategies, as well as other aspects of managing a spa retail operation. Other factors affect the cost of sales, including markdowns, pilferage, discounts, and merchandise movement (from retail to professional areas). Spa managers need to be aware of all of these factors, as retail can significantly boost a spa's profitability.

In addition, selling retail is not as labor intensive as performing a service. In small spa retail operations, the sales transactions are likely to be handled by the staff at the guest reception desk, which requires no additional staffing. In major spa retail operations, there will be a retail manager and sales clerks on staff. Generally these large spa retail operations will be designed into large resorts, where higher retail revenues are anticipated in the initial business plan for the spa operation. This is not an across-the-board statement, as some day spas may do a retail business of $500,000.

Fitness. Fitness is another special business consideration for a spa facility. On one end of the spectrum, few day spas will have a fitness component, while on the other end of the spectrum are club spas, for which fitness is the principal business of the facility. In today's fitness-conscious society, almost all resorts and hotels will include a fitness room, even if the property does not have a spa. There is revenue to be derived from a full fitness program at a resort, especially when the fitness area includes cardio and weight training; classes in aerobics, spinning, meditation, and tai chi; and perhaps such outdoor activities as guided walks, hiking trails, rock climbing, and rafting.

Most resort spas will charge the guests a 'day use fee' for use of the fitness facility, perhaps a spa swimming pool along with the sauna, steam, and whirlpool amenities and sometimes unlimited fitness classes. While this use fee is generally waived if the guest books a spa treatment, there are some resorts that have eliminated the use fee as resort guests sometimes perceive it as 'nickel and diming' them when they are already paying a very high room rate for their accommodations. In these cases, the hotel will allocate some portion of rooms revenue to the spa operation to underwrite the costs associated with staffing and providing amenities for the guests using the fitness facilities.

There are some other sources of fitness revenue, such as personal training sessions, fitness classes, and fitness evaluation programs, although these may account for only a small percentage of total spa revenue.

Memberships. The wild card in the fitness department is membership revenue. Some spas are ideally located either in an urban setting surrounded by office buildings full of potential members or in a resort community with many high-end residential homes filled with potential members. Overall, the fitness business is very competitive nationally in the United States, but there are people who are willing to pay the higher membership dues and initiation fees associated with a spa membership.

A spa director cannot wake up on any given day and say, "Let's start a membership program." The facilities must be designed to accommodate additional usage by members, with large gym spaces, perhaps additional fitness studios, and in most cases, a separate locker and grooming area for the members so that they do not disrupt the guests who are at the spa to receive a spa service. The membership might grant members access to the gym and to fitness classes, generally some discount on spa services, and in many cases, use of the property's pool or beach area.

There are dozens of varieties of membership programs and fee arrangements, but generally they will all include an initiation fee that might be $2,000, $5,000, or even $10,000 to $20,000, plus monthly dues that will be substantially more than what someone would pay at a local gym. The initiation fees include all one-time, non-refundable fees for activating a membership. These fees help offset the direct costs associated with obtaining the membership and orienting the new member and are generally recognized when the membership is sold.

However, if the profit from an initiation fee represents a substantial portion of the overall profit to be earned from a member, then the initiation fee and associated direct costs could be deferred and recognized on the spa income statement over the weighted average life of the membership (three to five years for example) rather than at the time the membership is sold, which is known as the **deferral method**.

According to the USFR, in the United States the Securities and Exchange Commission has advised public companies operating fitness facilities with initiation fees to follow the deferral method of accounting with respect to the revenue and associated costs of initiation fees.

Another financial scenario involves limited memberships. What happens when all memberships have been sold and the spa is limited to selling new memberships only as members resign? Suddenly, when comparing the operating results next year same month as compared to the prior year when the memberships were sold, the profitability of the spa is significantly less and requires comment to the statement of income. It becomes more difficult to make year-to-year comparisons. Thus, while it is appealing to claim all of the initiation fees on the month they have been received, it may be wiser to claim the revenue monthly over a year or several years, depending on the average length of time a person stays a member. For example, instead of recognizing an entire initiation fee of $22,500, it would be reported on the income statement over a period of time, such as three years, at the rate of $625 for 36 months.

Monthly dues, on the other hand, are a consistent stream of revenue that will improve a spa's overall profitability. For example, a spa with 100 members paying a weighted average of $150 a month based on the various types of memberships purchased (single, couple, family) provides the spa with $15,000 to cover fitness and spa operating costs.

Food and Beverage. Destination spas have an all-inclusive food and beverage component, in which all meals are included in the price of the guest's stay. At the other end of the spectrum, few day spas will include a café or restaurant, and perhaps 10 to 20 percent of resort spas will have a spa café or some form of food and beverage program within the spa area. The rule of thumb is that if the spa café is staffed by resort food and beverage employees and the food is prepared by the resort kitchen, then the revenue and associated costs belong in the resort food and beverage department. If, on the other hand, the spa staffs, orders, and prepares the food and beverages, then the spa will report both the revenue and expenses on a sub-schedule of the spa statement of income. Generally, the revenue and margin in a spa café are very small, but it is perceived by the guest as a wonderful addition to the spa experience.

Health and Wellness. Many spas will generate revenue derived from individual consultations and programs for spa guests conducted by an on-staff nutritionist or an independent contractor, including diet analysis, healthy cooking demonstrations, and shopping with the nutritionist programs. Some spas will also offer individual wellness consultations, including lifestyle coaching, stress reduction, smoking cessation, weight loss, acupuncture, herbal medicine, or other individual subjects. If guest demand is significant, the spa may have these counselors on staff or, more typically, will have a contract with professionals in the local area with whom the spa will negotiate a revenue-sharing arrangement. Thus, if a private consultation were to cost the guest $200, the contracted professional may be given 50 to 60 percent of the charge and the spa would keep the remainder as income. Revenue derived from these sources is generally modest, but having consultations available for the guests heightens the overall spa program.

Exhibit 7   Percentage of Revenue by Service Offering

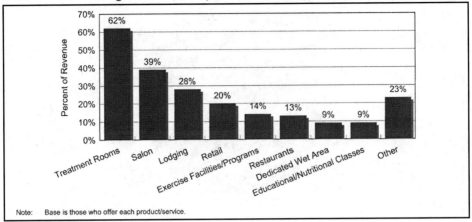

Note: Base is those who offer each product/service.

Source: ISPA 2007 Spa Industry Study

Contributors to Spa Revenue

The 2007 ISPA Spa Industry Study found that treatment rooms (with services including facials, massages, body treatments, and hydrotherapies) are the most significant contributor to revenue among spas that offer them. On average, treatment rooms account for almost two-thirds (62 percent) of a spa's total revenue. Exhibit 7 shows the percentage of revenue allocated to each of the different service offerings among those who offer that service. Salon is the second-largest contributor, averaging 39 percent of revenue among those who offer it. Retail brings in 20 percent of revenue.

Looking at the spa industry as a whole, 93 percent of a spa's revenue comes from the three top service offerings, with treatment rooms leading the way at 59 percent. Salon is second at 18 percent of revenue, with retail at 16 percent. Exhibit 8 shows the average percentage of revenue for the entire spa industry, and also outlines revenue allocation by spa type.

Cost Centers

As stated above, the spa industry is highly labor intensive, with labor costs of the spa's service providers taking the largest share of a spa's revenue. Other cost centers include support labor, **indirect operating expenses**, and **undistributed operating expenses** in the areas of administration, marketing, and facility maintenance and utilities.

Labor Costs

Spas are extremely labor intensive. Every single spa guest receives treatments from an individual service provider, who is supported by a significant staff of support employees. Spas are not like a local retail store where one might find a single employee working a check-out station for an entire department or a restaurant where

Exhibit 8   Average Percentage of Revenues for Entire Industry

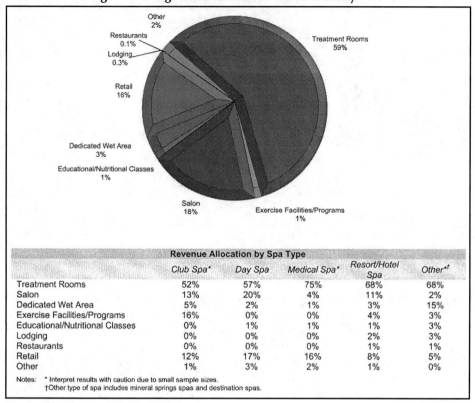

Revenue Allocation by Spa Type					
	Club Spa*	Day Spa	Medical Spa*	Resort/Hotel Spa	Other*†
Treatment Rooms	52%	57%	75%	68%	68%
Salon	13%	20%	4%	11%	2%
Dedicated Wet Area	5%	2%	1%	3%	15%
Exercise Facilities/Programs	16%	0%	0%	4%	3%
Educational/Nutritional Classes	0%	1%	1%	1%	3%
Lodging	0%	0%	0%	2%	3%
Restaurants	0%	0%	0%	1%	1%
Retail	12%	17%	16%	8%	5%
Other	1%	3%	2%	1%	0%

Notes: * Interpret results with caution due to small sample sizes.
         †Other type of spa includes mineral springs spas and destination spas.

Source: ISPA 2007 Spa Industry Study

a server will typically handle four to six tables. Even the comparison to a 'personal service' business, such as a doctor's office, falls short. While each patient will see an individual physician for only a few minutes, a spa guest will be with a spa professional for the entire treatment time, which could last an hour or longer. Attorneys see each client, but are able to generate significant billable hours without seeing the client at all. Perhaps a spa is analogous to a financial planner, but typically a planner will work independently without having a significant support staff.

This intense labor commitment makes controlling costs and achieving a reasonable profit a challenge for a spa director. According to the *ISPA Compensation Workbook*, total compensation in the range of 50 to 60 percent of annual revenue is desired positioning for a spa. The workbook notes that if the overall compensation of a spa operation, including raw payroll and benefits, consistently exceeds 60 percent of revenue, that spa will not be able to sustain reasonable profitability. Thus, the most important cost ratio in the business is service payroll to service revenue.

As a result, the most important business cost decision for a spa facility is to find the appropriate compensation program to attract, motivate, and retain staff, while remaining competitive with the marketplace and producing a sufficient return on the owner's investment to open and operate the spa facility. All compensation elements have a cost. Base pay, commission, fee-for-service, service charge, and tips/gratuities all require cash from the business. There are some hidden costs to compensation as well, including taxes on tips, healthcare costs, and paid-time off, which require careful planning and estimating. Few spas can be economically viable over the long run if **total compensation** costs for all employees exceed 60 percent of annual revenue.

On the other side of the coin, the *ISPA Compensation Workbook* notes that spas may not be able to attract and retain qualified staff if they share less than 45 percent of the annual revenue in the form of total compensation. Market pressures during the spa industry's explosive growth period will set the lower limit of compensation, because a spa that designs a compensation program that is not competitive within its market will find itself with no staff.

Once the balance is achieved between sharing enough revenue in the way of total compensation to attract and retain qualified employees and also remain financially sound, the key becomes the spa's ability to increase revenue through an increased number of clients, pricing structure, and strategies to increase revenue per client. Each of these activities will require the active attention and focus of management.

Professional Compensation. Compensation plans for spa professionals and service providers may be straightforward or complicated, depending on the layers of compensation and incentive bonuses that a spa offers. Several elements of their total pay must be factored into the equation including these possible elements:

- **Base hourly pay:** This base pay is a guaranteed hourly rate paid to the service provider regardless of whether or not they are performing a treatment. An hourly rate is sought by therapists as it usually ensures full-time employment and the ability to qualify for any spa benefits provided to full-time workers.

- **Commission on services:** This is a type of variable pay program element, with the service professional's earning determined by the revenue he/she generates by performing services and selling products. When a service provider is compensated through commission only, the pay delivery is referred to as **full commission**. Often, the commission will be blended with base pay with a lower commission percentage. If fully-commissioned employees might receive a 30 to 40 percent share in the revenue they generate, the **blended commission** might be 20 to 25 percent. One of the challenges with percentage-based commissions is that payroll costs will remain a fixed percentage of any increases in pricing and there is no opportunity to increase the spa's margin on treatment revenue.

- **Fee-for-service pay:** This is a variation on the percentage commission structure. Instead, a fixed amount is assigned to each treatment offered on the spa menu of services and the service provider is compensated a fixed amount for performing that service. For example, a fee-for-service on a $100 Swedish massage may be $24 or $26. The advantage of fee-for-service occurs when the spa increases prices and that $100 massage now costs $110, but the fee would remain the same. This practice enables a spa to increase its profitability when raising service prices, because the service provider's portion remains the same, sending the additional dollars to the bottom line.

- **Commission on retail sales:** It is also a customary spa industry practice to provide therapists with commissions for retail products they sell. After all, it is the advice of the esthetician to the guest following a facial that will drive the sales of skin care products or the hair stylist who recommends a special conditioner to the client to repair their sun-damaged hair that prompts the guest to buy that product. In some cases, service providers earn a small percentage of the retail sales for everything they sell. In a more sophisticated program, therapists are told at the time of hire that part of their job responsibility is to sell products to the guests at some acceptable threshold expressed as a dollar amount per treatment. In these cases, no commission is paid unless the minimum sales per service requirement is met, but a higher commission may be offered once the service provider exceeds that threshold over a period of time.

- **Gratuities, tips, and service charges:** Regardless of the term used to define these charges, guests have traditionally paid them directly to the therapist. From a spa owner and manager perspective, it is important to recognize that this is a part of the compensation package. Additionally, tips in the United States are considered to be part of wages, and the employee and employer are each required to pay Social Security and Medicare taxes on tip income. A best practice is for all credit card tips to be paid out as part of the service provider's paycheck, with all applicable taxes withheld. Cash tips must be reported at least weekly by the service provider to the employer, with the employer withholding the applicable taxes. Two prevalent questions related to gratuities in the spa environment are whether therapists should be permitted to keep all of their tips or share a portion of them with other spa staff members who assist with treatments and who might not be tipped directly by the guest, and whether gratuities should be automatically added to the price of a spa service or left to the discretion of the guest.

While there are clearly two schools of thought concerning whether an automatic service charge should be added to the guest's bill to cover the gratuity as opposed to leaving the amount of gratuity up to the guest, there has been a trend toward adding a service charge equal to 15 to 20 percent of the cost of the spa service. The advocates of the service charge argue that tipping is one less thing the guest has to think about and it makes accounting for tip income and the billing transaction easier. Advocates of leaving tipping to the guest's discretion believe that tips should be earned and tip amounts should rightfully vary based on the quality of the service. The important thing is that gratuities are an important component of therapist compensation and should be communicated at the time of hire while explaining the spa's compensation structure. Some professionals feel that tipping devalues the professionalism of the work they do, particularly in the area of massage therapy. They ask the question: "Would you tip your dentist, chiropractor, or acupuncturist?"

It is also important to remember that, in the United States, the IRS has determined that the automatic/non-discretionary service charges are revenue, and spas must report them as revenue, pay sales taxes on the service charge amount, and record the service charges distributed to employees as a payroll expense under "distributed service charges." The IRS logic is that service charges are really higher prices; if a spa did not have a service charge it would

Exhibit 9   Effective Compensation Rate—Fee for Service

a.	Client Paid Fee	$100
b.	Service Commission	$50 (50% of Client Paid Fee)
c.	Employer Portion of Social Security	$3.83 (7.65% of $50)
d.	Sub-total	$53.83 (54% ECR)
e.	Healthcare[1]	$4.29
f.	Paid-Time Off [2]	$3.85
g.	**Total Compensation Paid per Treatment**	**$61.97 (62% ECR)**

ECR = Effective Compensation Rate

1. Assuming Annual Client Fees (service revenue) of $70,000 and individual healthcare costs of $3,000, or 4.29% of service revenue

2. Assumes two weeks (10 days) of vacation and 10 holidays for a total of 20 days at $134.62 per day ($35,000 target commission divided by 260 total annual work days), which equals $2,692, or 3.85% of the client service revenue of $70,000

Source: *ISPA Compensation Workbook,* p. 12

simply increase its prices. The issue of service charges and optional gratuities is one that spa management must review and determine what is best for the financial health of the spa as well as the compensation of employees. The *ISPA Compensation Workbook* examines this issue in greater detail.

- **Incentive pay:** While it has been customary to include incentive pay in the form of bonuses to salaried managers of a spa, there is a growing trend of including spa team incentives for the entire spa staff as an element of the compensation program. Incentive pay is a variable pay program that is paid at least annually and sometimes more frequently, and which is linked to the performance of the spa and possibly the performance of the individual employee. Typically, incentives are paid on a curve, with a partial payout made if a minimum performance level is reached (target payout), and more paid when the budgeted or expected financial performance exceeds the expected level. The purpose of incentive pay is to focus the entire spa team on the financial expectations of the spa and to make the spa team recognize how each of them contributes to the overall financial performance of the spa.

In addition to the pay structure of compensation, the spa must add the costs of providing **benefits** for those therapists and other spa staff members who meet the qualification requirements. Benefits are generally classified into three major categories: health and welfare benefits, which include health, life, and disability insurance, and other related programs; paid time off, which includes vacation time, sick leave, and holidays; and retirement benefits, such as an employer contribution to a 401(k) savings plan.

It is important for spa management to figure in benefits, service charges/gratuities, and commissions on retail sales when planning compensation to ensure that actual costs are at 50 percent of total service revenue. Exhibit 9 demonstrates the **effective compensation rate** (ECR) for a service provider who is paid a 50

Exhibit 10   Effective Compensation Rate—Service Fees/Gratuities/Tips

a.	Client Paid Fee	$100
b.	Client Tip	$15 (15%)
c.	Total Client Revenue	$115
d.	Service Commission	$50 (50% of Client Paid Fee)
e.	Tips	$15 (15% of $100)
f.	Employer Portion of Social Security	$4.97 (7.65% of $65)
g.	Sub-total	$69.97 (61% ECR)
h.	Healthcare[1]	$4.29
i.	Paid-Time Off [2]	$3.85
j.	**Total Compensation Paid per Treatment:**	**$78.11 (68% ECR)**

ECR = Effective Compensation Rate

1. Assuming Annual Client Fees (service revenue) of $70,000 and individual healthcare costs of $3,000, or 4.29% of total client service revenue
2. Assumes two weeks (10 days) of vacation and 10 holidays for a total of 20 days at $134.62 per day ($35,000 target commission divided by 260 total annual work days), which equals $2,692, or 3.85% of the client service revenue of $70,000

Source: *ISPA Compensation Workbook*, p. 13

percent commission on services, plus employer contributions to Social Security and Medicare and contributions to health care and paid time off. Exhibit 10 factors service charges/gratuities/tips into the ECR equation, while Exhibit 11 goes a step further by showing the ECR when commissions on retail sales are added to the employee's compensation.

In each case, managers need to consider adjustments to keep their actual costs to 50 percent of total service revenue. For example, in Exhibit 9, options include not providing healthcare or paid time off, and lowering the commission rate to 47 percent, or keeping the benefits and lowering the base commission to 39 percent. In Exhibit 10, achieving the 50 percent benchmark can be achieved by eliminating healthcare and paid time off and lowering the commission to 39 percent, or keeping the benefits and lowering the commission to 31 percent. In the third example (Exhibit 11), the balance can be maintained by doing one of the two options above, plus lowering the retail commission rate from 10 percent to 9.3 percent.

Treatment Departments' Supervision. At minimum, a spa will have one service provider designated as a **lead**. If the spa is sufficiently large, there may be a lead massage therapist and a lead for the estheticians. The lead's tasks may include interviewing new team members, orienting new staff, and training new and existing staff. Other responsibilities might include monitoring the inventory of products used by the service providers to ensure that they are at proper par levels and ordering product. Finally, they are often responsible for scheduling.

Many treatment modalities require extensive continuing education and certification by the training center. Typically, a lead professional will hold several certifications for a variety of treatment modalities and can test any service provider claiming to be an aromatherapist or Thai massage certified. If a lead therapist/professional has certifications then it is imperative that they are practicing

Exhibit 11   Effective Compensation Rate—Retail Revenue

a.	Client Paid Fee	$100
b.	Client Tip	$15 (15%)
c.	Client Retail Purchase	$20
d.	Total Client Revenue	$135
e.	Service Commission:	$50 (50% of client-paid fee)
f.	Tips	$15 (15%)
g.	Employer Portion of Social Security:	$4.97 (7.65% of $65)
h.	Healthcare[1]	$4.29
i.	Paid-Time Off [2]	$3.85
j.	Sub-total Service	$78.11 (68% ECR on service)
k.	Retail Commission	$2.00
l.	Employer Portion of Social Security	$ .15 (7.65% of $2)
m.	Sub-total Retail Commission Rate	$2.15 (11% ECR on retail)
n.	**Total Compensation Paid per Treatment:**	**$80.26 (59% ECR for all revenue)**

ECR = Effective Compensation Rate

1. Assuming Annual Client Fees (service revenue) of $70,000 and individual healthcare costs of $3,000, or 4.29% of revenue
2. Assumes two weeks (10 days) of vacation and 10 holidays for a total of 20 days at $134.62 per day ($35,000 target commission divided by 260 total annual work days), which equals $2,692, or 3.85% of the client revenue of $70,000

Source: *ISPA Compensation Workbook,* p. 14

and keeping their own skills up to par. Most service providers are passionate about their profession and want to work in an environment where they are continually learning new modalities and expanding their knowledge and skills. The leadership of the lead therapists will create this environment. Leads are generally working supervisors, therefore they are compensated at a premium for their supervisory time and will also schedule themselves to provide services. Because they are working in the department, as well as supervising, their expenses are included as a cost of their department on the spa's financial reporting schedules.

Support Labor

While this is also a payroll or compensation cost, support labor is considered separately, as the employees in this category are not directly involved in the delivery of an individual spa service, but instead support the massage, skin care, hair, nail, health and wellness, and in some cases, fitness departments. The departments that support the delivery of spa services, as identified by the USFR, include:

- Guest Reception/Spa Front Desk
- Reservations
- Concierge
- Attendants/Host/Hostess
- Housekeeping
- Supervision

Spa Snapshot: How did you create your spa's current tipping policy, and how is it working?

The Spa at Moody Gardens is a relatively new spa. When we opened we decided to add an automatic 18 percent service charge to all services. The service charge includes gratuity to the therapist. I feel this policy has worked wonderfully for our establishment. Our therapists are compensated appropriately, our guests like the idea of not having to figure out what is correct when tipping, and every now and then you have someone that wants to leave additional gratuity above the 18 percent. Coming from another location previously that had an automatic gratuity and seeing it not work, I attribute our success to knowledge. We inform all guests when booking their appointments the price of the service and the additional 18 percent that we add. Our guests know what to expect when they come. No surprises.

—*Stephanie Vandecaveye, Spa Manager, Moody Gardens Hotel, Spa and Convention Center*

At the Spa at the Broadmoor, we tip by charging a 20 percent gratuity to all of our à la carte services at time of check in. We emphasize to the guests that this may be modified at their discretion following their services. Of that 20 percent, 17 percent goes to the technician who performs the services. The remaining 3 percent goes to a tip pool for our concierge and valet staff. This works well in almost all situations. We get one guest out of 100 who balks at paying this before their services. When we compared our salaries with those in the recent ISPA wage survey, for our category we performed a good bit above our regional average.

—*Ella Stimpson, Spa Director, The Spa at the Broadmoor*

Iatria Day Spa is still old-fashioned in that we leave it entirely at the client's discretion. Many spas add on an arbitrary gratuity. We still feel like the client may leave it if they like. We have tip envelopes at the checkout counter should they choose. It works very well. In fact, many of our therapists make more than the 15 percent if we had made tipping mandatory. We believe that our clients appreciate having the choice.

—*Erika Mangrum, President, Iatria Day Spa*

I look at these services as being performed by professionals, not lower-level service people who live on tips. My feeling is that it raises the level of the profession to not have tips. So I designed our policy to be one where the gratuity is included in the price, thinking that would make it

(continued)

easier for the clients. We at first did not accept tips when people wanted to leave something more, but after an ISPA [Knowledge Network], one of the participants who did customer service training explained how it was important to have a means for the clients to thank the people who have done the work for them. Now our policy is that we inform the clients of our policy in our written information and signs in the spa. If someone offers a gratuity to the therapist, we tell them to graciously accept it. If someone wants to leave a tip at the front desk, our reception staff is trained to explain the policy. But if the client says they did such a good job that they still want to leave this for them, we thank them.

—Judy Hohn, President, Serenity, The Rejuvenating Day Spa

After several different ways of handling tips, we went through a Labor and Industry audit in 2003. This was eye opening for me and changed what we do with tips. All tips must be given in cash or a personal check written out to the technician. We let clients know this at the time of booking, as a part of our script. The tips are collected at the front desk (if not given in the rooms) in envelopes marked with the tech's name. I stopped processing tips on credit cards because the fees we are charged were almost impossible to deduct from the tips. If the charge is under $15, the fee is higher. The staff revolted when I deducted the processing fees before they got the tip. Eliminating credit card processing has stopped this.

—Dorothy Andreas Tuel, President, The Sewickley Spa

We purchased a spa that formerly had a "no tipping" policy, so allowing the staff to accept tips made a great first impression with my therapists! I also wanted to make sure that the non-tipped employees were rewarded, as their contribution greatly affects the overall experience that is reflected at tip time. Because they see substantial tips—we just changed the policy and are already seeing $5,000+ per month in tips—but don't get the benefit of them, the opportunity for conflict is great. We discussed a tip split, but ultimately, the therapists decided that they would prefer to reward the non-tipped employees with free services like massages, facials, manicures, and pedicures. Now, the front desk and laundry staff are pampered, appreciated, and look great, the therapists feel like they are giving back to the team, and our guests benefit from the supportive team environment. As an added benefit, the front desk staff has a better working knowledge of the treatments and specialties of each therapist so they can make better recommendations to our guests.

—Heidi Lamar, Owner, The Lamar Everyday Spa

Source: *Pulse*, July 2005

Exhibit 12 The Spa Reception Desk

Command Central: The Spa Reception Desk

A comparison between a spa guest reception desk and the front desk of a hotel will add perspective on the amount of activity that takes place at the spa guest reception desk.

For a 250-room resort running 100 percent occupancy and an average length of stay of 2.5 days, the resort front desk would handle approximately 100 check-outs and another 100 arrivals.

That same resort has an average-size spa with 15 treatment rooms, three hair stations, two manicure and two pedicure stations, and schedules treatments from 9 a.m. to 9 p.m. The 12 spa treatment hours would generate 180 guest registrations and check-outs from the treatment room and another 87 arrivals for salon services and 87 check-outs following the guests' appointments (this assumes seven stations, with the salon operating for 10 hours and an average service time of 45 minutes) for a grand total of 534 guest arrivals and departures on that sold-out day, compared with 200 at the resort front desk.

Even factoring in the likelihood that the average number of treatments for a spa guest might be 1.2 to 1.4, which would reduce the actual number of guests at the spa to a number somewhere between 380 to 440 guests a day, that is still nearly twice the number handled at the resort front desk.

These support positions have important roles to play in the financial success of the spa. Even though they do not provide direct therapeutic services to guests, their interactions with guests and other staff members ensure that the spa operates in ways that boost productivity and profitability.

Guest Reception/Spa Front Desk. As with a hotel, the spa guest reception is the command center of processing reservations, checking guests into the spa, settling guest accounts, and often assisting guests with retail purchases from merchandise displayed in the spa lobby. In a small spa, it is likely that the guest reception desk will also control hair and nail appointments in the salon and settle those salon accounts following the guest's service. In a large spa that includes a sizable salon with several hair stations and an extensive nail department, there would typically be a second guest reception desk in the salon itself to handle salon guest appointments. Large spas may also have a reception desk dedicated to the skincare and retail areas. Exhibit 12 details the complexity of operating the reception desk of a large spa.

Spa Reservations/Programming. The term *reservations* is generally used by day spas and resort spas, where guests book a single appointment for a service or a number of appointments on the same day. The term *spa programming* is generally used in destination spas, where the guest is staying for several days and the programmer coordinates the accommodations, meal program, and all of the various elements from fitness classes to spa program attendance with the guest, as well as booking his or her spa service appointments.

A reservation department should be staffed by skilled telephone communicators who are able to accept reservations over the phone, answer general questions about the spa's facilities, and be completely conversant about each of the spa's treatments, easily quoting pricing and availability on the guest's requested day. Twenty-first century reservationists must also be adept at working with specialized spa software systems that manage reservations, treatment rooms and stations, and service providers.

Again, there is an interesting analogy to a hotel reservations department. When accepting room reservations, the agent must control two factors, room type and date. This would be the same for spa reservationists to control spa treatment room type: a massage room, skin care room, Vichy shower, hydrotherapy, or multi-purpose room, plus the hour and date being requested. Spas, however, have a third variable element in the reservation process and that is the therapist scheduled and certified to perform that service.

To give an example, a new spa had just opened with fourteen massage rooms. The spa was able to include Shiatsu on its menu of services as it had hired a therapist who was certified in this massage modality. The reservation system was not set up to control therapist availability, so the spa's staff arrived one morning to discover that the reservations staff had booked ten Shiatsu massages on the same day at the same hour with only one therapist trained to perform that service.

Spa reservations can be a very complicated process. When calling for a hotel reservation, the guest may inquire as to the guestroom's features, including Internet access, plasma TV, irons, and bedding, but those are fixed components of all guestrooms. The caller to a spa expects the reservation personnel to be very familiar with and able to accurately describe each of the treatments and services on the spa menu, along with the products used, complimentary services, and suggestions to help design the guest's day.

A spa reservationist is the front line sales agent for the spa. He or she suggests to the caller who is booking a massage appointment, "I would recommend that you consider a nice exfoliating salt scrub before your massage as your skin will feel so great that you will walk out of the spa after the two treatments feeling like a new person," or "I see that our nail staff has an opening right after you get your hair done. May I schedule that for you as you will walk out feeling your best." That suggestion or upsell can have a dramatic effect on the average number of services per guest ratio and will increase spa revenue. Often, spa reservationists are given bonuses based on upselling.

Spa Concierge. In many medium-to-large hotel/resort and destination spas, a concierge desk or office will be planned near the guest reception desk to provide support for the reception staff and to assist guests who have questions about the spa's offerings, taking pressure off the reception staff and providing guests with a higher level of experience. The types of duties a spa concierge at a resort spa might perform include:

- For those resort guests who have purchased a two- or four-day spa package, writing a welcome for the party and placing it in the guestroom, plus making sure that any special spa amenities are waiting in the guestroom at arrival.

- Inviting the package guest to the concierge office to personally review the guest's itinerary for the days they are at the resort and conducting a personal tour of the spa facilities.

- Meeting with walk-in guests who have questions, while the reservations office handles phone inquiries, thus taking pressure off the reception desk.

- Meeting with spa guests who experience a problem during their visit, as it is much more desirable for the complaint to be discussed at a semi-private concierge desk as opposed to standing at the reception desk in front of other spa guests.

The spa concierge is generally a senior guest reception agent who has gone through additional training to handle sales opportunities and guest challenges.

Spa Attendant/Host/Hostess. This support position has responsibility for maintaining the cleanliness of the spa's guest and employee areas and ensuring that guest supplies are stocked. The attendant's duties may include:

- Beginning guest spa experiences as guests move from the reception lobby into the core of the spa through the locker area. The attendant will generally start by giving guests tours of the locker and relaxation areas.

- Issuing guests lockers, robes, and sandals and instructing guests on securing their valuables.

- Providing ongoing housekeeping of the locker, relaxation areas, and wet lounges of the spa and ensuring that the grooming counters, showers, and towels are stocked and pristinely clean.

- Escorting guests to the relaxation lounge and informing guests who their therapists will be and how they will be picked up for their treatment.

- Perhaps serving guests water, teas, or snacks from the hospitality station and keeping the station clean and refreshed.

In a day spa, the attendant is generally referred to as the host/hostess. This person will generally seat the guest in the reception lobby, ask if the guest wants any water or snack, serve the guest, and then escort the guest to the treatment room.

Housekeeping. Generally, spas will use one of two approaches for janitorial and housekeeping service. While spa attendants, fitness staff, retail personnel, and spa technicians are responsible for cleaning and tidying their own areas, the general cleaning of the spa facility, including things like polishing the floors, vacuuming, and window washing must be completed after the spa's last appointment or early in the day before the spa opens. In some cases, the spa will hire its own housekeeping personnel and in others the spa will contract with an outside service to provide janitorial services. In the case of many resort spas, the housekeeping duties will be handled by the resort/hotel housekeeping department and the spa will be rebilled on the spa departmental schedule a charge from housekeeping for the labor and materials used to clean the spa facilities.

Supervision. The final category of support labor is supervision, which includes spa management and working support supervisors. The labor costs for the working lead therapists are included in their respective departments, not in this supervision category, as the therapist leads do generate revenue within the departments they supervise. Some spas will have a salaried spa services manager who does not perform services and devotes his or her entire attention to selecting, training, and maintaining standards for massage and body work, skin care, and hair and nail departments, in which case that payroll expense would be charged to this support labor schedule.

The common positions included in the support labor category include assistant spa director, spa manager, guest reception supervisor, and lead attendant. A large spa salon with many hair stations and a large nail area would be managed by a salon manager, who would in most cases perform management functions exclusively and not work as a stylist or a working supervisor. The USFR includes this manager on the schedule for support labor/supervision.

Resort and destination spas would include the spa director on the support labor schedule. For day spas, the position of general manager or spa director would be recorded on the Administrative and General Expense schedule, because of the principle of Undistributed Operating Expenses, which is discussed later in this chapter.

Indirect Operating Expenses

A spa's operating expenses fall into two categories, direct and indirect. The direct expenses are those professional treatment products that are specifically used in the delivery of treatment department services. These include the direct professional products of the skin care treatments, such as cleansers and masks, plus treatment-specific supplies used by the skin care technicians, such as paraffin wax, brushes and utensils, waxing strips, and eye pads. Those expenses are recorded on the financial reporting schedules for the departments that use them.

The **indirect operating expenses** of a spa are for those items that cannot be identified for use in a specific treatment, but are either used in a number of treatments from the four treatment departments or are used throughout the spa and salon. A couple of examples will help clarify the distinction between direct and indirect operating expenses. It is easy to determine that massage oils should be charged to the massage department, but what about the robes that are used by the guests during their visit? The guest could be having a massage or a facial or perhaps a facial and a pedicure. It would be meaningless to try and establish how much of the cost of robes should be charged to each treatment department. The same applies to grooming amenities such as shower gel, cotton pads, razors, and deodorant. These supplies are for use by all spa guests, thus the costs are recorded as an indirect expense.

In accordance with the USFR, indirect operating expenses include the following:

- Ambience—Items that create the sensory environment of the spa, such as background music, candles, aromatherapy oils, and diffusers.

- Contract services—The cost of activities that are outsourced, such as janitorial services, window washing, and carpet cleaning.

- Dues and subscriptions—The cost of memberships, such as ISPA or the local chamber of commerce, and the cost of subscriptions to newspapers and magazines employees of the spa use.

- Equipment rental—The cost of equipment rented for use in the spa.

- Guest clothing—Robes, sandals, workout attire, salon smocks, disposable swimsuits or wraps, and turbans the spa provides for guest use.

- Guest supplies—Locker room area supplies and amenities provided to spa guests, such as shampoo, body lotion, razors and shaving cream, cotton balls and swabs, and guest-use hair dryers, combs, and brushes.

- Hospitality—Items provided for the guests' hospitality, such as bottled water, fresh fruit, juices, herbal teas, coffee, brewing supplies, cups, utensils, and napkins.

- Laundry—For spas that outsource laundry services, this includes bills and invoices from outside laundries. In resort facilities with an in-house laundry, the expense is a part of the overall laundry operational costs assigned to the spa division, determined either by poundage of linen processed for the spa or percentage of time used for spa laundry. For small operations that have their own washers and dryers, the account would be charged for the laundry chemicals used to process linens.

- Licenses and fees—Federal, state, and municipal licenses for the spa facilities, including music licenses.

- Linen—Sheets, towels, treatment table covers, blankets, and bath mats used in the spa.

- Operating supplies—This includes cleaning supplies, printed forms employees use, paper supplies like facial tissue and toilet paper, and office supplies.

- Professional development—Costs, other than time, connected with employee training, including training materials, supplies, instructor's fees, and outside seminars and conferences.

- Telecommunications—Telecommunications expenses that can be directly related to the spa, such as monthly telephone charges, telephone equipment charges, cell phones, and pagers.

- Uniforms—Purchased or rented uniforms for spa employees, and the costs of cleaning and repairing employee uniforms.

There is significant variation in how spas record their operating expenses. For example, some hotel companies do not charge the spa anything for laundry processing while others do, and others charge the spa for any advertising that it may do while others absorb advertising costs as part of the resort's expenses, so it has been difficult to determine industry standards. One of the benefits of adhering to the principles set forth in the USFR is to bring spas into consistency in recording expenses and revenue, which could prove useful in establishing industry benchmarks.

Undistributed Operating Expenses

The use of **undistributed operating expenses** by spas is an adoption of the financial reporting traditions within the hotel industry and is a clear distinction in how resort/hotel and destination spas report their financial results as compared to day spas, which are individual business units that must record everything from taxes to credit card commissions and the energy bills against spa revenue, while resorts/hotels and destination spas do not do so.

To understand the reasoning behind the use of undistributed overhead expenses, readers must go back to 1925 and 1926 when the Hotel Association of New York City met to create the first edition of the *Uniform System of Accounts for Hotels*. During the discussions, the "Principle of Accountability" was adopted, whereby only a limited number of expenses would be charged to each revenue department. The expenses would include those over which the department manager would have significant control and were able to be accurately determined. Expenses for things like the human resources staff and energy and marketing were put into the categories known today as Undistributed Operating Departments of Administrative and General, Marketing, Energy, and Property Operations and Maintenance.

To demonstrate, while it would be possible to allocate the monthly gas or electric bill to each revenue center by installing dozens of energy sub-meters throughout a hotel or creating some reasonable but artificial allocation determined by a clerk in the accounting office, by the time the bills were broken down to so many areas, who would be ultimately responsible for controlling energy costs? How would a resort spa director feel about seeing an energy line on their department schedule when they would have little control over that expense?

The arguments around the table back in 1926 that said hotels needed to treat restaurants as IBU's (Independent Business Units) and should charge every expense to the restaurant in the same way a free-standing independent restaurant must do. Those arguments were trumped by the Principle of Accountability, which has stood the test of time and is still in place 80 years later. In the same way that hotel dining rooms appear to have an advantage over the financial discipline of a free-standing restaurant, so too does a resort/hotel spa have a similar advantage over a free-standing independent day spa.

It is for this reason that there is a significant difference in the profits reported by hotel/resort spas, which averaged a 23.6 percent average profit (23 percent median profit) according to ISPA's 2007 *Spa Industry Study*, with many large spas generating a departmental profit of 30 percent or even 35 to 40 percent, while day spas averaged 16.1 percent average profit (10 percent median profit), although it must be acknowledged that there are a significant number of day spas that have much higher profitability—some exceeding 20 percent. An individual who is considering opening a day spa must have a well-defined concept, an excellent business plan, an outstanding location, and be extremely diligent in the financial management of the spa. This may also be why so many day spas are therapist owned, as they can generate additional income by performing services themselves.

The reason for this large difference in profitability between resort and day spas is the undistributed operating expense of **occupancy cost** for day spas. This typically includes rent and other related charges from a landlord, such as common area maintenance, property taxes, and insurance. Because day spas are often in higher rent retail areas, if this expense is too high as a percentage of total revenue, it can destroy a day spa's profitability.

This is an expense that must be controlled in the business planning process. If the spa cannot generate revenue sufficient to support its rents, then it should not be built in the first place. The amount of acceptable rent falls into a range based upon the service and retail traffic that can be expected at the location. If retail revenue is expected to be high, then a rent to revenue factor of 10 percent is acceptable. In lower traffic locations, six to seven percent rent to total revenue should be the limit to ensure profitability.

Build out, which is the cost of what it will take to bring an empty, unimproved space to operational status as a spa, and **leasehold improvements** (improvements to a rented property made by the lessee) also affect profitability for day spas. At a resort spa, build out is for the whole property, and payback is also for the property as a whole, not just the spa area. The spa is an amenity investment for the resort, and build out and improvements enhance that investment. The resort spa does not have to "pay back" the resort for these improvements. For the day spa, though, every penny spent in build out and improvement comes off the bottom line. The day spa has to pay back its investment on its revenue alone. For that reason, it is vital for day spa owners and managers to know the payback period and determine whether the spa can afford the project.

It is important to highlight the types of expenses that are included in the undistributed operating expenses to gain an appreciation of the types of activities that must be charged against spa revenue in a day spa business. Exhibits 13, 14, and 15 list the expenses for the Administrative and General, Marketing, and Facility Maintenance and Utilities areas as contained in the *Uniform System of Financial Reporting for Spas*, which explains each line item in detail.

Although there have been no spa financial surveys conducted to report industry-wide experience for undistributed overhead expenses, informal surveys have suggested that the costs for these areas would total between 8 to 12 percent of total spa revenue.

Putting It All Together

All revenue and costs described in this chapter are recorded on the statement of income, which provides a financial snapshot of the spa. The statement of income shows the total sales by product or service category (massage, skin care, hair, nails, etc.) for a stated period of time, the expenses incurred in generating those sales, and the profit earned or the loss incurred as a result of those activities. The chapter appendix contains sample statements of income for a resort spa and a day spa.

A resort or destination spa will most likely have a finance department that prepares the spa's financial statements. In smaller day spas, the spa director may use the services of a CPA to help with all of the necessary financial and tax data. It is imperative that a spa director is able to analyze, summarize, report, and interpret financial information.

Although a spa is a business with purpose at its very core, it is still a business and to be successful in the delicate balance of business and purpose, the leaders

Exhibit 13   Administrative and General

Administrative and General—Schedule 14	
	Current Period
PAYROLL AND RELATED EXPENSES	
Management Salaries	$
Administrative Salaries and Wages	
Total Salaries and Wages	_____
Payroll Taxes and Employee Benefits	_____
Total Payroll and Related Expenses	
ACCOUNTING EXPENSES	
Audit and Other External Expenses	
Payroll Processing Expenses	
Other Accounting Expenses	_____
Total Accounting Expenses	_____
OTHER EXPENSES	
Bank Charges	
Cash Over/Short	
Contract Services	
Corporate Office Charges	
Credit and Collection	
Credit Card Commissions	
Donations	
Dues and Subscriptions	
Human Resources	
Information Systems	
Legal and Professional	
Licenses and Fees	
Loss and Damage	
Meals and Entertainment	
Operating Supplies	
Postage	
Professional Development	
Provision for Doubtful Accounts	
Security	
Telecommunications	
Travel	
Other	_____
Total Other Expenses	_____
TOTAL ADMINISTRATIVE AND GENERAL EXPENSES	$ _____

Source: *Uniform System of Financial Reporting for Spas*, p. 82

must have sharply honed financial skills. While owners and investors will be attentive as the spa director tells them in an owner's meeting about all of the wonderful treatments the spa is offering and how they are making a real difference in people's lives, as with all businesses, the spa will always be judged first and foremost by the financial results of the previous month and will be expected to sustain reasonable profitability over continuous months and for years. The real test is to sustain financial success month after month, year after year.

Exhibit 14   Marketing

Marketing—Schedule 15

	Current Period
PAYROLL AND RELATED EXPENSES	
Salaries and Wages	$
Payroll Taxes and Employee Benefits	
Total Payroll and Related Expenses	
OTHER EXPENSES	
Advertising Broadcast	
Advertising Print	
Agency Fees	
Collateral Materials	
Complimentary Guests	
Contract Services	
Direct Mail	
Dues and Subscriptions	
In-House Promotions	
Meals and Entertainment	
Postage	
Professional Development	
Special Events	
Telecommunications	
Trade Shows	
Travel	
Other	
Total Other Expenses	
TOTAL MARKETING EXPENSES	$

Source: *Uniform System of Financial Reporting for Spas*, p. 87

Additional Reading

Compensation Workbook for the Spa Industry, ©2004, ISPA Foundation

Retail Management for Spas: The Art & Science of Retail, ©2005, ISPA Foundation

Uniform System of Financial Reporting for Spas, ©2005, American Hotel & Lodging Educational Institute

Key Terms

benefits—Programs sponsored by employers that protect employees in the event of illness or injury; provide time off; and provide opportunity to save money for the future.

blended commission—A pay structure that includes base pay plus a commission.

boutique spa—A small hotel or resort spa with fewer than 10 rooms, but which provides a complete range of spa services and amenities.

Exhibit 15 Facilities Maintenance and Utilities

<table>
<tr><th colspan="2">Facility Maintenance and Utilities—Schedule 16</th></tr>
<tr><td></td><td align="right">Current Period</td></tr>
<tr><td>PAYROLL AND RELATED EXPENSES</td><td></td></tr>
<tr><td>Salaries and Wages</td><td>$</td></tr>
<tr><td>Payroll Taxes and Employee Benefits</td><td>_____</td></tr>
<tr><td>Total Payroll and Related Expenses</td><td>_____</td></tr>
<tr><td>OTHER EXPENSES</td><td></td></tr>
<tr><td>Facility Maintenance Expenses</td><td></td></tr>
<tr><td>Building</td><td></td></tr>
<tr><td>Contract Services</td><td></td></tr>
<tr><td>Dues and Subscriptions</td><td></td></tr>
<tr><td>Equipment Rental</td><td></td></tr>
<tr><td>Equipment Repair</td><td></td></tr>
<tr><td>Grounds and Landscaping</td><td></td></tr>
<tr><td>Heating, Ventilating, and Air Conditioning</td><td></td></tr>
<tr><td>Licenses and Fees</td><td></td></tr>
<tr><td>Locks and Keys</td><td></td></tr>
<tr><td>Operating Supplies</td><td></td></tr>
<tr><td>Sauna, Steam, and Pool Supplies and Repairs</td><td></td></tr>
<tr><td>Trash Removal</td><td></td></tr>
<tr><td>Uniforms</td><td></td></tr>
<tr><td>Other Repairs and Maintenance</td><td>_____</td></tr>
<tr><td>Total Facility Maintenance Expenses</td><td>_____</td></tr>
<tr><td>Utility Expenses</td><td></td></tr>
<tr><td>Electric</td><td></td></tr>
<tr><td>Gas</td><td></td></tr>
<tr><td>Water</td><td></td></tr>
<tr><td>Other Fuels</td><td>_____</td></tr>
<tr><td>Total Utility Expenses</td><td>_____</td></tr>
<tr><td>TOTAL OTHER EXPENSES</td><td>_____</td></tr>
<tr><td>TOTAL FACILITY MAINTENANCE AND UTILITIES EXPENSES</td><td>$ _____</td></tr>
</table>

Source: *Uniform System of Financial Reporting for Spas*, p. 87

build out—The cost to bring an empty, unimproved space to operational status as a spa.

commission on services—A variable pay program provided to individuals who perform services, with the employee's earnings determined by the revenue he/she generates. This is often expressed as a percentage of the cost of the service.

cost centers—Departments that support the proper functioning of revenue centers.

deferral method—The practice of spreading income (as from a membership fee) over the life of the membership, rather than at the time it was paid.

effective compensation rate—Employee compensation expressed as a percentage of total revenue when taking into consideration base pay, commissions, tips/gratuities/service charges, and retail commissions.

fee for service—A commission structure based on a per-treatment fixed dollar amount and not a percentage of revenue.

full commission—A pay structure under which the employee is paid only as a portion of the service revenue he or she generates.

gratuities—Additional payment to a service provider by a guest in appreciation of excellent service.

incentive pay—A variable pay program that is paid at least once annually or more frequently, that is linked to the spa's financial performance and/or the performance of the individual employee.

indirect operating expenses—Items that cannot be identified for use in a specific department, but are used in a number of treatment departments or are used throughout the spa and salon.

Marking up the item by 100%

keystone—Initial markup of a retail item by doubling the cost of the item.

lead—A working supervisor in a spa service department.

leasehold improvements—Improvements to a rented property made by the tenant or lessee.

occupancy cost—Costs related to occupying business space, including rent, build out, maintenance, repairs, etc.

revenue centers—Departments that generate income for the spa through the sales of services or products to guests/clients.

service charges—An additional fee added to a customer's bill, often in place of voluntary tipping.

signature massage treatments—A treatment that was created by and for a particular spa, for which it is known.

tips—Additional payment to a service provider by a guest in appreciation of excellent service.

total compensation—The total value of base pay, annual variable pay, and benefits.

undistributed operating expenses—Costs necessary to maintain the production of income from operation of the business.

Review Questions

1. How does financial success benefit a spa's mission?

2. Which spa departments are revenue centers?

3. Which spa departments are cost centers?

4. What are some of the accounting issues surrounding membership and initiation fees?

5. What factors are included in determining spa employee compensation plans?

6. How do benefits and retail commissions affect the effective compensation rate?

7. What is the difference between service labor and support labor?

8. What are indirect operating expenses?

9. What are undistributed operating expenses?

10. How do rent and build out affect a day spa's profitability?

Appendix A: Sample Summary Statement of Income

SUMMARY STATEMENT OF INCOME

	Net Revenues	Cost of Sales	Payroll and Related Expenses	Other Expenses	Income (Loss)
SPA DEPARTMENTS					
Massage	$ 1,446,000	$	$ 829,000	$ 45,000	$ 572,000
Skin Care	523,000		299,500	41,000	182,500
Nail	199,800		108,400	6,600	84,800
Hair	206,000		115,400	10,500	80,100
Total Spa Contributions	2,374,800		1,352,300	103,100	919,400
INDIRECT EXPENSES					
Indirect Support Labor			255,200		255,200
Indirect Operating Expenses				190,000	190,000
Total Indirect Expenses			255,200	190,000	445,200
SPA AFTER INDIRECT EXPENSES	2,374,800		1,607,500	293,100	474,200
Memberships	174,000				174,000
OTHER OPERATED DEPARTMENTS					
Fitness	198,800		200,900	22,900	(25,000)
Food and Beverage	99,000	32,100	44,800	18,000	4,100
Retail	515,600	268,000	108,600	22,700	116,300
Rentals and Other Income	58,500				58,500
Total Operated Departmental Contributions	871,900	300,100	354,300	63,600	153,900
INCOME BEFORE UNDISTRIBUTED EXPENSES	3,420,700	300,100	1,961,800	356,700	802,100
UNDISTRIBUTED OPERATING EXPENSES					
Administrative and General			101,300	65,300	166,600
Marketing			34,200	64,900	99,100
Facilities Maintenance and Utilities				128,000	128,000
Total Undistributed Operating Expenses			135,500	258,200	393,700
INCOME BEFORE FIXED CHARGES	$ 3,420,700	$ 300,100	$ 2,097,300	$ 614,900	$ 408,400

Fixed Charges	89,000
INCOME BEFORE DEPRECIATION, AMORTIZATION, INTEREST AND INCOME TAXES	319,400
Depreciation and Amortization	80,000
Interest Expense	30,000
Gain or Loss on Disposal of Property	(50,000)
INCOME BEFORE INCOME TAXES	259,400
Income Taxes	75,000
NET INCOME	$ 184,400

Source: *Uniform System of Financial Reporting for Spas*, p. 188

Appendix B: Sample Day Spa Statement of Income

Budget to Actual Report: Salon Division

Apr-08 USD Division Neill=3150 (Jefferso	TY-Actual Apr-08	% Sales	TY-Budget Apr-08	% Sales	YTD-Actual Apr-08	% Sales	YTD-Budget Apr-08	% Sales	YE Projected	YE Budget
Gross Revenue										
Service Income	171,766	78.00	219,097	79.00	2,395,755	76.50	2,248,534	77.90	2,395,755	2,248,534
Retail Income	31,958	14.50	40,767	14.70	514,294	16.40	464,548	16.10	514,294	464,548
Gross Revenue	203,724	92.50	259,864	93.70	2,910,049	93.00	2,713,082	94.00	2,910,049	2,713,082
Tip Income	19,683	8.90	22,567	8.10	276,058	8.80	228,921	7.90	276,058	228,921
Discounts	(3,151)	(1.40)	(5,197)	(1.90)	(55,535)	(1.80)	(54,871)	(1.90)	(55,535)	(54,871)
Total Net Revenue	220,256	100.00	277,234	100.00	3,130,572	100.00	2,887,132	100.00	3,130,572	2,887,132
Cost of Goods Sold										
Salon/Spa Retail	19,664	61.50	21,199	52.00	262,901	51.10	241,565	52.00	262,901	241,565
Professional Products	11,127	6.50	10,955	5.00	152,064	6.30	111,127	4.90	152,064	111,127
Cost of Goods Sold	30,791	14.00	32,154	11.60	414,965	13.30	352,692	12.20	414,965	352,692
Service Payroll	76,234	44.40	92,938	42.40	1,051,642	43.90	942,766	41.90	1,051,642	942,766
Inventory Adjustment	2,058	0.90	1,036	0.40	(773)	-	10,509	0.40	(773)	10,509
Total Cost of Goods Sold	109,083	49.50	126,127	45.50	1,465,834	46.80	1,305,967	45.20	1,465,834	1,305,967
Gross Profit	111,173	50.50	151,106	54.50	1,664,738	53.20	1,581,165	54.80	1,664,738	1,581,165
Direct Expense										
Payroll										
Incentives	2,106	6.60	2,242	5.50	20,149	3.90	25,550	5.50	20,149	25,550
Employee Benefits	3,618	1.60	7,030	2.50	78,847	2.50	72,551	2.50	78,847	72,551
Non-Service Payroll										
Administration	-	-	-	-	(535)	-	-	-	n/m	-
Client Services	2,957	1.30	4,773	1.70	48,335	1.50	49,263	1.70	48,335	49,263
Retail	14,384	45.00	14,587	35.80	174,983	34.00	166,225	35.80	174,983	166,225
Other Service Payroll	5,695	2.60	-	-	12,115	0.40	-	-	n/m	-
Total Non-Service	23,036	10.50	19,361	7.00	234,898	7.50	215,488	7.50	234,898	215,488
Tip Payroll	19,683	11.50	22,567	10.30	276,058	11.50	228,921	10.20	276,058	228,921
Payroll Taxes	8,946	4.10	10,830	3.90	126,634	4.00	111,767	3.90	126,634	111,767
Recruitment	-	-	50	-	83	-	600	-	83	600
Vehicle Leases	-	-	-	-	4,038	0.10	-	-	n/m	-
Workers Compensation	1,359	0.60	2,199	0.80	28,191	0.90	22,692	0.80	28,191	22,692
Total Payroll	58,749	26.70	64,278	23.20	768,897	24.60	677,569	23.50	768,897	677,569
New Academy Program Payroll	1,544	0.70	-	-	51,106	1.60	-	-	n/m	-
Total Payroll	60,293	27.40	64,278	23.20	820,003	26.20	677,569	23.50	820,003	677,569

(continued)

Appendix B: *(continued)*

Apr-08 USD Division Neill=3150 (Jefferso	TY-Actual Apr-08	% Sales	TY-Budget Apr-08	% Sales	YTD-Actual Apr-08	% Sales	YTD-Budget Apr-08	% Sales	YE Projected	YE Budget
Departmental										
Supplies										
Office & Equipment	364	0.20	439	0.20	4,092	0.10	4,486	0.20	4,092	4,486
Professional	968	0.40	1,299	0.50	16,678	0.50	13,181	0.50	16,678	13,181
Postage	-	-	59	-	14	-	702	-	14	702
Telephone	1,538	0.70	1,791	0.60	18,038	0.60	21,497	0.70	18,038	21,497
Training	91	-	458	0.20	7,423	0.20	5,500	0.20	7,423	5,500
Travel & Meals	99	-	306	0.10	2,613	0.10	3,667	0.10	2,613	3,667
Vehicle	343	0.20	525	0.20	1,809	0.10	6,304	0.20	1,809	6,304
Total Departmental	3,403	1.50	4,877	1.80	50,667	1.60	55,337	1.90	50,668	55,337
Advertising										
Advertising	1,568	0.70	2,065	0.70	15,485	0.50	24,778	0.90	15,485	24,778
Printing	38	-	416	0.10	2,094	0.10	4,987	0.20	2,094	4,987
Total Advertising	1,606	0.70	2,481	0.80	17,579	0.60	29,765	1.00	17,578	29,765
Promotional										
Dues&Subscriptions	-	-	35	-	267	-	421	-	267	421
Merchandising	277	0.10	483	0.20	6,223	0.20	4,987	0.20	6,223	4,987
Promotional	-	-	97	-	616	-	997	-	616	997
Total Promotional	277	0.10	615	0.20	7,106	0.20	6,406	0.20	7,106	6,406
Shipping & Warehouse										
Indirect Expense										
General Management										
Cleaning										
Janitorial	2,163	1.00	1,026	0.40	22,718	0.70	12,317	0.40	22,718	12,317
Salaundry	1,426	0.60	2,096	0.80	21,005	0.70	21,632	0.70	21,005	21,632
Equipment Rental	1,078	0.50	816	0.30	13,164	0.40	9,796	0.30	13,164	9,796
Insurance										
Umbrella & IM	-	-	139	0.10	-	-	1,667	0.10	-	1,667
Professional Fees	81	-	174	0.10	1,978	0.10	2,090	0.10	1,978	2,090
Repairs & Maintenance										
Building	1,026	0.50	491	0.20	10,676	0.30	5,889	0.20	10,676	5,889
Equipment	823	0.40	19	-	2,781	0.10	222	-	2,781	222
Rent	17,850	8.10	17,850	6.40	214,200	6.80	214,200	7.40	214,200	214,200
Utilities	2,082	0.90	2,262	0.80	32,974	1.10	27,145	0.90	32,974	27,145
Total General Management	26,529	12.00	24,873	9.10	319,496	10.20	294,958	10.20	319,496	294,958

Appendix B: (continued)

Apr-08 USD Division Neill=3150 (Jefferso	TY-Actual Apr-08	% Sales	TY-Budget Apr-08	% Sales	YTD-Actual Apr-08	% Sales	YTD-Budget Apr-08	% Sales	YE Projected	YE Budget
Finance										
Amortization										
Non-Compete	-	-	2,491	18.60	27,400	20.60	29,888	20.00	27,400	29,888
Bad Debt	180	0.10	381	0.10	2,840	0.10	3,928	0.10	2,840	3,928
Bank Fees	3,667	1.70	4,596	1.70	48,522	1.50	47,431	1.60	48,522	47,431
Depreciation										
Computer Equipment	38	-	192	0.10	460	-	2,307	0.10	460	2,307
Furniture & Fixtures	1,807	0.80	851	0.30	21,681	0.70	10,216	0.40	21,681	10,216
Leasehold Improvements	523	0.20	2,737	1.00	2,450	0.10	32,846	1.10	2,450	32,846
Machinery & Equipment	204	0.10	554	0.20	2,449	0.10	6,647	0.20	2,449	6,647
Other Finance	529	0.20	60	-	1,088	-	621	-	1,088	621
Over/Short	167	0.10	-	-	4,317	0.10	-	-	n/m	-
Taxes&Licenses	2,072	0.90	1,538	0.60	22,026	0.70	15,877	0.50	22,026	15,877
Total Finance	9,188	4.20	13,400	4.80	133,235	4.30	149,760	5.20	133,235	149,760
Total Direct Operating Exper	65,579	29.80	72,252	26.10	895,355	28.60	769,076	26.60	895,355	769,076
Total Indirect Operating Exp	35,717	16.20	38,274	13.80	452,731	14.50	444,718	15.40	452,731	444,718
Total Operating Expense	101,296	46.00	110,525	39.90	1,348,086	43.10	1,213,794	42.00	1,348,086	1,213,794
Net Operating Profit	9,877	4.50	40,581	14.60	316,652	10.10	367,371	12.70	316,652	367,371
Non-Operating Income (Expense)										
Income										
Interest Expense	(94)	-	(391)	(0.10)	(224)	-	(4,698)	(0.20)	(224)	(4,698)
Net Non-Operating Income (E	(94)	-	(391)	(0.10)	(224)	-	(4,698)	(0.20)	(224)	(4,698)
Net Income Before Taxes	9,783	4.40	40,190	14.50	316,428	10.10	362,673	12.60	316,428	362,673
Net Income After Taxes	9,783	4.40	40,190	14.50	316,428	10.10	362,673	12.60	316,428	362,673
Allocations										
Salon Earnings	9,783	n/m	40,190	n/m	316,428	n/m	362,673	n/m	316,428	362,673

Source: Paris Parker Salon/Spa, Jefferson, La., Courtesy of Neill Corporation

Chapter 8 Outline

The Spa Industry's Human Resource
    Challenge
        Sources of Spa Industry Managers
        A Well-Kept Secret
Advantages of a Spa Career
Challenges or Disadvantages of a Spa
    Career
Skills and Aptitudes of Spa Professionals
Career Opportunities
        Entry Level/Support Positions
        Professional/Technical Level Positions
        Managerial Level Positions
        Other Spa Careers
Spa Careers for the Future
        Medical Spa Technicians
        Life Coaches
        Age-Specific Specialists
        Holistic Health and Wellness Profes-
            sionals
        Green-Collar Jobs
        Technology Specialists
Training, Education, and Licensing
        Training
        Education
        Licensing and Certification
Compensation and Benefits
        Compensation
        Benefits
Beginning a Spa Career
There's a Spa Career for You

Competencies

1. Identify the advantages and
   disadvantages of a career in the spa
   industry. (pp. 289–295)

2. Identify important positions at all levels of the spa industry. (pp. 295–309)

3. Identify future career trends in the spa
   industry. (pp. 309–311)

4. Describe the education, training, and
   licensing requirements of various spa
   careers. (pp. 311–317)

5. Describe the types of compensation
   and benefits offered in the spa
   industry. (pp. 318–320)

6. Identify ways in which people begin
   a career in the spa industry.
   (pp. 320–323)

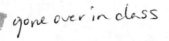 *gone over in class*

8

Spa Careers, Vocations, and Professions

"Spa work as life work offers a well-trained, reflective, and compassionate individual an ongoing opportunity to really facilitate and enhance others in their efforts and struggles to regain balance, harmony, and health .... In many ways a career in spa work is more than just a career because spa work touches the very essence of being human and human becomingness ... Spa as a profession manifests meaning, success, purpose, reward, and fulfillment."

Prof. Jonathan Paul DeVierville, Ph.D., Director, Alamo Plaza Spa at the historic Menger Hotel, San Antonio, Texas

T HE WORLD OF SPA is one of the fastest growing **service professions**. As more and more people embrace the concepts of wellness and healthy lifestyles, the need for spas continues to increase, and with that, the need for well-qualified personnel and a skilled work force at every level is becoming more apparent. Spas are looking for passionate people with the right combination of personality, skills, training, and education, who are able to provide and deliver the spa experiences that spa guests and consumers are seeking. The spa industry as an occupation, vocation, and profession offers countless career opportunities and work options for the right people with the right interests, aptitudes, skills, and heart.

The Spa Industry's Human Resource Challenge

The International SPA Association discovered a number of human resource challenges when conducting research on the spa industry. Many regions across the United States and Canada are experiencing a significant shortage of qualified people with a high level of skills. This is particularly true of directors and management staff.

According to the ISPA 2007 Spa Industry Study, there is a definite shortage of people working in the industry, with 72 percent of spas reporting at least one open position, and many spas having openings in several job categories. Exhibit 1 shows the percent of spas with open staff positions.

The ISPA study also looked at the average number of unstaffed positions by job title, both overall for all spas and among those that have open positions. The figures (shown in Exhibit 2) reveal a shortage of almost 24,000 massage therapists in the United States, other non-management positions with a shortage of 14,500 to 16,500, and at the management level, an estimated 6,600 spa director/manager openings.

Exhibit 1   Percent of Spas With Open Staff Positions

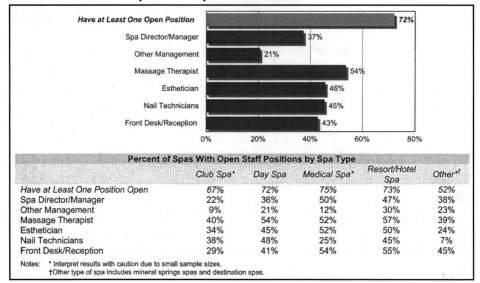

Percent of Spas With Open Staff Positions by Spa Type					
	Club Spa*	Day Spa	Medical Spa*	Resort/Hotel Spa	Other*†
Have at Least One Position Open	67%	72%	75%	73%	52%
Spa Director/Manager	22%	36%	50%	47%	38%
Other Management	9%	21%	12%	30%	23%
Massage Therapist	40%	54%	52%	57%	39%
Esthetician	34%	45%	52%	50%	24%
Nail Technicians	38%	48%	25%	45%	7%
Front Desk/Reception	29%	41%	54%	55%	45%

Notes: * Interpret results with caution due to small sample sizes.
              †Other type of spa includes mineral springs spas and destination spas.

Source: *2007 Spa Industry Study*, ISPA

Exhibit 2   Number of Unstaffed Positions

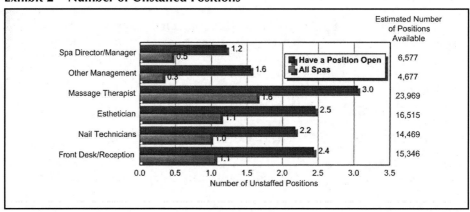

Source: *2007 Spa Industry Study*, ISPA

The general feeling is that the root cause of the spa industry's long-standing human resource challenge stems from the huge demand partnered with inadequate industry education, which has had trouble keeping pace with industry growth.

Sources of Spa Industry Managers

Colleges and universities, along with industry groups, consultants, and massage and esthetics institutes have all geared teaching and education toward meeting the industry's labor challenges. While most spas work closely with their suppliers to educate staff on treatments, materials, and protocols, spas themselves are now stepping up their efforts to provide more in-house training and development programs to prepare employees for career paths that lead to management.

However, without widespread opportunities to pursue a spa management degree at higher education institutions, spa managers must be recruited from the ranks of hospitality, business, marketing, and health care management. Many of today's spa leaders, managers, and owners arrive at their positions from varied avenues, educating themselves to the spa industry along the way.

Within the resort spa business, managers have often been appointed to the spa from within other areas of the resort, or promoted from the position of spa management assistant to spa director. Often, new spa directors and managers had strength in one area, but were weak in another—such as possessing strong business management skills, but knowing little about the intricacies of the spa business. Or, when an assistant was promoted, he or she often knew the spa, but was not strong in the business-minded characteristics required of a successful spa director.

Spa managers and owners have often been hands-on practitioners with an entrepreneurial spirit. However, the qualities that make someone a good esthetician or massage therapist are usually not the same qualities held by a strong business manager. As a result, the manager/owner struggles to run a successful operation. The lead therapist, esthetician, nail technician, or fitness instructor helps the managers who do not know their department's culture, and this experience propels the leads into assistant manager roles, which sets a career pathway for eventual spa management. However, since most massage and esthetics schools do not include business courses in their curricula, those who have been promoted to management from the ranks of therapists often feel ill-prepared for their new careers.

A Well-Kept Secret

Perhaps another reason contributing to the shortage of employees in the spa industry is that not enough career-seekers know that these jobs exist. Jack Morrison, managing director of Elmcrest College in North York, Ontario, Canada, and president of Leading Spas of Canada, has stated that the spa industry needs to make people aware of the myriad career opportunities that spa represents.

"If you were to go into virtually any career guidance office in any educational institution in North America and say, 'Tell me about careers in the spa industry,' chances are the person you ask will have zero to very little knowledge and they almost certainly would not have spa on their career recommendation list for students," Morrison said. "The industry has done a good job of promoting the therapeutic mind/body/spirit values of their products. In fact, they've done such a good job that that the first single-minded thought that enters the brain when the word 'spa' is spoken is that of self-indulgence. Nobody's first thought is 'great career paths.' With many other industries facing the same demographically-driven labor crisis, until the spa industry starts promoting spa careers on a competitive level, today's labor challenges will get worse. How on earth can we hope to fill today's and tomorrow's void if nobody has spa on their career radar screen?"

Advantages of a Spa Career

Spas focus on health and wellness, not only for clients, but for those who work within the spa environment. A professional looking for a career where health and wellness are valued and where there are opportunities to practice healthy living will find a home within the spa industry, where all of these are embraced. This is a field of service that enables people to pursue a passion for service, creativity, and helping others, while both teaching and practicing a lifestyle dedicated to health and wholeness.

The spa industry is a supportive environment for those who are "people persons." Those in the world of spa work with other people in ways that make connections and provide healing. The people who enter the industry are also people who are caring, creative, and committed to other people. For many, it is a calling as much or more than it is a job.

Continuing education and training are a high priority in the spa industry. Training is continual, whether in specific product uses, training modalities, customer service, or new treatments. Product suppliers offer training programs to impart product knowledge, and there are spa trade shows, spa magazines, online programs, and other educational opportunities both inside and outside the spa. Many spas offer mentoring and sponsor ongoing educational opportunities for staff to increase their skill levels. If life-long learning is important, a spa career is a great choice.

Other advantages to a spa career include receiving spa treatments from co-workers or perhaps receiving discounts on products and services. **Cross training**—being able to work in multiple departments, or work as a lead professional and a manager—is another benefit of working in the spa industry.

Challenges or Disadvantages of a Spa Career

Work hours for spa professionals may begin earlier or extend beyond the regular hours of spa operation to prepare the facility for guests and to clean up after the day is over. Work time includes days, nights, weekends, and holidays. First appointments may begin at 8 A.M. and the last might not end until 10 P.M. Flexibility is vital. Because the spa's priority is serving the guest, spa employees must be willing to work to accommodate guest needs. Staff members may be asked to work a split shift, on-call hours, holidays, or after closing. Someone who desires a traditional 9-to-5 work week may not be happy with spa schedules or changing work time environments.

Managers also have long and often non-traditional hours. Many resort or destination spas have a manager on duty (MOD) shift. The person in that role may have to stay on property overnight, which can be a challenge for his or her personal life. Managers may need to be flexible regarding travel, either for professional conferences or off-property retreats. During holidays, work schedules are also a challenge, with managers coming in very early or staying late.

Everyone working in a spa, from managers to professional staff to locker attendants, works together to ensure that all areas of the spa are clean, welcoming, and presentable to guests. Spa staff members are also responsible for keeping their

Spa Snapshot: What is your greatest satisfaction in doing your job?

At this place in my career, I get the greatest satisfaction in helping young managers and technicians grow in both their career path and as individuals who make up an exceptional team.

—*Wendy Clark, President, I-Bella*

My greatest satisfaction is when people recognize the true health benefits of a spa experience. Whether that information comes from a guest, or from a great story that is written about the spa experience – seeing how it benefits real people is exciting for me.

—*Darlene Fiske, Owner, The Fiske Group: Public Relations & Marketing Strategies*

Seeing guests embrace the spa lifestyle. Watching their shoulders slowly drop as they start to relax after entering the spa. Seeing younger staff attacking their jobs with gusto because they believe in it, that it's not just a job.

—*Wanda Love, Director of Sales & Marketing, Santé Spa*

Knowing that I am helping individuals stay sustainable in their careers longer by teaching business skills, body mechanics, and other self-care strategies.

—*Debra Koerner, Chief Operating Officer, imassage, Inc.*

I love that I work in a field that is based upon touch and caring intentions. It gives me great satisfaction to coach people on a day-to-day basis on how to best make people feel good, feel healthy, and on how to love and take care of themselves daily.

—*Sara Cruncleton, Ihloff Salon & Spa*

own work spaces clean and stocked, wiping down equipment, counters, and supplies, removing dirty linens, and restocking clean linens. The spa industry is not a place for those afraid to get their hands dirty or who expect others to clean up after them. Next to spa services, spa hygiene is the most important value in a spa environment. In fact, the two cannot be separated.

Spa work is also very physically demanding and requires a great deal of stamina. And, while an advantage to a spa career is working directly with people as opposed to being isolated in an office, it may also be a disadvantage, as spa professionals must be consistently and authentically present to every guest or client, no matter how they are feeling personally or how long they have been working that day.

When ISPA asked a group of spa professionals what they liked least about their jobs, their answers included:

- Dealing with unreasonable demands
- Having too short a time to spend with each client before and after service
- Labor intensiveness
- Repetition
- The long days
- Weekend, holiday, and night hours

Skills and Aptitudes of Spa Professionals

The breadth and depth of the spa industry's vocations and professions means that there can be an ideal, if not perfect, job for just about everyone. Taking inventory of one's own professional and personal needs and goals can help one decide on a career. Glamour, flexibility, making a difference in others' lives, educating others, learning, creativity, healing—spa has all of these, somewhere and at some time. For example, massage therapists' work is more clinical, while a spa designer's job is more creative. Discovering one's personal style may help a job seeker decide on a course of professional development that is right for them. For instance, the massage department is generally quiet and nurturing, while the salon area can be loud and more social.

Spa careers require a combination of head and heart—business and financial acumen plus people skills and empathy. Many people do not naturally possess both of these, so building a spa career involves a commitment to developing the business side of one's work style, the emotionally sensitive side, or both.

In the world of spa, technical skill is prized, but not at the expense of good communication skills, active listening, empathy, and sensitivity to others. As one spa director noted, "I am not looking for the best deep tissue therapist in the state. I am looking instead for someone who genuinely cares for each guest, who is interested in giving their best, and someone who fits well into our spa family."

Desirable traits of those who work in the spa industry include compassion; interest in health and wellness for themselves and others; acceptance of all body types and physical conditions; the ability to make people feel comfortable; sensitivity to others' needs; a thirst for knowledge and keeping up with the latest technologies and trends; a well-groomed appearance; high standards of cleanliness, health, and safety; passion; and talent for motivating others.

Spa technical professionals like massage therapists, estheticians, hair stylists, and nail technicians provide treatments and services for spa clients or guests. This requires a thorough knowledge of their areas of expertise; understanding of the human body, mind, and spirit; and willingness to learn a particular spa's specific treatments. Strong communication skills and ability to learn and convey product and service knowledge are needed. Because spas have various philosophies and missions, it is important for job seekers to find a spa that aligns with their core values. The reciprocal is also true in that it is very important that the spa hire those people who are aligned with its core values.

Working in a spa means being part of a team, working together for the good of the clients, one's fellow workers, and the business. Spa professionals must be punctual, organized, efficient, and detail oriented. They need to be good problem-solvers, and eager learners. For some positions, feeling part of the team can be more difficult; for example, a massage therapist or esthetician can spend hours alone behind closed doors with clients, having little staff interaction during working hours. Managers and spa directors must work with staff members to ensure that everyone feels included in the life of the spa.

The spa experience is not only the services provided; it is also creating the ideal environment for the guest. Guests should feel special, calm, nurtured, welcome, and comfortable. It is important for every member of a spa's staff to be authentically present with each guest, whether they are the first or last guest of the day, whether they are a first-time client or a veteran spa-goer. Spa staff must also be authentically present to one another, from the director to the therapists to the receptionists and locker attendants.

Career Opportunities

Spas offer a wide range of career opportunities from entry-level positions through upper-level management. The number of employees at any given spa varies based on the type of facility and extent of services offered. For instance, the staff of a destination spa may include positions for nutritionists, chefs, restaurant staff, and individual fitness instructors for a variety of activities, as well as the massage therapists, estheticians, and nail technicians found in a day spa. In a smaller spa, a single person may have responsibility for several tasks (retail sales, front desk, reservations, etc.), while a larger spa might staff each of those positions separately.

It is important to recognize that spas use different terms for the various positions in a spa. It is also important to understand that different spas will have a different division of duties associated with each job title. The following should be viewed as general descriptions.

Entry Level/Support Positions

Guest reception. The front desk offers guests their first impression of a spa. Front desk or guest reception employees must be friendly, knowledgeable about the spa and all spa treatments offered, and able to welcome clients and make them feel comfortable. They handle phone calls, make appointments, and greet walk-ins. Depending on the spa, they may also maintain the reception area, sell retail products, or monitor the inventory of supplies. In addition, they may provide orientation for guests, handle payments for services, or, in some cases, retail purchases. The person in this job may be called a front desk receptionist, front desk associate, or simply receptionist. (See Appendix for sample description.)

Reservationist. This employee schedules appointments and answers phones. He or she answers guests' basic questions about spa services, processes, and procedures. This person must be able to deliver accurate information to guests and be able to describe and support all the offerings from the spa menu. In some spas, this job may be done by the guest receptionist or front desk associate.

The spa guest receptionist offers guests their first impression of the spa by providing a warm welcome that makes guests feel comfortable.

Retail Sales Clerk. This person is responsible for the sale and service of all retail products to guests and for maintaining the retail area in a clean and orderly manner. The clerk must know the features and benefits of all retail offerings, product sales, and promotions, and how to effectively recommend products that meet the needs of the guest. Some knowledge of spas and spa products and previous retail sales experience is needed. It is important to understand that in most situations the initial product recommendation will be given in the treatment room by the therapist. In this case, the retail clerk's role is primarily as closer of the sale. (See Appendix for sample description.)

Lead Spa Attendant. The person in this role supervises attendant coworkers, including scheduling and training, and ensures guests are comfortable in the community areas. He or she is responsible for the cleanliness of locker, shower, grooming, wet, and relaxation areas, and ordering supplies and inventory.

Spa Attendant. This employee greets and orients guests to the locker area, conducts tours, and performs routine housekeeping to maintain the locker, shower, grooming, wet, and relaxation areas. The attendant issues lockers and guest supplies, and stocks guest supplies and inventory. In a day spa, this position is often known as spa host or hostess. (See Appendix for sample description.)

Spa Concierge. This employee welcomes guests to the spa and ensures that they are comfortable, providing any information needed for their visit and answering questions. The concierge may schedule, confirm, and change appointments, assist with retail sales, answer telephones, and update guest records. The concierge may assist the receptionist. He or she may also take care of duties such as selling gift certificates or providing extra services for the spa's VIP guests.

Spa Fitness Attendant. This employee instructs guests in proper use of fitness equipment, assists in providing non-technical fitness information, and provides fitness assistance to guests. The attendant monitors fitness supplies and equipment, conducts guest tours of the area, cleans machines, and is responsible for upkeep of the fitness area. Previous experience in a health club or spa environment and knowledge of weight and cardio equipment is useful.

Spa Restaurant/Café Server. In a spa that provides food service, this employee takes food and drink orders, serves guests food and drink, and may prepare food or beverages. Other responsibilities may include handling payment transactions, maintaining the cleanliness and safety of the area, or delivering orders to other areas of the spa.

Housekeeping Attendant. This employee cleans the spa facility, including treatment rooms, common areas, and bathrooms, and may clean some public areas. In a resort spa, these tasks may be done by the hotel's housekeeping department rather than by the spa.

Administrative Assistant. This employee provides non-executive clerical support to departments within the spa and reports to the spa director.

Professional/Technical Level Positions   *Requires Certifications*

Lead Esthetician. This position supervises esthetician service providers, including scheduling, hiring, and overseeing continuing education and training. In addition to these supervisory duties, he or she may provide skin care treatments. He or she ensures compliance with treatment protocols and may provide input on new treatment offerings. Those in this position will generally have three or more years of experience, with advanced training/certifications and licensing, which will vary by state and country.

Esthetician. Estheticians cleanse the skin by giving facials, full-body treatments, and makeup application. They may also perform hair removal through waxing or laser treatments. Employment for estheticians is expected to grow by 34 percent over the next 10 years because of increasing interest among consumers in skin care, according to the U.S. Bureau of Labor Statistics. According to Associated Skin Care Professionals (ASCP), the number of graduating estheticians doubled between 2001 and 2005. An ASCP survey of licensed estheticians found that 71 percent of estheticians work at least part of their day in a day spa or salon. Some 22 percent work at least some of the time in medical spas or doctors' offices. This position requires several hundred hours of course work to achieve licensing, which is required in most U.S. states. Requirements for licensing vary substantially from state to state and internationally, as does course content. For example, in Canada manicure and pedicure are standard components of an esthetics program, and while this vocation is heavily regulated in some provinces, it is virtually unregulated in others. It is therefore important that aspiring estheticians ensure that the school they choose to attend provides courses and course content that will adequately prepare them for licensing in the state or province where they wish to work. (See Appendix for sample description.)

Lead Massage Therapist. This person supervises massage and bodywork therapists, including scheduling, hiring, and overseeing continuing education and training. He or she may provide massage and bodywork treatments. He or she also ensures compliance with treatment protocols and may provide input on new treatment offerings. This supervisory role could require at least three years of experience.

Massage Therapist. Massage therapists provide massage services to guests. They may specialize in several modalities of massage and other bodywork treatments, each of which requires specialized training. Massage therapists need to be able to communicate effectively with their clients, work quietly, accept all body types, and practice good self-care. Because massage is the most requested service in spas in the United States, the job outlook is strong. According to the U.S. Bureau of Labor Statistics, employment for massage therapists is expected to grow faster than average (20 percent) from 2006 to 2016 as more people learn about the benefits of massage therapy. Most U.S. states require massage therapists to be licensed, but requirements vary widely from state to state. In addition to any state or country level licensing, massage therapists may take additional training and certification in specific styles of massage. (See Appendix for sample description.)

Nail Technician/Manicurist. A nail technician provides manicures, pedicures, polishing, nail extensions, and performs professional hand and foot treatments, including basic hand and foot massage. According to the U.S. Bureau of Labor Statistics, growth in the number of nail salons and full-service day spas will create many job openings for nail technicians. Employment is expected to increase by 28 percent between 2006 and 2016. A nail technician treats and polishes guest's nails and performs professional hand and foot treatments and basic hand and foot massage techniques. Certification or licensing is required in most states and countries. (See Appendix for sample description.)

Hair Stylist. This professional provides scalp/hair treatments, such as haircuts, styling, chemical services, and therapeutic hair and scalp treatments for guests. They work closely with guests to find the most flattering styles for their hair, listening to the guests' needs and also making suggestions. They are artistic and creative. They also advise guests on how to care for their hair and scalp to keep them healthy. They keep up on the latest trends and styles. Certification and licensing is required in most states and countries. Career prospects are strong in this profession, as both women and men are taking a greater interest in personal grooming. (See Appendix for sample description.)

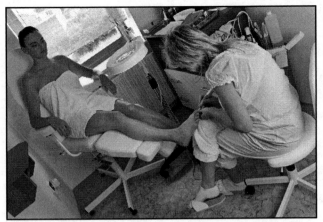

Employment opportunities are strong for nail technicians, because of the growth in the number of full-service day spas, according to the U.S. Bureau of Labor Statistics.

Cosmetologist. Cosmetologists work with clients' hair, skin, make-up, and nails. They have a variety of personal appearance skills and keep up with trends in personal grooming and appearance. Licensing is required and involves completing education and passing a state board examination.

Fitness Instructor. This person teaches fitness classes and instructs guests in a variety of fitness components. He or she generally has at least one year of experience; certification may be required. There are several certifying bodies for fitness instructors, including the American Council on Exercise, National Academy of Sports Medicine, and American College of Sports Medicine. Many specific exercise fields, such as Pilates, tai chi, and yoga, also have their own specialized certifications. This job area includes personal trainers, group exercise instructors, fitness directors, and instructors for a variety of activities including tennis, golf, hiking, aerobics, dance, yoga, and Pilates. According to the U.S. Bureau of Labor Statistics, jobs for fitness workers are expected to increase much faster than the average for all occupations, because of rapid job growth in health clubs, fitness facilities, and other settings where fitness workers are employed, including spas. (See Appendix for sample description.)

Nutritionist/Dietitian. In spas offering nutritional services, a nutritionist or dietitian provides nutritional instruction and consultation for guests and staff. Dietitians must earn at least a bachelor of science degree and must then serve an extensive internship (usually one year) in either a medical or management setting. A dietitian is registered with the American Dietetics Association and must follow a series of continuing education credits each year with recertification every five years. Nutritionists are not held to the same level of education and certification. According to the U.S. Bureau of Labor Statistics, jobs in this field are expected to grow during the twenty-first century, mostly due to the increased emphasis on

reflections

Jason de Caprio: Everything I Was Looking For

Jason de Caprio is a stylist and educator for Noelle Spa for Beauty and Wellness. Raised by Noel and Peter de Caprio, founders of Noelle Spa for Beauty and Wellness, he has spent his life in the beauty industry and participates in the management of the renowned day spa.

My mother was one of the instigators of me becoming a hairdresser, even though ultimately it was my choice. I explored other options in high school; I thought I was going to become a chef, so I got a job in a restaurant—for one night. And that was that. The restaurant was not my cup of tea, but I loved cooking.

I was going to explore sculpting and art. I thought about that for a while, but I knew I wanted to have a lucrative business and make some money while I was alive. I know that most artists are struggling through their life trying to create and get recognized when they pass away—that's when they start making all the money. I figured I didn't want to do that.

The entire time, I was working in the salon. My mom was here, my dad was here. I was learning how to shampoo and how to do customer service. I started shampooing when I was 13 years old. I loved working on the women and shampooing their hair. And, the tips at the end of the day were awfully nice.

When I finished high school, my mother took me to a salon and hair cutting event one weekend in Long Island. I was talking with (several salon professionals including the son of another spa owner). He got a hold of me while my mother was at the show and started talking to me about what the beauty business was like. After that conversation, I decided it really was all of the things that I was looking for. It was sculpture, it was lucrative, it was being around people, and really seeing your effects. One of the things about the cooking industry that I didn't like was that you made all the food for the people and you never got to see them enjoy it. Cutting hair, you actually got to see the response from the people you were working with. That's what really changed my mind and made me go into the beauty business.

Another reason I got into being a hairdresser was because I thought there wouldn't be any homework. I thought that there wouldn't be any e-mails or phone calls or paperwork, but as I'm being longer in this business, it's certainly showing up.

I've been cutting hair for about 12 years now. The haircutting was always something that would challenge you. Every day you come into work and you're trying to perfect your skill. You're trying to perfect your talents. You're trying to cut a bob in a different way, or blow dry in a different way. Every day you came to work, something was different that you could challenge yourself with.

Now that I'm into management and looking at the business more in depth, it changes every day also. There's always a new challenge: Who didn't show up? Why didn't someone go get the half and half for the coffee? How come the stations weren't cleaned? Every day, it's something different.

---

healthy eating, public interest in nutrition and health education, and the needs of an aging population. More and more spas are offering nutritional counseling to their guests, as well as providing classes in healthy cooking and eating.

Not Your Average Job

The world of spa welcomes people with myriad talents and gifts to share with others. A few of these more unusual job titles include:

Director of Flora and Fauna: Trisha Shirey is director of flora and fauna at the Lake Austin Spa Resort in Texas. She designs, cultivates, and oversees the resort's organic herb and vegetable gardens, an organic orchard, and flowers throughout the grounds. She teaches classes in pressed flower design, potpourri, and herbal swags to guests at the resort, and also teaches cooking classes and aromatherapy classes. Shirey enjoys sharing her gardens with guests and encourages them to take home seeds and cuttings to start or add to their own gardens. She loves to be able to garden organically and to show guests that toxic chemicals are not necessary to have great gardens.

Optimal Performance Training Specialist: Scott Fedisin has been the optimal performance training specialist at Sea Island Resorts in Georgia since 2006. With a 16-year career in health and fitness training, his focus at the resort is fitness assessment and golf stretching. He assists guests looking to lose weight, develop a fitness plan for healthy living, and sharpen their golf game.

Astronomy Guide: John P. Kolb Jr. is an astronomy guide for the Red Mountain Spa in Utah. Kolb leads the most popular activity at Red Mountain, the "star parties," teaching guests about his lifelong passion, astronomy. Throughout his working career, Kolb found time to attend seminars and visit observatories and museums around the world and shares his vast knowledge with the spa's guests. He also shares his positive outlook and his heavenly approach to daily living.

Director of Sleep Programs: Rubin Naiman, Ph.D, is the director of sleep programs for Miraval Resort, Tucson. Naiman approaches sleep and dream issues comprehensively, from a body, mind, and spirit perspective. A distinguished expert on sleep and dreams, Naiman provides workshops, lectures, and individual consultations where he analyzes sleep patterns to create a personal, customized plan for optimal sleep and dreaming. His activities with resort guests include "The Secrets of Mindful Sleep" and "Healing Sleep and Dreams."

Managerial Level Positions

Do not require certifications but is normally run by those who are

Spas have many opportunities for those who aspire to management. It is important to note that not all spas include every position or layers of management. In some spas, the spa manager might be the top position, and in smaller spa settings, there might not be a treatments manager or services manager.

Spa Director. The spa director has overall responsibility for the spa and sets the strategic vision, provides leadership, and sets the guest experience standards for the entire spa culture. He or she is ultimately responsible for the daily operations of the spa, including, but not limited to, reservations, guest reception, all services, retail, fitness, and staffing. The director leads and supervises managers and other staff and is accountable for the spa's financial performance. The director is responsible for forecasting, budgeting, payroll, expense control, monthly statement of

reflections

Cheryl Hartsough: From Dietitian to Spa Director

There wasn't a degree in spa management when I was in college in the early 1980s. I knew I wanted to be in disease prevention. I chose to become a registered dietitian and was considering medicine. Then I landed a job at the University of Southern Florida as a dietitian for the food service department and started a wellness program for the faculty and students after graduating with a BS in Clinical and Community Dietetics from University of Florida. I also worked with a cardiac rehabilitation program and many sports/wellness/certification programs. I traveled lecturing coaches and sports teams in sports nutrition for Gatorade.

I served as consultant to the food service departments of a few different spas, then went full-time into the industry at a destination spa in Miami called Doral Saturnia. My natural progression in the spa world seemed to encompass all of my other job descriptions and it was nice to just have one job. I started in the spa world as a nutritionist specializing in spa cuisine and worked six years full-time at Doral, then six years at PGA National Resort & Spa in Palm Beach Gardens. I eventually went into traveling and consulting in spa cuisine throughout the United States, Europe, and Asia for many four and five star resorts. I went into spa management as there was a shortage and I couldn't travel as much with my children.

I spent many years learning from some of the best directors in the country and went into management in 1997 as a wellness director in Aspen, Colorado. It was one of the first medical spas with many new offerings such as cardio and metabolic testing, sound therapy, and Pilates.

My next position was as wellness director at the Nemacolin Woodlands, a Feng Shui spa. I've now been a spa director for seven years at Gurney's Inn Resort & Spa in Montauk, New York. I'm constantly humbled because this is an industry that you can never know everything and you must keep up with the latest trends and staff development. I'm never bored and some days are tough, but I love what I do. I know that we help guests achieve their many relaxation/fitness goals and that is rewarding.

---

income, management, and strategic planning to achieve profitability. Ideally, this position would require at least four or more years' management experience, spa management experience, and a college degree. However, with several thousand open management positions in the U.S.-spa industry, owners often need to consider hiring a director with transferable management skills from a prior career, as well as knowledge gained through spa-specific education. A background in either esthetics or massage may be helpful, but is not necessary.

Assistant Spa Director. This person's primary responsibility is to assist the spa director in setting and maintaining the leadership and guest experience standards. He or she provides direction and supervision to staff in the daily operations of the spa. Direct operational accountability may vary with specific needs but generally includes all areas, depending on the spa's organizational structure.

Spa Manager. In a larger spa, this person performs duties under the spa director, often with responsibility for operational logistics, overseeing the coordination of guest and staff requests, and assisting with budgeting, forecasting, payroll details, scheduling, staffing, overseeing product inventory, and ordering supplies and equipment. In the absence of a retail manager, this person may also oversee the spa's retail operations. (See Appendix for sample description.)

Retail Manager. This person oversees day-to-day operations of the retail area, with responsibility for supervising and training retail staff, selecting and cataloging product inventory, and ordering.

Spa Treatments Manager or Manager of Therapy Services. This manager oversees and monitors all facets of spa treatments operations; interviews, hires, schedules, trains, supervises, and evaluates therapists and estheticians; supervises ongoing program development and staff training in treatments; and maintains inventory control for all treatment areas. This person may be the lead therapist or else works closely with that position.

Fitness Director/Manager. This person oversees the day-to-day operations of the fitness facility; manages fitness instructors and personal trainers; designs class offerings and schedules; sets operating standards; may personally provide fitness instruction; and participates in membership sales and programs where applicable.

Reservations Manager. This person supervises reservations staff and the telephone and Internet-based call center for the spa, and is responsible for scheduling and training reservationists. He or she is knowledgeable about all spa treatments and services. Strong communication skills, attention to detail, and an ability to maximize revenue opportunities for the spa are essential.

Salon Manager. This person oversees the day-to-day operations of the salon, ensures safety of salon patrons, and may perform services. Hairstylists and nail technicians report to the salon manager. The salon manager will work closely with the spa manager to coordinate services between the spa and salon.

Spa Sales or Group Sales Coordinator. Large resort spas at a property that hosts large groups will have a spa group coordinator to work with the meeting planner on spa usage. This person makes individual appointments for group members, coordinates VIP amenities, and encourages sales of spa services like chair massages or group fitness events for attendees. This position may also include coordinating the spa's involvement in local charity events and speaking to local organizations. (See Appendix for sample description.)

Spa Membership Manager. In club spas or spas that have added a membership opportunity, the membership manager meets prospective members, processes applications, and develops and distributes membership collateral materials. He or she is the spa's contact person for members, and may plan special members-only events and promotions.

Spa Chef. In spas offering food service, the spa chef is responsible for the spa cuisine menu, ensuring that food and beverage preparation meets spa cuisine standards set by the spa. This position generally requires three or more years' experience and a degree from a culinary school.

The spa's reservations manager trains reservationists like this one and shows them how to maximize revenue opportunities for the spa while providing guests with detailed and accurate descriptions of spa services.

Restaurant Manager. In spas offering food service, the restaurant manager oversees the operation of the food service operation, including managing the servers, bussers, and other food service employees.

Other Spa Careers

While the spa industry needs people to work within spas, there is also a need for others knowledgeable about the spa industry to work in related careers that support and advance the world of spa. These careers may be a logical choice for a spa professional looking for a new challenge, or for someone who wants to use their talents in the spa industry without direct guest contact.

Spa Designers. Spa design is important whether building a spa from scratch, renovating, or expanding an existing spa. Designers must understand the needs of the spa, operational flow, treatment areas, warm and inviting spaces, and materials that are appropriate for use in the spa (e.g., surfaces that can be easily disinfected and won't absorb oils).

Designers must understand how to incorporate water features and nature into their design and be especially aware of environmental stewardship and sustainability issues. Spa designers who understand how massage therapists and estheticians work can design ergonomically friendly treatment rooms that are both practical and inviting to clients. Spa designers must listen carefully to the needs and goals of the spa director and create spaces for both the front and back of the

A chef in a spa prepares nutritious, delicious food for spa guests.

spa—with adequate storage, office, and staff areas, and ample room for guests to relax. A spa designer would generally graduate from an interior design program and have experience in general practice before deciding to specialize in designing for the spa environment.

Product Representative. Working for a spa product, supply, or equipment manufacturer or vendor after working as a spa professional allows one to use working knowledge of the business to effectively present the company's product in relation to its use in the spa industry.

Manufacturer/Supplier. Someone has to develop, produce, and distribute the products used in spas. The possibilities are endless for those with a product vision plus knowledge of spa needs. Spa products include everything from lotions, oils, and serums to linens, uniforms, loungewear, CDs, and books.

Educator/Trainer. Spa professionals with strong communication skills and the ability to teach may decide to become a spa educator, either leading training within their own organization or offering educational programs to other professionals or spas. There are increasing opportunities for instructors at massage, cosmetology, and esthetician schools. As colleges and universities begin to incorporate spa

Spa Snapshot: How did your career lead you to the spa industry?

"I was 21 years old, just gave up on my acting career and started with a makeup company in a retail store. Then I decided I wanted to do more skin care than retail. I went to esthetics school, got my license, and started to work for Aveda. Several years later, I realized we had a beautiful spa and excellent service but couldn't seem to find proper attire. And that is how Fianna Spa Fashions was created. We wanted to stay with the Aveda philosophy so we designed a natural, eco-friendly uniform line. Four years later, we are going strong, trying to educate spas of the importance of natural instead of synthetic uniforms. I am so glad this is the industry I work in!"

—*Amy Brooks, President, Fianna Spa Fashions, Arvada, CO*

"I started my career as a public relations executive in a private sector bank in India at a time when the finance industry was booming and the job was highly demanding and stressful. Doctors recommended that I slow down and I took up yoga and Ayurveda to help cope with stress. Within a few months of embracing an Ayurvedic lifestyle and regular yoga practice, I began to feel more energetic, look younger, and generally enjoy good health. It was then that I felt the calling to do something related to health and wellness. I began by joining an Ayurveda resort to help with marketing. In the time that I was there as marketing manager, I also learned about spa therapies and administration, and from there the next step was to set up a full-fledged spa using Ayurveda as the basis. That is how Emerge Spa came about, and today we are offering health and wellness to many people who are looking for relaxation and rejuvenation to help them cope with stress."

—*Vinita Rashinkar, Spa Director, Emerge Spa, Nazarbad, Mysore, India*

"Almost everybody asks me this question when they hear I have a medical degree. Why would a doctor leave the medical world and join the spa world? Well for me, spa and medicine are actually connected, interrelated. This is how I made my transition from one to another, as a necessity for my patients: I started to apply Ayurvedic techniques and reflexology in treating them, looking for ways to complete the standard medical treatments. I felt that my hands can make a difference, and I decided to study more in depth and learn new ways of applying my knowledge. I had an opportunity to join a newly-opened spa in Jordan as a spa therapist, and I took it. This was the first real spa training [I had], and I got forever hooked."

—*Maria Micu, Spa Director, The Rosseau, a JW Marriott Resort & Spa, Minett, Ontario, Canada*

Source: *Pulse,* September/October 2007

Spa manufacturers and suppliers provide spas with professional and retail products specifically tailored to the needs of the industry.

management courses into their curricula, there will be additional opportunities for educators.

Spa Consultant. Beginning in the late 1980s, the demand for adding spas to resorts and hotels was far greater than the supply of people who knew anything about spas. Several key spa professionals of that era switched careers and became spa consultants, guiding development projects and educating the builders and operators of new spas in the complexities of creating and operating functional, profitable spas.

Spa consultants may be called upon at various stages of a development or operations project to assist in a variety of ways. Most commonly, the spa consultant guides the development process, taking the spa from conceptual exploration through design development to final construction documents and equipment and supply specifications. They conduct feasibility studies for proposed projects, conduct market surveys and prepare three-to-five year spa financial projections, and develop opening operating supplies and equipment (OS&E) plans and budgets. Many projects involve spa consultants all the way through to opening, including training of staff and development of operational guidelines and protocols. Some consultants specialize in operations, training, marketing, or turnaround projects. Spa consultants play an important role in streamlining the spa development process, providing training and education, and troubleshooting operational challenges. This position is one undertaken by senior spa professionals with many years of professional experience opening and operating spas.

Spa Snapshot: When or how did you know that spa was where you were meant to be professionally?

Seeing the positive results of applying my business acumen to this industry and having a lasting impact on growing and improving the spa lifestyle.

—*Loren Stone, CEO, Sovereign Hospitality*

On my first day of training at Lake Austin Spa Resort 13 years ago, I went to a Nia dance class, did water aerobics in the pool overlooking Lake Austin, and ended "training" with my very first massage. How could you not LOVE an environment and an industry dedicated to making people feel good!

—*Darlene Fiske, Owner, The Fiske Group: Public Relations & Marketing Strategies*

I was born into this world with a mother who is a massage therapist; a father who is a yoga instructor, sound healer, and importer of Tibetan bowls. When I was five, my parents took me to a psychic who made a cassette recording with many predictions. I didn't listen to this cassette again until an era when cassettes were almost no more—my early 30s.

I never imagined working in this industry. I was in the field of special event production: fireworks, hot air balloon launches, Broadway theater, and rock concerts. Then one day while producing events for a hotel, I was told the racquetball courts would become a two-level spa, and then I would be working within it. What a shock—I never imagined going to university to manage manicures and pedicures, among other things. This opportunity was a blessing in disguise, because the career and moments that have developed since this day are priceless.

It's amazing to listen to the original psychic's tape and see my career occupation, personal relationships, and nearly 25 years of life unfold as originally predicted. It's all incredibly fascinating and truly was meant to be.

—*Sean Handler, Director of Sales, Solace Spa/Boyne USA*

I was in the high-tech industry for 20 years and the stress was unbelievable. Spa was the one place where I could recharge the batteries in short order, to face another week of off-the-scale pressure. Toward the end of my high-tech days, I considered opening a spa as I figured I was not the only stressed-out exec around.

—*Angela Cortright, Owner, Spa Gregorie's*

(continued)

I was intrigued by it initially, but the real a-ha moment for me was attending my first ISPA conference. Experiencing the warmth and commitment of the global spa community was extraordinary.

—*Wanda Love, Director of Sales & Marketing, Santé Spa*

My background is in theater and I began working in a day spa right after college in order to save up money before moving on to New York to become a famous actress. After working in the spa for about a year at the desk, I realized how similar the spa employees were to the "theater people" I was used to working with. I had an easy, comfortable connection with them and also with the way that they could "communicate" to their guests through touch and movement. It all felt very similar to theater or art and I believe that is why I felt that connection.

—*Sara Cruncleton, Ihloff Salon & Spa*

Spa Careers for the Future

As spas continue to grow and certain types of spas become more popular, spa careers and job options will increase and expand. New opportunities will arise in existing jobs and in other areas such as those listed below.

Medical Spa Technicians

One trend in spa careers is a greater focus on medical spa procedures, requiring a more targeted scientific background in addition to traditional esthetics. According to the ISPA 2006 Spa Industry Update, medical spas are the fastest growing spa segment in terms of locations, with a growth rate almost double the next closest segment.

Laura Todd, director of the Institute of Advance Medical Esthetics at the University of Professional Sciences in Richmond, Va., has a bachelor's degree in biology and is working toward a master's degree in education. She combines and applies her knowledge of science and skin care to the next generation of estheticians. "New technology is always out there. If you don't stay on top of it, you become obsolete. … We need an education that not only teaches present-day information, but future information as well," said Todd.[1] Todd was appointed to the first four-year esthetician's seat on the Virginia Board for Barbers and Cosmetology. From her work, in July 2007, Virginia became one of only two states to offer a two-tiered licensure for estheticians.

Because of varying state regulations, those who work in medical spas with laser technology or who perform certain paramedical procedures may be required to hold medical credentials or licensing in order to practice in a spa. This could open the way for medical professionals who are seeking a new career path, or for spa professionals who wish to expand their skills and training.

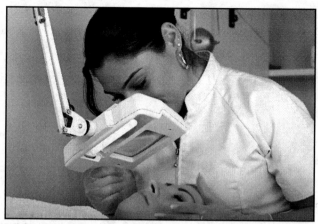

With medical spas growing faster than any other spa segment, there will be a continuing need for spa professionals trained in medical specialties.

Life Coaches

Spa consumers are no longer viewing spas merely as a place to indulge and pamper themselves. Rather, the spa is part of their overall plan for health and wellness. Spa-goers may look to life coaches who work at a spa for advice and direction in shaping a personal wellness plan for all aspects of their lives. Some destination and resort spas are already offering this service, and it should continue to become more popular.

According to the International Coach Federation, a coach partners with a client in a creative process that inspires a person to maximize his or her personal and professional potential. Coaches help people improve their performances and enhance the quality of their lives. They are trained to listen, observe, and customize their approach to individual client needs. They help clients find their own solutions and unlock natural creativity and resourcefulness.

Age-Specific Specialists

As more people embrace spa as a lifestyle, the spa industry may see a need for spa professionals who specialize in working with specific population segments, such as teenagers or the elderly. Spa professionals who have knowledge of services and treatments best suited for targeted populations will be able to provide value-added services for their clients.

Holistic Health and Wellness Professionals

Looking into the future, spas will continue to provide guests and clients with more in-depth access to health care that is focused on prevention and wellness, rather than reactive treatment of disease. Dissatisfaction with the current state of Western medical practice and restrictions of primary health care systems will give spas the opportunity to offer alternative health care and wellness programs for a growing number of people. Forward-thinking spas will look to leaders in the field, such as Miraval and Canyon Ranch, for models of integrating a broad spectrum of medical professionals into their staffs.

For example, Canyon Ranch lists among its specialists: cardiologists, herbal medicine practitioners, acupuncturists, behavioral health therapists, chiropractors, dermatologists, exercise physiologists, movement therapists, nutritionists, physical therapists, podiatrists, and women's health specialists. Medical professionals who become disenchanted with the constraints that insurance companies and hospital policies place on their practice of medicine may find a welcome home in the spa world.

Green-Collar Jobs

Sustainability and environmental stewardship are a high priority for spas today and into the future. Professionals with the knowledge and skills to assist spas with implementing environmentally sound policies and procedures and who can teach spa guests and clients to integrate eco-friendly practices into their own lives will be much in demand.

Technology Specialists

The future of spa includes a greater focus on technology, both for spa management and for spa marketing. Both IT professionals and marketing professionals who are savvy in the use of social networking tools like blogs, podcasting, e-newsletters, and sites like MySpace and Facebook may find a niche using their skills in a spa environment. Those who develop spa-specific software applications will also be in demand as spa professionals turn to technology solutions to help them streamline the administrative aspects of their jobs.

Whatever the future holds, there will certainly be ample career opportunities in the spa industry for men and women with an interest in helping others achieve health and wellness through the services offered by spas.

Training, Education, and Licensing

The spa industry is a wonderful place for people who enjoy learning. Training and education are high priorities among spa professionals. For some positions, such as massage therapists and estheticians, this training and education must take place before obtaining a job, but learning does not stop once work begins. Spa directors and managers provide training to employees on spa procedures and protocols and vendors provide training on how to use their products and equipment. Spa directors also benefit from continuing education to fill in gaps in their industry knowledge. For instance, a spa director with a background in the hospitality industry may benefit from achieving certification as a massage therapist or esthetician, both to better understand employees in those departments, to be better able to make decisions about treatments and products, and to increase his or her professional marketability.

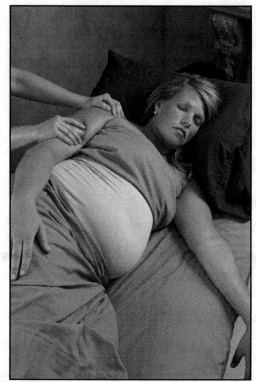

Spa technical professionals may need to pursue additional training and/or certification to be able to perform particular treatments, such as prenatal massage, Rolfing, or shiatsu.

Training

Training benefits the individual, their place of employment, and ultimately the spa guest. Training and education keep spa professionals current in their field and enhance their skills. Many spas reimburse or provide assistance for employees to take seminars, classes, and workshops to learn new techniques and skills that will enhance the spa experience for guests and expand the spa's treatment menu.

The International SPA Association Foundation offers educational programs and certifications for spa professionals. Their programs include *Supervisory Skill Builders for the Spa Industry*, which prepares supervisors for the Certified Spa Supervisor examination. There is also a course in *Retail Management for Spas* that leads to a certificate of completion, and an e-learning course in risk management that provides a certificate of completion.

Some spa and hospitality companies operate their own training programs to prepare employees to work in their facilities. In 2007, Shangri-La Hotels and Resorts opened a spa training center in Manila, Philippines, to train therapists to fill positions in the company's CHI spa brand. The program teaches therapist skills,

Spa Snapshot: Whether you are personally paying for your continued education or offering classes as compensation for your staff, how do you measure the return on investment?

At The Well Spa, we have money allocated in our professional development line of the budget to decide who in the spa and what services we want to allocate for classes and professional growth. This past year we were having a hard time finding a nail technician. This is a hard market to find staff in. We decided to invest in one of our desk associates. We posted the opportunity just like it was a position open in the spa; interested parties applied, and we chose one employee to send to nail school.

Our return on having an additional nail technician was returned to the spa in approximately three months, and it sent a message to the entire staff that we want to grow from within. It has proven more successful than waiting for an applicant. We measure success by this investment through one question on the associate opinion questionnaire ("I feel that management at this spa invests in my continued education.") and the yearly scores on employee satisfaction. Employee satisfaction drives success with the guest and our revenues!

—*Jennifer Di Francesco, Spa Director, The Well at Miramonte Resort*

I personally pay for my team to attend education, and I also compensate them for attending. I do, however, have them sign an education contract that holds them responsible for repaying me should their position be terminated or if they leave the spa. I measure the return on investment by sheer numbers as it relates to what I sent them for – usually increases in add-on services, up-sells, and of course, retail. If it is a business class, what I have found is a general increase in enthusiasm and attitude and of course a better understanding of what it really takes to run a successful business. That, of course, is priceless.

—*Alayne White, Proprietress, Alayne White Spa, Inc.*

Training is an ongoing procedure at our spa. If someone has downtime, someone else will grab him and give training. At the monthly team meeting, one hour is devoted to kudos, applause, and new information. The second hour is devoted to training by department. Employees are rewarded for keeping up with training by receiving free outside training. Each quarter, the owner circles classes in the junior college catalog; any team member who takes any of those classes gets the registration fee, tuition, etc., paid for by the spa. We do not track the return on

(continued)

(continued)

investment. Education is as important for the growth of an individual and a business as air and food are for a human.

—*Mimi Barre, Founder/Owner, International Skin & Body Care*

I feel very strongly that continuing education is something that should be part of the ongoing training of the individual spa and not left up to the individual. In addition to building additional skills, classes are also a place that service providers can interact with their peers, learning about what makes each person unique and how they fit into the puzzle that makes a team. When I am assessing if the training was successful, I am looking to see if staff is excited about the training during and after. After the training, I look to see that there is a real change, either in technique, skills, or behavior. With a spa investing around 50 percent of their budget in staff payroll, it only makes sense to me to take a small percentage for training to ensure that the 50 percent is not squandered on untrained and unmotivated staff.

—*Jenean LaRoche, Spa Director, Nob Hill Spa*

When it comes to continuing education, it is my belief that investing in yourself or in the lives of someone else is invaluable. You can't put a price on education. I teach a segment of the University of California Irvine's Spa Management and Hospitality Program, and I see the return on my investment with my students in how they excel in this industry as leaders. Their passion for the industry through their time and investment adds further legitimacy to what we do and is making everyone take a serious look at the spa industry as a whole.

—*Maureen Vipperman, CSS, ACC, BS, Glen Ivy Hot Springs Spa*

We offer continuing education for any staff member that has been employed for at least six months in good standing and is full-time. If there is an educational opportunity that is mutually beneficial for the staff member and the resort (meaning it applies to an offering already on the menu or one we would like to add), we will pay for the class. The staff member signs an agreement that if they remain with the resort for at least a year after completing the class, their class is paid in full. If they leave for any reason prior to a year, they will pay back a prorated amount. Staff members see it as a great benefit, especially since the credit assists them with their recertification/license renewal requirements.

We are very selective about the trainings we approve, but there are several modalities, such as stones, lymphatic, cranial, table Thai, etc., that are the most requested services we offer, so having additional staff trained means we are instantly able to accommodate more guest requests.

—*Deborah Waldvogel, Director of Spa Development and Operations, Sedona Resorts*

Source: *Pulse,* November 2006

reflections

Anne Bramham: From Make-Up Artist to Global Spa Educator

One might say I stumbled into my life's work. In my early twenties, a well-known British makeup artist, Barbara Daly, opened a training center in London. Thinking that a career as a makeup artist could be quite glamorous, I signed up for classes. One morning there was a lecture on the lymphatic system and I remember thinking that the secret of life, the secret to rejuvenation, was being revealed to me, and I was thrilled by the discovery. I began to study anatomy, physiology, and the power of touch and rehabilitation therapies.

Three decades later, I'm still studying—still very much a student—but my career has taken me into management and teaching. My early years in the spa industry were spent in my native England where I owned and operated a day spa. In the early 1980s, we moved to the United States.

In my first years in the States, I opened and managed a few residential/club spas in South Florida. In 1989, I was on the opening team of the "Waters of the World" Spa at PGA in Palm Beach Gardens. Soon after opening, I set up the Bramham Institute at the PGA Resort. A few years later, I moved the Institute to my own spa in West Palm Beach and began teaching classes in different spa therapies. In 1996, I founded ASTECC (the American Spa Therapy Education & Certification Council), to provide therapists with the integrative tools to effectively implement individualized, result-oriented spa treatment programs. In the past ten years, I've taught ASTECC components to numerous spas across the United States and Europe, including leading training at Spa Montage in Laguna Beach, California, the first spa to train in the entire ASTECC curriculum.

---

customer service skills, and the CHI brand philosophy. Some students in the program also receive spa management training.

Other professional organizations and associations also offer training programs, online seminars, web-based training, and professional certification. Spa trade shows, spa magazines and professional journals, and membership in associations for professional areas of expertise also provide opportunities for continuing education.

Education

There are career and technical schools that specialize in the education and training of massage therapists, estheticians, and cosmetologists. In addition, some colleges and universities are offering courses in various aspects of spa operations and management. These courses may be part of the hospitality management program, the sports and leisure department, or the health and wellness department. The first university to offer spa management classes was Cornell University, where Dr. Mary Tabacchi began teaching business-related courses in spa management in 1986. While most schools offer only selected courses related to spa topics, a few have developed complete program tracks dedicated to spa management education.

Since 2000, Elmcrest College in Canada (see Exhibit 3) has focused its curriculum solely on spa education. Its full-time program in spa management is based on

Exhibit 3   Elmcrest College Profile

In 2000, Elmcrest College, a private career college in Toronto, Canada, was created to focus solely on spa education. Its curriculum includes high standard full-time programs in massage therapy, esthetics, and three levels of spa management based on the challenging requirements of the industry as opposed to just meeting the minimum needs of the government for program approval.

After three years of development and testing, its spa director diploma program was launched in 2003. This represented the first full-time spa management program in North America from a school specializing in nothing but spa education. Graduates from this very intense strategically oriented program enjoy international job offers and placements.

According to their Web site at www.elmcrestcollege.com, students choose to attend Elmcrest for the following reasons:

*   Flexibility to choose from three levels of spa management education - Spa Customer Service Professional Diploma, Spa Leadership Program, Spa Manager/Director Diploma Program.

*   Curriculum based upon hands-on management experience with their sister company, Elmwood Spa

*   Extensive field trips in spa environments so students have real-life exposure to their future career

*   Access to the experience of Elmcrest's management team, who play prominent roles in many spa associations in Ontario, Canada, and internationally

skills and attributes identified as being essential in a spa director/manager. Some other schools that have developed spa management curricula include:

*   Arizona State University was one of the first American universities to offer a spa management certificate program, earned through the Exercise and Wellness Department at it Polytechnic campus in Mesa, Arizona.

*   University of California, Irvine, Extension offers an instructor-led, online certificate program in spa and hospitality management, designed for those seeking management positions within the spa industry.

*   Hocking College, Nelsonville, Ohio, offers a program in International Spa Operation & Management within its hospitality department. Students can pursue one of two tracks within the discipline: spa business or spa technician.

*   University of Derby, Buxton Campus, in England, offers a diploma program in International Spa Management. Students learn and work in the full-service Devonshire Spa, which was developed by the school on the site of the former Devonshire Royal Hospital, in the spa town of Buxton.

In the United Kingdom, Habia, a government-approved standards setting body for hair, beauty, nails, and spa therapy, creates the standards that form the basis of all qualifications including National Vocational Qualifications, apprenticeships, diplomas, and foundation degrees, and industry codes of practice for

Exhibit 4   Spa Careers Licensure, Training, and Exams

Profession	License required in most U.S. states	Training Hours	Exam
Cosmetologist	Yes	1200-2100	Yes
Estheticians	Yes	250-1500	Yes
Hair stylist	Yes (Cosmetologist)	1200-2100	Yes
Makeup artist	Yes (Esthetician or Cosmetologist)	600-2100	Yes
Massage therapist	Yes	125-1000	Yes
Nail technician	Yes	300-600	Yes
Personal trainer	No	n/a	n/a

Excerpted from www.spabeautyed.com Career Center

the United Kingdom. This organization has created standards for spa education that include a mix of practical therapist training and spa management skills. The suggested course content includes modules on management topics, spa therapies, science, research, and other spa-specific topics.

Licensing and Certification

Most professional careers in the spa and beauty industry require some kind of license to practice. This may include passing an exam and completing a certain number of training hours, set by a state, provincial, or national regulatory board. **Licensure** can vary greatly depending on one's location around the world. Exhibit 4 lists some examples of the training hours necessary in the United States to obtain licensure in a particular career field.

In the United States, estheticians are required to be licensed in 49 states, plus Washington, D.C., Puerto Rico, and the U.S. Virgin Islands. (Connecticut is the only state without licensing.) Two states, Utah and Virginia, have a two-tiered system in which 600 hours of training are required for a basic license, and another 600 hours for a master esthetician license.

For massage therapists, 38 U.S. states and Washington, D.C., require licensing, and more states are moving toward passage of licensing regulations. In 2007, the Federation of State Massage Therapy Boards introduced the Massage and Bodywork Licensing Exam (MBLEx), which is recognized in several states. To earn a license, some states also accept passing scores on the examination portion of **certification** from the National Certification Board for Therapeutic Massage & Bodywork or the American Organization for Bodywork Therapies of Asia. In addition, certain massage modalities require massage therapists to have additional training and certification.

Because licensing and certification requirements can vary widely from state to state, country to country, and discipline to discipline, those pursuing licensure should research the requirements for their professional goals. The end of this chapter lists several organizations and certifying and licensing bodies.

Exhibit 5 Total Industry Employment in the United States

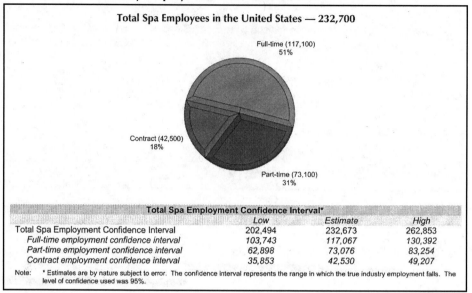

Total Spa Employees in the United States — 232,700

Full-time (117,100)
51%

Contract (42,500)
18%

Part-time (73,100)
31%

Total Spa Employment Confidence Interval*			
	Low	*Estimate*	*High*
Total Spa Employment Confidence Interval	202,494	232,673	262,853
Full-time employment confidence interval	*103,743*	*117,067*	*130,392*
Part-time employment confidence interval	*62,898*	*73,076*	*83,254*
Contract employment confidence interval	*35,853*	*42,530*	*49,207*

Note: * Estimates are by nature subject to error. The confidence interval represents the range in which the true industry employment falls. The level of confidence used was 95%.

Source: *2007 Spa Industry Study,* ISPA

Compensation and Benefits

Spa employees are commonly compensated in one of two ways: a traditional employer-employee arrangement or the less traditional, but still common, contracting spa–**independent contractor** relationship. According to the ISPA 2007 Spa Industry Study, only 18 percent of U.S.-spa employees (42,500) are **contract workers**, while the rest are traditional employees, either full-time (117,100 or 51 percent) or part-time (73,100 or 31 percent). Exhibit 5 shows this breakdown.

Compensation

In the employer-employee arrangement, the employee works for a spa full-time, part-time, or on-call. The employer provides a set **compensation**, outlines working hours and conditions, provides uniforms, provides benefits, and arranges for the payment of payroll taxes. Employees are expected to follow the spa's policies and procedures. Employees typically receive benefits in addition to regular compensation. These benefits can include medical insurance, dental insurance, 401K plan, paid time off (vacation, sick days, personal days), use of spa facilities, and discounts on services and products. Spa employees can receive all, few, or none of these depending on the structure of the spa.

Independent contractors are not employees. They are responsible for paying all applicable taxes and generally have more freedom in their working hours and schedules than employees. Independent contractors are often expected to provide their own supplies and uniforms. It is understood that independent contractors will follow spa policies and protocols and support the mission and philosophy of the spa when acting as its representative.

The decision to engage in an employer-contractor versus an employer-employee relationship is not arbitrary. The U.S. Internal Revenue Service (and the IRS equivalent in many other countries) has very strict rules about what constitutes a contractor-employer relationship that most spas would have great difficulty meeting. The consequences of working under a contractor-employer agreement when one can't meet the IRS test for an independent contractor can be literally devastating to the spa and threaten its existence.

Several possible wage structures may be used by spas to compensate employees and independent contractors. These include:

Commissions on Services. The person is paid a specific amount agreed upon at the time of hire, when a service is provided. Commission can be a percentage of the value of the service provided or a fixed dollar value commission for the service.

Hourly. An employee (not an independent contractor) is "on the clock" and paid an hourly rate whether providing a service or not. Hourly employees may be expected to perform other duties to assist with the spa's daily operations. In some cases, an employee's hourly rate may vary according to the function they perform. For example, many spas have a training rate that is lower than the employee's rate when performing his or her core function.

Hourly Plus Commission. An employee receives an hourly wage for time worked plus an additional commission when providing a service. The commission and/or hourly rate may vary with the service performed.

Contracted Wage. Cruise ships and seasonal resorts may require spa professionals to sign a contract that outlines the obligated time commitment of employment. The specified time may also include a base minimum salary.

Commission on Retail Sales. A person may earn additional income from selling products or supplies to guests. These products typically complement the service that the guest received. Commission structures vary depending on the department or the work environment. They can be set as a percentage of the item's retail price, or set on a scaled percentage based on total retail sold by the individual or a group of individuals.

Bonus. A bonus may be offered to staff, above and beyond other wages. This may be in the form of extra days off, a percentage of retail sales, or a percentage of services performed by those with excellent performance.

Tips/Gratuities/Service Charges. Most spas have tip policies to assist guests during their spa visit and provide consistency in spa practices. Tips may be included in the service, in which case a percentage of the service charge is contributed to the staff member's wage per service. Alternately, tips may be at the guest's discretion and either added to their service voucher or paid directly in cash to the staff member at the conclusion of the service.[2]

Managerial level employees of a spa are typically paid a salary, rather than an hourly wage.

Benefits

While **benefits** packages are most commonly offered to full-time employees, some spas may offer benefits to part-time and on-call employees to enhance the attractiveness of working for a particular spa.

In addition to typical benefits such as medical insurance, 401K plans, and paid vacation and sick time, spas may offer any of the following to employees:

- Payment for continuing education, either in full or through an annual dollar allowance. Continuing education may be defined by the spa and generally covers professional skill development and learning new skills or techniques.

- Use of the spa's facilities, such as trading services with other professionals, using the fitness or pool areas, or attending workshops.

- Free or discounted services, meals, products, and supplies.

- Seasonal resort or cruise ship benefits may include room and board and travel expenses to/from the resort or ship.[3]

Beginning a Spa Career

While it may seem that a technical specialty like massage therapy or esthetics would be the logical opening to a spa career, these are not always necessary to spa success. For those looking to become spa managers, it may be possible to work up to a management position by starting at a lower-level position, learning the business, and then advancing in the field. For example, working as a front desk supervisor, guest receptionist, or concierge provides an opportunity to interact with virtually every aspect of a spa, including customers, staff, treatment menus, computer systems, and retail products.

A degree in life sciences, recreation, psychology, business, hospitality, or marketing could prove useful in a spa career, as would relevant professional experience in these and other areas, such as retail sales, office administration, marketing and public relations, accounting and finance, and hospitality management. All of these areas have skills that are transferable to a spa career. Exhibit 6 offers suggestions for preparing oneself for a career in the spa industry.

Because specialized full-time spa management programs and spa management tracks within other college programs are so new, the industry may be slow to embrace and acknowledge the high-level management and financial skills of graduates from these programs. Often they also bring a wealth of valuable transportable skills and attributes they might possess from earlier careers before entering the spa industry. Yet most spas still want to hang onto the established methods of starting these highly skilled and capable graduates as hourly employees with no specific path to a management position. By being aware of this potential challenge, students can learn to set their own minimums in terms of position and remuneration. They must learn to sell themselves and their skill sets.

For students in a technical school or college-level spa management program, participating in an **internship** program or forging a mentoring relationship can be a good way to get started in a spa. When participating in an internship program and/or **mentoring** arrangement, it is important for students to ensure they

Exhibit 6   Tips and Tricks for Getting a Spa Job

These are tips and suggestions from the top recruiters in the industry, Lori Hutchinson, John Korpi, Christian Mayr, and Ron Folkman:

- Do as much research as you can. Read as many articles as you can. The greater your knowledge of the industry, the more confidence you can instill as a professional in your field.

- Know the technical parts of the job. An understanding of the job from the therapist's viewpoint gives you a wealth of knowledge which remains a mystery to most of the people who will be doing the hiring.

- Be informed of trends. What's hot, what's happening, what's in, what's out.

- Visit spas. Especially the competitors of where you wish to be hired. This gives you insight into trends and also a basis for comparison among different properties.

- Know who's who. Since the advent of the Internet, information is much more readily available. If you already know the names of the key managers, owners, and investors, you will be more comfortable in an interview and it will be much easier to come across like an insider.

- Even if you are not in the spa industry, you can develop skills and experience as a supervisor and manager of people.

- Take some courses.

- Seek out a mentor who can take you under their wing.

- Work with a consultant. You can learn vicariously by working closely with someone who is an expert in the field.

- Seek out internship programs where you can get educational credits for working in a spa environment.

- Experience is more important than education, but both are important. Take a look at what you are lacking and work on rounding out what you have to offer.

- This business is all about people. Show your passion and your personality.

- Your voice should instill a spa feeling. Keep it soothing and calming.

- Do not be afraid to talk about your feelings.

- You might not know how to give a massage yourself, but you should know how to receive a massage. What makes a good massage?

- Do not bite off more than you can chew. Take career steps that you will be successful at. Do not rush into a position that you cannot succeed at.

- Learn as much as you can about retail selling.

- A good business sense from any industry can be applied to the spa industry.

- If you need a foot in the door, start at the front desk of a spa. This is the best place from which to learn the business.

Source: *Fab Job Guide to Become a Spa Owner,* Jeremy McCarthy and Jennifer James (2006, FabJob-Guides)

Spa Snapshot: How do you use interns in your company, and where do you find qualified candidates?

"The Spa at Laguna Cliffs is located 30 minutes south of the University of California at Irvine, which now offers a spa management program. During this program, the attendees are encouraged to work within a spa so they can gain practical experience in all areas pertaining to this ever-growing industry. With all new employees and interns, we complete our basic two/three-week training where they will experience spa services, instruction, and use of our gym, working as a spa attendant and finally moving onto the spa reservations desk, at which point we then place them where they are most suited. Our goal is to try and provide as much experience and knowledge to the next spa generation, as well as gaining help from an extra pair of willing hands."

—*Jane Lohmann, Spa Operations Manager, The Spa at Laguna Cliffs, Dana Point, CA*

"The Spa at Silverado allows massage interns to do their practical hours at our spa. It allows the spa staff to get massages and take care of themselves, and it gives the intern the hands-on hours they need to graduate from school. It also works out very well if the intern is a great candidate for employment; once he or she has graduated from massage school, we then interview and hire them. We work closely with three Bay-area massage schools that have a great curriculum and produce quality therapists."

—*Yalda Teranchi, Spa Director, The Spa at Silverado, Napa, CA*

"Our local technical college has a program called Early College High School. They are high school students who actually attend college and take college-level classes as well as finish up their high school degree. They are students who would otherwise not attend a four-year school, and they are giving them this great opportunity to learn a trade and enter the work force. We had two awesome interns this summer, Katelynn and Natasha. Katelynn aspires to be a massage therapist (15 years old) and Natasha wants to be an esthetician (also 15). We assigned them a mentor here at the spa who met with them weekly. They had regular job duties like folding sheets, taking clients back, helping therapists and front desk staff during busy times. They acted like a spa attendant basically. Each week we set up a time for them to spend with our nail technicians, in the Vichy shower, or with an esthetician so they got a well-rounded view of a spa career."

—*Jessica Durivage, Regional Spa Director, Hibiscus Spa at Myrtle Beach Marriott, Myrtle Beach, S.C.*

Source: *Pulse,* January/February 2008

are working in a supportive environment with someone they quickly respect and whose skills and attributes they would like to emulate. Interns should take the opportunity to talk with their coworkers to see if they are happy and enjoy working there. In the wrong environment or in the hands of a poor mentor, students run the risk of picking up bad or ineffective habits, but in the right environment, an internship can be a positive growth experience.

Aspiring spa professionals should not overlook opportunities as **expatriates**. Spas are expanding all over the world and jobs are offered in many exotic locations. While this may not be a lifetime career option, international jobs offer an opportunity to explore other parts of the world, learn about indigenous treatments, and get acquainted with other cultures. Most countries require some sort of certification for spa professionals. Although U.S., Canadian, and European certifications may be accepted in most countries, organizations such as SIBTEC offer international certifications. Salaries in international destinations may not be comparable to what a spa professional might get paid in North America, but often include lower taxes, free housing, and insurance benefits that compensate for lower wages.

There's a Spa Career for You

The spa industry is waiting for soulful, caring individuals who love people and who want to make a difference in the world, one life at a time. Technical skills, business savvy, and an ability to read people are traits that will take people far in the world of spa.

Education and training are keys to advancing in the spa industry, but there are still areas of spa education that need to catch up with the demand for spa professionals and managers. New college and university programs will help to fill gaps in the shortage of spa managers and directors, but spas must be willing to accept the graduates of these programs and give them the opportunity to succeed.

Learning about the spa industry, meeting and networking with spa professionals, being willing to work hard, and exploring the myriad opportunities available in day, resort, destination, medical, fitness, club, and cruise spas will guide the career seeker on an exciting journey to spa success.

Endnotes

1. Elizabeth Ulrich, "Face to Face," *Skin Inc.*, March 2007, p. 160.

2. Spa Professional Career Guide (ISPA), pp. 25–26.

3. Spa Professional Career Guide, p. 27.

Key Terms

benefits—Non-wage compensation provided to employees to increase their economic security.

certification—Formal recognition by an independent body of professional peers of an individual's qualifications in a profession or a professional organization, often by having the individual meet qualifications such as passing an examination.

compensation—Payment made to an employee in return for the work they perform for the employer.

contract worker—A person who provides goods or services to another entity under terms specified in a contract. Contract workers retain control over their schedules, the jobs they accept, and the performance of their job. Also called an independent contractor.

cross training—Learning job skills in an area outside one's current position in order to broaden one's marketability and usefulness to an employer.

expatriate—A person temporarily or permanently residing in a location other than the country of which they are a citizen.

independent contractor—A person who provides goods or services to another entity under terms specified in a contract. Contract workers retain control over their schedules, the jobs they accept, and the performance of their job. Also called a contract worker.

internship—An unpaid job performed in order to get career experience in a given field.

licensure—The process whereby a governmental authority, in accordance with state statute, determines the competency of individuals seeking to perform certain services. Licensure grants individuals the authority to engage in an area of practice, based on demonstrated education, experience, and examination.

mentoring—Career guidance and development of a younger professional by an established, more experienced professional in that career field.

service professions—Careers that are based on the concept of serving or helping people.

 # Review Questions

1. What are some of the advantages and disadvantages of a career in the spa industry?

2. What skills and personality traits are important for success in a spa career?

3. What spa jobs are available at the entry level, technical/professional level, and managerial level?

4. What training and educational opportunities exist for those interested in a spa career?

5. What role do licensing and certification play in spa careers?

6. What are the various ways in which spa employees and managers may be compensated?

7. How does someone begin searching for a career in the spa industry?

Internet Sites

For more information, visit the following Internet sites. Remember that Internet addresses can change without notice. If the site is no longer there, you can use a search engine to look for additional sites.

American College of Sports Medicine
www.acsm.org

American Council on Exercise
www.acefitness.org

American Dietetic Association
www.eatright.org

American Massage Therapy
Association
www.amtamassage.org

American Spa Therapy Education &
Certification Council
www.astecc.com

Arizona State University
www.poly.asu.edu/saas/wellness/spa

Associated Bodywork & Massage
Professionals
www.massagetherapy.com/careers/
index.php

Associated Skin Care Professionals
www.ascpskincare.com

Australasian College of Natural
Therapies
www.acnt.edu.au

Comité International D'Esthétique Et
De Cosmétologie
www.cidesco.com

The Commission on Dietetic
Registration
www.cdrnet.org

Commission on Massage Therapy
Accreditation
www.comta.org

Day Spa Association
www.dayspaassociation.com

Elmcrest College
www.elmcrestcollege.com

Federation of State Massage Therapy
Boards
www.fsmtb.org

HABIA
www.habia.org.uk

Hocking College
www.hocking.cc.oh.us/academics/
schools/hospitality/international_spa/
index.htm

Hospitality Careers.com
www.hcareers.com

International Coach Federation
www.coachfederation.org

International SPA Association Job Bank
www.experienceispa.com

National Accrediting Commission of
Cosmetology Arts and Sciences
www.naccas.org

National Certification Board for
Therapeutic Massage and Bodywork
www.ncbtmb.com

National Cosmetology Association
www.ncacares.org

National Strength and Conditioning
Association
www.nsca-lift.org

NSCA Certification Commission
www.nsca-cc.org

Pilates Method Alliance
www.pilatesmethodalliance.org

ResortJobs.com
www.resortjobs.com

Spa Jobs (International spa
  recruitment)
www.spa-jobs.com

Spa Jobs (a division of the Health Care
  Jobs Store)
www.spajobs.com

Spa Salon Staffing
www.spasalonstaffing.com

University of California, Irvine
http://unex.uci.edu/certificates/
business_mgmt/mgmt_supervisory_
skills/spa

Yoga Alliance
www.yogalliance.org

Chapter Appendix
Sample Job Descriptions

FRONT DESK RECEPTIONIST JOB DESCRIPTION

Reports to:

Department:

Job Summary:

The Spa Front Desk Receptionist is responsible for the reception area at the spa. Includes the greeting of all guests, answering phone calls, assisting guests with questions regarding spa services and products, booking all appointments, checking the guest into the computer system and charging for services performed.

Duties and Responsibilities:

- Be on time for your shift.
- Properly open and close spa each day according to Standard Operating Procedures.
- Accurately book, change and cancel spa appointments.
- Acknowledge and greet everyone who enters and leaves spa facilities.
- Provide detailed descriptions of spa treatments, packages, services, facility features and hours of operation.
- Utilize spa computers with skill and proficiency.
- Maintain a Spa Desk Bank.
- Answer the phone promptly and use the guest's name throughout the phone conversation.
- Actively promote the spa, treatments, services, sessions and retail, as well as programs, promotions and/or discounts available.
- Maintain eye contact when addressing external and internal guests.
- Handle guests' questions and concerns professionally and courteously.
- Provide accurate, appropriate and immediate responses to all requests by guests, ensuring complete guest satisfaction.
- Maintain a clean; safe, fully stocked and well organized work area.
- Develop ability to work without constant direct supervision and remain at assigned post for extended periods of time.
- Maintain a positive attitude and contribute toward a quality work environment.

- Regularly attend, participate in and support training/staff meetings for the spa.
- Assist in all areas of spa operation as requested by management.
- Communicate to management any and all occurrences involving staff or guests in the spa that require attention.

Position Requirements:
- Must be detail-oriented and have ability to multi-task.
- Ability to be efficient and productive in a fast-paced environment.
- Must have enthusiasm and possess excellent customer service skills.
- Must possess basic math and money handling skills.
- Enjoy working with people and possess a friendly and outgoing personality.
- Excellent communication, listening and computer skills.
- Must be a team player.

Education and Experience Requirements:
- Will vary by employer

SPA ATTENDANT JOB DESCRIPTION

Reports to:

Department:

Job Summary:

The Spa Attendant is responsible for orientating guests to the spa facilities, greeting guests as they enter the facilities, and providing personal guest service. They are responsible for keeping the lounge areas neat, clean and stocked with all amenities.

Duties and Responsibilities:

- Be on time for your shift.
- Issue spa lockers, robes and slippers to guests and then escort guests to their lockers.
- Provide orientation tour, explaining spa amenities offered and answering guests' questions.
- Maintain a safe, clean and well-organized spa environment through consistent monitoring of the locker/facility area.
- Stock locker room supplies and amenities and maintain accurate supply lists and inventory sheets.
- Review guest appointment/schedules as needed.
- Actively promote the spa, treatments, services, sessions and retail, as well as programs, promotions and/or discounts available.
- Maintain eye contact when addressing external and internal guests.
- Handle guests' questions and concerns professionally and courteously.
- Provide accurate, appropriate and immediate responses to all requests by guests, ensuring complete guest satisfaction.
- Develop ability to work without constant direct supervision and remain at assigned post for extended periods of time.
- Maintain a positive attitude and contribute toward a quality work environment.
- Regularly attend, participate in and support training and staff meetings for the spa.
- Assist in all areas of spa operation as requested by management.
- Communicate to management any and all occurrences involving staff or guests in the spa that require attention.

Position Requirements:

- Ability to be efficient and productive in a fast-paced environment.

- Must have enthusiasm and possess excellent customer service skills.

- Enjoy working with people and possess a friendly and outgoing personality.

- Excellent communication and listening skills.

- Must be a team player.

Education and Experience Requirements:

- Will vary by employer

MASSAGE THERAPIST JOB DESCRIPTION

Reports to:

Department:

Job Summary:

The Massage Therapist administers professional massage and body treatments to our guests. They must have a thorough knowledge of numerous massage modalities, possess a general understanding of body treatments and be willing to train in our spa's specific massage and body treatment offerings. They must possess excellent communication skills and be able to learn the product and service knowledge necessary to effectively provide wellness solutions to meet the needs of our guests. They must hold and maintain a current state license.

Duties and Responsibilities:

- Be on time for your shift, prompt with each appointment and perform services within the appropriate time allotted for the service.
- Provide consistent professional massage and body treatments in accordance with spa protocols and accepted certification practices.
- Effectively inform and educate our guests about specific wellness concerns.
- Be flexible with your schedule, supporting the needs of the spa.
- Properly care for equipment and use proper amounts of product to assist with cost controls.
- Have complete knowledge and understanding of all services and products offered.
- Uphold the standards of sanitation and sterilization as directed by law and the spa's policies and procedures.
- Perform prep work, properly clean and restock room as required.
- Communicate to management any and all occurrences involving staff or guests in the spa that require attention.
- Actively promote the spa, treatments, services and retail, as well as programs, promotions and/or discounts available.
- Handle guests' questions and concerns professionally and courteously.
- Provide accurate, appropriate and immediate responses to all requests by guests.
- Possess the ability to work without direct supervision.
- Maintain a positive attitude and contribute toward a quality work environment.

- Regularly attend, participate in and support training and staff meetings for the spa.

- Assist in all areas of spa operation as requested by management.

- Communicate to management any and all occurrences involving staff or guests in the spa that require attention.

Position requirements:

- Must have enthusiasm and possess excellent customer service skills.

- Enjoy working with people and possess a friendly and outgoing personality.

- Excellent communication and listening skills, as well as basic computer knowledge.

- Must be a team player.

Education and Experience Requirements:

- Must hold and maintain a current state license

ESTHETICIAN JOB DESCRIPTION

Reports to:

Department:

Job Summary:

The Esthetician administers professional facials and waxing services to our guests. They must possess a thorough knowledge of the skin, have excellent facial massage and skin extraction techniques, possess excellent cleanliness and sanitation skills and be willing to train in our spa's specific facial treatment offerings. They must possess excellent communication skills and be able to learn the product and service knowledge necessary to effectively provide wellness and beauty solutions to meet the needs of our guests. They must hold and maintain a current state license.

Duties and Responsibilities:

- Be on time for your shift, prompt with each appointment and perform services within the appropriate time allotted for the service.
- Provide consistent professional facial and body treatments in accordance with spa protocols and accepted certification practices.
- Be flexible with your schedule, supporting the needs of the spa.
- Properly care for equipment and use proper amounts of product to assist with cost controls.
- Have complete knowledge and understanding of all services and products while educating and training guests in these areas.
- Actively promote home care programs, meeting minimum retail sales goals.
- Uphold the standards of sanitation and sterilization as directed by law and the spa's policies and procedures.
- Perform prep work and properly clean and restock room as required.
- Communicate to management any and all occurrences involving staff or guests in the spa that require attention.
- Actively promote the spa, treatments, services, sessions and retail, as well as programs, promotions and/or discounts available.
- Handle guests' questions and concerns professionally and courteously.
- Provide accurate, appropriate and immediate responses to all requests by guests, ensuring complete guest satisfaction.
- Communicate to management any and all occurrences involving staff or guests in the spa that require attention.
- Possess ability to work without direct supervision.

- Maintain a positive attitude and contribute toward a quality work environment.
- Regularly attend, participate in and support training and staff meetings for the spa.
- Assist in all areas of spa operation as requested by management.

Position requirements:

- Must have enthusiasm and possess excellent customer service skills.
- Enjoy working with people and possess a friendly and outgoing personality.
- Excellent communication and listening skills, as well as basic computer knowledge.
- Must be a team player.

Education and Experience Requirements:

- Must hold and maintain a current state license

NAIL TECHNICIAN JOB DESCRIPTION

Reports to:

Department:

Job Summary:

The Nail Technician performs professional nail, hand and foot treatments. They must possess a thorough knowledge of the nails, including a basic knowledge of hand and foot massage techniques and a neat application of polish. They must possess excellent cleanliness and sanitation skills and be willing to train in our spa's specific nail service offerings. They must possess excellent communication skills and be able to learn the product and service knowledge necessary to effectively provide beauty solutions to meet the needs of our guests. They must hold and maintain a current state license.

Duties and Responsibilities:

- Be on time for your shift, prompt with each appointment and perform services within the appropriate time allotted for the service.
- Provide consistent professional nail, hand and foot treatments in accordance with spa protocols and accepted certification practices.
- Be flexible with your schedule, supporting the needs of the spa.
- Properly care for equipment and use proper amounts of product to assist with cost controls.
- Have complete knowledge and understanding of all services and products while educating and training guests in these areas.
- Actively promote home care programs, meeting minimum retail sales goals.
- Uphold the standards of sanitation and sterilization as directed by law and the spa's policies and procedures.
- Perform prep work and properly clean and restock work area as required.
- Communicate to management any and all occurrences involving staff or guests in the spa that require attention.
- Actively promote the spa, treatments, services, sessions and retail, as well as programs, promotions and/or discounts available.
- Handle guests' questions and concerns professionally and courteously.
- Provide accurate, appropriate and immediate responses to all requests by guests ensuring complete guest satisfaction.
- Possess ability to work without direct supervision.
- Maintain a positive attitude and contribute toward a quality work environment.

- Regularly attend, participate in and support training and staff meetings for the spa.
- Assist in all areas of spa operation as requested by management.

Position requirements:
- Must have enthusiasm and possess excellent customer service skills.
- Enjoy working with people and possess a friendly and outgoing personality.
- Excellent communication and listening skills, as well as basic computer knowledge.
- Must be a team player.

Education and Experience Requirements:
- Must hold and maintain a current State license

HAIR STYLIST JOB DESCRIPTION

Reports to:

Department:

Job Summary:

The Hair Stylist performs professional cuts, styles, chemical services and therapeutic hair and scalp treatments. They must possess and maintain knowledge of current hairstyles and trends. They must possess excellent cleanliness and sanitation skills and be willing to train in our spa's specific hair and scalp service offerings **(IF APPLI-CABLE)**. They must possess excellent communication skills and be able to learn the product and service knowledge necessary to effectively provide beauty solutions to meet the needs of our guests. They must hold and maintain a current state license.

Duties and Responsibilities:

- Be on time for your shift, prompt with each appointment and perform services within the appropriate time allotted for the service.
- Provide consistent professional hair treatments in accordance with spa protocols and accepted certification practices.
- Be flexible with your schedule, supporting the needs of the spa.
- Properly care for equipment and use proper amounts of product to assist with cost controls.
- Have complete knowledge and understanding of all services and products while educating and training guests in these areas.
- Actively promote home care programs, meeting minimum retail sales goals.
- Uphold the standards of sanitation and sterilization as directed by law and the spa's policies and procedures.
- Perform prep work and properly clean and restock work area as required.
- Communicate to management any and all occurrences involving staff or guests in the spa or salon that require attention.
- Actively promote the spa, treatments, services, sessions and retail, as well as programs, promotions and/or discounts available.
- Handle guest's questions and concerns professionally and courteously.
- Provide accurate, appropriate and immediate responses to all requests by guests ensuring complete guest satisfaction.
- Possess ability to work without direct supervision.
- Maintain a positive attitude and contribute toward a quality work environment.

- Regularly attend, participate in and support training and staff meetings for the spa.
- Assist in all areas of spa operation as requested by management.

Position requirements:

- Must have enthusiasm and possess excellent customer service skills.
- Enjoy working with people and possess a friendly and outgoing personality.
- Excellent communication and listening skills, as well as basic computer knowledge.
- Must be a team player.

Education and Experience Requirements:

- Must hold and maintain a current state cosmetology license

FITNESS INSTRUCTOR/PERSONAL TRAINER JOB DESCRIPTION

Reports To:

Department:

Job Summary:

The Fitness Instructor is certified to lead classes and perform Personal Training sessions and private classes for the guest. They are fitness professionals with extensive experience in the fitness field. The Fitness Instructor must be knowledgeable of all fitness offerings at the spa, hold current certifications and have previous experience. They must possess excellent customer services skills in order to provide the highest quality environment and instruction that will meet the needs of our guests in the area of health and exercise.

Duties and Responsibilities:

- Be on time for your shift, prompt with each appointment and perform sessions with total focus on safety, attention and timeliness.
- Provide consistent professional fitness class and personal training sessions in accordance with spa protocols and accepted certification practices.
- Be flexible with your schedule, supporting the needs of the spa.
- Properly care for equipment and maintain fitness equipment.
- Maintain a clean, well-organized and stocked fitness area.
- Have complete knowledge and understanding of all fitness offerings while educating and training guests in these areas.
- Perform administrative duties in a complete, organized and accurate manner.
- Communicate to management any and all occurrences involving staff or guests in the spa or fitness area that require attention.
- Actively promote the spa, treatments, services, sessions and retail, as well as programs, promotions and/or discounts available.
- Handle guests' questions and concerns professionally and courteously.
- Provide accurate, appropriate and immediate responses to all requests by guests ensuring complete guest satisfaction.
- Possess ability to work without direct supervision.
- Maintain a positive attitude and contribute toward a quality work environment.
- Regularly attend, participate in and support training and staff meetings for the spa.
- Assist in all areas of spa operation as requested by management.

Position requirements:

- Must have enthusiasm and possess excellent customer service skills.

- Enjoy working with people and possess a friendly and outgoing personality.

- Excellent communication and listening skills, as well as basic computer knowledge.

- Must be a team player.

Education and Experience Requirements:

- Must have National Certification

RETAIL CONSULTANT JOB DESCRIPTION

Reports to:

Department:

Job Summary:

The Spa Retail Consultant is responsible for the sale and service of all retail products to guests. They are responsible for maintaining the retail area of the spa in a clean and orderly manner. The Retail Consultant should be knowledgeable of the features and benefits of all retail offerings, product sales and promotions. They must understand how to effectively recommend products to meet the needs of our guests.

Duties and Responsibilities:

- Be on time for shift.
- Properly open and close retail area each day according to Standard Operating Procedures.
- Acknowledge and greet everyone who enters and leaves the retail area.
- Actively promote and provide detailed descriptions of retail products, sales and special promotions.
- Assist guests with appropriate retail selections.
- Handle product inquiries and returns professionally and courteously, ensuring complete guest satisfaction.
- Utilize spa retail sales system with skill and proficiency.
- Maintain Retail Bank.
- Regularly crosscheck physical inventory with computer inventory to manage/avoid shrinkage and to ensure appropriate inventories are available.
- Regularly create and change product displays to promote various products, seasons and holidays.
- Meet monthly/quarterly sales goals as outlined by management.
- Actively promote the spa, treatments, services, sessions and retail, as well as programs, promotions and/or discounts available.
- Maintain eye contact when addressing external and internal guests.
- Handle guests' questions and concerns professionally and courteously.
- Provide appropriate and immediate responses to all requests by guests.
- Maintain a clean; safe, fully stocked and well organized work area.
- Ability to work without direct supervision and remain at assigned post for extended periods of time.

- Maintain a positive attitude and contribute toward a quality work environment.
- Regularly attend, participate in and support training/staff meetings for the spa.
- Assist in all areas of spa operation as requested by management.

Position Requirements:

- Ability to be efficient and productive in a fast paced environment.
- Must be detail and multi-task oriented.
- Must have enthusiasm and possess excellent customer service skills.
- Must possess basic math and money handling skills.
- Enjoy working with people and possess a friendly and outgoing personality.
- Excellent communication, listening and computer skills.
- Must be a team player

Education and Experience Requirements:

- Will vary by employer

SPA SALES MANAGER JOB DESCRIPTION

Reports to:

Department:

Job Summary:

The Spa Sales Manager is responsible to manage and oversee the day-to-day operations of the Sales department; maximizing services and retail revenue by promoting the spa to predetermined target markets in order to achieve overall sales objectives. The Spa Sales Manager should be knowledgeable of the features and benefits of all Spa services and retail offerings, product sales and promotions. They must understand how to effectively recommend services and packages to meet the needs of our guests. Utilize strong communication, sales and presentation skills to effectively promote service and sales efforts. Comply with all corporate reporting requirements, conference calls, and procedures established for the Spa Sales department.

Primary Duties and Responsibilities:

- Be on time for shift.
- Assist in the preparation and updating of the marketing plan.
- Implement strategies and tactics according to the marketing plan.
- Plan public relations activities and events.
- Plan sales campaigns.
- Manage the spa's loyalty program.
- Prepare sales reports.
- Assist in the development and updating of the spa menu.
- Manage all resources in spa to maximize profits and long term growth.
- Meet monthly/quarterly sales goals as outlined by management.
- Actively promote the spa, treatments, services, sessions and retail, as well as programs, promotions and/or discounts available.
- Maintain eye contact when addressing external and internal guests.
- Handle guests' questions and concerns professionally and courteously.
- Provide accurate, appropriate and immediate responses to all requests by guests.
- Ability to work without direct supervision.
- Maintain a positive attitude and contribute toward a quality work environment.
- Regularly attend, participate in and support training and staff meetings for the spa.
- Assist in all areas of spa operation as requested by management.

Position Requirements:

- Ability to be efficient and productive in a fast paced environment.
- Must be detail and multi-task oriented with the ability to handle constant deadlines.
- Must have enthusiasm and possess excellent customer service and selling skills.
- Must possess basic math and money handling skills.
- Enjoy working with people and possess a friendly, positive and outgoing personality.
- Excellent communication, listening and computer skills.
- Self motivated with a strong sense of ownership.
- Must be a team player.

Education and Experience Requirements:

- Minimum of 5 years spa sales experience in an international standard spa.
- Degree: Business Degree in Sales and Marketing.
- Recognized sales courses an advantage.
- Business writing including press releases and marketing content.

SPA MANAGER JOB DESCRIPTION

Reports to:

Department:

Job Summary:

To oversee all aspects of the spa operations and implement strategies to achieve performance targets. The Spa Manager should be knowledgeable of the features and benefits of all Spa services and retail offerings, product sales and promotions. They must understand how to effectively recommend services and packages to meet the needs of our guests. Utilize strong communication, sales and presentation skills to effectively promote service and sales efforts.

Primary Duties and Responsibilities:

- Prepare, implement and update business and marketing plans.
- Manage the financial budget, control costs and prepare revenue and expense reports for owners/board of directors.
- Ensure the spa's operating procedures and policies manuals are implemented and updated as required.
- Supervise daily spa operations and liaise with department heads to ensure cleanliness, maintenance and service standards are upheld.
- Assist in the development and updating of the spa menu.
- Manage client feedback.
- Reference and abide by the Spa's Standard Operating Procedures, Policies & Forms Manuals.
- Actively promote the spa, treatments, services, sessions and retail, as well as programs, promotions and/or discounts available.
- Handle escalated guests' concerns professionally and courteously.
- Ability to work without direct supervision.
- Maintain a positive attitude and contribute toward a quality work environment.
- Regularly attend, participate in and support training/staff meetings for the spa.
- Assist in all areas of spa operation as requested by management.

Position Requirements:

- Ability to be efficient and productive in a fast paced environment.
- Must be detail and multi-task oriented with the ability to handle constant deadlines.

- Must have enthusiasm and possess excellent customer service and sales skills.

- Must possess basic math and money handling skills.

- Enjoy working with people and possess a friendly, positive and outgoing personality.

- Excellent English communication, listening and computer skills (mid-advanced level).

- Self motivated with a strong sense of ownership.

- Must be a team player.

- Willing to work varied shift hours including nights, weekends and holidays.

Education and Experience Requirements:

- Minimum of three (3) years spa management experience in an international standard spa.

- Proven skills in operations management, financial reporting, human resource management, public relations & marketing, retail management, customer service and industry analysis.

- Beauty/spa therapist qualification an advantage.

- Business administration qualification an advantage.

Chapter 9 Outline

A Spa Director's Roles and Relationships
    Relationships with Staff
    Relationships with Guests
    Relationships with Owners and
        Upper-Level Management
Similarities and Differences Among Spa
    Types
    Resort Spas
    Destination Spas
    Day Spas
A Day in the Life of Three Spa Directors
    Day in the Life of a Resort Spa Director
    Day in the Life of a Destination Spa
        Director
    Day in the Life of a Day Spa Director
A Career That Makes a Difference

Competencies

1. Identify a spa director's relationships
    with employees, guests, and owners/
    managers. (pp. 349–353)

2. Contrast management and operations
    at destination, resort, and day spas.
    (pp. 353–355)

3. Describe typical points of interaction
    that occur during a spa director's day.
    (pp. 355–379)

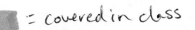 = covered in class

9

A Day in the Life of a Spa Director

SPA DIRECTOR CAREERS are more rewarding and more challenging than many people realize. Spa directors—whether of day spas, resort spas, or destination spas—must master many diverse skill sets to be successful. Their areas of responsibility encompass financial management, human resources, training, retail management, safety and security, information technology, guest relations, sales and marketing, and operations. While working to achieve a profitable operation, they must also meet the sometimes competing needs of employees, guests, and owners. On the same day, a spa director may have to deliver a presentation at a Chamber of Commerce meeting, counsel a therapist who is distraught, evaluate a new product line, tactfully resolve a guest complaint, and run a load of towels to the local laundromat when the spa's laundry breaks down.

Spa consultant Sylvia Sepielli has likened a spa director to a swan. This lovely and majestic bird is the picture of serenity, calmly and gracefully gliding across the water. What people don't see, however, are the swan's feet, frantically paddling with all their might to keep the swan on course. Spa directors "paddle with all their might" so that guests experience a calm and serene spa visit.

Another spa consultant calls the career of spa director "one of the most demanding positions out there," but also "one of the most rewarding, exciting, mind-expanding, life-enhancing journeys possible. Where else do you have the chance to explore every corner of your creative, leadership, and business talents … to make such a difference in the lives of the people you touch, while at the same time living the good life inside the thriving health and beauty phenomenon?"[1] Another comparison identifies a spa director as a symphony conductor directing all of the moving parts within the spa. A spa director is "host, cop, mom, confidante, punching bag, referee, and superstar. The spa director is also subject to the praise, indifference, or wrath of everyone they supervise or to whom they answer."[2]

The important qualities that spa directors need include the following:

- Personal and professional fortitude
- Recruiting and hiring skills
- Organization
- Crisis management
- Sales and marketing

Spa directors' work must appear effortless, like a graceful swan, even though both the swan and the spa director are "paddling with all their might" beneath the surface.

- Financial management
- Leadership
- Passion and vision
- Realism
- Commitment to long hours and hard work
- Ability to lead and motivate people

A Spa Director's Roles and Relationships

Key elements of spa directors' jobs can be broken down by the various groups with whom they interact.

Relationships with Staff

Many of the duties of spa directors involve the employees of the spa, from hiring and disciplining them to scheduling and training them. Spas are labor-intensive businesses—the employees are an integral part of the service being delivered to guests. Guests visit spas to experience the touch of the massage therapist's or estheticians' hands, the skill of the nail technician's file, and the advice of the nutritionist or fitness trainer. Even the cheerful greeting of the receptionist can affect guests' perceptions of their spa visit.

The director's tasks of recruiting and hiring the right employees, motivating them, counseling and training them, and scheduling them effectively help to ensure that guests are satisfied, employees are happy, and the spa is profitable. It is one of the spa director's missions to guide staff to become caring members of the spa team and to be creative problem solvers. The director implements ongoing skills training to maintain service standards and to provide staff with the confidence they need to deliver a memorable spa experience. He or she evaluates employee performance and develops plans to help employees achieve their professional goals. The director ensures that the staff is informed about all aspects of the spa's operations through regular meetings and open communication. His or her attention to the details of risk management ensures that the spa is a safe place for all employees. In addition, the spa director's efforts toward bringing new clients to the spa and existing clients back benefits employees by providing them with meaningful and rewarding work. Above all, the spa director is a role model for the staff.

Relationships with Guests

Spa directors are the public faces of their spas. They hear guests' praise when things go well and handle their complaints when things do not meet the guest's expectations. The director's job includes identifying guest needs and then coaching the staff to meet those needs in ways that keep guests coming back and recommending the spa to their friends. They also monitor guest satisfaction and take action when clients are dissatisfied. A spa director must be a diplomat, realizing that while the customer may not always be right, the customer is always the customer. Spa directors keep abreast of the latest spa trends and refine their menu offerings to attract new business and keep existing guests returning. Additionally, the spa director makes decisions about the spa's retail offerings, which are designed to provide guests with a continuation of their spa experience at home.

The spa director is responsible for making sure that the spa lives up to its customer promises. In its marketing efforts and messages to guests, each spa presents its vision. The spa director needs to ensure that vision is a reality when the guest arrives. For example, if the spa touts itself as featuring therapies that stem from Native American culture and traditions, but then offers a menu with a mix of Japanese, Thai, and Native American therapies and sells products that do not pertain to that Native American theme, it does not fulfill a focused mission and will disappoint the guest. Word-of-mouth marketing is a powerful tool. When the spa meets and exceeds guest expectations, the guest will talk about his or her experience and encourage other guest visits. Likewise, if the guest has a negative experience, he or she will also spread the word and hurt the spa's business. The spa director must manage the guest experience in order to create an effective advertising vehicle through word-of-mouth marketing.

Relationships with Owners and Upper-Level Management

While spas perform services that enhance the health and well-being of guests, they are also businesses with the expectation of making a profit. The spa director's responsibilities to the spa owner are focused on overseeing activities that control expenses and increase revenue. In some cases, the spa director acts in place of the

reflections

Karen Korpi: A Spa Director's Personality

Karen Korpi was the first corporate spa leader for a resort hotel company. The vice president of Ritz-Carlton's spa division, she has grown the brand from one spa to 45 in less than ten years.

Before that she owned her own consulting company and worked for numerous spas in all segments of the industry.

It takes quite the personality to be a spa director. It's a complex business. You have nine different businesses that you're running under that little three-letter word "spa." You have to be an expert or make sure that you hire properly to manage the whole salon piece—the whole licensing and certification and the different personalities there. It's the same thing with the massage business, skin care, fitness, retail, recreation. You also run housekeeping, front desk, and reservations. It's like a mini-hotel. Instead of the rooms turning every night, it's the rooms turning every hour, so it is volume, volume, volume.

The spa professional's personality: If you drew a circle and cut it in half, on the one side you'd have a dollar sign and on the other side you'd have a heart. This person has to have strong business acumen in order to drive the public relations and sales and marketing and manage the financials to achieve. On the other side, this person has to have the heart and soul to be able to be in this business. The spa director almost becomes a psychologist or caregiver to the service providers.

I always say there is a definite need. It is a paternal kind of need, whether you are a parent or not, in how you manage the staff because the only way the spa makes money is having the right service providers. You have to nurture and care for them. It's a balance. Then you have to be able to manage up with your general manager, with ownership, or corporate or that type of thing. It's quite a profession.

---

owner who wants to own a spa but doesn't want to deal with the details of daily operations. The owners may be counting on the spa director to have the inside knowledge and experience to make their business generate a reasonable profit and remain successful and competitive.

It is the spa director's job to carry out the owner's overall mission for the spa. The director must maintain standards of operation and service set by owners. Spa owners may not always come from within the spa industry, so the director must stay abreast of advances in the spa industry and keep the spa owners up-to-date on trends, opportunities, and advances in product lines and equipment, as well as the spa's needs for any capital improvements. The director must also educate owners unfamiliar with the spa industry about the nuances, unique aspects, and reasonable benchmark expectations within the spa industry.

With an eye on profitability, the director must maintain an efficient operation and establish a realistic return on investments made in the business while still meeting the owner's expectations of quality. The director must also be able to interpret profit and loss statements and understand all areas of accounting. Within

---

Spa Directors' Most and Least Favorite Aspects of Their Jobs

A survey of 45 spa directors asked them to identify what they liked most—and least—about their job. Here are some of their answers:

What do you like most about your job?

- Constant variety and diversity, never having a normal day.
- Creativity, growth, and new concepts.
- Customer relations and dealing with people.
- Seeing the staff grow and develop.
- The diversity of doing a lot of things and no routine.
- The opportunity to create an environment where guests and staff are happy.

What do you like least about your job?

- Constant staff "counseling."
- Doing the budget and working within the budget.
- Guest complaints and dealing with difficult guests.
- Having no back-up for myself.
- I find that service providers are more emotionally high maintenance than employees in other industries.
- Paperwork, paperwork, paperwork.
- Too many priorities.
- Strong weekend business and the conflict with family time.
- Trying to hire qualified staff.

Source: Spa Director and Spa Technician Profile Survey, October 2001: ISPA Conference, Palm Springs, California. A Project of the ISPA Research and Development Education Committee.

---

a resort setting, spa directors may report to the resort hotel's upper-level managers, who may know much about the hotel business, but little about the spa business. In addition to meeting the goals of the spa, the director must also meet the goals of the resort and work to mesh the two entities into a cohesive partnership.

Similarities and Differences Among Spa Types

Different types of spas present their directors with unique challenges and opportunities. These range from attracting guests to developing programs to meeting revenue goals. Knowing how resort spas, destination spas, and day spas differ may help a spa professional choose which spa segment is right for them.

Resort Spas

Resort spas are part of a larger resort hotel experience, as an **amenity** to be combined with the guest's use of the property's other amenities such as golf, tennis, or gaming. Resort spa guests are usually casual spa-goers, seeking spa treatments to complement their overall vacation experience. Resort spas typically attract a mix of male and female guests, as well as families. Because the spa is one of several resort amenities, spa services are priced à la carte.

Most resorts also attract many meetings and conferences that contribute from 40 to 60 percent of total hotel occupancy, which can positively or negatively influence a spa's business. The typical program for a resort meeting is a two-and-half day meeting with either a full day or an afternoon available for recreational activities. Therefore, the spa will have the benefit of one busy day or afternoon during a meeting, but must find ways to attract business when conference attendees are tied up in meetings. For this reason, most resort spas also serve as a day spa facility that welcomes local residents for treatments.

Many of the resort spa's expenses are handled as a cost of the overall resort property as an undistributed overhead expense, such as energy costs, marketing, and credit card commissions. Resort spas can also tap into the hotel's resources, such as the hotel's human resources department, which has already established policies and procedures, and its marketing department. The property's housekeeping, laundry, and maintenance departments are there to assist the spa operation, eliminating the need to include those departments under the umbrella of the spa.

However, an additional challenge that resort spa directors face is that they often report to senior hotel managers who know how to run a hotel but don't understand spa operations. The expectations of resort spa owners and operators can range widely, from being seen strictly as a necessary amenity or guest service that helps put "heads in beds" with little expectation of stand-alone profitability, to being seen as a stand-alone profit center that is not only expected to carry all of its own direct costs, but also to be responsible for the costs incurred when using the services of other departments, such as housekeeping.

Destination Spas

Destination spas typically attract guests for a specific time period, ranging from two or three days to a full week or two, for an all-inclusive, totally spa-focused retreat. Guests visit a destination spa for a specific program that focuses on health and wellness, whether that means working on a fitness and nutrition program, reducing stress, or testing oneself physically at an adventure spa. In addition to spa treatments, a destination spa offers a complete program of activities, such as wellness classes, hiking, yoga, fitness classes, and lectures. The destination spa in the United States is typically an adult environment that attracts more women than men, although many destination spas in Europe are family getaways. Healthy spa cuisine is on the menu; some don't serve caffeine or alcohol.

Destination spas usually charge guests based on a program rate that includes all-inclusive accommodations, all meals, fitness programs, educational programs, and lectures, as well as a set number of treatments as part of a guest's stay. In destination spas, the director's scope of operation is that of running a hotel as well as a spa. Areas of responsibility are broader in scope than those of a resort/hotel spa director, and include sleeping rooms and associated departments (such as housekeeping and maintenance) along with food service, retail, fitness, and activities.

Day Spas

Day spas offer people a spa experience in their own community, without having to travel and make overnight accommodations. A day spa may start as a salon that rents additional space and adds treatment rooms to provide customers with massage, body work, and skin care as an opportunity to enhance the salon's positioning and to increase revenues. Most day spas have a strong hair business that pollinates the growth of the spa side of the business. Relying on hair guests to experience the spa services strengthens the overall growth volume of the day spa. It is easier to convert a hair guest to become a spa guest than the other way around.

A day spa operates as an independent business where everything from rent to property taxes are recorded as an expense of the business. This places a much higher demand on payroll and expense control to generate even a small net operating income. Day spas do not have the same captive audience as a resort and day spa. Guests have many options close to them when choosing where to spend their money. This puts greater competitive downward pressure on the prices that a day spa can charge.

The director needs to be responsible for everything from human resources and marketing to maintenance to laundry. Day spa directors do a lot of **guerilla marketing**. They meet with the local chamber of commerce, get on the radio, and host events in the community to attract business.

While some day spas are part of a larger corporate entity, most are owned by a single person or a partnership. According to the 2007 ISPA Spa Industry Study, 41 percent of day spas are sole proprietorships, while another 12 percent are partnerships. Small corporations own 44 percent of day spas, while only three percent are owned by major corporations. This means that most day spa directors operate independently to make decisions from hiring and product selections to marketing and training. Multi-unit and corporate day spas have the advantage of having these functions centralized and standardized, making these decisions easier for individual spa directors within those corporate entities. Exhibit 1 describes the kind of support provided by the Red Door day spa's corporate structure.

A Day in the Life of Three Spa Directors

Every day, spa directors around the world deal with the challenges of leading employees, managing profitability, and serving guests. While there are many types of spas, this chapter will follow hypothetical directors at three of the most common types of spas: resort spas, destination spas, and day spas. Actual daily activities for a spa director will vary from operation to operation and from day to day; the examples presented in this chapter are only a reflection of what a day might entail. There is no such thing as a "typical" day in the spa world.

Another point to note: with the rapid growth of the spa industry it is important to understand that job titles and specific roles and responsibilities can vary greatly from spa to spa. A director of operations, spa director, executive spa director, spa manager, general manager, or managing director may have very similar or distinctly different responsibilities, depending on the size of the company and the organizational structure.

Exhibit 1 The Corporate Day Spa Experience

The Red Door Spas' organizational structure differs from the majority of day spas. The company owns and operates more than 30 spas worldwide, from freestanding locations to mall locations to co-branded partnerships within hotels or resorts. This operation is supported by a large corporate office and infrastructure consisting of a CEO, vice presidents of operations, human resources, information systems, construction, warehouse, marketing, and retail. Each vice president of operations has a specific territory of "groups" of specific locations. This in turn supports the individual spa director with business issues and driving/controlling the business. Similarly, the spa director can call the HR department and receive support if a staffing situation occurs. Likewise, marketing provides support in creating events, collateral, and advertising efforts.

The day in the life of a spa director/owner revolves around communication, listening, relationship building, motivating, problem solving, decision making underscored by precision planning, consumer trend analysis, and organization and time management. Communication is key with direct reports in operations and training. Weekly one-on-one touch-base meetings focus on guest and associate relations, financial performance reviews, staff and room utilization, marketing and merchandising, training, staff retention, and development. Collaborative discussions determine initiatives and strategies to meet operational and financial objectives.

In weekly corporate staff meetings, each department head provides a status update. Generally the operators begin with a financial performance review and operational highlights. The director of supply chain management reports on in-stock levels of managed inventory and reviews any current supply issues. Concurrently, human resources, marketing, information systems, design and construction, real estate development each provide departmental information needed to operate a branded multi-unit day spa chain.

The Red Door Spas function as a paradigm in the day spa industry due to highly efficient, professional leadership. The general managers of the Red Door Spas are talented, experienced entrepreneurs running multi-million dollar businesses. They are the key operators managing the daily operational activities. The GMs drive the business through cultivated expertise in scheduling trend analysis, staff development, execution of marketing and merchandising programs, as well as providing an enhanced level of guest services.

The technical staff are the service providers and primary representatives of the brand name, image and reputation of the Red Door. To that end, Red Door Spas have a sophisticated, comprehensive training curriculum. Each one of the service departments—face, body, hair style, hair color, nails, retail, and guest services—is represented by a regional training manager.

The company's regional training managers are credentialed, certified, leading experts within their specific service category. They determine and maintain the level of technical expertise within each service department. The educational curriculum is broken down into new and continued technical training. For example, when a new technician is hired, the first 90 days of training are dedicated to the fundamental principles, applications, and modalities of the service.

Source: Chris Fields, Vice President of Operations, Red Door Spas

Day in the Life of a Resort Spa Director

Andrew Bruin has been the director of The Luxury Spa at Lakeside Resort for three years. Located in the Midwest, the resort draws both vacation and business travelers, with 70 percent group business and 30 percent social transient guests. It is known for its challenging golf course, elegant restaurant, and world-class spa. What follows is a typical day for Andrew.[3]

6 A.M. Start My Day. I arrive early at the resort to start my day by swimming laps in the pool. The exercise invigorates me for what is sure to be a busy day ahead. Despite the fact that I'll be 'on the run' most of the day, that won't count as the exercise I know is so important to both my physical and emotional health. I grab a quick shower, then head to the spa café for a breakfast of fresh carrot juice, yogurt, and whole-grain banana bread before handling my morning paperwork and leading the morning line-up and motivational meeting.

7:30 A.M. Office Time. In the quiet of my office, I review the night clerk's summary report, which is prepared by the resort accounting office. It reports the revenues for all departments, including the spa, for the previous day as compared to budget for the day and month to date. We were very busy yesterday, so the spa exceeded the budget plan for the day and we are now very close to catching up to budget for the month. I also pull up the shift logs from guest registration on screen to review everything that the guest registration agents have recorded. I see that there was an appointment missed for the late afternoon that was handled nicely by the desk staff, but I take out a note card and write an apology note to the guest, asking her to call me directly if she needs anything. There is also a note that the desk is low on service menus, so I add a reminder to my to-do list to check on the inventory when I pass the storeroom. I quickly check my e-mails and note that the hotel controller wants me to stop in this morning to approve a few invoices for processing.

After that, it's time for my morning spa walk-through to make sure everything from the treatment rooms, relaxation lounges, wet lounges, and locker areas is perfect. I pay special attention to the women's areas, as I never have a chance to inspect them once our first guests arrive. This makes my early morning walk-through especially important.

8:30 A.M. Line Up/Motivational Meeting. I meet with the spa's staff to prepare for the day's tasks. The daily line-up is a 15- to 20-minute motivational meeting to go over the events of the day and any special requirements and to emphasize the mission and vision. During this morning's meeting, I:

- Review positive comment/survey cards. "Ariana, Mrs. Conway wrote that after her massage with you, she felt better than she had in weeks," I read aloud. By singling out hands-on practitioners who were specifically praised by guests, I hope to bolster staff pride and remind them of the effect they have on each guest who walks through the door.

- Announce VIPs, including a writer from a regional travel magazine and the regional director of a company holding its winter meeting at the hotel. I provide specific instructions to the staff handling the VIPs, but also remind the entire group that each guest should be handled with such care.

- I remind the staff that media personnel may be either looking at angles for stories or visiting to see if we are what we say we are and if our services match up with our marketing and/or credentials. Unlike the writer we are hosting today, some may approach the spa anonymously, to review the spa without being noted as a travel writer.

- Group VIPs are often meeting planners or executives that the hotel qualifies as key to business. The hotel wants to make sure these VIPs have a flawless stay and experience at all of the hotel outlets (golf, spa, restaurants).

- Review the hotel occupancy forecast detailing the upcoming daily occupancy for the next 15 days. The sheet also lists all outlet hours of operation and groups and VIPs that will be in house. This sheet gives the spa's hands-on practitioners advance knowledge of potential high occupancy days for the spa, so they can plan to work other days than their scheduled days (with management approval) and meet the needs of the hotel and spa.

- Notify the staff of any technical difficulties. The hotel kitchen is short-handed today because of staff illness. We must make every effort to facilitate the ordering of lunches for our spa guests so they are not inconvenienced by the kitchen's staffing problem and so the kitchen is not inconvenienced by our requests (e.g., the front desk must give plenty of notice to the kitchen).

8:50 A.M. A Massage Therapist Calls in Sick. When I return to my office, I have a phone message that Sergei is home sick. This is a problem. When a staff member unexpectedly misses work, it's my job to make sure a replacement staff member is found immediately; canceling the therapist's appointments for the day is a last resort. Guests often plan a spa visit well in advance, eagerly anticipating the experience, and canceling that spa visit will disappoint the guest and leave a negative impression.

Each employee receives a copy of the spa's sick policy at his or her time of hire. Following policy, the sick employee should have contacted someone else to work for him or her. If a replacement was not available, despite all efforts to locate one, the spa director first tries to move the sick therapist's appointments to another therapist already on the schedule, where possible. I review the day's schedule. Sergei was supposed to have given four massages—three of them are for guests here with a business group, and one other is a guest vacationing at the resort. I don't want to have to cancel any of their appointments, especially the ones with the meeting group.

One of the challenges in calling a client to tell them the spa cannot honor an appointment is the client may be visiting the spa as part of a group. Such situations must be handled very delicately, because canceling one guest's scheduled appointments will many times upset and disrupt the whole group of spa guests. They may all request a discount in compensation and can easily leave with a negative impression of the spa and/or hotel. All efforts should be made to cover each of the appointments for the sick associate, thereby avoiding potential problems, or to encourage the guest to make alternate choices for his or her treatment time and/or desired treatment.

Fortunately, using our spa's scheduling software, I'm able to adjust the day's schedule to cover Sergei's appointments, although it means that Ariana will need to put in a full day instead of the half day she was originally scheduled for and Kaiyah's lunch break will be later than planned. I also have to call one of the guests to reschedule her to a different time. I offer her a 20 percent discount for having to change her original time.

9 A.M. Meet with Vendor for New Product Line. After juggling schedules and thanking Ariana and Kaiyah for going the extra mile, I hurry to a meeting with a **vendor** to consider a new product line for the spa. Retail sales play an important role in any spa's success, so I need to make intelligent choices about what I put on our shelves. Therefore, I've done my homework before this meeting. Some questions I asked as I investigated the potential line were: What are the ingredients? What research did the vendor have to back up their specific claims? What is the line's mission and/or background? Does it match the spa's identity and mission? Do the retail company's practices (environmental, material base) fit my spa?

I had secured product samples ahead of time to give to my staff to encourage ownership from them. I wanted to make sure that most of them liked it and would sell it. I had seen in other resort spas where a new director chose a new focus and replaced a line that was well liked by the staff, but the new line failed because the staff didn't want the change. Fortunately, my team approved of the new product and agreed that it would be an asset to our retail offerings.

At this meeting, I still had several questions for the vendor. These questions are important to consider when reviewing any new retail line:

- Does the line offer discounts, perks, and contests for our staff to motivate sales?

- What training support can we expect?

- Does the line have credibility and some history? Is this line used in similar high-end properties like mine? Reviewing the line's list of customers may reflect its success in the market.

- Does this line sell to salons and day spas or directly to consumers on its website? It is important that the line have some minimum requirements before entering an agreement with a new account and that they scrutinize me as much as I am investigating them! I hope the line has some exclusivity and does not sell at big box retailers. My guests want to know that they are purchasing an exclusive product when they visit us.

- What spas with operations similar in size, client demographics, and philosophy to ours are on this supplier's list? I plan to ask for the contact information for two or three customers so I can call to discuss their experiences with this vendor.

- What spas close to mine do they sell to? I want to seek exclusivity, asking the vendor to not sell the product to any other spa within a certain radius.

- What kind of marketing support does the company offer? Do they have a sampling program? Do they provide marketing materials such as bags, brochures,

Spa directors are members of a resort's executive team, which meets to ensure the smooth functioning of all departments at the property.

posters, and mailers? Do they offer a co-op advertising program? Do they provide regular product promotions our spa can participate in?

9:50 A.M. Guest Accident. As the vendor and I are wrapping up our meeting, my pager beeps. A spa guest has slipped and fallen in the locker room. I've got to go. I assess the guest and call security to conduct an initial overview. I ask the guest if he needs medical assistance, but he says he is fine and declines. Security for the hotel fills out the incident report and takes pictures of the guest's scraped knee. I have to complete paperwork to file documentation about incident. Security will follow up with the guest in two days to check the status of his injury.

[handwritten in margin: Fill out incident report]

10 A.M. Resort Executive Team Meeting. As spa director, I'm also part of the resort's **executive team**. This mandatory, weekly meeting brings together the resort's department heads to encourage a well-blended, team effort. It could easily last up to two hours. As the spa director, I will both receive and give information during the meeting. The general manager of the hotel, to whom I report, usually assumes the role of moderator. Forecasted revenues and overall financial performance are discussed for pace and variances based on the budget. General meetings are discussed such as employee orientation or any company-wide meetings. Upcoming events and marketing are discussed so staffing can be adequate for any events.

I present information on the month-end profit and loss statement, reviewing the figures for estimated and actual budgets with the resort's general manager and controller. I am prepared to discuss the spa's revenue for the week, any challenges with other departments (such as food and beverage regarding spa lunches for guests or on-site laundry), and the week's strengths. In this meeting, I gain perspective on the big picture – how the spa fits into the resort and how the spa and I complement the total effort for groups and transient guests. It's also important for me to stay aware of future occupancy, conferring with sales executives at this meeting regarding future groups.

For example, the hotel's convention sales director tells me that the hotel is sold out to a group in two weeks, but the group is in meetings all day for three days with no afternoons for recreation. The sales manager alerts all outlets that they need to staff accordingly. The wheels start turning in my head, trying to figure out a way to gain spa business from this group and the local market.

11:15 A.M. Observe Reflexology Training Session. Hunter, our lead massage therapist, certified in reflexology by the American Spa Therapy Education and Certification Council, is leading a reflexology training session for some of the massage therapist staff. The session started at 10:30 a.m., but I knew I'd be slipping in late because of the resort executive team meeting. The in-house workshop allows us to train new staff and review protocol with existing massage therapists to ensure consistent service for guests. Today's training session has been organized in shifts, so we can keep part of our staff on the floor meeting reservation demands, especially in light of Sergei's absence.

Sometimes it is very hard due to turnover to have all hands-on staff trained on every service our spa menu offers. On-going training is essential to maintain consistency among our staff and keep the spa operating at optimum potential.

Training and continuing education is critical in a resort spa setting as we train our staff to meet guests' expectations. There must be a level of consistency in each treatment so that each guest receives a similar service. Many guests visit the spa together and will compare or talk about their treatment, even if it was the same service. It is important that they receive consistent service, with every step in the treatment protocol followed by each therapist, even though their personal style in delivering the service may differ.

Training is also critical in a resort spa setting since it keeps the service providers learning so they stay sharp and work with intent and not get burned out or seem disinterested to the guests. I have found that almost all therapists are passionate about the opportunity for advanced training and want to work at a spa where they can constantly improve their skills. Continuing education may also be an incentive for the employee. The spa may opt to provide complimentary training/education after the service provider stays with the resort for six months and if they receive continuing education units (CEUs) for their license renewal based on the training. For training that occurs before the staff member's six-month anniversary, he or she is responsible for half of the cost of that education. At hiring, each employee signs an agreement, authorizing the resort to take out half of the cost of the education from his or her check.

11:30 A.M. Lead Meeting. The training session ends, and Hunter and I join the lead esthetician and cosmetologist for our weekly lead meeting. We discuss staff challenges, any issues with the physical plant, and ideas for improvement. I review and set goals for each lead to share with his or her staff.

This meeting prompts communication among the different areas of the spa. Good communication is necessary because many of the service providers are isolated in rooms all day with guests – they can very quickly feel that there is poor communication within the spa. Because the personalities are so different between salon staff (stylists, makeup artists, nail technicians) and massage therapists, estheticians and fitness personnel, the lead meeting is a good exchange of information and knowledge and helps each area learn and understand the unique needs and challenges within each department. I always come away from these meetings with a greater understanding and appreciation for my team.

12:30 P.M. Lunch. I eat at the associate cafeteria within the resort, where all resort associates eat. The resort provides a healthy, nutritious, delicious, and timely meal so associates don't have to go off property for lunch. This meal is typically provided to associates free of charge or for a nominal fee. After I eat, I stop by the controller's office to approve the invoices he has waiting for me.

1 P.M. Office Administration. Back in my office, I take some time to check messages and return calls. I ponder the stacks of paper on my desk—what should I tackle first? I decide to review inventory counts of marketing materials (brochures, postcards, business cards, stationery) and place a new order. It is imperative that the spa doesn't run out of marketing collateral. Inventories must be counted periodically to ensure we don't run out since lead time on these items may be one to eight weeks depending on the amount, complexity, paper style, etc. By staying aware of inventories, I can stay proactive in keeping the spa stocked, not reactive when we run out of something.

1:50 P.M. Spa Rounds. With paperwork for the day finished for now, I decide to conduct a physical walk-through of the facility to ensure that all systems are working and that the spa's flow does not have any challenges. I know that typically most of the treatment rooms will turn over from ten minutes to the hour to the top of each hour, so it is a great time for me to walk the treatment corridor and the dispensary to greet each of our therapists and check on their day. I check the locker room and verify that the daily maintenance checklist has been properly updated. I notice that one of the hampers is overflowing and call over one of my attendants to make sure it gets taken care of. I check the waiting areas, the whirlpool, and the meditation room for cleanliness and overall appearance, and check the temperature in the whirlpool and steam room. It's important that the spa facility is not only clean, but hospital clean, as guests expect a spa to be antiseptically clean. This ensures the right environment for a positive guest experience and eliminates any potential hazards.

Treatment protocol is important for the spa's service providers, but facility protocol is also essential for the successful performance of my support staff. Communicating my expectations and providing a list of standards and checklists establishes clear systems for the staff to follow. My job is to check to make sure those systems are running smoothly, according to the standards the spa has set and the expectations that have been outlined. As usual, I'm pleased, but not surprised, to see that everything is running as it should.

2:40 P.M. Handle Guest Complaint. Oh well. I guess everything is not running as it should. The front desk manager calls to tell me about a guest who is complaining that her pedicure did not meet her satisfaction. Guest complaints have to be handled delicately, with the spa director making every effort to rectify the situation for the guest, regardless of the validity of the complaint. Negative word-of-mouth advertising spreads quickly. I also have to make sure we don't open ourselves up to more complaints from nearby guests. A complaint about the spa will reflect on the property/resort as a whole, and if the guest is not satisfied with our handling of the situation, he or she may start to pick apart the resort.

I listen to the guest's complaint and repeat back what she has said. The guest complains that the nail tech talked to another nail tech during the entire pedicure and didn't pay attention to what she was doing. I ask her, "How can I make this right for you today?" I try to get the guest back in the pedicure chair to redo the polish with another nail tech. She doesn't have time for this, so I offer her something in compensation – her choice of a complimentary gift bag or a discount on the service. She chooses the gift bag.

Following my discussion with the guest, I meet with Jenna and Tori, the two nail techs involved, to discuss the guest's point of view and to help them understand the priority being placed on the guest. I ask the nail tech who provided the guest's pedicure to write a personal note of apology to the guest.

3 P.M. Meet with Retail Manager. Cherise, the spa's retail manager, meets me to review the past month's revenue, look at top 20 selling products, and discuss her challenges and concerns. I review her plan for increasing retail sales with a special promotion and through a special reward program for top-selling staff. It is very important to look at retail, inventory, and monthly shrinkage to determine whether the staff is recommending home remedies to continue the guest's spa experience once they leave the resort. We review each staff member's sales and determine what they are selling, and discuss ways we can assist them to identify other items that could assist their client's needs at home. The retail manager has just completed the spreadsheet of the month-end retail inventory taken just two days ago. I compare her numbers to the value on the balance sheet, and the inventory dollar variance is less than one percent—good news!

Our meeting also covers monthly inventory and shrinkage reports to see what is missing and why. We crunch some numbers to determine whether we have the right amount of product on the shelf (too little or too much)? Inventory management is crucial as we must (1) select the right inventory, (2) carry the right amount of inventory, and (3) manage cash flow in order to earn a profit.

We also discuss an upcoming visit from a visual merchandising expert who will ensure that our top items are being seen at eye level and the retail area doesn't look cluttered, but is still very inviting.

3:45 P.M. Greet Group Guests. The spa is fully booked at 4 P.M. and 5 P.M. by one of the groups meeting in the hotel. I always try to spend that critical time before the first people arrive and during their check-in to support my guest service agents, answer questions, escort guests to the locker areas, and generally, just be available so that everything starts off on the right foot. I love the look on guests' faces when I take the time to greet them and ask about what brought them to the resort. It's easy to tell they don't get that level of attention other places they've been, but being present to guests is one of the most important parts of a spa director's job.

4:00 P.M. Interview New Lead Massage Therapist (LMT). After spending some time with our guests, I remember that I've got an interview scheduled to find a successor for our lead massage therapist, Hunter, who is moving to Colorado. I'm almost hoping that the candidate is late because I'm searching for a minute to check e-mail, but I'm pleased to see that she is already here, completing some paperwork before our interview. Interviews are serious business. I must remember to follow established guidelines to ensure that I do not inadvertently discriminate against an applicant. I have ten standard questions ready, and try to remember that the interview should follow an 80/20 rule: The applicant talks 80 percent of the time; the interviewer talks for only 20. My job is to listen and consider the key indicators for a successful LMT at the spa:

- Ability to work in a team environment and at a fast pace
- Has good time management skills
- Can flow in an environment with a large number of working parts
- Ability to lead, coach, and mentor others

My list of standard questions for a massage therapist interview usually includes the following:

- What influenced you to become a massage therapist?
- Tell me a little bit about your base education and any postgraduate education you might have taken. What massage school did you attend? How many hours of education and how many hours of practical experience did you receive?
- What are some examples of how you practice good time management skills in your field?
- What would you say is unique about your style of massage? Has any modality or educator influenced your style?
- How do you assess what type of massage is best suited for your client?
- Tell me about a time when you had to work with a difficult guest.
- Why is working in a team environment important to you?
- Tell me how you lead/manage others. What is your leadership philosophy?
- Tell me about a time that you disagreed with someone at work. How did you resolve it?
- Where do you see yourself in five years? What additional education or understanding in your field would you like to have learned in that time?

Following the interview, I still need to verify the applicant's level of credentials and licensing, so I place a call to the resort's human resources office to coordinate our efforts.

5 P.M. Yield Management Meeting. It is late November and hotel occupancy is low, so it's time to look for ways to increase revenue and discuss how to market to any in-house groups. I join the hotel's general manager and managers from the rooms division, front office, group sales, and accounting in a small meeting room. The group sales manager had commented in the executive team meeting this morning that a group arriving in two weeks will not be candidates for spa treatments. I bring that up and ask whether spouses are expected to accompany the group's attendees. If so, I could approach them with a special offer through an e-mail blast before their arrival, special incentive cards in the rooms, and specific phone calls placed to each room, inviting the spouses to visit the spa (and thereby ensuring our business levels are adequate while the group is in house). If no spouses will be attending, I'll need to consider the opportunities that remain for the group in-house. Would the event organizer consider booking therapists to provide chair massages during breaks? Doing so will keep a few of my therapists busy and provide a point of contact with the guests. Or maybe the spa could promote its holiday gift sets and offer group members a discount. One of my fellow spa directors works at a resort that requires groups to include a required minimum number of spa treatments in the group's contract. Would that work here?

5:45 P.M. Visit Fitness Center. I walk over to the fitness area as a spinning class is scheduled to start at 6 P.M. I am interested in knowing how many guests have signed up and make sure everything is in order. It also gives me a chance to check on the cleanliness and set-up of the cardio and weight equipment.

6 P.M. Prepare for Next Day. I try to make sure that tomorrow starts smoothly by taking some time to prepare tonight. I review software for the next day's business and make sure staffing is in good order, and meet with the reservations staff to troubleshoot any potential issues. I double-check that F&B has been notified of a large spa group that will need lunch on the following day and that a spa gift basket has been ordered for in-room delivery to a VIP.

7 P.M. Deliver a Gift Certificate to a Charity Function for a Local Domestic Violence Group. I leave the resort, heading to a local charity event, where the spa is offering a gift certificate for an overnight stay at the resort and half-day spa package at a dinner and silent auction fundraiser. The spa and resort's donation is one of the featured prizes, so I receive recognition in front of the group for our contribution. The spa has achieved such a good reputation in the community – my staff and I are doing our jobs well!

A Day in the Life of a Destination Spa Director

Chloe Jamison is the managing director of a 20-year-old destination spa on the West Coast. The property caters mainly to women 35 and older and is known in the industry as an affordable fitness spa. The property has about a 65 percent repeat clientele with a maximum capacity of 82 guests and has more than 120 employees. Guests come alone or with a friend. There is very little group business and no meeting facility. There is a two-night minimum stay that includes accommodations, all spa cuisine meals and snacks, and the complete fitness program along with evening talks and various classes.[4]

7:30 A.M. Arrive at Spa to Hike with Guests. I arrive at the spa in time to join the guests on their morning hike. I enjoy having the chance to hike with the guests in the early morning. The trail is so beautiful with the shadows filtering through the

Spa Snapshot: Describe a memorable moment from one of your days.

As the general manager of Avon Salon & Spa, I was walking through the salon one morning and said hello to a customer who I had met at a business lunch some months ago. I said my hellos and noticed she had her dog with her (not an uncommon event at our spa) so I petted the dog and said "Good morning, Baby" to the dog. The customer then replied to me, "You are the best manager I ever met! I can't believe you care so much about me that you even remember my dog's name. I love it here and will tell all my friends this is the only location in NYC to visit." I did not confess to her, but I will tell you I had no idea the dog's name was Baby! It just seemed like a nice thing to call the little dog!

—*Wendy Clark, President, I-Bella*

There are just so many. They range from serious injury to a guest and making all our resources available to help the family and transport them to get out of town to different expectations expected from some of our international customers. One of my therapists was asked halfway through her 90-minute massage if she knew of anyone that gave happy endings. She was a bit shaken by the experience. As she said, he wasn't attacking her, but just bringing it up. It makes her nervous that she is not taken as a professional at a resort by this guest.

—*Loren Stone, CEO, Sovereign Hospitality*

I'm in my office at La Costa Resort and Spa and everything appears to be functioning smoothly, and then I hear screams of profanity coming from within the men's spa. What in the world was going on? I quickly headed in the men's facility, only to find a group of CEOs and retired gentlemen (I use that word lightly from the words coming out of their mouths), playing water polo (in a space very close to the massage treatment area). It was that day that I came to realize that everyone finds balance, relaxation, and tranquility in different places. For some it's an invigorating Thai massage, a soothing Swedish massage, or releasing tension and stress within an expressive profanity-filled game of water polo. Who would have known?

—*Sean Handler, Director of Sales, Solace Spa/Boyne USA*

Every day I am more convinced that a reality show on 'behind the scenes' in a busy spa would be a home run. Some of the excuses guests give for missing appointments, plus some guests are very "fragile." They have a meltdown if their nail tech is sick, and one demanded that her massage

(continued)

therapist come in to serve her, even though he was tending to his father's death the night before. Oh, and the devout Muslim woman who was praying in one of the toilet stalls. We gave her a private treatment room. But those are all dwarfed by the accolades and letters we get from people whose lives we have touched. We have also played babysitter, chauffeur, personal shopper, wedding planner, and personal assistant in the course of serving our guests – it is our honor to do so.

—Angela Cortright, Owner, Spa Gregorie's

A few years ago when we were opening a second location and I needed to train an entire staff of new spa therapists at one time, I began a month-long spa boot camp for their training. During many of these classes, I would end up being the model for the service being performed and therefore could give constructive feedback or continue talking and educating while receiving the hands-on treatment. At one point during this training, the conversation turned to our spa policy regarding inappropriate behavior in the spa and I got very serious when explaining our sexual harassment and inappropriate guest behavior policies and the importance of adherence to these policies. While talking, I suddenly had a mental picture of what was taking place and began laughing hysterically. My class, who were all trying to stay professional and who were also confused at what exactly I found to be so funny all stared at me until I finally explained: In what other business would anyone find it acceptable or even normal to have a stern conversation on sexual harassment or acceptable guest behavior from their NAKED boss!

—Sara Cruncleton, Ihloff Salon & Spa

trees and the sound of the stream creating a soothing rhythm to our walk. This is the perfect opportunity to share an experience with our weekly guests, to find out how their stay is going and what they hope to accomplish while they are with us. I like to find out who has been with us before and ask what it is about our spa that makes them return. For the first-timers, I ask how they found us and assure them that my door is always open if they need anything during their stay.

8:45 A.M. Visit Guests in Dining Room. Invigorated by the hike, I stop by the dining room to say good morning to those guests who chose not to participate in the hike and instead went to the gym for a morning workout. At a destination spa, the guests really expect personal attention from the entire staff, and especially from the director. It is impressive for guests to know the boss on a personal basis; it creates loyalty for what we are doing at our spa.

9 A.M. Review Reports and Handle Facility Issue. When I finally get to my office, I check my messages—voicemail and e-mail, as well as the mail from the front

At a destination spa, directors often interact with guests during an activity like yoga, a morning hike, or a fitness class.

desk. I review the revenue report for the previous day that the accounting office e-mailed to me. The controller has flagged that we're down a bit in revenue for additional treatments and private consultations, so I make a note to talk with our nutritionist and personal trainers about ideas for better promoting their services to guests. The controller's e-mail reminds me that he needs to stop by later to have me sign the checks for the week, and to approve several purchase orders. I hit reply and ask him to drop by my office after lunch.

The facilities manager pops into my office to review last night's property report and review projects for today. He brings up two issues, neither of them critical.

First, the kitchen ice machine failed. The facilities manager says that he ordered the broken part last evening. When it's delivered, he can install it—it's an easy fix. We won't need to get an outside supplier for ice. Second, one of our pedi spa chair basins cracked and leaked. After reviewing my options, I ask the salon manager to make note in our appointment scheduling software that the chair is temporarily out of order, so that no appointments are mistakenly scheduled for that chair. Back in my office, I review the purchasing document for the equipment to see if the warranty was valid past one year and call the manufacturer for a recommendation. We decide to repair the chair on our own because the warranty had expired. The facilities manager estimates that he can have the chair back in service within two days, and orders a replacement basin that is in stock from a local supplier.

10 A.M. Attend Renovation Meeting. I meet with the contractor to review layout and select tubs, fixtures, and doors for new bathrooms in four of our guest cottages.

We review costs and timelines and try to figure out the best time to take rooms out of service. To do this, I evaluate current booking trends compared with those from last year. In the past, we've been successful with starting construction at the end of a discount special. I negotiate with the contractor that if we start renovations in mid-September, we will be complete before Thanksgiving. My past experience is that we lose tradesmen as the holidays approach, which can delay completion by seven to ten days. I evaluate the impact to nearby cottages and discuss where the contractor will set up his work yard.

The cost of the project also includes the potential loss in revenue. I make a note to get the rooms blocked by the reservations manager. The facilities manager can use this opportunity to develop a punch list for each room to maximize other repairs and painting while the room is out of service. For example, during the bathroom remodel, the bedroom can be repainted or touched up and the interior and exterior of the windows can be re-glazed. We could install Wi-Fi and upgrade the landscaping near the entrance.

I also have to decide whether a discount is needed due to the disruption or whether the project can be isolated. In this case, it can be isolated. Noise should be minimal; all water to cottages will need to be shut down for a few hours; I have to decide what day and time are best and send a notice to guests in occupied cottages. I'll also have to figure out where to put a temporary walkway for one room to get around the construction fencing. It is best to start preparing for minor projects like this about four to six months in advance and major ones ten to 12 months in advance. I write a memo and e-mail it to the front desk, reservations, and the managers on duty as well as all department managers so everyone is abreast of the upcoming project.

10:45 A.M. Arrange Advertising for the Spa. I receive a call from a media broker with remnant space; the deadline is today. I negotiate the final rate for the ad layout. By the end of the day, I'll have to determine the best image to use, write copy, and send it to the broker. I file the information into my advertising file and add dates, magazine information, and cost to my yearly advertising schedule spreadsheet. The next steps include writing the incentive call to action for a full page ad layout, reviewing the legal contract, and signing the insertion order, then writing a purchase order for a graphic design request to submit to accounting. At a large resort with an extensive support staff, this task might be delegated to another department, but a smaller, independent property like this one doesn't have the luxury of separate in-house departments for every job. It's truly a case where the spa director has to be a jack of all trades—and master of them all.

11:05 A.M. Review Treatment Proposal. I review a proposal from the services manager for a new treatment, making some suggestions and evaluating pricing. I return the proposal to the manager for another round and suggest a time when I can experience the proposed treatment myself. Her proposal is sound; this treatment is one that can only enhance our guests' experience. I'm fortunate that the members of my management team are on top of spa trends and innovations and take the steps needed to keep our offerings fresh.

11:20 A.M. Work on Five-Year Renovation Plan. A reminder pops up on my computer calendar to continue working on the spa's five-year renovation plan. It is important to keep thinking strategically about the business. It can never be just business as usual. As an officer of the company, I must always stay on top of what to do next. Creating a concept list and incorporating department managers' wish lists into it gives a foundation for future planning and budget reviews. I must look at what might make the greatest positive effect on the guests, but also what just needs to be done and balance where to allocate time and money. For example, putting in a new kitchen floor will not improve the guests' overall experience, but it is definitely needed. It's important to be proactive in making repairs versus being forced into it by the health department inspector who might be picky about cracks or worn paint. It is always a balance between getting more life out of something or replacing it before it might fail.

12 P.M. Review Amenities for Rooms. It's nearly time for lunch, but the housekeeping manager pops her head into my office and asks for a few minutes of my time. She's been concerned about the quality of our room amenity products. She's done some background work and brings me samples and pricing from other companies. We need to ensure that whatever we select for the rooms fits in with the products we use throughout the rest of the spa, and also maintains the environmental standards to which we're committed. She leaves the samples with me and I agree to follow up with her by the end of the week.

While she is in my office, I commend her for the new training program she has implemented with the housekeeping staff. Weekly ESL (English as a Second Language) sessions have led to greater confidence among our Spanish-speaking housekeepers, and their tutors, selected from among other employees, have also increased their self-esteem by being selected as teachers. It's been a win-win for everyone, and it shows in the performance and demeanor of the staff.

12:15 P.M. Lunch. I finally head to the employee break room to have lunch with the staff. Lunch is spa cuisine, the same food the guests eat. Today there is a Chinese noodle salad with chicken and won ton crisps, with a side of ginger-poached pears. I savor the crunch of the cabbage and sprouts and marvel at how much better organic, free-range chicken tastes than factory-raised. I also grab a blueberry muffin from this morning's breakfast. The blueberries are grown right here in the spa's gardens, and the walnuts add valuable omega 3's to my diet. It's hard to believe that something so good is only about 100 calories. I stop by the kitchen to give feedback about the food. The ginger-poached pears were amazing—I had overheard some guests raving about them a few days ago, but this was my first chance to try them. They are definitely a welcome addition to the menu.

12:45 P.M. Work on Guest Communications. I sit down at my desk to write a response to a guest complaint. I've made certain to gather all the details before responding. In this situation, a guest felt embarrassed when the manager on duty asked her to stop using her cell phone around the pool. The guest's letter complained of feeling attacked and embarrassed and added that we did not follow up with her as she said she was promised after complaining to the owner.

Writing personal letters is one way in which spa directors keep connected with guests and show the level of personal attention that spa guests expect.

My research showed that two guests by the pool complained to the manager on duty about a guest on a cell phone by the pool. (We have a "no cell phones in public areas" policy). The manager on duty asked her to please not use her cell phone. After researching whether the guest's complaint about how we handled the situation was followed up on, I learned that the guest was sent a handwritten note from the owner apologizing and, two weeks later, she was sent a letter from the general manager responding to her written complaint on a guest comment card. My duty now is to write an additional follow-up letter to the guest, responding to her complaint about not getting a response letter. I use a pleasant tone, but back it up with copies of all correspondence to her. It is important to always start by apologizing and letting the guest know how sorry we are that we did not meet her expectations. There is a fine line to balance between giving the house away to please an angry guest and standing one's ground. Research and follow-up are keys to guest handling; you cannot always believe that what the guest says is exactly the way the situation unfolded. However, it is always important to handle guest concerns with the utmost respect and courtesy.

The rest of my correspondence is much easier. As managing director, I try to write a personal note to each of our guests from the previous week. I have a basic format for these letters, but I always customize them from the notes added to the guest history by other staff members. The best marketing is to turn our guests into advocates and to share with others how wonderful they feel after a week of total relaxation and rest coupled with invigorating exercise. This is one of my favorite tasks because it keeps me connected with our guests on a very personal level. I never want to lose sight of the guests; after all, they are our reason for being here.

1:15 P.M. Arrange Comp Stay for Writer. I respond to a request from our public relations firm for a complimentary stay for a travel writer who is working on a feature article about destination spas with a strong culinary focus. I always evaluate the timing and, if a suite is available, we try to put writers in our nicest accommodation; if one is not available, we ask them for an alternative date. Fortunately, we do have a suite available for the dates the writer requested. I have reservations book the room, request that a welcome gift be placed in the writer's room, and write a handwritten welcome note. The services manager will work with me to set up treatments for the writer.

1:30 P.M. Lead Weekly Management Meeting. I head to our weekly management meeting with all department managers, the general manager, and the owners. In this meeting, we review occupancy and current events. The reservations manager reads a list of all return guests' names for the week and any VIPs. We try to see if we need to have a heads-up for any particular arrivals. For example, this week Mrs. Miller is arriving and on her last stay she was unhappy that only the down pillows were removed due to her allergies and not the down duvet insert. Fortunately, the software program we use includes a screen for recording guest preferences, so we're prepared this time around. The housekeeping manager will cover this with her staff and make sure we make this guest happier on this visit.

2 P.M. Discuss New Product for Spa. I meet with the kitchen manager to discuss ideas for naturally-flavored water in our public areas. I review the look and taste of the product, as well as any health department requirements regarding refrigeration needs.

2:30 P.M. Donation Requests, Media Coverage. I evaluate donation request letters; we get about three per day. This is always a challenge as we are not just giving away a room, but all meals, classes, and even treatments, so any contribution is very expensive. We try to say yes to any requests that come directly from our guests for a charity they are involved in. We also support almost all local requests, although we are cautious about anything that has a strong religious or political overtone because of any implied endorsement.

While perusing the requests, I take a call from an editor who is fact checking an article for an airline's in-flight magazine. Because of our planned renovations, I ask when the article is scheduled to run and wonder whether to ask her to add a note about the construction to the end of the article. Fortunately, the piece will run after the renovations are done.

3 P.M. ISPA Board Conference Call. I review my travel calendar to schedule flights for an upcoming spa conference. Then I peruse notes for an ISPA board conference call, and join the call where we'll review current and upcoming projects. I've blocked out an hour for the call, but will have to leave by 4 P.M. to attend an off-site meeting. At this point in my career, it is important to give back to the industry, thus my volunteer service to the ISPA board.

4:30 P.M. Review Plans for Massage Room Upgrades. I meet with an interior designer in her office to review plans, colors, and furniture for our massage room upgrades. The meeting lasts a little less than an hour, and I feel that she has a clear vision of the atmosphere we want for the massage rooms. When I return to the office, I will write a purchase order for accounting to pay the designer for our meeting time.

5:45 P.M. Review Occupancy Report. Looking at my computer screen, a high-importance e-mail from the controller catches my attention. He is concerned that our advance booking pace is below target and suggests that we consider possible discount specials to generate additional occupancy. I review the occupancy report and financials he had sent earlier. Based on the reports, I evaluate down times and consider his suggestion. It's important not to offer too many discounts or return guests will not be willing to pay regular rates and will only come back during discounts. It's a balancing act.

I had hoped to go through the new product offerings for the spa boutique—they come in daily and if I don't keep up with them, I'll soon fall behind. But it doesn't look like I'll get to them today. I decide to delegate the task to Alan, the retail manager, and request a report on his top recommendations after he reviews the many product offerings I've collected in a file on my desk.

Instead, as long as I'm already on the computer, I review the upgrades needed for our website and consider possible layouts and designs of upgrades presented by a local web designer with whom we've contracted. We're not quite there yet, but his proposed designs are fresh and exciting and are sure to capture the interest of prospective guests. I e-mail a few suggestions and ask to meet with him tomorrow to discuss ideas in greater detail.

6:30 P.M. More Paperwork. It's time to clear some paperwork off my desk and review current issues of lodging and hospitality magazines. After walking the property again, I stop in to the dining room to visit with guests and ask how their day went.

7:30 P.M. Attend Lecture. After dinner, an author is doing a special presentation on his new book, which focuses on social isolation. I'm interested in what he has to say, so I call my husband and remind him that I will be late this evening as I want to attend the lecture. It seems like this happens to me a couple of times a week—I end up staying late.

9 P.M. Head for Home. As I drive away, I notice the entryway fountain in front of our building is not working. I call from my car to the front desk and ask that they put it on the evening houseman's board to check. I then write a note on my trusty car pad to check in the morning with the facilities manager. (I later find out that the pump has failed. Fortunately, there are 14 days left on the two-year warranty and the facilities manager is able to get a replacement pump the next day from our local supplier at no charge.)

A survey of spa directors asked: Can you describe your main passion for this business in approximately ten words?

Their responses:

- All encompassing.
- Desire to integrate spa and wellness into my own life, then the community and family.
- Fun doing something unique in the health care field.
- Mentoring.
- Provide authentic spa services to customers related to health and wellness.
- Seeing the guests transform while they are here.
- The ability to provide a complete wellness experience on a daily basis.
- This is what I trained for—it's my life.
- To see the integration of medicine in the spa industry and its effects on guests.

Source: Spa Director and Spa Technician Profile Survey, October 2001: ISPA Conference, Palm Springs, California. A Project of the ISPA Research and Development Education Committee.

Even with a start and end time to my day, the business is always on my mind. When I am in a store, I see things that might be good for us. On vacation in hotels, I can't help but critique how things are done and who makes the comfy chair in the room. The spa business gets in your blood and is hard to turn off. I wouldn't have it any other way.

Day in the Life of a Day Spa Director

Bailey Santiago is the director of the Something Special Day Spa and Salon, a 6,000 square foot spa with 20 staff members, located in a medium-size Northeastern city. Services offered at the day spa include manicures and pedicures, hair styling, facials, massage therapy, and waxing. Bailey has been the director at the spa's downtown location for five years; prior to that, she was the assistant director at Something Special's west side location.[5]

7:30 A.M. Leave for Work. My day always begins while driving to the spa. I mentally review what the day has in store, and prioritize my "to do" list in my mind. This may sound silly, but I always visualize a clothesline and mentally hang on the line my tasks for the day in order of importance. Needless to say, that priority list can change in a flash, but it helps me to keep my goals for the day in the front of my mind. Today, the items on my mental clothesline include welcoming a new massage therapist, arranging a spa party with a local restaurant, and ordering retail and professional products.

8 A.M. Perform Opening Duties. I arrive at the spa and begin preparing for the day. As the director of a day spa and salon, I have many hands-on duties that those unfamiliar with day spas might not think would be part of the director's job. They are not terribly glamorous, but they are necessary to the successful functioning of the spa. By leading through example, the personal care and pride I have in the spa's cleanliness and its smooth functioning rubs off on every spa staff member.

I say good morning to Paige, our hostess/spa attendant, and ask whether she needs any assistance with her morning set-up tasks, which include:

- Turning on lights and towel cabbies in the nail area

- Turning on all lights, bed warmers, wax pots, and towel cabbies in each treatment room

- Choosing a calming music CD for the relaxation area

- Making our signature comforting tea for the relaxation room

- Checking to make sure all rooms are stocked with headbands (esthetics only) and small and large towels

I make the tea (brewing it is nearly as soothing as drinking it), then fill my mug and walk to my desk. After the computer boots up, I print out the reports for the previous day's business and input the revenue on a spreadsheet for the spa's accountant. I work with a local accountant to prepare monthly financial statements for the spa, along with other tasks like filing sales tax reports and payments for the state. Together, we designed an input spreadsheet that I complete and forward to his office.

With that done, I count the change bank at guest reception and prepare the morning's bank deposit. Finally, I record the daily report of employee commissions for the 15 stylists, nail techs, estheticians, and massage therapists. I've found that it works best if the payroll records are completed daily; if I ignore that responsibility for a few days, it is easier to make mistakes. Our new spa-management software is wonderful, but it can only work with the data that gets put into it.

Calling up the day's schedule on the computer, I make a list of available spa services that I'd like the salon staff to upsell, then create a list of spa lunch orders for our receptionist to e-mail to the manager of the café down the street that provides us with catering services.

8:30 A.M. Service Providers Begin to Arrive at Work. The day begins with a staff "huddle" to discuss the day's opportunities and to reinforce our goals for retailing, client retention, and guest service. I believe in sharing the business numbers with the staff, and giving them retail and sales goals weekly. We're all in this together, and the spa's success depends on each member of the team. Since it's the beginning of the month, I hand out a monthly calendar that shows this month's product focus, upcoming trainings, benchmarks, and inspirational focus. This morning, I tell the staff that I had a call last night from one of our nail techs, Margot, who had gone into early labor and was headed to the hospital. I've called over to our west side location and arranged to have one of their nail techs, Felicity, help us out for a few weeks until Margot's replacement is scheduled to start. After the meeting, I work with Neveah, our front desk receptionist, to prepare new guest packets.

9 A.M. Greet Guests. I greet and welcome our first guests of the morning. I assist with check-in (waiver forms are given to each spa guest upon arrival) and make

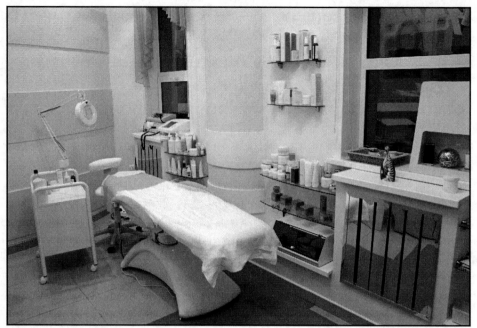

Spa directors check to ensure that treatment rooms have been properly stocked and set up for guest use.

sure that a neck pillow, water, or comforting tea is offered to guests in the relaxation area. New guests are given a tour of the spa, a task I try to handle when other management duties don't keep me away from interacting with our guests.

10 A.M. A Potential Problem Pops Up. A guest calls and says she is running 30 minutes late. Neveah tries to make the change in the scheduling program, but it doesn't look good. We're booked very tight today, and I'm not sure that we'll be able to accommodate our guest if she is late. Still, working over Neveah's shoulder, I make some suggestions for shifting service providers and changing the order in which some guests might receive multiple services, and we finally hit on a solution. It means that one of our stylists will have to take a late lunch, but at least the guest will be taken care of. Thank goodness for booking software that can handle the complexities of juggling services, treatment rooms, and service providers so effectively.

10:15 A.M. Felicity Arrives. Felicity, the nail tech from our west side spa, arrives to take Margot's shift. I thank her for being available on such short notice. She has filled in at our spa before, so I give her a brief reorientation, show her where we keep our nail supplies, and review her appointments for the day. After she is settled, I return to my office to add her to the spa management software, so that her appointments, commissions, and payroll will be correctly noted. I also note Margot's maternity leave, then pick up the phone and call the florist to deliver flowers to the hospital on behalf of the spa's staff.

A spa director might work with an employee to solve a schedule challenge using spa-specific software for managing appointments.

11:00 A.M. Upsell Services. I overhear Neveah, our receptionist, on the phone with a guest. "Yes, Ms. Hampton, we do have an opening on Thursday for a facial. I see that Richelle will also be in that day. Would you like me to schedule a brow waxing along with your facial? Yes? Thank you. We'll see you at 10:30 Thursday. Have a blessed day." I compliment Neveah on her pleasant phone manner and her initiative in upselling services to Ms. Hampton. When she first started, Neveah was nervous about using the spa-management software and learning all of the various services we offered, but now she is confident, poised, and efficient. She glows at my praise, then turns to answer another phone call with a smile on her face and in her voice.

11:15 A.M. Administrative Duties, Lunch, and Banking. Back in the office, I pull and post productivity reports, check my e-mail messages, and return calls. I confirm a meeting with a local restaurant regarding an upcoming spa party. I also begin to plan a Chamber event. Local marketing efforts like this can pay off if chosen carefully. Working with the Chamber of Commerce has been worthwhile for the spa. I try to participate in their events, network with local merchants, attend meetings, and do cross-promotions when appropriate. After grabbing a quick lunch, I head to the bank to make the daily deposit. While there, I mention to our representative that I will need to make a small draw on the spa's line of credit on Thursday, as payroll is due and with last weekend's snowstorm, revenues are a bit down and we will need some extra funds to make payroll. The good news is that next weekend's bridal event will bring in additional revenue, so I'll be able to repay the line of credit in just a few days.

1 P.M. Review Inventory and Order Products. Back at the spa, my next task is placing my weekly order of professional and retail products. We conduct a complete retail product inventory monthly, but I like to stay on top of our 20 best sellers to make sure that we are on par. I do all the ordering myself. I have a purchasing log that I use so that the accountant has something against which he can compare invoices. It works pretty well, but sometimes products get back-ordered, which can result in missed retail sales if we are out of something. Retail sales are critical to our financial success, so I watch the spa's **par levels** like a hawk. I also conduct a professional product inventory monthly, reconciling the number of services performed in each area with the remaining professional product on hand. This helps me keep on top of any possible **pilferage** or misuse of product that may signal a need for more training of our service providers in the spa's treatment protocols. This has been so much easier since implementing a new spa software system.

2 P.M. New Hire Training. It's time to begin orientation and training for Arlo, a new massage therapist. Arlo is a graduate of a nearby massage school. I've always had a strong relationship with the school, participating in open houses and career fairs, and accepting offers to be a guest speaker in any class that requested me. In return, the school sends me their candidates as they graduate. I keep a folder of résumés and applications in my file and try to stay in touch with good candidates. There is always more turnover in massage than among estheticians.

Working with Arlo, I use a comprehensive checklist I have developed for new employee orientation. He also receives an employee manual that managers at our two locations created with information from ISPA and with input from a local labor attorney. Arlo's initial training will be spread over three days.

We have all new employees spend a day working the guest reception desk to learn the appointment system and to complete check-in and check-out with customers. We are a small spa and everyone on staff needs to know how to run the computer system, especially with our new spa software, which we're all learning together. New employees also work a day as a host or hostess, where they are responsible for ongoing cleaning in the spa and salon, as well as restocking linens and products and keeping the refreshment station pristine. I find that the team has a much greater awareness of what it takes to keep the spa clean and orderly by spending one of their first days having to do the work.

I hope that this experience will set the correct tone and that Arlo and all new employees will have respect for and attention to detail for their own areas and not expect that someone else will clean up their messes.

4:30 P.M. Meet with Advertising Salesperson. A salesperson walks into the spa and asks to meet with me about a direct mail coupon program that she thinks will be a perfect advertising opportunity for our spa. "I'll bet she says that to everyone," I think. I spend a few minutes with her in my office to listen to her presentation, in order to decide if this is a good use of our marketing dollars. My inclination is that coupon advertising might cheapen our image and not really bring in any new business. Advertising is expensive and it needs to be the right vehicle to communicate the mission and vision of our spa. Day spas simply cannot participate in every local advertising offer, and I have a strict budget to allocate to advertising each month. If I did everything that was offered, we would be out of business.

5 p.m. Personal Meeting with Staff Member. Rita, one of our hair stylists, has a break between appointments, so I ask her for a few minutes of her time. I like to bring each staff member into my office for a ten to fifteen minute chat on a regular basis. I ask how her son's basketball season is doing and find out a little more about her two-day trip out of town last week, before turning our talk to business. I know that employees would rather work at a spa where the management is concerned about them as people and takes the time to learn what is happening in their lives.

5:15 p.m. Visit Retail Area. Glancing at the clock, I realize that I won't have time to fit in an exercise class and get a shower before an evening meeting. Instead, I spend some time in the spa's retail area, straightening product and reorganizing our CD rack to feature some new music we've recently added to our product line. I make a note in my PDA to work on a new merchandising display that will tie in with next week's bridal event.

6:30 p.m. Meeting with Restaurant. I gather information and collateral and leave the spa for a 7 p.m. meeting with a local restaurant. They are interested in scheduling a spa party for twenty-five guests. We discuss what services we can offer and how guests will move from one area to the next during the party.

7:45 p.m. Time to Head Home. As I leave the meeting with the restaurant manager, my cell phone rings. Erika, my closer, is panicking because the computer has "frozen" and she's not sure what to do. I had the same problem two nights ago and try to remember the steps that our tech support person walked me through to solve the problem. Rather than make matters worse, I tell Erika where to find the help desk number for our tech support service. She knows she can call again if necessary, but I'm hoping I can head home now and not have to return to the spa. "It worked," she says. I wish her a good night, then head for home.

A Career That Makes a Difference

Spa director is one of the most demanding and rewarding careers in the spa industry. The job requires an extensive knowledge of all aspects of spa operations, from financial management and human resources to facilities management and marketing and public relations. Through their interactions with employees, guests, owners, and executive management, spa directors chart a course for success for the spa and steer the business through myriad challenges and triumphs. They care deeply about the people around them, and model servant leadership through their hands-on participation in the life of the spa—teaching and coaching staff members, seeking to understand guests and exceed their expectations, and transforming the spa's vision into reality.

Endnotes

1. Leslie Lyon, "The Spa Director's Ever-Expanding Job Description," from www.4hoteliers.com, retrieved September 13, 2007.

2. Douglas Preston, "Becoming a Spa Director: 10 Important Skills You Must Absolutely Master," www.prestoninc.net, retrieved September 13, 2007.

3. Content for this section based on material provided by Ann Moloney Brown, spa director, Spa Shiki, Lodge of Four Seasons, Lake of the Ozarks, Missouri.

4. Content for this section based on material provided by Cathy Cluff, managing director, The Oaks at Ojai, Ojai, California.

5. Content for this section based on material provided by Elaine Trahan, spa director, Paris Parker Aveda Lifestyle Salon/Spa, Jefferson, Louisiana; Helga Surrat, president, About Faces Day Spa, Towson, Maryland; Annette Jankowski, spa consultant.

 ## Key Terms

amenity—Something offered for the convenience or enjoyment of guests.

executive team—A committee composed of the general manager and department or division heads of a property.

guerilla marketing—Unconventional marketing designed to get maximum results from minimal resources.

par levels—Levels of supplies or products needed to have sufficient stock on hand until the next delivery.

pilferage—Repeated stealing of small amounts of merchandise, often by employees.

vendor—A product supplier.

Review Questions

1. What are some traits of successful spa directors?

2. What type of activities do spa directors perform in relation to employees?

3. What are a spa director's responsibilities toward guests?

4. What is the relationship between a spa director and the owners or upper management of a property?

5. What are some similarities and differences between resort spas and destination spas?

6. What are some challenges faced by directors of day spas?

Chapter 10 Outline

Management: Building Blocks for Leaders
    Management Functions
    Management Skills
The Importance of Leadership
    Strategy I: Attention Through Vision
    Strategy II: Meaning Through
        Communication
    Strategy III: Trust Through Positioning
    Strategy IV: Self-Development
Good to Great
    Levels of Leadership
    Fiscal Leadership
    Becoming a Leader
    Disciplined People
    Disciplined Thought
    Disciplined Action
The Eighth Habit
    Find Your Voice
    Inspire Others to Find Their Voices
Spa Leadership
    Managing Healers
    Strategic Intent and Transformational
        Experiences
    Authenticity
    Communication
Spa Ethics
    Ethics Defined
    Theories and Approaches to Ethics
    Social Responsibility and Business
        Ethics
    Implementing Ethics
    Code of Conduct
    Ethical Issues in Spas
Finding Success

Competencies

10

Leadership and Ethics

THERE ARE MANY NOTES that create the music of a spa's success. The notes include the physical location, architecture, interior design, theme, business plan, treatments, and therapists, among other things. Once all of the instruments of an orchestra are brought together, it takes a conductor to masterfully blend them to create a symphonic masterpiece.

Just as an orchestra doesn't rely on a single instrument to play a moving symphony, neither does a spa succeed on the strength of a single soloist. Leadership is needed from many people in the spa organization and it is not the spa director alone who drives every decision to create the necessary environment. Rather, a spa leader is a disciplined, focused, consistent communicator whose goal is to take the spa from good to great.

Who is a leader in a spa? Ultimately, leaders are all people who display qualities of leadership to inspire those around them. Spa professionals such as leads, supervisors, managers, directors, executive directors, and general managers—to list just some of the titles commonly used in the spa industry—need to develop their leadership skills and to nurture the character traits that can make them great leaders. But the list doesn't end there. Each individual therapist, the spa receptionist, the person who cleans, everyone who works in the spa has the potential and opportunity to display leadership.

Managers are needed to see that things get done—to create procedures and processes and ensure that they are operating for the spa's best interest. Leaders, on the other hand, inspire each person in the spa to make it a place where guests find value and want to return. It is leadership that can take a spa from merely good to great.

This chapter will briefly explore traditional management concepts before moving on to a more in-depth look at some important leadership concepts that are specifically appropriate for a spa environment. Spas have a specific mission that requires a nurturing form of leadership different from many traditional forms of leadership. The chapter will also address the important subject of ethics.

It doesn't matter whether a professional is leading a spa in Germany, Japan, Chile, Canada, or the United States, leadership is a matter of character and principles. Leadership is not a matter of genetics or knowledge or circumstance. It is not static. No one wakes up one morning and declares, "I am now a leader." Instead, it is a lifelong process as all leaders continually reflect on their leadership qualities and strive for improvement throughout life's journey whether it involves the spa, their families, or their communities.

It is also important to note that the subject of leadership occupies shelf after shelf in bookstores across the globe. There are many theories and instructions on how to lead. This book focuses on those leadership traits and philosophies that spa professionals have identified as being particularly relevant to the spa culture.

While it is impossible in a single chapter to cover all leadership theory, this chapter will touch upon the evolution of theory while taking an in-depth look at the leadership concepts of Jim Collins and Stephen R. Covey. The theories of these two leaders were chosen as two examples of concepts that are particularly effective in a spa environment. They were chosen by spa professionals who have found their work to be inspiring. However, before this chapter gets into the heart of leadership, it will first touch upon management functions.

Management: Building Blocks for Leaders

When Larry Prochazka, marketing executive for Robbins Research Institute in Phoenix, Arizona, addressed a group of spa professionals in 2007 on the topic of leadership, he spoke in terms of balance—particularly the balance between managing and leading. Organizational activity consists of tasks (measurables, standards, delivery, procedures, structure, what is done, what is said, what is professed) and process (resistance, fear, attitude, buy-in, enthusiasm, how things are done, how things are said, how people show up).[1] In other words, spa professionals manage *things* and lead *people*.

In practical terms, this distinction means that while a professional can become a manager on the virtue of what he or she accomplishes, being a leader is in part determined by others and their willingness and acceptance of the professional's leadership. Whether others accept the leadership of a professional will depend in large part on how they manage and, even more importantly, how they behave and believe.

Management Functions

Henri Fayol, a French management theorist born in 1841 who developed the foundation for the field of management studies, grouped many different activities that managers perform into categories that are now referred to as **management functions**. Through the years, these functions have been grouped many different ways. Six common ones include:

- Planning
- Organizing
- Coordinating
- Staffing
- Directing
- Controlling

Planning establishes goals and objectives to pursue during a future period. These goals become the basis for short-range, annual operational planning and more specific objectives. It also encompasses such things as developing renovation plans or creating a marketing plan.

Organizing reflects how the spa intends to accomplish its goals and objectives. It involves the assignment of tasks, the grouping of tasks into areas, and the allocation of resources. Organizing also involves establishing the flow of authority and communication between positions and levels within a spa.

Coordinating refers to achieving an efficient use of resources to attain the spa's goals and objectives. Servicing the needs of a bridal shower party might require coordinating staff members from several different areas. Interfacing electronic point-of-sale terminals from the retail shop to the guest registration desk is another coordinating activity.

Staffing involves recruiting applicants and hiring those best qualified. All spas use basic principles of staffing such as defining jobs with job descriptions, recording personal qualities needed to perform the work in job specifications, considering several sources of job applicants, using job application forms to collect information, screening applicants, and offering employee orientation, training, and evaluation programs. Decisions about transfers, promotions, and other related actions are also part of the staffing process.

Directing involves influencing others to accomplish the spa's goals and objectives. In this context, directing means communicating goals and objectives throughout the spa and creating an environment that encourages everyone to perform at the highest level.

Controlling involves translating the spa's goals and objectives into performance standards and assessing actual performance against standards. This is necessary to determine whether the spa is on target to reach its goals and to take corrective actions as necessary.

Management Skills

While the functions of management attempt to categorize the many activities that managers do, another approach to management focuses on the skills that managers need to carry out their jobs effectively. Robert L. Katz offered a view of management in relation to three skills:[2]

- Technical skills
- Human relations skills
- Conceptual skills

Technical skills involve specialized knowledge of tools, techniques, methods, procedures, or processes associated with a specific type of activity. Human resources managers, marketing directors, controllers, and all spa managers apply a unique set of technical skills to their particular jobs. Technical skills for a spa director might include creating a monthly variance report, establishing inventory levels, or creating a treatment menu.

Human relations skills are the abilities of the manager to work effectively with people at every level in the spa. Managers need interpersonal skills that enable them to relate to guests, owners, peers, and staff members. Human relation skills for a spa director might include conducting a performance evaluation, training staff members, discussing a treatment plan with a guest, and responding to a guest complaint.

Conceptual skills involve a manager's ability to see beyond the technical aspects of his or her position. They include recognizing the interdependence of the various departments within the spa as well as seeing the bigger picture of how the spa fits into the community and the wider world at large. Conceptual skills include identifying a mission for the spa and ensuring that all elements in the spa are in harmony with that mission, tracking trends and understanding their effect on the spa and its guests, and could even include establishing a sustainability plan that ensures the spa operates on an eco-friendly basis.

The Importance of Leadership

Warren Bennis—an industrial psychologist, an advisor to four U.S. presidents, and a man who has been called the father of leadership theory—wrote a land-mark book (together with Burt Nanus) called *LEADERS: The Strategies for Taking Charge.* Bennis and Nanus interviewed 60 successful CEOs, all presidents or chairs of boards, and 30 outstanding leaders from the public sector. Bennis concluded that these people succeeded not by being managers, but by being *leaders.* While Bennis acknowledged that both management and leadership were important, he said there was a profound difference between the two:

> To manage means to bring about, to accomplish, to have charge of, responsibility for, to conduct. Leading is influencing, guiding in direction, course, action, and opinion. The distinction is crucial. *Managers are people who do things right and leaders are people who do the right thing.* The difference may be summarized as activities of vision and judgment— *effectiveness*—versus activities of mastering routines—*efficiency.*[3]

To make the distinction clear, Bennis quoted from an advertisement for United Technologies, headlined, "Let's Get Rid of Management," that ran in the *Wall Street Journal.* Here is what the advertisement said:

> People don't want to be managed. They want to be led. Whoever heard of a world manager? World leader, yes. Educational leader. Political leader. Religious leader. Scout leader. Community leader. Labor leader. Business leader. They lead. They don't manage. The carrot always wins over the stick. Ask your horse. You can lead your horse to water, but you can't manage him to drink. If you want to manage somebody, manage yourself. Do that well and you'll be ready to stop managing. And start leading.[4]

After their research was complete, Bennis and Nanus concluded that all of the 90 leaders they interviewed employed four basic strategies:

- Strategy I: Attention through vision
- Strategy II: Meaning through communication
- Strategy III: Trust through positioning
- Strategy IV: Self-development

Strategy I: Attention Through Vision

Leaders have clear ideas of what they want the spa experience to be for their guests. More importantly, they know what their spa is like today—what the spa delivers, how it performs, and what its strengths and weaknesses are. They understand what needs to be done to build upon the spa's strengths and to have discipline to make that happen.

Spa leaders know how the spa should look, how clients feel after spending a day there, and how the spa creates that feeling. Spa leaders know and understand these things—and are committed to seeing that they occur.

Spa leaders are *not* knights in shining armor who ride in with reverberating pronouncements on what the vision is and how it will be accomplished. Rather, they are more like the Arthur of legend who summoned all the knights to a round table where all were equal and where the vision for Camelot was forged by all present. Arthur held positional power much like spa leaders who have power from the position that they hold. However, the stories say Arthur chose a non-traditional leadership role: his knights were equals who would pursue his new vision. So the modern spa leader works together with the spa team to develop a vision or guest service promise.

A spa leader must be able to nurture an environment where all can participate in the spa's mission and vision, as well as work together to form the practices that support them. Spa leaders today do not create the vision in a vacuum, but work with their spa leadership team to determine how they can do the best job in the world. Leaders have an unyielding passion for the consistent delivery of the vision or service promise.

The spa's shared vision must be attractive and compelling—a long-term dream that stretches and motivates. To be effective, it should reach hearts and minds, raise spirits, and be a catalyst for action. To act as a catalyst, a vision must be owned by all those in the spa. Essentially, a vision is a shared view of the future. A vision is not static; it lives, grows, and evolves.

Strategy II: Meaning Through Communication

Bennis and Nanus pointed out that dreaming isn't enough. Successful leaders are able to translate dreams into reality by getting others to share their dreams, commitment, and enthusiasm.

Effective leadership is partially accomplished through effective communications. Some leaders write inspiring e-mails. Others hold meetings complete with models, drawings, and charts to get their ideas across. Many use analogies, comparing what they want things to be like to something that everyone already understands. Bennis pointed out that such communication has little to do with facts—rather, it concentrates on direction. The idea is to get everyone in the spa to share the same ideas and dreams so that they will all hear the same music and play the same tune—without having a song book in front of them, but because they know instinctively how the tune should sound.

Strategy III: Trust Through Positioning

Leaders not only communicate the vision in a way that gets everyone behind it, they know how to steer a constant and steady course in the direction they have laid out. People who work for effective leaders trust their reliability. They know that their leaders will do what they have said they are going to do.

Leaders communicate with spa associates a vision that helps them find their own path to success and harmony.

When Bennis and Nanus entered McDonald's founder Ray Kroc's office, he showed them an elaborately framed statement that he said was his favorite inspirational message. The same message was in every other executive's office at McDonald's, in a place where no visitor could miss it. The statement, originally written by former U.S. president Calvin Coolidge, reads:

> Nothing in the world can take the place of persistence.
> Talent will not; nothing is more common than unsuccessful men with great talent.
> Genius will not; unrewarded genius is almost a proverb.
> Education will not; the world is full of educated derelicts.
> Persistence and determination alone are omnipotent.

Effective leaders hold on to their principles, ideas, and visions, and are not deterred by obstacles, no matter how insurmountable they seem. The people who work for them know this and trust them to carry out their vision. In this respect, they are no different from the legendary generals in military history, whose soldiers knew that they would fight until they achieved victory and thus were willing to fight alongside them.

Strategy IV: Self-Development

Bennis believes that effective leaders are out on the front line leading the charge most of the time. "Our top executives spent roughly 90 percent of their time with others and virtually the same percentage of their time concerned with the messiness of people problems." He calls this "the creative deployment of self." Leaders know what they are good at and are constantly using their personal strengths to achieve their goals. At the same time, they understand their weaknesses and compensate for them. If they believe they can't compensate for their weaknesses (for example, by surrounding themselves with a staff competent in the areas in which they do not excel), they typically do not take the job. Leaders generally do this without being prodded. They have a strong feeling of self worth—who they are and what they can do—and they act based on that confidence in themselves and their own abilities.

reflections

Michelle Kinney: Communicating High Expectations

Michelle Kinney is the spa director for the Alvadora Spa at the Royal Palms Hotel in Phoenix, Arizona. She previously worked at the Red Door, conducting training across the country, developing product, and helping to open new stores. She was also general manager of a Red Door spa in San Francisco.

You have to know what your expectations are of yourself and what you want to accomplish. You have to work at that and set goals for yourself and set boundaries. I have boundaries on my personal life and how much time I need off, and goals for what I need for the Alvadora Spa.

My leadership style is that I have high expectations but I have a great team. What gets measured gets done. You have to constantly look at where you've been successful and where your team has been successful and implement those things into your training programs.

You have to be open and communicative with your staff. They have to know that you're both on the same team. I lead by example. I don't expect them to do anything I wouldn't do. I clean lockers, I check guests in, I take phone calls. Then I also expect them to come here and do their best every day—to love their job as much as I do.

At the same time, leaders value and respect others. They understand that you can't get others to follow you willingly unless it feels right to them. Leaders seldom criticize others.

Leaders are not afraid to make mistakes. They believe that making mistakes may be the best way to learn—not only about themselves but about their employees. This is where the key principle of **empowerment** was derived. Leaders will make mistakes. Some of these mistakes may even be costly. Employees who make mistakes learn from them and become better at doing their jobs. It makes their jobs more rewarding because they are given a chance to act like a leader. Sure, there are risks, but there are also rewards. Spas that encourage their employees to risk failure, and reward them when they succeed, develop a strong group of well-trained leaders who also know how to follow. In the best spas, all employees are encouraged to become leaders by taking customer problems into their own hands and solving them. They are empowered to solve them by being given the resources—whether money or the assistance of other people. This requires great trust on the part of their leaders so that they *can* be trusted. Bennis pointed out that leaders who trust themselves understand instinctively that it is necessary to trust others.

When undertaking self-development, leaders have a broad range of wisdom to draw upon. Exhibit 1 shares some leadership wisdom from a variety of sources.

Exhibit 1   Words of Wisdom

"Divorced from ethics, leadership is reduced to management and politics to mere technique."
—James MacGregor Burns, *Leadership,* 1978

"Perhaps the most central characteristic of authentic leadership is the relinquishing of the impulse to dominate others."
—David Cooper, *Psychiatry and Anti-Psychiatry,* 1967

"The real leader has no need to lead—he is content to point the way."
—Henry Miller, *The Wisdom of the Heart*, 1941

"The trust of the people in the leaders reflects the confidence of the leaders in the people."
—Paul Freire, *Pedagogy of the Oppressed,* 1968

"Your position never gives you the right to command. It only imposes on you the duty of so living that others can receive your orders without being humiliated."
—Dag Hammarskjold, *Markings,* 1955

"Leadership consists not in degrees of technique but in traits of character; it requires moral rather than athletic or intellectual effort, and it imposes on both leader and follower alike the burdens of self-restraint."
—Lewis H. Lapham, *Money and Class in America,* 1988

"The art of choosing men is not nearly so difficult as the art of enabling those one has chosen to attain their full worth."
—Napolean Bonaparte, 1802

"The best way to inspire people to a superior performance is to convince them by everything you do and by your everyday attitude that you are wholeheartedly supporting them."
—Harold S. Geneen

"In order that people may be happy in their work, these three things are needed: They must be fit for it; they must not do too much of it; and they must have a sense of success in it."
—John Ruskin

"You do not lead by hitting people over the head—that's assault, not leadership."
—President Dwight David Eisenhower

"A man who wants to lead the orchestra must turn his back on the crowd."
—Max Lucado

"No person can be a great leader unless he takes genuine joy in the successes of those under him."
—W.A. Nance

reflections

Michael Tompkins: Taking Care of Yourself First

Michael Tompkins is general manager at Miraval Resort Life in Balance in Tucson, Arizona. Tompkins was named 2007 New York State Hospitality and Tourism Executive of the Year while serving as vice president of hotel and spa operations at the Turning Point Resort and Casino. Before that, he was Director of Health and Healing and Associate Managing Director at Canyon Ranch and the assistant director of nursing at a health center.

I try to lead by example. In the spa world, that means because we are here taking care of people and changing people's lives, making sure that you take care of yourself first. That's one of the things that people tend to forget the most.

At Miraval, I've had a chance to reconnect with who I am as a person. I dedicate the first hour of my day to me. I exercise every day. In the seven weeks that I've been here, I've lost 30 pounds.

Beyond that, I think it is really important to work hard. I wouldn't expect people to work hard if I wasn't working hard. I think nurses are the backbone of the hospital because they work so hard. That's carried over into the spa realm. I come to work every day trying to work my best. I try leading in the manner that inspires the staff that works with me to do their best as well.

It's important to be who you are. That's one of the practices here at Miraval: Being who you are and being authentic. Being who I am and encouraging the staff to be who they are helps to instill the creative spirit.

Good to Great

In *Good to Great,* Jim Collins sets forth a model for leadership that many spa professionals feel makes sense for the culture in which they operate. Collins studied great companies with an eye to discovering what made them great. Specifically, he looked for those companies that started out as merely good and became great.

The good-to-great companies were those that:

- Had a transition point from good results to great results.
- Maintained the results for at least 15 years.
- Averaged cumulative stock returns that were 6.9 times the general market for those 15 years.[5]

When Collins started, he wasn't looking for leadership traits. In fact, as he gathered data, he was convinced that it wasn't the leadership that was going to be the key element, but the data kept pointing him in that direction.

He reported that his research team was surprised at the type of leadership necessary to take a company from good to great. "Compared to high-profile leaders with big personalities who make headlines and become celebrities, the good-to-great leaders seem to have come from Mars. Self-effacing, quiet, reserved, even shy—these leaders are a paradoxical blend of personal humility and professional will. They are more like Lincoln and Socrates than Patton or Caesar."[6]

Levels of Leadership

After conducting his research, Collins sketched out five levels of leadership:

- Level One: A highly capable individual makes productive contributions through talent, knowledge, skills, and good work habits.

- Level Two: A contributing team member contributes individual capabilities to the achievement of group objectives and works effectively with others in a group setting.

- Level Three: A competent manager organizes people and resources toward the effective and efficient pursuit of predetermined objectives.

- Level Four: An effective leader catalyzes commitment to and vigorous pursuit of a clear and compelling vision, stimulating higher performance standards.

- Level Five: This type of executive builds enduring greatness through a paradoxical blend of personal humility and professional will.

Collins found **Level Five leaders** at the helm of every company during the period in which it advanced from good to great. He wrote:

> "Level Five leaders channel their ego needs away from themselves and into the large goal of building a great company. It's not that Level Five leaders have no ego or self-interest. Indeed, they are incredibly ambitious—but their ambition is first and foremost for the institution and not themselves."[7]

If a spa is going to make the move from good to great, it must have leadership throughout the spa from people who are able to turn the focus of their ambition away from themselves and onto the goals of the spa. It isn't ensuring that there is a snazzy design on the spa's private label body lotion or the lush towels used in the grooming area that make a spa great, though both of those are elements of management. What makes a spa great is the experience it creates for the guest.

To successfully lead a spa, individuals must not rely on personal charisma and ability alone, but on the ability and soul of the entire staff to deliver a quality guest experience. Many of the spa greats do have tremendous charisma and it is their charisma that allows them to spread their message beyond their individual spas. However, it is not charisma alone that defines leadership.

Fiscal Leadership

One of the contributing factors to the maturation of the spa industry has been the increase in leaders who practice sound business skills. Level Five leadership is not about ignoring fiscal responsibility or disregarding the basics of management and business.

Spas, like other businesses, have to measure their success in part by the revenue they generate and their profitability. Spa leadership must respond to this challenge with a delicate balance that focuses on both financial results and the guest experience. Ultimately, it is this balance that will ensure the health of both. If a spa leader focuses only on costs at the expense of the guest experience, it leads to the commoditization of the spa. Once that happens, guests are unlikely to pay higher prices for service they could get in a spa that keeps the guest experience as its central focus.

True leadership is the ability to look beyond short-term financial gain. A person possessing the heart and soul of a leader is able to articulate the importance of a long-term vision and convince everyone working in the spa to work toward the spa's best interest. This isn't to say that a spa leader can afford to ignore short-term financial success. Many leaders are required to submit monthly financial reports. However, the spa leader will need to be able to eloquently articulate why the finances are where they are and why the decisions made are fiscally sound for the spa.

The quick and easy path to profitability includes such things as working short-staffed, buying fewer professional products, and extending the life of linens beyond their comfort. These things can tempt a spa manager who searches for financial answers by cutting expenses. Cutting expenses can improve the bottom line in the short term, but operating with minimal staffing and worn-out linens will not sustain profitability.

The more desirable approach to increasing the profitability of a spa is to increase revenue rather than reduce expenses.

The focus on the spa's long-term good does not mean that a spa leader is able to ignore basic management functions. Rather, it is assumed that a spa leader already possesses these skills or is committed to learning such essential managerial requirements as:

- Analyzing financial statements
- Forecasting and budgeting
- Practicing revenue management
- Creating marketing and public relations initiatives
- Developing a compensation program
- Managing retail inventory
- Maintaining a customer feedback system
- Practicing strong human resources skills
- Developing a sense of place and design
- Organizing the workplace and attaining efficiency
- Controlling risks in the workplace

Exhibit 2 provides a few samples of the professional development tools available to assist leaders with developing these skills.

Becoming a Leader

A Level Five leader embodies the skills needed to take a spa from good to great. This type of leadership can distinguish a spa from its competitors and make the spa a unique place that transforms the lives of its guests.

It would be unrealistic to expect that every spa leader would possess Level Five leadership abilities or that there would be a team of Level Five leaders. Rather,

Exhibit 2   Educational Resources for Spa Leaders to Develop Management Skills

> The International SPA Association has developed educational resources to provide spa leaders with the tools necessary to successfully manage important skills required of spa leaders, including:
>
> - Uniform System of Financial Reporting for Spas
> - Retail Management for Spas
> - Compensation Workbook
> - Risk Management for Spas
> - Supervisory Skill Builders for the Spa Industry
> - Financial Management for Spas
> - Spa Professionals Career Guide
> - Spa Operations Manual
> - Extensive Catalog of Research

it is the job of spa directors to develop themselves and their spa teams in reaching their potential.

The real mission for senior management isn't the acquiring of management skills but of mentoring their supervisors and managers in these skills to prepare them for senior leadership. The same goes for students who are considering a career in spas—the earlier they learn the skills to manage a spa, the better their chances of advancing to senior management.

Exhibit 3 offers some tips for acquiring the traits of a leader.

Jim Collins was asked whether it is possible to learn to become a Level Five leader. His response was that he believed there were two types of people: those who could never become a Level Five leader because they are too egocentric and measure everything by what their personal gain will be, and those who have the potential to grow into Level Five leaders. It is his belief that the latter group is larger and that they can become Level Five leaders through self-reflection, conscious personal development, a mentor, a great teacher, loving parents, a significant life experience, a Level Five boss, or any number of other factors. They are people who are concerned not with fame, fortune, adulation, or power, but with what they build, create, and contribute.

The traits necessary for a Level Five leader—personal humility and professional will—are those that many spa leaders will be more comfortable with than the traditional celebrity-style leadership. Celebrity-style leadership is one in which a leader is expected to be highly charismatic or a celebrity savior who will turn the company around through sheer force of will and their unique vision. Rather, successful spa leaders are those who are determined and committed to their ideals. They are quick to give credit to their team members while taking personal responsibility for things that go wrong.

Collins divides the leadership circle into three main concepts: disciplined people, disciplined thought, and disciplined action.

Exhibit 3   Tips for Acquiring the Traits of a Leader

- Remember: You *can* learn leadership skills.
- Take good care of your body and your mind.
- Think before you speak.
- Consider the feelings of those who work for you.
- Set goals and become accountable for achieving those goals.
- Make your employees feel important, defend your employees, and show support for them.
- Be positive, not negative.
- Keep cool even under pressure.
- Learn to see the spa as a whole. How do other areas within the spa operate? How can your area support the whole organization better?
- Adopt a "mentor," someone whose leadership traits you admire. Talk to your mentor about leadership issues, and learn as much as you can from him or her.
- Lead by example.
- Keep current on industry trends, especially those that affect your staff.

Source: ISPA Foundation, *Supervisory Skill Builders for the Spa Industry,* Leadership book, p. 9.

Disciplined People

New leaders often make the current spa team nervous. For decades, management theory attributed the nervousness of an old team to a new leader as resistance to change. However, much of the nervousness may be attributed to concern about whether the leader would first get to know the organization before making changes.

One precarious model for taking over a new spa is to charge in with a new direction or a vision developed by that leader alone. Under that model, the leader might even commit the cardinal sin of telling everyone on the spa team, "This is how we did it at my old spa"—a statement that begs the question, "If it was so great at your old spa, why did you leave?"

Spa leadership isn't about changing everything, nor is it about arriving with a briefcase of strategies. Rather, it is about the people. Collins says it is not the "what" that matters, it is the "who." He uses the analogy of a bus in taking a business from good to great, and

> **"Great vision without great people is irrelevant."**
> **—Jim Collins, author of *Good to Great***

getting the right people on your bus (and in the right seats) and the wrong people off the bus. It is then important to decide where to drive the bus.

What is new about the notion of assembling a great team? The idea of surrounding yourself with good people is an old and useful one. Although the idea is

Spa Snapshot: Who has been your mentor and why?

Without question, Kathryn Tuckwiller holds that title for me. Kathryn was the spa director at The Greenbrier when I made my entry into "spa world." I interviewed with Kathryn when The Greenbrier Spa at Savannah Harbor was opening and knew immediately that this was a woman who possessed extensive knowledge of the industry, related well to all walks of life, and was willing to take a chance on someone who had a strong business background but no hospitality experience. Kathryn invested her time and energy in my development and to this day continues to welcome me when I seek advice. She taught me not only the "how" of spa management but the "why." She was tough, yet realistic. She was demanding, yet supportive. She was firm, yet understanding. She was, is, and I have no doubt, will continue to be my mentor, both personally and professionally.

—*Liz Hutto, Spa Director, The Watermark Hotel & Spa*

I have been able to work with amazing mentors. One in particular who I think is such a great visionary of spa, products, and the growing evolution of spa and its metamorphosis is Kerstin Florian. She is a leader that I have worked around on many occasions since I was a young girl, and she had a profound affect on how I viewed my role in the industry and how the job of spa orchestrator should be approached. As a woman who started in a skin care background with her own business—growing her company from the ground up to today servicing some of the highest-end spas on spa programming, training, and product authenticity—she has great talent. Watching her and her eye for detail is inspirational!

—*Jennifer Di Francesco, Spa Director, The Well at Miramonte Resort*

Jim Root has been one of my biggest mentors. Dwayne and I attended an ISPA Roundtable (now known as ISPA Knowledge Networks) at the Diplomat in Florida several years ago when Jim did a presentation on building your management practices around your organization's philosophy. Not only did he share some amazing "best practices," but he gave us job descriptions, management reports, facility brochures, company history, checklists for technicians, etc. I have contacted him on various occasions throughout the years or seen him at ISPA events and he'll never really know how much he has inspired me or motivated me to stay true to myself and my vision for The Spa at West End.

—*Stacy Coulter, Owner, Spa at West End*

Source: *Pulse*, September/October 2005

Spa Snapshot: What characteristics does a spa leader need to embody?

A spa leader must have empathy. This characteristic must apply to dealing with staff situations and customer issues. A spa leader must be open-minded and embrace change. A spa leader must have the courage of their convictions in maintaining the culture of the organization while working with entrepreneurs.

—*Wendy Clark, President, I-Bella*

The ability to be versatile, think out of the box, be a trendsetter and not a follower, and not be afraid to be different.

—*Loren Stone, CEO, Sovereign Hospitality*

A spa leader needs to have vision for the future and good communication skills. Never underestimate the value of the spoken word and the power it has to move people and inspire change. A leader also needs to have compassion and understanding – we are dealing with people's emotions on a daily basis, and a leader is able to balance the mechanics of the business with the intangible and very personal elements of the spa experience.

—*Darlene Fiske, Owner, The Fiske Group: Public Relations & Marketing Strategies*

A visionary who embodies the ability to listen, motivate, energize, create, develop, and love; who possesses humility; understanding of others; is a healer and a business-minded individual.

—*Sean Handler, Director of Sales, Solace Spa/Boyne USA*

Passion, commitment, integrity, creativity, honesty, respectful, innovative, professional, intelligent, and a sincere generosity of spirit

—*Wanda Love, Director of Sales & Marketing, Santé Spa*

I think any leader needs to be authentic – walk the walk. But since we deal in the world of touch, we need to be especially sensitive to the needs and emotions of therapists because they need to be centered and happy in order to deliver the best service.

—*Angela Cortright, Owner, Spa Gregorie's*

I believe that patience, integrity, and compassion are all keys to being a good leader in the spa.

—*Sara Cruncleton, Ihloff Salon & Spa*

easy to grasp, it is a very difficult thing to do, and most companies do not do it well. This may be especially true in the spa world as the explosive growth has made it difficult to attract and keep qualified employees. Spa leaders must be extremely disciplined to ensure that only the right people are hired—not just those who will fill the empty job quickest.

It takes tremendous discipline in decisions regarding employee selection to take a spa from good to great. Twenty years ago, hiring decisions were principally based on skills, education, and experience, but not so today. Great companies are now placing more weight on character attributes, giving rise to an increasing use of behavioral assessment tools in the hiring process.

Skills and traits may be learned, but character, passion, ethics, and values are ingrained.

Disciplined Thought

Once the right people are on the bus, the next step is for a spa to face the brutal facts. This step leapfrogs the conventional wisdom that the management team should be gathered in a conference room to brainstorm the spa's direction with a hope that a lightning bolt of inspiration will stimulate the creation of a vision for the business.

According to Collins, the process does not start with a dream of what the team would hope the spa might be, but with a disciplined analysis of the facts of the spa's current operations and place within the market. It is a process that requires the spa team to accept the facts rather than to put the most positive or comfortable spin on them.

The Level Five leader creates an environment where the truth is openly stated without fear of blame. The truth is welcomed as important to the process of introspection and identifying the best answers. There are many ways to cultivate this type of environment. One way is to hold no-agenda meetings with groups of employees or managers, opening with a "what's on your mind?" or "what is happening in the spa?" These non-agenda meetings often result in healthy debate and a surfacing of the truth of the business situation.

It is natural for leaders in an organization to believe that they were selected because they have the answers. However, in the same way spa leaders seek to engage the spa's guest in the spa experience, it is a characteristic of good leadership to engage the team in the process of dealing with the facts of exactly how things are in the current moment.

A Level Five leader is able to take all of the complex facts and ideas and bring them into one unifying, simple driving vision that can be communicated to everyone. It is a vision to which everyone in the spa can stay committed over the long term. Collins said companies that achieve greatness can articulate simple answers to the following questions:

- What are you deeply passionate about?
- What can you be best in the world at?
- What drives your economic engine?

reflections

Thad Hyland: Inspiring Everyone on Staff

Thad Hyland is the former managing director of the Ojai Valley Inn and Spa in Ojai, California. He led the property to earning the five diamond designation from the American Automobile Association (AAA).

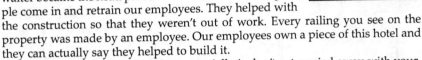

We take care of people, not in a patriarchal way, but in a respectful way. When something bad happens to someone at this property, we have a hardship fund and we help them. We were just voted for the fourth year in a row for L.A. County one of the best family businesses. We have child care; we have a great insurance program with low premiums; we have a health fair.

During our renovation, we retrained 250 people in construction arts. Our pastry chef was a welder, our head waiter became the head painter. We had construction people come in and retrain our employees. They helped with the construction so that they weren't out of work. Every railing you see on the property was made by an employee. Our employees own a piece of this hotel and they can actually say they helped to build it.

My philosophy of leadership essentially is don't get carried away with yourself. As a leader, you are a general practitioner and your associates and your department heads are specialists. If you have a problem with your throat, you go to a throat specialist. My maitre d' knows more about seating people and serving people than I do in the food and beverage realm. My chief engineer knows a lot more about high voltage electricity and I would not be in that manhole trying to flip a breaker. You have to hire for attitude, trust the people you hire, and trust that you did well.

Leadership is not a skill you're born with. It's a skill you have to learn. You never stop learning it and if you do, it's time for you to retire. Things change every day in this world.

We had an inspirational speaker come here about 10 years ago. At the end of the inspirational speech, the speaker asked (a question) through an interpreter of this lady who was in the front row. Her name is Nefertiti. The speaker asked, "Nefertiti, what job do you eventually aspire to? You're in housekeeping now. You just came from Mexico." Nefertiti looked at me—she'd only been here about a month or two—she pointed at me and said, "I want his job." And she's well on her way there now. She's our executive housekeeper of the hotel, speaks fluent English, is one of the best managers that I could ever imagine having. She's cross-training in the rooms division, but she went from not even speaking the language to there. Mentoring her is a pleasure. She had a passion from day one. She wants my job. I only hire people who want my job. Why would I want anyone else?

Disciplined Action

Collins also addresses a culture of discipline. When a spa's leader takes disciplined action, hierarchy, bureaucracy, and excessive controls are not needed. "When you combine discipline with an ethic of entrepreneurship," Collins wrote, "you get the alchemy of great performance."

reflections

Pam McNair: Each Spa Needs to Do What It Does Best

Pam McNair, the founder of Gadabout SalonSpas, is a visionary and one of the early day spa pioneers. She owns seven spas in the Tucson, Arizona, area and one in Italy.

As a day spa owner, I would like to leave the medi-spas to the doctors. We are not one of those day spas that wants to develop a medical spa. I think that over the past five years that has been a big question. Some have gone into medical spas and some have not. Some that have gone into medical spa services are now deleting them because they didn't have the information that they needed.

What if someone comes into your facility as a day spa and has a bad experience with a medical treatment? Does it not affect you? These are all questions that I had to ask myself because we have been solicited by doctors over and over again. They want to rent a room, develop a space, do laser treatments.

All I can think of is that personally our best interests have always been served when we do what we do best: that's servicing people with services that make them feel better when they leave than when they came. The downtime between a medical procedure and the feel good can be a week, ten days, or a month.

When we make everything look like it is great for everybody, we eliminate a lot of people. We made a decision a long time ago that we can't be all things to all people.

Bureaucracy is often created as a response to a few people who are doing things counter to an organization's mission. When policies and procedures are adopted to prevent such behavior, the creative spirit gets sapped.

For years, companies have invested thousands of hours developing job breakdowns or detailed standard operating procedure manuals for every function of the business that specify exactly how each function was to be conducted. Highly successful companies such as Nordstroms didn't have those standard operating procedures, but did have a standard statement that their employees would use their best judgment at all times. This creates disciplined action within a framework of intention, and employees do their jobs to accomplish the shared, driving vision.

Most standard operating procedures are designed to instruct employees on "what to do." Likewise, most training focuses on what or how to do something. Think of the difference that could be made if leadership focused on *why* something is done. This would provide the discipline to accomplish the basic service intention while creating a culture of freedom and responsibility within the spa. As Collins suggests, by getting the right people on the bus and the wrong people off, an organization doesn't need to create those rules that kill success.

All of this is not to say that all standard operating procedures should be thrown out. There are some that are necessary in order to create a framework for the overall experience at the spa. However, standard operating procedures should be used to communicate the spa's vision and a good leader is able to foster a balance between the procedures and the service intent that each staff member should bring to work each day.

Level Five leaders create a culture of discipline without being tyrants. They are not the ones who discipline, but rather they set an example of extreme self-discipline in which the spa is committed to sustained results, not responses to strong personalities.

Finally, Collins addresses technology as a factor in the success of great companies. Technology must be used to accelerate a company's momentum, not to create it. A spa can't adopt a new technology with the idea that the technology will create its success. Rather, it must know the direction it is headed in and use whatever technology is necessary to get it where it wants to go. If the technology fits immediately into what the spa is passionate about, what it can be best at, and what drives its economic engine, then the spa needs to adopt the technology or be a pioneer in implementing it. If it does not fit within those three circles, then the technology may not add value to the spa.

The Eighth Habit

There are now 8

Stephen R. Covey, author of *The Seven Habits of Highly Effective People,* followed up his highly successful book in 2004 with *The 8th Habit: From Effectiveness to Greatness.* His original seven habits were:

- Be proactive
- Begin with the end in mind
- Put first things first
- Think win/win
- Seek first to understand, then to be understood
- Synergize
- Sharpen the saw

Covey groups the first three habits under the expression "make and keep promises," the next three under "involve people in the problem and work out the solution together," and the final one as the commitment to increasing competency in the four areas of life: body, mind, heart, and spirit.

Covey encourages readers to find their own voices and inspire others to find theirs. This is fueled by one great overarching purpose: serving human needs. Covey emphasizes that leadership is not a position, it is a choice. Leadership is the very core of who a person is and something that individuals develop and refine throughout their lives.

> **"Being effective as individuals and organizations is no longer optional in today's world. It's the price of entry to the playing field. But surviving, thriving, innovating, excelling, and leading in this new reality will require us to build on and reach beyond effectiveness. The call and need of a new era is for *greatness*. It's for *fulfillment, passionate execution,* and *significant contribution.*"**
> —**Stephen R. Covey,** *The 8th Habit*

Leadership isn't the function of position. It is really the exercise of choice demonstrated through initiative and influence. People are not things needing to be motivated and controlled. They are four dimensional beings: body, mind, heart, and spirit. Society is no longer in the industrial age where leadership was thought to be a position that controlled, managed, and used the old carrot-and-stick in order to motivate people. Instead, the modern world is the information age where leaders respect their employees as whole people in a whole job who are paid fairly, treated kindly, and used creatively while being given the opportunity to serve human needs in principled ways.

Find Your Voice

Covey describes "voice" as each individual's unique personal significance: "Voice lies at the nexus of *talent* (natural gifts and strengths), passion (those things that naturally energize, excite, motivate, and inspire a person), need (including what the world needs enough to pay someone for), and conscience (that still, small voice within that assures a person of what is right and that prompts a person to actually do it)."[8]

His concept of voice is tied up with an individual's search for meaning and the path that they choose in life. He says that people choose one of two paths: the path to mediocrity or the path to greatness. Mediocrity occurs when people get caught up in their ego, indulgence, competition, and in being a victim. "Travelers on the upper path to greatness rise above negative cultural influences and choose to become the creative force of their lives."[9]

According to Covey, each person was given three gifts at birth that allow them to discover their voice. They are:

- The freedom and power to choose

- The natural laws or principles that are universal and never change

- Four intelligences/capacities

Freedom to Choose. Understanding that each person has the freedom and power to choose involves shunning a culture that is caught up in blame and victimhood. Whenever something happens, individuals have the power to choose their response and this choice will determine the quality of their life.

Natural Laws or Principles. Wisdom is found when people make the choice to "live by principles or natural laws rather than going along with today's culture of quick fix." Covey points out that principles such as fairness, kindness, respect, honesty, integrity, service, and contribution are universal and timeless. They transcend culture and are self-evident.

Four Intelligences/Capacities. Our nature is made up of four different types of intelligence: mental, physical, social/emotional, and spiritual. Mental intelligence is often referred to as IQ, the ability to reason, analyze, use language, think abstractly, visualize, and comprehend. Physical intelligence embodies all those things that bodies do without any conscious effort. It is the intelligence that runs our bodies' systems, such as breathing, circulation, and fighting disease. Social or emotional intelligence is often referred to as EQ and is a person's self-knowledge, self-awareness, social sensitivity, empathy, and ability to communicate successfully with others. Spiritual intelligence is "the central and most fundamental of all intelligences because it becomes the source of guidance of the other three. Spiritual intelligence represents our drive for meaning and connection with the infinite, Covey states.

Inspire Others to Find Their Voices

The process of inspiring others to find their voices is the heart of leadership. At the most basic level, Covey says, leadership "is communicating to people their worth and potential so clearly that they come to see it in themselves."

An organization, he says, is "made up of individuals who have a relationship and a shared purpose."

All spas have problems—very often the same problems, just with different personalities and characters. However, most problems have common roots. Those roots are found in the people that make up the organization. Spas can design all sorts of systems to control problems, but if they don't draw out the full potential of people, they're not going to succeed.

Covey also points out that personal leadership and leadership within an organization are knit together:

- Modeling (conscience): Set a good example.
- Pathfinding (vision): Jointly determine the course.
- Aligning (discipline): Set up and manage systems to stay on course.
- Empowering (passion): Focus talent on results, not methods, then get out of people's way and give help as requested.

Finally, he summarizes things with the words focus and execution. Leaders need to be focused on what matters most and then committed to executing what needs to happen.

Spa Leadership

Before moving on to ethics, there are some additional leadership concepts applicable to spas:

- Managing healers
- Strategic intent and transformational experiences
- Authenticity
- Communication

Managing Healers

Spa professionals frequently talk about how leadership in a spa is different than in other operations because of the types of people that look to the spa manager for leadership. Spa professionals must have the heart of a service provider and model how they want employees to treat guests.

reflections

Pam McNair: Inspiring Others to Reach Their Full Potential

I have more of a philosophy about leadership than any other area in our business because I believe it is a moral issue. I believe moral leadership is the future of any industry. If I don't hold my co-workers with respect, if I don't allow them to learn (if they don't already know) good self-esteem, how to communicate, how to listen to those voices that are in our heads that tell us all the time that we can't do something—then I'm not being a good leader.

The majority of people in our industry come to this industry as a last resort. They are sent to beauty school or cosmetology school or esthetic school because they didn't feel like they could qualify for college. They don't feel as though they can have another professional future. Maybe they weren't the best students in the world, and I'm saying this (despite the fact that) we now have college graduates who are working in this company in all areas. But as an industry, that is not who came to work here. It is really important for us as leaders to know whom we lead. All these great books and philosophies that you can read about and all these plans that you can set in motion, if who you are training doesn't fully understand the benefits to them to learn it, you isolate them. You continue that pattern of making people feel less than because you don't respect the fact that they can learn the information that is necessary to make them live with their full potential. Sometimes that means that after they've reached their full potential, they move on. But who of us wants to live in a stagnated place? If you can offer people a successful career in your company no matter what your company is, then there will be fewer who move on. But once you stagnate and stop teaching and stop learning yourself, you eliminate that whole ability to become something that maybe you never thought you could be. That's hope, that's inspiring, that builds passion in what you do.

Most of us are passionate about what we do because we see that we can be successful at it. Passion dies quickly if you don't think you can make it to the finish line. I believe as a leader my job is to teach those qualities and that culture to the people right around me whom I lead and then allow them to lead the next generation of people or the next group of technicians so that it isn't all about me and my ideas. It's about letting people learn what you know, being consistent with it, and letting them assimilate it and possibly teach it to the next generation of people in their own life. It doesn't always have to be taught the same way to learn the lesson.

Success is partnering with the people in life that you're with. Be open to the ideas and concepts of other people—that there may be a better way than the way you have. Analyze it, then let them go ahead with it, support it, and give them credit for it. That elevates their self-esteem and their ability to have a successful experience.

That's what moral leadership is.

Spa staff come to the spa from many walks of life. They are often people who want to help others. They are often people who are sensitive and open to emotion and the hurt that other people feel. As they minister to the needs and hurts of other people, they are going to have specific needs as well. The nature of the work that technicians do requires that they give of themselves all day long, every day. They need to have a way to "fill back up" and to take care of their own emotional needs

reflections

Elaine Trahan: When the Personal Affects the Professional

Elaine Trahan, spa director for Paris Parker Aveda Lifestyle Salon/Spa, is also a salon coach with more than 12 years of sales, training, and human resource experience. She customizes team building programs and conducts one-on-one coaching for businesses to increase motivation, set goals, establish priorities, and become change agents in their industry.

As a director, I have learned through experience that we hire for skills, but that what we really get is the person's whole life. The old paradigm that you leave your problems at the door is totally unrealistic.

I was assigned an experienced massage therapist. He was intensely frustrated because he and his new wife had just bought a new home and had a baby. Now the pressure was on him to produce. He was placed in our Leadership Circle because of his past experience and intellectual capital.

At one of the monthly meetings, I was delayed by the commuter interstate being shut down due to a fatal accident. During the meeting, he criticized my not being on time to the meeting in front of the entire team. This negative behavior by a designated leader was less than cohesive to the team and resulted in the group shutting down. When I did finally arrive, I could tell that the energy was extremely non-productive. I carried on with my planned agenda. He stayed after the meeting to repeat his negative comments to me personally.

Before I could address his comments, another team member who had witnessed the behavior offered her perspective voluntarily on how his behavior had flattened the team. Her questions to this leader were: "What was your intention? As a leader, your role is to constantly support the entire Leadership Circle. It takes a village to create a successful business to support each other moment to moment. What you did was less than leadership. It was actually counterproductive and you said it with negative tone."

As a result, the leader took responsibility for his words, tone, and body language and apologized to me. He expressed his extreme frustration around creating abundance for his new family and asked me not to take it personally. He has since resigned from the Leadership Circle and has chosen to concentrate on expanding his clientele to create abundance for his family. In addition, he apologized to the entire team at our next monthly meeting. He now has balance and focus that serves his life.

---

if they are going to be able to continue giving. The spa leader can play a crucial role in this.

That said, it is also important that the spa professional draws lines that he or she does not cross. At some spas, the owners or managers end up being held hostage to the demands of employees. At other spas, managers are insensitive to the unique needs of spa employees. The healthy spa environment is one where the spa leader is able to draw a balance and everyone is able to operate in a nurturing, appropriate fashion.

Spa professionals are expected to model the behavior that they want to see in the staff. They are expected to walk the walk and talk the talk of the spa world. It's not enough to tell the guest about a healthy lifestyle; leaders must model that behavior or the staff will see the disconnect. Leaders will be more effective if they reflect the mission.

Spa leaders are expected to be far more empathetic than leaders in other industries. The leadership must be heart centered. As one spa professional said, "They'll let you get away with eating at a fast food restaurant, but they won't let you get away with walking on people."

It is also important to note that some of these healers in the spa industry may eventually want to move up into management and become leaders. They will have to learn how to balance the business side of the spa with the nurturing, healing side.

Strategic Intent and Transformational Experiences

There are two great pieces of advice for leadership that speak directly to the spa world:

- The power of intention
- The power of transformational experience

Power of Intention. Everyone has had a service experience in which it is obvious that the service provider is following a script with little interest or passion for what he or she is saying. The words roll out in memorized fashion with little to no power or concern behind them. "Hello, my name is Rachanee, I'll be your server this evening."

Leaders must create ways to engage guests. The truly engaging experience surfaces only when the spa employee decides to enrich *how* he or she performs each activity. This means that spa leadership must work with the entire spa team to empower each individual team member to identify and use personal intention when interacting with the guest.

An acting instructor once said, "For every piece of work, one must describe his intention using the phrase 'in order to'." The same question must be asked in a spa environment. Why is each task being done? There should always be an answer that begins with "in order to." For example, the spa receptionist has a task that can be very repetitive and may result in monotone scripts. However, the purpose of that job is to truly engage the guest. How the engagement happens depends on the personal intention of the employee in that position. The spa leader could meet with reservationists and talk about their intention while talking with guests. This type of leadership can make the reservationist's job of entering the appointments into the computer or writing them on the scheduling sheet become incidental to the intention of "in order to provide the guest with treatment recommendations that match their needs" or "in order to extend the guest experience by suggesting complementary services or amenities."

Leaders must engage in creating a strategic intent with goals that are focused on making a real difference in the lives of spa guests and creating meaning for employees.

Power of Transformational Experience. The idea of transformational experience stems from the origins of U.S. spas in places like Canyon Ranch, Rancho La Puerta, and the Golden Door. Spa-goers would spend a week or more in programs to accomplish specific results like losing weight, completing a health evaluation, having personal time to focus on exercises, getting away from day-to-day demands, and putting life back into perspective.

Today's spas—indeed most of today's service businesses—realize that they have gone beyond simply providing a service to providing an experience that is in some way meaningful or transformative. Spa leaders must create the environment in which these transformational experiences can take place, not just for their guests, but for their employees as well.

Authenticity

Authenticity has long been a buzz word in the spa world. A spa that offers authentic treatments gains attractiveness in the eyes of consumers, while one that makes false claims causes harm to itself and to other spas.

However, authenticity does not begin and end with the spa treatment menu. Authenticity is a key quality of successful spa leaders. While there are many suggestions for effective leadership styles, there is no one-size-fits-all template any more than there is a single spa that meets the needs of every potential customer. Nor is leadership simply a garment that is put on or shrugged off at the entryway to the spa.

Being an authentic spa leader is as much about who a person *is* as it is what he or she *does*. Spa leaders can't simply play the part of leaders, they must be genuine in who they are and allow their natural strengths to help them lead.

Bill George, author of *True North* and *Authentic Leadership,* wrote that there are five dimensions of an authentic leader:

- Pursuing purpose with passion
- Practicing solid values
- Leading with heart
- Establishing enduring relationships
- Demonstrating self-discipline[10]

He further writes that each person's life story is what makes them unique as a leader. Being true to oneself and to each person that one comes into contact with is at the heart of authentic leadership. Truly authentic leaders, he explains, are those who are true to themselves by being the same person no matter where they are. They develop themselves as human beings and relate to others as human beings whether they are at work or at home.

Communication

Communication is the successful exchange of information from one person to another. Good communication is vital to a leader's success in the spa industry. The good news is that anyone can learn to communicate better. Communication is a skill and good communication requires practice.

People are known by what they say and how they listen—in other words, by how they communicate. A successful leader doesn't have to possess the communication skills of an evangelist such as Billy Graham or a charismatic U.S. president such as Ronald Reagan—although that wouldn't hurt—but they must have solid communication skills.

Many leaders use storytelling as the primary means by which they communicate their vision to their followers. The telling of stories provides listeners with mental maps that allow them to know what is important and how things are to be achieved.

Organizational leaders can use storytelling to paint the big picture, to teach management values, and to reinforce or change the company's culture. Memorable stories can also act as potent change mechanisms because they generate belief and encourage behavioral and attitudinal mind-shifts. Clearly, storytelling should be part of any leader's communication repertoire. If one does not already have the ability to tell stories effectively, like other communication skills, one can develop the ability through training and practice.

There are three primary channels or elements of communication: vocal, visual, and verbal. Vocal is the voice of the speaker and includes vocal variety, quality, rate, volume, and vocalized pauses. Visual is what a person sees when they look at the speaker. It includes eye contact, posture, gestures, and facial expressions. Verbal refers to the actual words of the speaker.

Nonverbal communication consists of the vocal and visual elements. It is *how* people say something, not *what* they say.

Vocal Communication. Each person's voice has unique characteristics. These characteristics should help spa leaders, not work against them, when they speak with employees or guests. The following vocal characteristics can be developed:

- **Variety.** It's difficult to listen to a person who never alters the tone or inflection of his or her voice when speaking. People who speak in a monotone sound uninterested. Using **variety** in tone adds interest and enthusiasm.

- **Quality.** It's important for spa leaders to have good vocal quality. This means the voice should not be nasal (through the nose) or breathy (shallow because too much air is escaping as the person speaks). Good vocal quality adds authority and believability to the words spoken.

- **Rate.** A spa leader should speak at a rate of speed that allows people to understand and remember what is being said. The rate should not be too fast, especially if the message includes many details or technical information. On the other hand, if the information is not technical, the rate should not be too slow, or listeners may become bored or offended, assuming the speaker is talking down to them.

- **Volume.** An important environmental element of a spa is a quiet atmosphere. A leader may choose to raise the volume of his or her voice to emphasize a point. Always talking loudly can have a negative effect on co-workers, but never speak so softly as not to be heard.

- **Vocalized pauses.** Vocalized pauses are made when speakers interrupt their message with "uhm," "er," or "ah." Vocalized pauses happen when speakers repeat phrases such as "you know" or "like." Leaders must make a deliberate effort to eliminate vocalized pauses from their speech because it sounds as if they're unsure of themselves. A spa leader always wants to speak with confidence.

Visual Communication. When people communicate, they get a great deal of information by looking at one another. The following elements can help or hinder communication:

- **Eye contact.** Eye contact is looking at a person while speaking with him or her. It is perhaps the most powerful form of nonverbal communication. When you use eye contact in communication, you're really saying, "I'm interested in you. I'm paying attention to you." Eye contact is a compliment to the other person. Alternatively, when leaders fail to make eye contact, the listener generally thinks they are unsure of themselves, lying, uninterested, or uncaring about the person with whom they are speaking.

- **Posture** is how people hold and carry their body. Posture sends very clear messages. For example, a person standing or walking with rounded shoulders or slouching sends a message of being tired, unassertive or bored. Spa leaders should carry themselves with ease and confidence. This means standing upright with shoulders back in a relaxed manner. They should carry their body as if they feel good about themselves, and their co-workers will get the message.

- **Gestures.** Gestures include moving hands, arms, shoulders, and even one's head while speaking. They can be used to help explain or support what is being said. Gestures add information and variety and impart information. For example, if employees play with their hair, chew on their lips or fingernails, or repeatedly fold and unfold a tissue, it might mean they are uneasy. People can reveal nervousness by repeating movements, including swinging their feet or drumming their fingers. One common gesture is crossing one's arms in front of one's chest. This can indicate anxiety, disagreement, or the desire to protect oneself. Be careful to consider the gesture in the context of the entire situation. Crossed arms might simply be a more comfortable position for a person.

- **Facial expressions.** The expression on a person's face reveals a lot about their attitude. Most people look at a person's face when they are talking. Facial expressions can communicate whether a person is happy, sad, angry, or confused. Facial expression is very natural, but some people avoid using it. These people use a "dead-pan" expression, showing no feelings through facial expression. Not only is it uninteresting to talk to a person with a dead-pan expression, but it also makes us uncomfortable because it's so unnatural. It is important to remember that facial expression is not always reliable. Many people have learned to fake a certain facial expression when they think it is expected. Also, facial expression does not always match the words a person is speaking. When this happens, people tend to believe the facial expression over the words.

Verbal Communication. Verbal communication is what a person actually says when speaking, not how the person says it. The following guidelines can help a leader's verbal communication to be more effective:

- Keep it simple. The most important guideline is to keep one's communication simple. What is the one main idea that the listeners need to remember? Leaders should state it simply and clearly.

- Explain or provide an example. Speakers should first state the point they're trying to make and then express the point in different words to explain it. They might also present an example or illustration.

- Use clear, direct words. The point of speaking is to have the listeners understand the message. Therefore, use language that can be easily understood. Choose words that are the exact, appropriate meaning for what you want to say.

- Respect your listeners. Leaders should keep the listeners' interests in mind and let them know how the information can help and how to apply it. When speaking with one individual, spa leaders should use the person's name. People are complimented when their names are used. Leaders should always treat their listeners as people who are important.

- Repeat the main idea. Before finishing a message, leaders should repeat their main idea to emphasize it and help the listeners remember it.

- Check for understanding. Leaders should occasionally ask whether they can clarify anything or whether the listener has any questions.

Listening. Many people believe hearing is listening. That is, if they can hear what a person is saying, they're listening. Listening goes far beyond just hearing, however. Good listening involves four distinct steps:

- Paying undivided attention
- Attaching meaning
- Evaluating the message
- Responding and remembering

It is also important to ensure that the place where the listening is taking place is conducive to good communication and appropriate to the level of importance of the message. A performance evaluation or discipline session would not be conducted in the hallway as the therapist was on the way to greet a guest, but that might be a moment to praise them for solving the previous guest's problem.

A good listener is an active participant in the communication process. Good listeners are involved verbally, nonverbally, mentally, and physically.

Listeners get involved verbally by using verbal responses to a speaker. They can encourage the speaker by occasional comments such as "I see," "Tell me about that," or "That's interesting." They can ask the speaker questions when a point is not clear or when they want more information. They can also get involved verbally by using a technique called paraphrasing. When they paraphrase, they repeat to the speaker in their own words what they think he or she has said. Paraphrasing allows listeners to check with the speaker to see whether they have correctly understood what was said.

Listeners get involved nonverbally by giving speakers good nonverbal feedback. This means using good eye contact—looking at the speaker as he or she talks, giving appropriate facial or head responses, such as a smile or a nod of approval. Active listeners also observe the speaker's nonverbal behavior. How the speaker says something may be more important than the actual words spoken. Observing the speaker's nonverbal behavior helps the listener find the feelings hidden behind the speaker's ideas.

Listeners get involved mentally by trying to pick out the main idea being presented. Active listeners summarize the points the person is making and ask themselves whether there are things the speaker is saying that are unclear or about which they want more information.

Listeners get involved physically by taking notes. They may need to write down a few facts for later reference. Another good retention method is for the listener to report or repeat what they hear. This makes them more likely to remember the information. Listeners do need to take care that the notetaking doesn't become the focal point—it should be an aid to later memory, not a way to occupy the listener so that some of the speaker's message goes unheard.

Poor listeners have bad habits that can be broken. Several common bad listening habits include:

- Interrupting. This is a clear message to the speaker that what the listener has to say is more important than what the speaker is saying. Hearing a person out is a wonderful compliment. It says, "I value what you have to say."

- Prejudging. When listeners prejudge, they assume they know the point the person is making rather than waiting until it has been said.

- Script-writing. This is when a listener mentally prepares his or her response while the other person is still speaking. Good listeners concentrate on the speaker and what he or she is saying.

- Reacting emotionally. Everyone has **emotional triggers**—words, issues, or personalities that seem to excite or irritate them. When a co-worker sets off an emotional trigger, spa leaders need to try to concentrate on the issue, not the emotion.

Spa Ethics

No discussion of spa leadership is complete without a discussion of ethics. Imagine the following situation taking place in a hotel spa:

> The lead therapist storms into the storage closet where the retail manager is taking an inventory of professional product. "Look at this!" she said angrily. "Yesterday, the spa manager told us the commission structure was going to stay unchanged, and here's an e-mail from the hotel general manager ordering that retail sales commissions be given only to retail sales clerks, not to therapists."
>
> "That's terrible!" the retail manager says. "Where'd you get that e-mail, anyway?"
>
> "The spa manager once asked me to print out a document for her and I remembered the password. I read her e-mail occasionally so I know what is happening. That woman is such a liar!"

In the situation above, the spa manager should not have shared her password and if she knew about the changes to the commission structure when she told her supervisors there wouldn't be any, she acted unethically by lying. The therapist acted unethically by using the manager's password, reading and printing the manager's e-mails, and showing the copy to a co-worker.

An ethical environment helps to create a place of trust where managers and employees tell the truth and respect each other. Ethics support a life of leadership and turn it into a transformative experience for guests and employees.

Ethics Defined

Philosophers through the centuries have attempted to define **ethics**. Ethics can be described as choosing the better choice between two rights. It can be described as what ought to be. It can be described as the study of moral principles concerning rightful conduct based on a culture's most deeply held values.

Being ethical involves more than just obeying laws and regulations. Being ethical means having moral principles that guide one's behavior. Stealing an employee's idea and telling someone else it was original, excluding some employees from departmental lunches, or telling ethnic jokes may not be illegal in all cases, but they certainly are not ethical. Being ethical is doing the right thing when nobody's looking.

Having a sense of ethics also means seeing the larger principle involved in small actions. For example, most spa employees would recognize that accepting sexual advances from a guest, taking home spa equipment such as a paraffin warmer, or taking money out of the till is wrong. However, would those same employees equally regard as wrong such things as punching a time card for someone else, making personal calls on the spa's toll-free lines, or taking professional products home?

The spa world faces several ethical challenges, some of which are shared with other businesses, while others are unique to the environment and concerns of spas. Exhibit 4 is the code of ethics that ISPA has developed in cooperation with spa professionals. Other third party professional bodies have also established professional ethics standards that govern the actions of spa staff. For example, massage therapists in Ontario, Canada, are regulated by the College of Massage Therapists of Ontario (CMTO). The CMTO has a very strict code of ethics, breach of which would cause a registered massage therapist to lose his or her registration and ability to practice as a registered massage therapist. Likewise, financial controllers might be governed by strict ethics that are a requirement to practice under particular accounting designations. Between personal, company, association, and government laws, there are often several sets of ethical standards to which people must adhere. Exhibit 5 shows the code of conduct and ethics that the International Medical Spa Association developed for its members.

Before delving into specific ethical issues for spas, this chapter will first address ethics in a broader sense.

Ethical discussions focus on the "right thing to do" or the "wrong thing to do." When used in this way, "right" and "wrong" are ethical terms. However, "right" and "wrong" are not always used in the ethical sense. For example, we could say

Exhibit 4 Code of Ethics

ISPA Member Code of Ethics

- Member will be guided in all activities by truth, accuracy, fairness, and integrity.

- Member pledges loyalty to the Association and agrees to pursue and support its objectives.

- Member pledges to keep informed on the latest techniques, developments, and knowledge pertinent to professional improvement.

- Member will help fellow members reach personal and professional fulfillment.

- Member will utilize every opportunity to enhance the public image of the spa industry.

Exhibit 5 Code of Ethics

International Medical Spa Association Code of Ethics

1. A member of the International Medical Spa Association and staff will provide competent care; delivered with respect for its clients' dignity and rights.

2. A member of the International Medical Spa Association and staff will provide only those treatments, products, and services that are safe, effective, and of the highest quality.

3. A member of the International Medical Spa Association and staff will uphold the highest standards of professionalism, be honest in all professional interactions, and shall not engage in fraudulent, deceptive, or unethical practices.

4. A member of the International Medical Spa Association and staff will make a commitment to on-going education, to the application of that knowledge toward improving services and treatments, and to making the most accurate information available to its clients and the public as a whole.

5. A member of the International Medical Spa Association and staff will respect the rights of its clients and staff to confidentiality and privacy.

6. A member of the International Medical Spa Association and staff will adhere to the laws, rules, and regulations governing the provision of treatments and services as required by the state in which it operates.

7. A member of the International Medical Spa Association and staff will respect and value the community in which it operates and look for opportunities to actively support and improve the health and well-being of that community.

Source: The International Medical Spa Association, www.medicalspaassociation.org. For more information, call 201-865-2065.

that the right way to set up a book display in the spa's retail area is with the cover facing out, not the spine. There is no ethical or moral dimension to how we display the book, but there is when we discuss photocopying pages out of the book to give to spa guests who are not purchasing the book.

So what exactly puts something in the "moral" or "ethical" category? Ethical or moral norms concern a group's deeply-held values, the things most cherished and things most despised. As such, ethics involve actions that are believed to either greatly benefit or greatly injure people, organizations, or social structures. Ethical or moral norms are held to be more important than other values such as self-interest or material comfort. If there is a conflict between "doing the right thing" and doing something that is wrong, but makes us wealthier, or more comfortable—we should do the right and ethical thing.

Theories and Approaches to Ethics

Utilitarianism. Some ethical theories argue that the *consequences* of an action make it either moral or immoral. Thus, an action that leads to beneficial consequences is right and moral, and one that leads to harmful consequences is wrong or immoral. Utilitarianism holds that an action is morally justified to the extent that it maximizes benefits and minimizes harm or costs. Thus, the moral thing to do in any situation is that action that can be reasonably seen to provide the greatest *net* benefit for all concerned, when the expected costs are subtracted from the expected benefits. To do something else is to behave unethically, and the more an alternative action maximizes net costs or net harm, the more immoral it becomes. The shorthand often used to describe utilitarianism is that it calls for "the greatest good for the greatest number of people."

Kantian Ethics. Immanuel Kant, an eighteenth century German philosopher (1724–1804), developed an approach to ethics very different from utilitarianism. Kant argued that the consequences of an action are irrelevant to a moral evaluation of that action. His theory proposed that actions are moral or immoral because of their very nature, not because of their consequences. For Kant, their nature stems from the type of rules they follow, and it is on the basis of the rule followed that an action can be morally judged.

For Kant, it is the motivation behind an action that makes it morally worth praising or condemning. Moral actions are undertaken out of a sense of *duty*— which means you do it because you know it is the "right thing to do." Actions that are undertaken simply because you enjoy them, for example, do not take on a moral character, even if they result in many positive benefits for others. Likewise, actions can be immoral even if they result in positive benefits for others. For example, a spa could claim that a signature facial was based on an ancient healing tradition even though it was simply the result of a staff brainstorming session. The guest might still reap the benefits of the treatment, the estheticians might have more work, and the spa might make more revenue. However, under Kantian ethics, it would still be immoral because of the nature of the false claim.

Ethic of Justice. "Justice" is a word often used when making moral judgments. Most people believe in justice and oppose injustice, but what exactly does this mean? Usually, justice is thought of as "being fair." Justice requires that people treat others fairly and treat like cases alike. Justice is a comparative term: it involves comparing cases and making sure that we are not discriminating or treating people differently who are alike in relevant respects. To a certain degree, our notion of justice is based on the notion of individual rights. A violation of an individual's rights is considered an injustice.[11]

Social Responsibility and Business Ethics

It is important to distinguish between social responsibility and business ethics. The concept of social responsibility suggests that "at any one time in any society there is a set of generally accepted relationships, obligations, and duties between the major institutions and the people. Philosophers and political theorists have called this set of common understandings 'the social contract.'" This contract differs among societies and may change over time. For example, today we expect that businesses will take care (1) not to pollute the air or the water, (2) not to damage the ozone layer, (3) to offer fair wages and employee benefits, (4) to provide a satisfactory product or service at a reasonable price, and (5) to participate in making the community in which they operate a better place. These are not ethical considerations—they are part of a "deal" that says that consumers expect companies to act in this manner because they are part of society.

Many spas recognize this and have stated publicly their belief that it is good business to be a good citizen. They support local arts, raise funds for charities, and put some of their profits into the communities that have made their success possible.

Implementing Ethics

Business ethicists agree that without ethical leadership at the top of an organization, dishonesty multiplies rapidly in the lower ranks. Managers who fail to communicate ethics to their employees send the unspoken message that it is acceptable to cheat. That doesn't mean that every employee will behave dishonestly. The honest ones will stay honest, but they will become demoralized and move on.

When managers are unethical, or tolerate unethical behavior, business suffers. It is very easy to rationalize breaches of business ethics by saying, "Who'll ever notice?" or "Who's it going to hurt?" or "It's just a drop in the bucket." But there's a big connection between ethics and the bottom line.

Most people know right from wrong. The difference between ethical and unethical people is that the ethical ones *care* about being ethical.

Experts also stress that you can't expect to respond ethically to larger issues if you don't exercise your sense of ethics on the smaller ones. One way to exercise your sense of ethics is to consider hypothetical situations and decide how you would respond ethically to them. Discussing these circumstances with fellow workers can help you resolve what to do when these situations arise.

Tips for acting ethically:

- If employees are doing something unethical that they have learned from the leader, the leader needs to admit he or she was wrong and model appropriate behavior. For example, the leader could say: "I used to run personal mail through the postage meter, too, but it's wrong. I wrote a check to the spa to cover the past charges and I don't do it anymore."

- Offer employees a reminder of the rules that govern ethical behavior: "I know you wouldn't take home spa bathrobes, but taking home professional product is just as wrong, and won't be tolerated."

- Learn to say no: "I know we've been friends for a long time, but I can't hire your son because he's not qualified for the job."

- Clearly communicate and model adherence to the policies and rules of conduct. Be sure to discuss the spa's commitment to ethics during employee orientation and make ethics a topic in the employee handbook.

- Make sure employees know the legal requirements of the job. For example, make sure therapists have the correct certifications for any service they perform.

- Don't ask employees to do something that is unethical or illegal, such as running personal errands for management during working hours.

- Discuss ethics periodically during team meetings.

- Acknowledge or reward employees who demonstrate ethical behavior. This reinforces leadership's commitment to ethics in a positive way.

Even with laws and spa policies and rules, ethical behavior is an intensely personal decision for every manager and employee. There are no easy guidelines that apply equally well in all circumstances. Ethical philosophers often talk about the moral duty of taking into account the interests of all stakeholders in arriving at a decision.

Stakeholders are all who are affected by the outcome of a given decision. These could be employees, one's boss, the owners of the company, the families of employees, or the community in which the spa operates. Sometimes managers or employees who are forced to implement unethical policies become whistleblowers and let other stakeholders or authorities know what is happening regarding an unethical action or plan.

In their book *The Power of Ethical Management*, Ken Blanchard and Norman Vincent Peale list three simple questions that they believe managers should ask themselves when making a decision:

1. *Is it legal?* Will I be violating either civil law or company policy?

2. *Is it balanced?* Is it fair to all concerned in the short term as well as the long term? Does it promote win-win relationships?

3. *How will it make me feel about myself?* Will it make me proud? Would I feel good if my decision were published in the newspaper? Would I feel good if my family knew about it?

Code of Conduct

Ethics and conduct are two concepts that play important roles in spas. Spas around the world are devoted to enhancing the overall well-being of their guests through professional services that encourage the renewal of mind, body, and spirit. To achieve this, spa professionals must respect the needs and limits of their guests

Spa Snapshot: What are some of the most difficult ethical decisions you make?

Treating all cases equally to the customer and the staff.

—*Loren Stone, CEO, Sovereign Hospitality*

I embrace the assumption that 99 percent of the people who cross your path (guests, employees, vendors) have the best of intentions. I am going to treat 100 percent of them as honorable individuals. It is difficult when you come across the one percent who truly take advantage of your operation; however, it is not worth treating them any differently than an honorable individual.

—*Sean Handler, Director of Sales, Solace Spa/Boyne USA*

We're very strict on making any unsubstantiated health claims, so we are constantly reviewing what product/equipment reps are claiming about their product and securing appropriate test results and documentation to support the claims before sharing any of them with guests.

—*Wanda Love, Director of Sales & Marketing, Santé Spa*

and staff. As part of the service encounter, they must act responsibly with regard to important issues that affect comfort and safety.

The International SPA Association and the ISPA Foundation partnered with the Resort Hotel Association to develop a Code of Conduct so that spa goers are aware of their rights and responsibilities once they enter a spa. The intent was to enhance the level of comfort for spa-goers. "Consumers want to be free to express their expectations and concerns and feel safe in the process," said 2006–2008 ISPA Chairman Jim Root. "With the development of this new code, both parties are able to share in the responsibility of creating an engaging and empowering spa experience."

The code of conduct reads:

As a Spa Guest, it is your responsibility to:

1. Communicate your preferences, expectations, and concerns.
2. Communicate complete and accurate health information and reasons for your visit.
3. Treat staff and other guests with courtesy and respect.
4. Use products, equipment, and therapies as directed.
5. Engage in efforts to preserve the environment.
6. Adhere to the spa's published policies and procedures.

As a Spa Guest, you have the right to:

1. A clean, safe, and comfortable environment.
2. Stop a treatment at any time, for any reason.
3. Be treated with consideration, dignity, and respect.
4. Confidential treatment of your disclosed health information.
5. Trained staff who respectfully conduct treatments according to treatment protocols and the spa's policies and procedures.
6. Ask questions about your spa experience.
7. Information regarding staff training, licensing, and certification.

Ethical Issues in Spas

Each day spa managers are faced with a variety of business decisions with ethical overtones.

Linda K. Enghagen surveyed 113 four-year colleges and universities on ethical issues in hospitality and tourism. While a total of 35 different issues were raised, the ten that were most mentioned were:

- Managing an ethical environment
- Relations with customers and employees
- Honesty
- Employee privacy rights
- Alcohol/drug testing
- Environmental issues
- Relations with foreign governments
- Codes of ethics and self-governance
- Employee abuse of alcohol or drugs
- Conflicts of interest[12]

These issues reflect the academic perspective. Industry leaders have cited many other ethical concerns. These include:

- Sustainability
- AIDS in the workplace
- Advertising claims
- Concealing income from the Internal Revenue Service
- Kickbacks
- Raiding of competition's staff
- Meeting the needs of customers and employees with disabilities
- Adequate safety and security measures

Spa Snapshot: What is the most pressing ethical issue that spas face on an ongoing basis?

Delivering what they say they can deliver in products and services. There are too many products out there that claim to help with anti-aging or improve this or that. I know that a lot of these products and treatments are to latch onto the trend, but can we be sure that they all are delivering the results that we claim?

—*Loren Stone, CEO, Sovereign Hospitality*

Therapy is all about the individual. There is no place for EGO inside a spa. Communication, confidentiality, and boundaries are never to be compromised.

—*Sean Handler, Director of Sales, Solace Spa/Boyne USA*

There is a decided lack of commitment to safety and hygiene standards in favor of reducing costs. There are also unsubstantiated health claims on products and equipment.

—*Wanda Love, Director of Sales & Marketing, Santé Spa*

I think that corporate-owned spas will always have the ethical challenge of doing what is right for the guest/environment/community vs. what is right for the bottom line.

—*Angela Cortright, Owner, Spa Gregorie's*

- Adequate health practices
- Guest medical history and well-being
- Personal dignity

This text will look at a few of these issues.

Sustainability. Preserving and protecting the resources of the planet has become a topic of major importance. Spas, which have always been about restoring and regenerating the human body, spirit, and mind, also must ensure that they are contributing to renewing planetary resources. There are many elements to **sustainability**, from energy management to waste reduction to design. Spas, which are about water by definition, also have a responsibility with regard to water conservation.

The very nature of what spa means builds in an additional layer of responsibility to foster the health of the environment. It actually becomes part of the spa experience when the spa is dedicated to a healthy environment. A spa might grow its own organic foods or selectively choose the materials that make up the spa, making only those choices that limit the environmental footprint.

AIDS in the Workplace. AIDS is a good example of how prejudice and hysteria have affected some managers' ability to make fair and impartial decisions. Some people believe that AIDS carriers ought to be identified through testing, so that they can be informed and prevented from spreading the disease. But as columnist William Schneider points out, "What about their right not to be forced to learn whether they are under a probable sentence of death?" There are other rights involved as well. Should employees who have tested HIV positive, but have no symptoms of AIDS (and may never have) be hired or promoted? One could argue that they may not be able to stay in a position long enough to benefit the employer, but no one knows how long a person in this situation will remain healthy, and to deny him or her a well-deserved job or promotion seems unfair by any standard. The issue is most often not one of promotion but simply of keeping one's job. It is illegal in the United States to discriminate against AIDS-infected workers, since (1) they are considered "disabled," and (2) their condition cannot be transmitted via food or casual contact, according to the latest scientific studies.

Advertising Claims. The purpose of advertising is to sell products and services. Most people understand this and therefore are skeptical about advertising claims. Most people rely on recommendations from friends, relatives, and peers when making spa plans, and the claims made in brochures, advertising, and on websites may not be believed.

There is a difference between exaggerated claims and outright deception. Spas that advertise that they are "on the beach" should be on the beach and not across the street from it. If a rate is advertised, it should be one that is readily available and not one offered only every third Tuesday if the esthetician feels like coming in that day. Likewise, when spas claim to have a certain amount of square footage, that square footage needs to be of the facility devoted to the spa. Is it acceptable for a property to claim that a fitness room converted to a treatment room is a spa? Resorts in particular must be careful about what they claim.

Unlike a television set or a sweater, which can be returned if it is not satisfactory, a spa treatment is not returnable and represents an investment in time that cannot be replaced. Spa professionals have a moral duty to disclose all of the relevant details of their spas so that guests can make a fair judgment as to whether their expectations are going to be met.

Sanitation. Guests put their trust in spa professionals that the spa environment is safe and healthy. They rely on the spa to follow strict sanitation rules to prevent diseases from pedicure stations or wet lounges and shower areas. Products should not be used past their expiration dates and treatment rooms should be thoroughly cleaned and sanitized between guests, with all linen changed and washed.

Spa Treatment Claims. Spa professionals must be careful about claims they make about their treatments and the treatment origins. If a particular treatment is described in the spa menu, then that is the treatment that should be offered. The treatment must have the tradition and heritage that the menu claims. There have been spas that have made up fake treatments or used a treatment they had no right to use. When a spa develops proprietary treatment protocols, they are not to be used by a therapist who leaves for another spa. Issues have also arisen about whether some treatments are truly indigenous or taking advantage of the interest in a culture without truly drawing from the culture.

Likewise, spa professionals need to carefully examine the claims made by product representatives. Does their product do what they claim or are the claims exaggerated?

Some spas have struggled with therapists who hand out business cards for their own private business to their guests at the spa property. Soliciting private business is generally considered unethical.

Guest Medical History and Well-Being. Spas collect health and medical information for a good reason. Certain physical conditions may suggest the need to modify or even refuse treatment. Spa professionals need to help the guest make the best choices. Management has a responsibility to ensure that spa staff understands what medical and health conditions preclude which treatments. Professional staff members receive training in this area, but reception and technician employees should also be familiar with contraindications.

Also, some things shouldn't be talked about. Staff must avoid giving a diagnosis if they are not qualified to do so. They also must be careful that they don't impose spiritual or political beliefs on their clients. They also should not allow guests to talk them into providing services or treatments for which they have not received training or certification.

Government regulations also exist in many countries that dictate how health information can be used. In some countries it may be illegal for some types of medical information to be gathered, stored, or shared with any except specific care-providers. Spa professionals need to be aware of these laws and aware of their guest expectations. It may not be illegal for therapists to talk about their guests' physical ailments outside of the workplace, but it could very well be unethical.

Personal Dignity. Protection of personal privacy is a constant concern in spas. Many treatments require partial or complete undress. In many cultures, removal of clothing carries a sexual connotation, inappropriate to a spa environment. Also, no one wants to be caught in a state of undress unexpectedly.

Spa is a high-touch industry that provides personal services. This, too, may generate discomfort or embarrassment in guests. There are three ways to protect guests' personal privacy:

- Restrict access to treatment areas
- No phones
- Employee discretion

It is equally important to protect staff members' personal dignity from unethical situations that can arise from guests. The warm intimacy of the spa environment is rich soil for social misunderstandings, miscommunications, and "advantage-taking" behavior. At times, it may be necessary to refuse to serve a guest, or to terminate a service before it is finished. There are some circumstances that require a therapist or manager to say no. Perhaps the guest becomes unwell during treatment. Perhaps the guest arrives emotionally distressed or behaves inappropriately. Intoxication, offensive language, sexual misconduct, or even medical emergencies may precipitate the need to stop the treatment or service.

There are many policies, procedures, and guidelines to help with ethical issues that spas must create and adhere to. These can include providing private changing areas; offering robes, towels, and closing doors; explaining draping techniques and treatment protocols before starting treatment; and making sure guests know the clothing requirements of each service. Guests should be allowed plenty of time to change and told that they may wear more clothes if they choose.

Staff should follow standard protocols for draping, exposing only the part of the body being treated. Therapists should also understand cultural differences regarding modesty, touch, and treatment techniques.

Finding Success

Leaders help to cultivate the heart and soul of a spa. They are the humble, determined drivers who can steer a spa to greatness while uplifting the spirit of employees and guests. It is a role that is a sacred trust for the dual tasks of ensuring a spa's success while creating serenity and renewing the hearts, minds, bodies, and souls of all who enter its doors.

The spa leader is a person who can relate to others with empathy and who can live the message of spa in an authentic, passionate, and ethical manner.

Leadership implies the need to guide and influence—rather than to order—employees to undertake specific actions. The role of the leader is fast becoming that of a facilitator and coach (one who assembles resources and provides guidance) as opposed to the dictatorial taskmaster of yesterday. The leader who is flexible will likely be better able to provide an environment that is nurturing and effective.

What makes a leader a success? We'll close this chapter with words from spa leaders throughout the industry on how they define success:

"For me, success is not acquiring things and a lot of money. Success is having financial freedom and flexibility, absolutely loving what you do, and hopefully having a career like mine in that my love and passion for what I do impacts on other people. Passion, persistence, professionalism, and power equals success."

—*Sheila Cluff, owner and founder of The Oaks at Ojai*

"My degree of success is measured by the friendships I've made. I don't view my success on monetary or business or where I've come in my career, but more in the connections I've made with the people in my path."

—*Michael Tompkins, general manager of Miraval Life in Balance*

"We like a little edge. We want to be confronted. We want to test ourselves, not unduly, not by trying to climb Mount Everest necessarily, but in an everyday sort of thing. We like to grow and think that we are becoming more intelligent and having a little more wisdom about life every day ... It's been a full life. What else do you need?"

—*Peter de Caprio, owner, Noelle Spa for Beauty and Wellness*

"I've always known that success is only sweet if you're there with other people. If you get wherever you think you're going and you're all alone, you're a failure. My definition of success is realizing what is possible and then, with help, achieving your full potential for now. That is not a forever thing."

—*Pam McNair, owner, Gadabout SalonSpas*

"Part of my intention is to move away from being controlled and motivated by those things that are being motivated by fear. Success is being as present as I can be, living with a sense of reward as I understand the opportunities in my life that are truly rewarding. My sense of success is to go deeper to understand truth."

—*John Lopis, CEO of The Lodge at Woodloch*

"Success is balance. It's coming to work and loving my job every day. I love what I do."

—*Michelle Kinney, spa director, Alvadora Spa at the Royal Palms Hotel*

"If I look back at my day and everyone I touched during that day was happy with how I treated them; if the contact I made with each one of those people was good, that's success. If I don't have any remorse about how I handled anyone or how I treated anyone, I think that's pretty successful."

—*Jason de Caprio, hair stylist, Noelle Spa for Beauty and Wellness*

"To be successful is to wake up in the morning and know that you have to face a day that you're going to give as much as you can in order to succeed. When I lay my head down at the end of the day on my pillow, I feel like I've accomplished everything that I could for that day, and I have to be well with that. I have to be good with that. To me, that's success. Just live it."

—*Jana Westerbeke, vice president, Gadabout SalonSpas*

"My definition of success is getting my message out there. When you have made a change in someone else's life—that to me is more important than anything else I could ever do."

—*Dr. Howard Murad, founder, Murad Inclusive Health System*

"The successful leader or manager isn't the person who can last the longest in a day and occupy a desk. It's the manager that manages smartly, manages their time, and communicates with the individuals they're leading. So that (the individuals they are leading) have a general idea of what the goal is and they are able to use their own personality and ingenuity to accomplish this."

—*Thad Hyland, former managing director, Ojai Valley Inn and Spa*

 # Endnotes

1. Notes taken from ISPA Roundtable in June 2007, Washington, D.C., with Larry Prochazka as the speaker.

2. Robert L. Katz, "Skills of an Effective Administrator," *Harvard Business Review,* (September-October, 1974), pp. 99–102.

3. Warren Bennis and Burt Nanus, *LEADERS: The Strategies for Taking Charge* (New York: Harper & Row, Perennial Library Edition, 1986) p. 21.

4. Bennis, et. al. p. 22

5. Jim Collins, *Good to Great*, (New York: HarperCollins Publisher, 2001), p. 3.

6. Collins, pp. 12–13.

7. Collins, p. 21.

8. Stephen R. Covey, *The 8ᵗʰ Habit: From Effectiveness to Greatness*, (New York: Free Press of Simon & Shuster, 2004).

9. Covey, p. 28.

10. Bill George, *True North*, (San Francisco: Jossey-Bass, 2007), p. xxxi.

11. For a more complete discussion on the types of ethics and their significance, read Karen Lieberman and Bruce Nissen, *Ethics in the Hospitality and Tourism Industry*, 2nd ed., (Lansing, Mich.: American Hotel & Lodging Educational Institute), 2008.

12. Linda K. Enghagen, "Students' Perceptions of Ethical Issues in the Hospitality and Tourism Industry," *Journal of Hospitality & Tourism Research*, Vol. 15, No. 2, (1992), pp. 41–50.

Additional Reading

Bennis, Warren, and Burt Nanus, *LEADERS: The Strategies for Taking Charge* (New York: Harper & Row, Perennial Library Edition, 1986).

Collins, Jim, *Good to Great*, (New York: HarperCollins Publishers, 2001).

George, Bill, *True North* (San Francisco: Jossey-Bass, 2007).

Lieberman, Karen, and Bruce Nissen, *Ethics in the Hospitality and Tourism Industry*, 2nd ed., (Lansing, Mich.: American Hotel & Lodging Educational Institute), 2008.

Woods, Robert H., and Judy Z. King, *Leadership and Management in the Hospitality Industry*, 2nd ed., (Lansing, Mich.: American Hotel & Lodging Educational Institute), 2002.

Key Terms

communication—The successful exchange of information from one person to another.

conceptual skills—Abilities of managers to see beyond technical aspects and recognize the interdependence of the various departments within the spa.

controlling—Translating the spa's goals and objectives into performance standards and assessing actual performance against standards.

coordinating—Achieving an efficient use of resources to attain the spa's goals and objectives.

directing—Influencing others to accomplish the spa's goals and objectives.

emotional triggers—Words, issues, or personalities that excite or irritate a person.

empowerment—Giving employees the authority to make decisions and work choices without direct input from managers.

ethics—Making the better choice between two rights. The moral principles that guide behavior and choices.

human relations skills—Abilities of managers to work effectively with people at every level of the spa.

level five leaders—A concept developed by Jim Collins that describes leaders who build greatness through a blend of personal humility and professional will.

management functions—Categories that describe the activities management performs. They include planning, organizing, coordinating, staffing, directing, and controlling.

nonverbal communication—A combination of vocal and visual elements. It is how something is said, not what is said.

organizing—Determining how to accomplish goals and objectives.

planning—Establishing goals and objectives to pursue during a future time period.

staffing—Recruiting applicants and hiring those best qualified.

stakeholders—Everyone who is affected by the outcome of a given decision.

sustainability—Preserving and protecting the resources of the planet.

technical skills—Specialized knowledge of tools, techniques, methods, procedures, or processes associated with a specific type of activity.

variety—Changing one's tone or inflection when speaking.

verbal communication—What a person actually says when communicating.

visual communication—The physical cues a person gives when speaking. It includes such things as eye contact, posture, gestures, and facial expressions.

vocal communication—The sound, variety, and quality of a person's voice.

 # Review Questions

1. What are the basic management functions?
2. What are the basic types of management skills?
3. According to Bennis and Nanus, what are the four basic strategies that leaders use?
4. What are the levels of leadership according to Jim Collins?
5. What are the three main concepts of the leadership circle according to Collins?

6. What are Stephen Covey's seven habits of highly effective people? What is the eighth habit?

7. What three gifts do all individuals have that can help them find their voices?

8. Why is authentic leadership important in the spa setting? What are the dimensions of authentic leadership?

9. What are the primary elements or channels of communication?

10. What are spa ethics?

11. What are some of the major ethical concerns found in spas?

 ## Internet Sites

For more information, visit the following Internet sites. Remember that Internet addresses can change without notice. If the site is no longer there, you can use a search engine to look for additional sites.

9 Biggest Causes of Spa Leadership
   Failure
www.spatrade.com/knowledge/idx/
0/288/article

Authentic Leadership Institute
www.authleadership.com

Center for Authentic Leadership
www.authenticleadership.com

Discover Spas with Julie Register
www.discoverspas.com/news/
spaleadershipindex.shtml

Jim Collins
www.jimcollins.com

Leadership Styles Assessment Test
www.yourleadershiplegacy.com/
assessment.html

Lypomassage Code of Ethics
www.lypossage.net/1011942.html

Medical Massage Code of Ethics
www.medicalspaassociation.org/
index.asp?submenu=ethics

Mind Tools Leadership Assessment
www.mindtools.com/pages/article/
newLDR_01.htm

Stephen R. Covey Community
www.stephencovey.com

True North Leadership
www.truenorthleaders.com

Index